Jeff:
a sexually realized spiritual odyssey of stepping into love

McMillin Publishing, LLC
P.O. Box 8396
Ennis, TX 75120

Visit our Web site at www.mcmillinpublishing.com
ISBN: 0-9717951-5-0

Library of Congress Cataloging in Publication data:

Printed in the U.S.A.

FIRST EDITION
Out of respect, some of the names have been changed.

Author Photo by Korby Banner

For my best friend Richard
whose life in service to others
exemplifies the love
that this journey has taught me to own.

Though not the complete truth.

Every event contained in these pages is completely true.

Jeff:
a sexually realized spiritual odyssey of stepping into love

❖ ONE ❖

Dear Jeff:

Something happened to me yesterday.

Some paradigm shifting, untellable something happened!

Oh God! Now I have to write this letter that I will probably never send you.

Even though I know I must, because you have to know about the something,

Because I need you to.

....I have a new friend. His name is Ted. We have been seeing each other for about six months now. He is a very nice man....And ...

I want to jump right in and tell you about the something that happened. Because I feel as though, if I express it, it will carry the same power for you as it did for me.

But, it won't will it?

No. It can't, can it?

Of course not,

Of course not,

Of course not.

DAMN IT!

So now,

Even though I know that,

For the sake of my sanity I have to tell you,

I don't think I can.

Because what if you don't understand?

And because, definitely, I'm afraid.

I'm afraid that if I try to tell you what happened,

If I express it out of me,

In order to give it to you,

It, and you,

Will be gone.

And I don't want gone,

Any more.

I want here, now, always, and,

I want it forever, even though it's disabling me.

And so here I am fumbling with the words,

Unsure of whether or not I am willing,

To stop clinging to: "the happening."

Unsure and unknowing about anything, except this:

I am whole again!

And it is because I have pulled all my pieces back together, that I now understand I was apart.

And it is because there is no longer any reason to cry that, as I type, and caress the keys, my eyes pour tears upon my hands.

And it is because I have ceased to believe love is something that just happens to you — an uncontrollable event full of the dramatics of romanticism — that I am swirling in the heady vertigo of,

Your memory.

It is because of all these things that "the happening" happened,

While I was in my new friend's arms,

Deep in the wee hours of Valentine's morning.

We were rocking, in the in and out, of the rhythm of love,

When I held my breath,

Closed my eyes and ...

Oh!

You won't understand.

I can't say it.

I just don't know how,

To tell you.

Even though I am so good at telling.

Even though I know how to put words to music, to say love with syllables, to communicate the crescendo with a phrase, what happened last night is too absolute to be described,

And I just can't.

And,

I just have to,

Because it is also,

Too all-sweeping to brush aside.

Besides,

I feel as though I have been in this place before,

And know that it will return,

Again and again,

And again and again,

And again and again and again,

If I do not honor it,

With recognition.

And though I don't want it over,

Again,

I don't want it over again,

Forever without end.

I want instead to make it mine,

To honor it,

And turn it into something I can bear.

So, I dare not, pretend it away,

Unless I want to become someone else,

Someone who never loved you,

Someone,

Empty,

Inside.

"I DO NOT,"

Wish to be hollow.

I wish to be filled with honor for the truth, even though honoring the truth, will break the chain,

Of my reactions,

For in the past I have always pretended away, by changing me.

But, if I do break the chain of my reactions, by not changing,

Then I change and become someone else.

Because the change of not changing away from, is the mother of re-creation, that is re-creating me,

Into becoming the someone else that I, maybe, do not wish to be.

Shit! Choosing not to follow my old pattern of choosing to become someone else leaves me no choice but to choose to become another,

Someone,

Who maybe never loved,

You,

But only thought she did.

Some,

One,

With open eyes,

Calls me to wear her skin.

She calls and calls and tempts me to risk,

Becoming,

Different than the different,

Shifting sands of buried heads with ostrich feathers,

And pirate's dead, enemies, known as treasures,

Buried deep in the soil of me.

And so in answer to her call I choose to unearth my truth and write to you. And yet, though I believe the path to my salvation will be found in your company, in the telling of "the happening."

If you read of the experience without the evolution of the story, without the revelation "the happening" gave me,

My words will have less meaning,

Than the self-absorbed meanderings of a prepubescent teenage girl who yearns for the affection of some impossible to meet film star completely unaware of the marked difference between the actor and the character he portrays. And,

My experience will seem fanciful rather than universally true.

So I sit looking at the computer,

Wanting to impart the power of the implosion,

Outward.

I am deciding,

What to say,

Waiting for inspiration,

Oscillating.

And suddenly I feel like the whole thing is an undoable, stupid, messed up, total waste of time.

I find myself speaking to myself, in an overloud voice. "*I won't write this letter after all.*" As if I'm telling myself to believe, what I have to say. As if I could just let it go, press delete and walk away from the computer,

With nothing saved!? Erasing any possibility I might have for salvation.

And again," *Why am I writing about salvation?*" my voice jumps into the dance of incredulity. "*Is that what I am after? Is it possible?*" I feel aghast!

"*I don't even believe in salvation. Saved from what?*" I find myself talking to my computer?! Correction, I find myself asking it questions.

And getting answers!!

"*Just what is going on here?*"

"Birth."

And hearing the clarity of a response, I whisper, with the screaming delight of excited fear, " *What kind of something is this?*"

Why are my hands writing without asking permission from my mind? And why am I still thinking in denial as though I didn't just hear someone else in my head?

Someone else?

Or a previously hidden me?

With answers to my questions,

About saving,

She?

"There's that ridiculous concept again. I don't believe in right and wrong. And I definitely don't believe in being spiritually saved, especially by some invisible female entity in my head. I most particularly don't believe in being saved from the act of original sin in which I definitely don't believe. Of course I guess I could possibly believe in saving myself from myself. Hey, maybe that's it? Maybe myself, is just me, thinking too loud, and sounding like a person in my head?"

"Are you trying to fake yourself out by deciding that I am just another aspect of you? Looks like you're afraid that I am more than that. C'mon, you're afraid that I am someone with something to teach that you don't want to learn. You want me to be you so that I can be just as probably wrong as you are, which is always a possibility anyway. Right? Look, why do you want to believe you need to be saved from yourself?

That you are your own enemy?

That can't feel good.

And how can we be saved,

At all, from anything,

That is nothing more than a game of pretend,

We call life?"

"Man! Not only am I talking to my keyboarding fingers but "we've" become an eavesdropping on me "we" and, according to what I'm hearing, "we" are starting to agree, this… she…. and me…... All this focus on "the happening" is making me nuts. This whole letter is just a lot of crazy, talk…typing,"

"Is that what you think I am? Just a lot of insane self propelled finger typed hieroglyphics on a monitor?"

"That's it! I'm turning it off. Music in my head is one thing but this…OK Jeff forget the letter. I'm out of here."

It seemed I was making a decision to stay the same by walking away.

And you know me, once I decide, I do.

Actually I guess you don't know me because you knew me,

Before I began to become,

This new me.

And with that realization,

I froze in place and stopped,

Typing,

In present tense.

I walked away from the computer,

Because,

Like always,

Walking away from the things I couldn't control,

Was the part I followed through on.

However, I didn't turn it off.

Because,

Like always,

Turning things off,

Was a skill I had not chosen to acquire,

A fact, which was in fact, the reason for all this nonsense.

So perhaps considering the sameness of my behavior I was overzealous in believing that anything very notable had begun to change in me,

And perhaps nothing very notable had begun to change in me because I still hadn't decided to honor "the happening" by telling its truth,

Because I was still unsure of how to say what I hadn't yet learned.

So, like always, I didn't delete or power down just in case, I couldn't actually follow through, and turn it off.

Which is fortunate because,

It seems that following through,

Really meant talking to you,

With everything turned on.

And besides, like always, my fingers craved to type.

And I succumbed to the craving when,

With the computer humming a come-love-me lullaby,

I tried to put my grandsons to bed.

Grandsons? Me?! Can you believe it, Jeff? I have four of them now.

Two of them:

Jory (my first baby Tsara's first baby) and Dakota (Deja's boy),

Were in my bed — directly behind me — laughing and giggling and brightening up the room that held my computer as I sat back down to unfold at my desk.

Jory and his brothers and Tsara were all living with me. Dakota often visited. And Dakota and Jory were in my bed because Dakota didn't have his own space in my home.

So, at my suggestion, he usually claimed mine. Which set Jory up for a little bit of jealousy, especially since he never got to "nighty-night, don't let the bed bugs bite" next to me on my threadbare pull-out couch because it wouldn't be fair to his brothers,

Who were also afraid of bugs and would love the comfort of my attention. Besides,

Jory never got to, because my home was his home. He saw me all the time whereas Dakota was a visitor in need of maximum exposure. I just didn't want to become an at-home sleep-aid habit for the munchkins I lived with. "Anyway," I often reasoned to myself "If I let Jory then I'd let his brothers and we'd all run out of room."(Which was a problem their mother had almost nightly.)

But that evening was different. That evening I tried to ease Jory's jealousy by saying they could sleep together in my room since the other guys had already conked out. It was kind of like having a sleepover with them bunking out in my boudoir.

And as I was ineffectively trying to settle them into slumber the computer tempted me away from caring if they slept.

I wanted!

I placed my hands at the ready on the keyboard and told Jory he could only stay in the room with Dakota if he stopped stirring things up and at least pretended to go to sleep.

I started to type while the children babbled and Jory...forgot to pretend,

Himself into believing he was tired.

I didn't care.

I was immediately immersed in my writing, unperturbed and only vaguely aware of the Jory-induced trampoline antics, the "George Of The Jungle" mating howls and the "Wipeout" drum duets being performed behind my back.

Then, whenever the sounds did break into my writing reverie, I merely refused to engage in dealing with my grandsons' awakeness,

By smilingly surmising that "Jumping Jory" was a sleepwalking gymnast: as long as I didn't look.

Funny, Jeff, that you don't know any of my grandchildren, not even one of them.

Of course you already know of Jory (We talked about him several times on the phone.) and you may even have seen him on that nationally aired, and aired again, episode of "Man Alive," the documentary about me and my family,

But that's not the same as hugging,

Mr. hyperactive,

While he tries to run away.

Can you believe he's five now?

That so much time has passed?

Since we last talked?

Have you and your wife survived that argument?

Have you had children?

Do they have your eyes?

Those sparkling sea blue eyes,

Bright and happy as a cloudless day?

Do you remember the day you moved into my house?

Do you remember the night,

On the day you moved out,

When I took the kids camping?

I spent the night seeking comfort cocooned in a blanket by the fire that taunted me with the memory of your eyes,

By seeming to dance blue instead of orange.

I was waiting to know.

I had said my piece, given you my position and then left you to make the decision,

Alone. And free to leave,

Easily. Without me.

I hoped you wouldn't,

Go.

But the fire told me you would,

Be gone when I got home.

The fire was right,

You were.

And my room,

Our love lair,

Echoed empty.

I breathed deeply,

Hyperventilating,

Crying,

Seeking the smell of your clean,

Soap scented skin.

The room that was once again mine, stood still,

Lifeless,

Thick,

And stuffy with sadness.

It stank of dank,

Death,

And mildew.

And I fell into the pre-Jeff familiar,

Nothingness.

So that coming home without you felt like coming home,

To that oft abandoned cave,

I used to know.

...I remembered us...

As I remember us now.

Do you?

Remember,

The day,

Two weeks after we started seeing all of each other,

When I tried to stop.

I had just come out of an abusive marriage. I was trying to understand, to learn to understand, the meaning of kindness. I saw unfairness and abuse everywhere and nowhere and you said something, I don't even remember what it was, but I took it to mean that you might one day possibly, maybe, be cruel.

So I told you that I didn't know if I knew anything, but that in case I did, you should go away, because you might be abusive.

I ran. You followed.

You called me from the donut shop on the corner, the same one that my daughter used to work at, and begged me to see you. I told you there was no point in trying, that I felt old and ugly when you joked about my age, that you made me feel more, than the six years your senior I was already ashamed of.

You said something that made me hear the surprise in your heart.

You seemed,

So sorry,

So self-reviled,

As though these insensitivities to me,

Had been previously undiagnosed personality parasites.

Then you — having never seen your warts before — found them and, without hesitation, plucked them out.

I let you come over and gave you five minutes,

Within which to convince me, of your earnestness.

When you got to my house I was so scared,

So afraid to not know,

What to do.

You came into my living room, your eyes gone gray and sad. You didn't speak. You looked lost without me.

I stood leaning on the archway to my room, trembling.

You reached your arms to me but made no move to close the space between us. Your rough, sensuous, oversized hands beseeched me in the silence.

You looked heavy. Wrung out. I ever-so-slightly shook my head no, to send you away.

And you crumbled to your knees.

As the strongest of men.

And whispered, "Baby please!"

I tried to speak but my words were soundless.

"*Why?*" my lips begged. "*Why me?*"

"Because," you choked, "When you see me, your face lights up."

And I was yours...Because you loved how I loved you.

Oh Jeff my mind is free-falling with so many memories of you.

I've been re-infected, am caught by "the happening,"

Inside a tornado of infatuating love,

So much more intense than when cupids arrow first tore into me,

And speared my attention,

Onto you.

It's because of last night and "the happening" that I am no longer in remission.

It's because of last night that I cry,

And laugh, and fall out of control.

Do you remember that night you moved in?

Once we got your bed put together and your things put away there was a moment of awkwardness like we didn't know what came next. You had stayed in my home so many times and yet, now that you lived there, I didn't know what to do with you.

I was ecstatic. Full. So amazed to be living with love that it burst out of me. We were naked. And the kids I'm certain were in the living room listening through the door. How crazy it must have sounded. I was energized with sex and lusty with joy. I played Native American music and danced around, in and out of my billowing blanket, knowing that wild abandon makes no mistakes.

You were laying on my — our — bed: an audience to my absolute delirium you seemed to delight in whoever I chose to be. Your smile sparkled. Your eyes watched me surf the dance of life on my wafting waves of wool.

Then finally after nine or ten haunting chant songs, all eight of my kids piled into the room seeking to witness the demise of their mom who had been replaced by a raving lunatic.

Jaws dropped, frowns took shape, judgment was passed and giggles ensued.

And we glowed, knowing how much more grown up we were, now that they thought we weren't.

Ah! Children! My children! What a burdensome blessing they have come to be.

You know Jady doesn't even talk to me anymore. I guess six years with a new mother just isn't enough time to fall in love for a teenage girl.

Maybe I didn't care enough,

To accept her the way she was,

And tried too hard to make her,

Who I thought she should be.

Or maybe there was nothing I could do,

Maybe, I just wasn't lovable enough,

For her to love,

Me back,

Beyond the time when we lived together.

I was lovable enough for you,

Before, during and even — I believe — after.

Thank you.

Remember the night we were talking about how nice it was to sleep in a waterbed but how much better it was to make love on the floor? We were pleased with our setup. My futon, folded up into a couch against the wall, was great for the raw animal sex of earlier that evening. Meanwhile, as we talked ourselves into sleep, the warm gentle rocking of the water mattress sang such a sweet harmony to the spooning sway of our lazy second-shift lovemaking.

Our conversation drifted onto the history of the waterbed. Do you remember how that went? What you said?

The bed had been Cill's. She was, like you, my lover friend.

I explained it to you, the whole story. The way I had been so full of the need to sleep with a woman, so caught in the fantasies and desires. The way I had been so ashamed of my nature, so sure that I was bad.

Then, when the counselor from the woman's shelter had been unaffected by my confessions of bisexuality, I felt naive, but vindicated, better, than I'd thought I was.

She hadn't even blinked, never gave sinful a moment's consideration. She just looked at me and responded with an unconcerned, "So?" as though still waiting for the interesting part of the story.

And so,

I released myself of the self-abasement, the judgment, that my husband had instilled.

And I recounted — to you — how wonderful my first successful same-sex experience had been.

The girl's name was Marg. We attended the same acting school. She was beautiful, with long dark hair, firm round breasts, sensuous thick lips, huge, thoughtful, doe-brown eyes.

She reminded me of my sister,

And of myself.

Though the eyes were different.

She approached me as a friend.

Later after several weeks of deliberation on the subject of,

'Should we? Could we? Would we?"

We became lovers,

And did.

I had thought that being with a woman would be easy. After all, I reasoned, I was a woman, therefore, do to her what I liked done to me.

Right?

Wrong!

She was different than me, liked the pace slower, had sensitive nipples and...well, I don't really know, I never actually figured it out.

But I liked it,

I liked trying,

Loved receiving.

In fact until you,

Sex had never been better,

Than the not-sleeping part,

Of sleeping with Marg.

Because, as much as she was different, she was also the same.

I remember everything!

We had taken our clothes off and necked a little, grinding and rubbing and pretending passion, until I got tired of the pretense and stopped her. I had gotten to this point before with other girls and it never felt good, never lived up to my fantasies.

But then nothing ever lived up to my fantasies, so, no surprise.

We both agreed that it just wasn't working and stared at the ceiling for a cigarette or two. I rolled over onto my tummy, to fall asleep. Marg began to tickle-trace, softly, connecting all the little moles and freckles on my back. My buttocks rippled with waves of erupting goosebumps. I lay perfectly still and allowed her body to guide me through the actions.

And though I have intensely sexy memories of her feathery soft hair whispering on my thighs, what truly made the experience so heady, so overwhelmingly amazing, was the discovery of the,

Me...In her.

Up until that moment I had felt that men were only pretending to like to look at my slimy, ugly genitals. That they were only putting up with touching me, in order to get to the part that they wanted, the part where I touched them back.

That's why enjoying oral sex from a man was impossible. I was too worried, too afraid that I might be smelly and wet.

I just felt dirty, too dirty to relax.

"Besides, my God, what if he swallowed me! Never mind that, what if I taste as bad as he does!?"

With that in mind, I certainly never wanted to share my flavor. And I could not be reassured by a man's telling me of my deliciousness, since I was easily the first one to lick my lips and lie to reassure him. I falsely touted him as tasty because I believed that the truth about my revulsion was way too cruel to tell.

Thus, since there were lies in the assurances I gave, I heard lies in the assurances I got.

I wanted so to trust in and see the beauty through their eyes, but how could I, when I'd never seen the beauty through mine, though I'd always pretended I had?

And it wasn't just my body parts that I was pretending to not be grossed out by.

Penises reminded me of withered, dehydrated, veiny sausages. And to make matters worse these chubby little wieners never went anywhere without their friends; a set of miniature water balloons buried under the excess skin of a bulldog's coat, the sight of which made me want to stand up, salute and sing:

"*Do your balls hang low? Do they wobble to and fro? Can you tie them in a knot? Can you tie them in a bow? Can you throw them over your shoulder like a continental soldier? Do your balls hang low?*"

As I marched out of the room,

To the painful sound of swollen bags and squeezing pipes.

Sex organs might make music for some. But for me — until I met Marg — everything was out of tune, dissonant, silly, funny,

And anything but sexy.

I never had orgasms except when masturbating and assumed the reason for the difficulty to be my own troubled headspace.

I believed that this euphoria, never achieved by me,

In the hands of any man, was an inadequacy, a flaw, in me,

The recipient of other than my own two-fingered love.

And then I found myself faced with the mystery of a woman and the impossibility of knowing whether or not I was doing anything at all the way she liked it,

That's when I came to realize that; a woman's body is no child's toy.

Thankfully, Marg, the musical genius, was nowhere near a child.

She knew how to play me. It became pleasurably obvious that she, unlike all the men I'd been busy not sleeping with, knew how to unravel my discomfort with her gentle easiness of pure focus. It felt like acceptance. And that acceptance felt clean. And that clean was what made her able to gift me with the euphoria of orgasm in the company of another, the euphoria that had always previously escaped me.

And she kissed, the way, I like, to be kissed.

And so I relaxed, possibly even before she began,

To more than kiss me.

I tried to pay attention, in spite of the passion, tried to know what she was doing so that I could do it, too. But it was hard to see with pleasure in my eyes,

Hard to see with my head thrown back, my eyes closed, my body tensed,

Hard to see as my mind raced with sensations and I lost the art of studentship.

Hard to see. . so hard to see, so when she lay back to await my touch,

I prayed for the miracle of instruction and fumbled around,

Like a gauche tourist attempting to pilot her angel guide.

I was made aware of my own ignorance because of her expertise.

I wondered how a man could know what it takes to please a woman,

When I, another woman,

Didn't even know,

What it took, someone else,

To please myself.

Fact is, if Marg hadn't already known how to take me there, I couldn't have shouted directions. I simply never would have arrived.

So, though I wanted to return the favor, surprisingly, I had no store of knowledge from which to draw. I couldn't even find her clitoris and I was too shy to look. I was way too busy trying to pretend I already knew. Way too busy being cool, smooth, sexy,

Uncertain, afraid,

That when I found it,

I would have no idea what to do with it.

Ironically, sleeping with a woman, gave me a new respect, a new patience level and a new commitment to men. I vowed to memorize the map that was me, to give better instructions and be a better navigator whenever I came across another fumbler like myself.

I vowed,

To moan out my approval as they ferreted through my body trying to find their way.

"But first," I thought, "I'll have to create the map by traveling the terrain. I must have the experience before I can turn it into a memory.

So, I'll just lay back and let her portage while she explores my body another nine or ten times. That way she can help me solidify what it is, exactly, that I like."

And she did,

Solidify,

All the peaks and valleys.

Until finally I discovered that part of what I liked, was her.

And I understood man's fascination,

With the awesome heat and fiery potential of the volcano.

More than her sensual warmth and gentle explorations of my body, more than the titillation of the naughtiness of what we were doing, more than learning what buttons did what on my heaving self, more than anything she gave me,

She gave me the ability,

To be OK,

With the me in her,

That was totally delighted by the her in me.

I placed my hands on her breasts, felt their heaviness, ran my thumb along the nipple. My mouth lingered and kissed, nibbled and bit, my fingers stroked and massaged every inch of her body. Her skin was hot and smooth, and with each new piece of anatomy, I saw and felt as though I were touching me.

She was lying on her back and I was on my side while my fingers twined and twisted playfully on her body. I leaned over her and kissed her face, her eyes, her nose, her mouth.

I faced her in the dark, her long hair, nose, mouth, vagina, the same as mine.

It was so erotic to feel the hot, secret flesh inside her body, as it opened and closed, held and let go, pulled and released, pulsing like the heartbeat to some pagan ritual. It was so amazing to discover that nothing, not a smell, not a taste, not a touch, not even a sound was repulsive or ugly or even undesired.

And I felt,

As I felt,

That I was feeling me,

And finding me sexy.

So Marg taught me that it was exciting to be with a woman, possibly even for men. And that made me a much, more, exciting woman, for everyone.

Until I met my husband, who screamed and yelled and called me names in order to make me a better person and strip it all away.

And again I believed that women were ugly, though I wanted them still, more and more,

The more he named it sick.

Until I tried to get his homophobia out of me, after he'd gone, by confessing myself to the counselor, who found my sins uninteresting,

As sins,

But tempting,

As a predisposition.

So, of course, later when the counselor and I began sleeping with each other, I questioned her motives for being so blase about my fetishes. I considered that her acceptance of my quirks was possibly a technique for getting me in her pants.

However, doubting her felt uncomfortable, while at the same time the self-acceptance that her teachings gifted me with did not. Thus, I chose to trust her complete conviction that bisexuality was normal. I listened to the reassurance and trusted in the expertise, of all the mentors from the women's shelter, even as I ran into most of them at the same gay clubs that my newly-made-intimate counselor was introducing me to.

I saw these coincidences not as proof that these women were all anti-men, but as my introduction to a larger, more open-minded society.

My therapist/lover showed me where all the other predisposed women were. She introduced me to the `scene" and, like so many other bi-curious wanna-bes, I fell into it with desperate fervor.

And again I felt lost in the ways of women.

I would wander around the bars, trying to look beautiful, unsure of how to proceed.

I felt awkward.

Should I flirt?

Should I wait to be noticed?

Should I forget about it?

I was shy.

Me!??

What a lesson.

One night I walked into my favorite "lesbians only" club and was surprised to discover no music and only a few people. It was strangely quiet. I saw a woman sitting at the bar. I sat beside her. She was small, cute, a little bit butch. She asked me why I was there.

I looked at her and finding familiarity in her masculine edge I thought, 'What the hell, it works with men,' and said, "*I was hoping for sex.*"

She pushed the hood of her parka back to more clearly expose her face. She smiled, showing off a slight overlap in her two front teeth and said, "Ya? Well. I'll screw ya!"

I was surprised at the term 'screw' having previously seen that as a heterosexual activity,

And followed her home.

It was different with her than it had been with Marg or the prettily perfumed, slightly overweight spousal abuse counselor. This girl was less sweet. No long hair lay across my thighs as her tongue discovered my need, no scent of Opium or White musk tickled my nose. No liquid aroma of woman permeated the room. Her smell did not enter into me and tantalize my brain cells for she seemed to have none. And so I stayed separate from her, and instead of using her for the heady ride of sensual sex, became her friend, as she became my friend with whom I had sex.

Cill was funny. I love funny.

In fact I think funny is about the sexiest thing there is,

On a man, that is.

On Cill the funny overtook the feminine.

Sex, with Cill, was like an extension of her attitude: a great game to be had by all. And so we played upon her bed till the night ended and I found myself exhausted from laughing, not even sure if I'd gotten around to climaxing, definitely sure that I didn't really care.

I raced home trying to beat the sunrise and the rising of my sons. I was happy and worn out and feeling good about knowing Cill who made me feel happy and worn out and good about knowing me.

The third time I romped with my darling butch she offered me a keepsake: her beautiful wood-framed, king-sized waterbed. Cill said she didn't want it anymore and that she had already ordered a new bed, one that didn't require a surfer's license whenever the moon was full.

The offer came,

On the day after,

The first time I'd slept with you.

You were new to Toronto and sharing a house with Mike and — oh, I can't remember the other guy's name, Clint or something like that — anyway, you had no bed, just a mattress on the floor.

You were in my head, stealing my focus, keeping me tipsy. I told Cill that I had just bought a $500 futon and didn't need her waterbed, but that I had a friend who could use the offer if she didn't mind my giving it to him. She looked at me, steady and silent for a few minutes. She knew I was talking about you. I'd been talking about you the whole night.

She said she was sick of the whole waterbed experience.

And there we were a year later, sleeping on that same bed in my home, with the futon folded up and set to the side. "Life is strange!" we laughed. Talking about Cill had added an extra something to the room.

God! I can feel it all.

Your soft, soft, soft, warm skin was framing my back and wrapping around me, your strong arms and large hands encircling me from behind, your breath in my ear, your penis so long and hard inside me that it was no longer yours, it had become a part of my body.

You had filled me, holding at bay the empty feeling, the hungry, the pain, the echo of the void.

Your palm slid, with gentle command down my slim belly, until the heel of your hand found my clitoris and held me in position, making every part of me a part of you. I arched.

The future belonged to my body now. It tensed, tighter, tighter, tighter. I held my breath. I threw my head back, threw open my mouth, my throat, my lungs and my belly. The scream came. Ripping through my body. And out into the room.

We never moved. We lay there drinking each other's sweat through our pores. Still. Quiet. Re-assembling ourselves.

From somewhere the moment came, when you kissed my ear and whispered a question. "Do you still need to sleep with women?"

It seemed a strange question, considering that you knew I was still sleeping with women. *"I don't know. I guess so."*

I don't remember how we got from that moment to the next one I recall. I just see the look on your face as you tried to be OK with my appetite.

I just remember how sincerely you offered to,

"Would it help if I put on women's underwear?"

As foreign as the offer was to your masculine pride.

You even looked a little sheepish, slightly embarrassed, wanting to please me, to not confine me and yet, to not share.

Who am I that I had this effect on you?

How is it that it wasn't enough?

To hold us to each other?

When we first met in September of 1990, over eight years ago, I didn't even really notice you. I was working a new gig and it was only my second night singing at the Player's Lounge. You came in with your roommates. At least I think that's who you came in with. You were all pretty drunk. In fact, that was almost the only time I ever saw you drunk.

And it was the only time I ever got you to sing along with me.

So the man I met was not the man I would later decide to know,

Or I wouldn't have decided to know him.

Because, though I remember thinking that your golden hair shimmered like sunlit strands of silk,

I also recall discounting that drunken, unruly man in the audience.

And, since you were that, you were no one to remember,

Though I did,

And though I do.

So I thought of you as I sang at the club that I hadn't sung at long. In fact I hadn't sung anywhere long. This club was my very first gig for money.

I was an old beginner,

That got her start because,

The first time I ever crooned in public had been that August, a few weeks before meeting you, when I belted out "House of the Rising Sun" at the club across the street.

"House of the Rising Sun" was the only song I knew, though the guitar player had thought I would be received better if he introduced me as though I was a professional. And he was right.

After the song the owner of the Players Lounge, who just happened to be in the audience, offered me a regular gig.

I loved the idea,

Needed the income,

And time,

To learn how to sing,

In one key per song after song.

I pretended that I was booked for the next two weeks.

I had to pretend I was booked to buy the time I needed to do some problem solving and score myself a singing lesson or two.

The owner and I settled on a schedule of Wednesday, Thursday, and Friday nights from nine till one, a fee of four hundred and fifty dollars per week for as many weeks as I wanted...to let him touch my breasts when he handed me the money.

I had fourteen days to create a style, get some equipment, a band or maybe some back-up music and memorize, or at least become familiar with, four hours" worth of songs.

Piece of upside-down and backwards cake!

Luckily, karaoke had just arrived in Toronto. So I bought a $3000 machine using my credit called bullshit: a promise, a smile and a willingness to pay high interest.

Then I learned some songs and, having never seen one, used my instincts to create a sing-a-long old English pub type night of open mic entertainment.

My style labored out of me in frantic bursts of desperation that weren't fully delivered till the end of my premier performance,

After those first few painful moments,

When,

I stood at the mic,

Vulnerable,

Voiceless,

And trying to disappear.

A friend in the audience mouthed the words to me,

Helping me,

By filling in my blank.

So I began,

To croak...And in dying I lived again.

I couldn't tell whether or not I was staying in key. So, just in case my singing was awful, I danced to keep them interested.

I danced, and danced and danced, because dancing, I can do.

I had a problem remembering lyrics even when I was the composer. So as a safety net I carried the words folded up neatly in my hands. I was prepared to unabashedly read melodically to the music.

Except I was so busy entertaining the folks that I forgot to look at the paper. That's why, whenever I lost my place, I either made up the words or I stuck the mic in someone else's face. True, I was trying to draw the people into my circle of song, but I was also using them as cover, for me. Admittedly, I was pretending to help them when who I was really helping was myself.

Thus, as was always the case,

I loved helping,

Others,

Learn what I needed most to know.

We all learned to sing.

Sometimes, when the limelight of my choosing people to sing with the mic in their mouths, frightened folks, I held them, stroked their backs and loved them into trying.

And that's what I remember most about the first night I ever saw you smile at me:

Loving people into trying.

And that became me,

My style,

As we all sang off-key,

Especially you and I,

Until because of the loving, we found harmony, and didn't anymore.

Until when, because of the loving, we fell back into dissonance and did, sing off key,

Again.

Jeff, I love you,

Actively. Even now.

This love in me is not a love from the past, a kind of dormant dead thing, like the silverware in the cupboard that you pull out and shine up on weekends. It's here with me now, tingling and alive, because of "the happening" that happened last night.

Actually "last night" is no longer true.

The sun has come up, the grandkids are asleep, and "the happening" is already a day into the past.

It looks like Dakota peed my bed again. Oh well, at least I wasn't sleeping in it this time.

So much has changed since we last talked,

How is it that I am still the same?

As when we didn't talk?

That's the thing I miss the most!

Our silence!

Remember how you used to come to the club, at least for a few songs, almost every night that I was there? You didn't talk; just had a beer, watched me, and left.

You never sang again,

Or got sloppy with alcohol,

Just had a beer, watched me and left.

After a while I started to watch for you,

Having picked your silence,

Out of the boisterous crowd.

It's never been hard to get a man. In fact, the men and I had had each other so often that I'm sure I was way into the triple digits by the time I watched for you. Truth be told, sometimes men even paid me. And once you've been paid to make love as if everyone is someone special, they are. That's when all the rules change. So each person was special and each person was the same and there was nothing especially different about you.

You were just another guy to get,

Because I knew better than to fool myself into believing in anything more.

I had been drawn to your kind of silence before. It never panned out, never delivered the promised still pool of deep tenderness. Most often the silence simply meant that the person had nothing to say...not even with their hands.

Still, I watched for you.

I even began to sing particular songs to attract you. You became the reason for the job; long after the job had served its purpose. It was painfully delicious waiting for you to seek my company outside of the club, like the anticipation of that first kiss with a new beau.

I've never liked that nervous, "can't make sense of what you're saying because I'm waiting to kiss you" feeling. Usually I kissed first at the beginning of a date just to avoid it. So I considered asking you out to short-circuit the agony. But I had a rule against dating audience members.

So, because of my rule, I primped, and circled, and danced around, waiting for your move, ready to reject you,

Once or twice.

You had a beer, watched me and left.

I primped.

You had a beer watched me and left.

I circled.

You had a beer watched me and left.

I danced.

You had a beer watched me and left.

I wondered if you also had a rule against dating,

Your audience,

The performer?

I watched you,

Come in,

Have a beer,

And leave.

My desire obliterated,

Any respect I may have had,

For my own rules,

Or yours.

So the next time when,

You had a beer and watched me,

I intercepted your leaving.

I broke the silence,

And gave you my number,

Hoping that you wanted it.

I waited for your call,

In the silence as yet unlearned.

And waited for your call,

In the uncertainty!

And waited for your call.

In the hope,

That you would stop the waiting,

And call.

You didn't.

But,

You did,

Come back to the club,

With friends.

This time,

Just like the first.

You had a beer,

Watched me and,

I flippantly teased you for not putting an end to my misery.

"*Afraid*???" I ran my finger along your arm.

"Nah, working." You smiled.

And hope, which springs eternal, sprang.

I gave you my number,

Again,

Just in case you'd lost it.

I don't remember how long it took you,

While I waited.

I just remember,

It took you long,

Two days maybe three,

'Til we finally got together.

At which point the memories jumble into a mixed-up pile of perfectly captured still picture portraits.

But you know what I can't remember, Jeff?

I can't remember what we did before we did it that first day.

Did we go out or did you just take me to your place? I feel as though we must have gone out but the image is gone from my recollection.

I can't even see the picture of our sex so I have no idea how it went,

Though, knowing what I know now, I'm sure it was fine.

It must have been.

In fact, it must have been,

Too good, too incredible,

To be indelibly captured by my mind.

I am certain of this,

Because,

Of the way I felt afterward,

Which is the part I do remember.

For that was the hook that captured me.

I was caught by, and imprisoned in, the feeling pool of the radiating warmth of our after-sex glow,

That,

Never,

Ever,

Left,

My skin.

I was owned by the mouthwatering deliciousness of your kiss,

That tasted clean, soft and free as a mountain stream.

Your mouth always drew me in, absolved me, cleansed my palate.

And my memories of that first day begin when we were done and you carried me, naked, perfect, from your bedroom to the living room. You curled me onto the couch and snuggled me into a blanket. Then, as always, you took care of me, without ever making me feel as though I couldn't take care of myself.

I can't help but sigh into the memory of the feeling of being naked under the blankets,

Of being warm and sexy and appreciated,

While you cooked for me.

You did everything so easily, so silently. You never asked me to notice how you treated me and so I can't forget.

Your hands.

As they passed me the plate, or reached under the blanket.

Or shaved my legs.

It may seem like nothing to you but I can't help remembering the way you shaved me: not on that night but on other nights.

My life was so hard, so much to do, so many kids with so much need, so little money, so little time. I would end my days asleep in my clothes, too tired to undress. You would come find me, hold me, let me sleep.

Then, in the morning, after the kids had gone to school, you would take me home, to your home, and bathe me.

And somehow, you would do all that, without disturbing my need for independence.

Somehow you were able to care for me completely without ever making me feel as though I couldn't care for myself. Somehow.....

Some .....mmmmmmm.....how!!!

The memories purr!

You would wash me.

And you would shave me.

Such a private thing.

I never knew a razor could feel so tender.

I think about it often, the way the blade touched me, the soft short strokes, like feathers upon my skin.

Your hands were huge, callused and manly. The veins were pushed up and pulsing.

You were infinitely gentle, even as you cleaned the blade between strokes.

The razor looked so small in your fingers. I lay in the bath watching your face, that seemed to see me as perfect and so I was.

And though you grew hard with desire, your eyes never changed, except to twinkle with pleasure. I saw no animal, no pretended adoration, no anger, no emptiness, just me.

I began to smell like Irish Spring and shaving cream as you smoothed the hair away from my underarms and legs. Moving the blade from shin to thigh, taking care, seeing me, spreading my legs, always with permission. You moved the skin to eliminate the folds and kept me safe.

You shaved me so softly. Pulling gently on the hair, so gently that I felt it everywhere. You coddled the scissors, and trimmed me.

Sometimes you brought food to the tub and fed me while I soaked, sometimes you washed my hair, sometimes we turned the shower on and you got in. Always we made love.

And somehow no matter how, tired, belabored or poor I was, while I was yours, there was so much love in my life, that I felt rich, and afraid, of not being..... so.

Shit!

The mood was just broken by my life.

As I've been writing this some time has passed and my duties have intruded on me. As always I've had chores to do and children to care for. Even so, it's been easy, at least the writing has.

But responsibility is getting hard.

Overwhelming in fact!

To remember you like this,

With no gap between the then and now.

Writing has kept me crying,

Inside the past,

Trying not to be,

Loving every minute of it.

And loving every minute of it, I have to write because, as I told you, not writing, not telling you what happened, would keep me inside the past without my knowing it. And "the happening" would keep happening, over and over, dropping the past into the present, making me cry forever and ever and ever,

Without end,

Trying not to,

Loving every minute of it.

But being inside the writing is an assault on my senses and, as I also told you, I feel like I did at our beginning: the way I couldn't clear my head, couldn't think, couldn't function, couldn't stop breathing you, with every thought.

So, I'm changing my external environment to keep me safe, from the car accidents and cut fingers that befall preoccupied parents.

And, to keep me safe,

Inside the fog,

Of seeking your silence.

I've come to the cabin to be alone. That way I can take the journey of this letter to it's natural end, without scaring the children. Tsara is watching my boys, and hers. She is my other half. My first-born helpmate.

How old was she when you and I first started? Sixteen? She's going on twenty-five and a mother of three now. Can you believe it? Dar will be eighteen. That seems even more incredible. That he could be an adult and still not be able to talk, at least not well enough for others to understand.

Four boys and four girls and none of us normal. What a life I've led,

Am still leading,

Looking for connections.

❖ TWO ❖

My new friend- his name is Ted- followed me to the cabin last night. I was driving a little faster than usual, trying not to impede his sporty, high-performance silver-bullet BMW. I was concerned, because on occasion, Ted had displayed an annoyance with the tardiness of other drivers not nearly as slow as myself. A fact of which I was conscious because it **was** a sporty, high-performance silver-bullet BMW, not because he'd asked me to be.

So I sped up out of a created concern that shouldn't have mattered to me even if it did (though I'm sure it didn't) matter to him. However, the choice seemed to make itself, as I drove, caught in a weird kind of deja vu.

I am used to deja vu, you know that. So that's not what made it weird. It was not because it felt like I had been in that moment before but because it felt like I, and Ted and someone else besides Ted, had been there together, at different moments, all at once.

Before.

It was almost like an overlapping of times and lives or perhaps the simultaneous immersion into a past life deja vu overlapping the memory of a precognitive thought.

I knew that Ted belonged somewhere in the picture, but I was driving and couldn't follow the images to figure out the message.

It felt ominous and I was wishing Ted wasn't with me, though being with him is good. A fawn dashed in front of my truck, just a baby, streaking into my headlights, wanting to cross the road. I have miraculously missed so many deer in my life, but this one leapt into the preoccupation of my thoughts too late to be seen. I hit him. I can still feel the feeling of weighted flesh impacting on the hood.

Why had I wasted time trying to remember the foretelling instead of watching the road? I sat in the truck, with my hands over my face, afraid, crying,

And deciding him alive.

Why hadn't I let him pass through us?

Why had I made the impact solid?

What good is understanding how to do it,

If I couldn't remember how to do it,

Ever again?

'Why is it that every time something miraculous happens,

It happens only in the inkling of a thought?'

I thought,

As I thought of that time I told you about,

When, while I was thinking about the fact that nothing is actually solid at the molecular level,

That the only difference between wood which I cannot penetrate and water which I can-

Is whether the molecules are doing the two-step or the jive-

Something happened.

While I was thinking that if matter is really as Einstein surmised, simply frozen energy like a floor full of choreographed dancercules packed tightly in a row then,

There are no real beginnings or endings to things, making us all,

Every one of us, sundry threads of the same cloth,

Differentiated only by the varying vibrations of our various patterns.

And thinking that,

We are all just molecular changes melding and moving from one to the other, like the colors of a rainbow, blending and shading, recreating, becoming,

The appearance of difference,

I'd had the thought, that a close-up look at molecular activity,

Would blend the edges of the object of my attention into a fuzzy connectedness.

And I began to sense that the truth was even much more awesome,

Than edges,

That bleed.

I felt the shimmering electricity of all life blended and interspersed into one space.

I breathed with the rock and lay still with the hummingbird.

I focused on the interspersed atoms that weave in and out in sparkly life, like a great computer that flashes on and off in a breathtaking display of binary brilliance.

I saw the illusion of,

Dead,

And separate,

And one at a time.

I tried to re-engage into concrete,

Thought,

(Another illusion).

'So it follows,' I reasoned, 'Since no thing is really an alien substance to any other thing, there's no need for bumping and crashing.'

'Maybe,' I contemplated, 'if elements coexist in the same space and time with no need to adhere to, combine with or bump up against the elements of any other substance in that same space and time,

They only do so because we want them to.

Like flexing our muscles just to experience the flex.

Since all the work is done in the mind. Maybe we are the creative chefs of that recipe to manifest reality whether we know it or not. Maybe molecules are simply the minions of mind-controlled thought particles obeying orders from the brain. Maybe we can manipulate our molecules into standing apart, and allow others to share our space and pass through us.'

And while immersed in these ideas,

A truck crossed into my lane, to avoid a box that fell out of the truck in front of him, and me with a carload of sleeping children, believed,

I had no choice but to,

Try it.

I pulled the molecules apart,

And passed him through,

Our car and us.

While poor Brandessa, who stirred awake, was frightened into nightmares that lasted for years.

That sensation, when the truck and the man inside it whooshed through us, was an unforgettably awesome,

Millisecond of shared oneness.

What a rush!

Of tingles, and goose bumps.

I'd done it!...Once.

I was never able to repeat the miraculous event again.

A tale which my various banged-up cars is sure to tell.

And the only difference that I can see between that time when the car remained un-chafed and all the other times when my vehicles sustained injuries,

Was assumption.

My assumption that I knew how to do it,

And my decision to remember to assume.

A decision I apparently forgot to make when the dear baby deer jumped into my path,

Out of nowhere,

As if I'd called it there,

To symbolize the fleeting, fragility of something new.

And as Ted's BMW pulled next to me to see if I was OK,

That dizzying deja vu washed over me again.

And I wondered if Ted was thinking of Lisa,

His last lover, to hit a deer.

Was it just another sign of our sameness,

Lisa's and mine?

And if our sameness was another sign,

Of repeated patterns, of constant choice,

What did it mean?

That Ted and I belonged together?

Hurting things,

Causing damage?

Proving,

That

Love bites,

Love bleeds,

It's bringing me to my knees.

Love lives,

Love dies,

It's no surprise,

Love bites.

Words from a **Def Leppard** song crashed into my head.

I tried to shake it away.

I just didn't want any more echoes,

Of pain,

Especially by me,

To myself.

I've become so vulnerable, Jeff.

And "the happening" just keeps happening,

Especially in bed.

Ted wanted to come back to the cabin again tonight,

But I asked him to stay away, said I'd be writing.

I think I have to be alone with you until I'm not anymore.

This cabin reminds me of the time we went to your uncle's cottage.

Remember? My boys were at camp, my girls old enough to be alone, my cell phone and pager both out of range. It was a crisp summer day at a typical Canadian cottage and you showed me how to keep the bugs away by swinging a leafy twig while we walked. We wrapped ourselves in a blanket naked together in front of the fire and re-discovered our perfection, our soft molding oneness, wondering how we could have broken up.

And your kisses! You know, my mouth salivates when I think of your clean kisses: no cigarettes, no drugs, no alcohol, (most of the time).

The perfect seal between your lips and mine, not too wet, not too dry,

Your tongue always cool, mine always hot,

Your face always soft, no whiskers or pain.

And I think of Ted and his fast growing facial hair,

And wish you were here.

But even you are married now,

And there'd be no way to avoid hurt,

Dirtying it up,

With someone else's pain.

You know, Jeff, no matter what you might think, you never hurt me.

That trip to the cottage is a perfect example,

Of what happened to us, and of why I love you.

The canoe, remember the canoe?

It was such a gorgeous day, so full of hot sunlight, so blue like your sparkling eyes, reflected on the water and staring from the sky. We were out in the canoe, you paddling in happy silence, me soaking up the sun. I lay into the protected rocking of the boat, and lost the coolness of the Canadian breeze. I started sweating, playing audience to your chest muscles as they moved beneath your tank top: a lazy pleasure to watch you work.

You set the paddle down. And removed you shirt. You twirled it into a band and tied it around your head to keep the sweat from your eyes. I teased you, complained that women don't have the same rights as men, said that I was hot too. You smiled.

I looked at the jet skiers approaching from the distance and challenged, "*What if I took my top off too?*"

You smirked with a kind of "Go ahead" look in your eyes.

So, I did.

And that's what I love.

That you never said don't.

You never told me not to,

Not once,

Not ever.

You never made fun of my odd ways

In any fashion that I could hurt myself with.

I can't tell you how often I remember with amazement the way you would be standing talking to me and I would lay on the floor, without provocation, and put my legs up for you to hold. You never asked me why I did that, which is good because I didn't have a reason. I just liked the feeling of lying on the floor at your feet while you held my legs up in the air and continued talking.

That's what I mean by your silence. And that's what I mean by my weirdness,

And the beauty of your acceptance, of me;

That you never protested.

And that your silence

Was never a quiet complaint used to hurt me,

But instead always a solitude shared.

Oh, sure we often talked.

But we also often didn't.

And that's how I blossomed, in the quiet perfection of our tranquility,

Our stillness,

Our love.

I think that with you and I,

It was not that we shared surface level common interests,

But that we lived together in the depths of quiet singularity,

That made us,

Us.

So, when the time came to leave your uncle's cabin, when the trip was over and we headed back to town in silence, I should have been happy. But I knew it was coming, had been feeling it for hours, had even pushed our leaving to an earlier time. My children needed me! I could feel it. And sure enough as we got into cell range the alarm bells began to ring.

We looked at each other. I answered the call,

Remembering why we no longer lived together.

It had been so exciting having you live with me. Mundane things became special. Things like walking through the grocery store and hearing the sound of my inner voice shout "I HAVE A MAN!"

And understanding,

That it really meant, "For the first time in my life, I not only have the man that I want, but I still want to have him!!"

Mundane excitement.

Like waking up every day for three days to the sound of you mowing my two-and-a-half acres of neglected lawn, making it easier for the neighbors to like me.

Like running and playing through the house, rolling around like teenagers and making the kids feel old.

Like touching and nibbling into orgasms so big that I screamed loud enough to attract the police.

Like laughing, watching you try to eat my one-pot wonder vegetarian slop.

So great.

So quick to

End.

I was tired, having been unable to sleep the night before. You wanted to treat me special, help me, let me sleep in. You put my four special-needs sons, all lined up in a row, in the front seat of your truck and headed for the zoo. I watched you out my window, watched you working to try and get them to sit still. It was...

AWESOME!

Even my own mother wouldn't baby-sit Dar.

And Rye got kicked out of every daycare or nursery school I put him in.

I knew you had no idea what you were doing, that you were just trying to help, that you wanted to immerse yourself into my life.

I was too full of wonderful to sleep!

In fact too full of wonderful,

Was what had kept me awake all night.

And remembering what had kept me awake,

Reminded me of my not-a-dream dream,

And the psychic information it had contained.

So I phoned my friend and asked him if he had placed a foreign titled, face down, blue, hard cover book on the nightstand beside his bed, the night before.

He had.

I felt powerful.

Like I could know anything.

But the powerful feeling lasted only for a minute.

Because suddenly, I knew too much,

More, than unimportant visions with the blue book value of repossessed love,

And became rock-heavy tired,

The way I always am when I'm afraid.

And so I slept.

Until you came back,

And threw yourself on the bed,

And mumbled, loud enough for me to hear,

Quiet enough for you to not feel like a jerk,

"They're so dumb. I never wanted, my sons...dumb."

And I knew that living together was over.

I walked straight to my desk and wrote down what I hoped were the winning lottery numbers. Because right then, I needed something besides my children to look forward to.

And needed, even more,

Something for my children to believe in, as they looked forward.

My poor babies had been rejected so often by so many people. First, their natural parents, then their foster parents, then my husband, my family, their teachers and eventually my friends,

And finally you.

I wish it had stopped there, that I had dated no more, that my children never again searched the eyes of a man and hoped for a father. But they did search, because it didn't stop, because I continued to look, to experiment, to expose their hearts to wishes.

My new friend is another example of maybe. Of all the possibilities should the world be different. And once again my children, though they have become jaded, have begun seeking to seek, to reclaim their love-ability.

I love my children.

But my sons are boys who already have me, so I am not what they are looking for.

They want a dad.

Now.

As they did then.

Know please that I do not,

Not love you,

Because you didn't love them.

Though I sometimes wonder what it would have been like if you had.

Sure we left each other because you didn't love them,

Enough.

But I still love you,

Because you loved me.

It's enough that you did.

You know what, Jeff?

You never bugged me.

Not even when I needed to justify losing you.

I was never annoyed by your habits,

Never irritated by your way,

Never hated you for being human.

You never bugged me.

And that is not a little thing.

And neither were the problems that my kids caused,

Little things.

So, there we were, driving home from the cottage,

When my phone rang,

A little ring.

The mom in me was in trouble,

Again.

Rye had been kicked out of camp and apprehended by Children's Aid,

Again.

You can get used to anything, so my panic was minimal.

"*Why?*" I asked.

Apparently Rye had been running and screaming and VVRROOMING at the top of his lungs all night long. On the second night the exhausted camp counselors gathered Rye's brothers together and asked for advice. They had been trying to reach me but none of the numbers I had left were of any use to them. So they turned to my other children for help.

"Does he do this often?"

"Lots and lots."

"What does your mommy do when he acts like this?"

"Tie him up."

And I was in trouble.

Again.

Poor Rye, he was just too wound-up to stop moving, even for sleep. Dar was the same. Something about autism and sleep doesn't mix. However, Rye was close enough to normal to get in a lot more trouble than Dar.

Because Rye was close enough to normal to be irritating.

And because Rye was dangerous.

Because he was fixated on so many hazardous things like heaters and furnaces and tailpipes and hanging out of second story windows. And of course there was that destructive savant in mechanics that led him to want to take everything apart but never put it back together again.

He was my challenging little "Houdini from Hell" whom no lock could keep in, or out, or even slow down.

Sleep deprivation, destructiveness, fixations and an inability to restrain themselves are common complaints with autistic kids. People who deal in children's services should know all about it. But they seldom do. So people like me, with children like them, get in trouble.

Of course I'd known this would happen, had seen it coming. That is why I had had the doctor prescribe a bed harness to keep Rye safe and make him stop sneaking out in the night and going into other people's houses looking for heaters.

He was only four years old. He needed to be contained somehow.

I knew how to prevent Rye from getting out at night but I also knew that whatever method I used needed to be approved of by a recognized professional. Otherwise I'd be called abusive and my son would be considered at risk. How ironic!

Because my son was at risk I had to keep him safe, which put my son at risk of my keeping him safe, which put me at risk, of getting in trouble for preventing him, from running the risk, of coming to harm.

So I had gone to the extra trouble to involve the doctor and make my parenting legal. The contraption he sold me was pathetically ineffective. However, it **was** medically prescribed, which made it superior to anything I could come up with in its ability to keep me out of jail.

So I bought the harness for my protection from accusations, and created my own device for Rye's safety from fires and falls. This type of social politicking wore me out even more than my kids did.

I felt that I should have been able to be honest and just do what was best for my son without fear of persecution.

But the undesirable world of "Woe Is Me" is papered in, "Should Be Able To's" so I just dealt with it by accepting the fact that such was not the life for the single Canadian mom of four special-needs sons.

Of course before accepting came venting.

Every time.

Poor, Jeff, as always you got stuck ducking the verbal diarrhea as I spewed and ran off at the mouth all the way home. I jabbered on and on about how the professionals weren't very professional and had no idea what kind of damage apprehending my children would do to my children. I just wanted to be trusted, to do what was best for my son, to be allowed to teach him, without always having to explain myself. I wanted to be a person who was a parent not an administrator of programs.

I wanted, I vented.

I wanted, I vented.

I wanted!

I vented!

And vented!

And vented!

I knew that technically I could have gotten in trouble for the homemade safety ties. After all I hadn't used that unbelievably useless medically prescribed bed harness but my own version of a child's straight jacket: a men's shirt put on backwards with the arms brought around the back and tied to the shirttail between the legs.

I knew I could get in real trouble and that's what pissed me off. I hated this horrendous waste of time and emotional strength. My one consolation was that I had thought ahead.

The way I figured it, the existence of a prescription was enough of a legitimizer to cover the butts on the plethora of asses the governmental system was about to make me deal with, thereby giving their reports the necessary validity that would keep them from investigating the issue too diligently.

I was virtually certain that the verdict of my innocence would be upheld even though I was guilty,

Of creative parenting,

As long as I pretended that the "official" harness was the one I'd been using to curtail my son's nightly excursions. And in fact, this form of decoy was the exact purpose for which I'd bought the dumb thing. It had come in handy after all.

In other words I had learned to do the bureaucratic bullshit dance of deflection

With fervor.

But I was angry at the need to learn.

I had no tolerance for the camp's issues with my parenting particularly since they were reporting me for handling what they hadn't been able to. And particularly since I didn't even use that shirt jacket anymore.

It had done its job.

And given credibility to my threats,

Proving to Rye that I could stop him from getting up and running off, making his attempts at escape futile, making him willing to willingly stay, in order to avoid being forced to,

Start sleeping, he slept,

At least three hours every night.

So, by the time the camp heard about restraints, there were no restraints to hear about.

And Alannis Morisette with one hand in her pocket and the other one giving a high five pops into my head.

Isn't it ironic?

Don't ya think?

It wasn't a problem until it was no longer a problem.

But I'm rambling.

Still,

Telling you things you already know,

Again,

Things upon things.

You knew it all,

And more.

And that was the problem.

With me and mine,

There were always,

Too many problems.

So, you took me home and dropped me off.

I dealt with the authorities and never had time to cry, for us.

It must have seemed so different to you in the beginning. It never occurred to me, till just now, that my life might have appeared easy and my finances plentiful. I mean there I was living on the most expensive street, in the most expensive town in North America. I had two cars, eight (Correction, Deja became my child later. I guess it was only seven) children, a nanny, a singing, stand up comedy and acting career.

By contrast you had just moved to town in a beat-up yellow truck, carrying simply a mattress and a few clothes. You were straight out of college having returned to school after several years on the oil rigs in Alberta and fortunately for me your first job in this new field brought you to the television station in Toronto. But man, things were so expensive in Toronto compared to out west; you must have felt a little intimidated.

And there I was, rich.

In appearances.

Until you looked closer.

And found poor.

But that first invitation to play in my excessively large house must have been a mind blower.

Remember making love in the spare room with the kids at school and the maid vacuuming outside the door? Remember the Jacuzzi? With the suds completely filling the room?

Our bodies, hot and tight together, melted the bubbles and massaged each other clean.

That was the last time anyone ever used the Jacuzzi.

Rye broke it two days later.

And that is why success and money for me have been fleeting.

My children break things.

And I can never keep a job because my children need me at home,

Or at school,

Or at camp,

Always accessible,

To fix the damaged goods.

But then you know that.

And you know that they are not the children of your dreams.

But they are my children and I dream for them often.

As they stretch beyond their disabilities,

To become their idea of normal.

I am in AWE!

I've never even pretended I could do that.

But then you know that too.

Remember the time we went to Buffalo New York in search of karaoke tape and a wireless microphone? We were walking down the hall of our hotel room, I saw the length of carpet beckon me and, without questioning the urge, began to cart wheel down the hall. I say began because I never finished the wheel. Half way through the spin I lost my balance, and not being much of a wheeler any way, my body crumbled into a heap on the floor.

You never said a word about it. Just reached down, grabbed my hand and continued walking while you talked, uninterrupted, as though nothing peculiar had happened.

Never mentioning my absurdity.

That's the thing I remember on an almost daily basis.

That your silence was created by the fact that

I didn't bug you either.

Because you accepted me.

And it wasn't as though you didn't notice my strangenesses:

The strangenesses, I didn't know I had.

Until that day,

When we were sitting in the C.F.T.O. news truck in downtown Toronto, talking about wanting to move to the States, eating lunch and waiting for the phone call telling you to uplink to satellite feed.

And I saw something that you had already seen.

There was a lady crossing at the intersection in front of the truck. She was wearing a faded, worn-at-the-knee, pink jogging suit. Her socks were multicolored and rolled at the ankles. Her out-of-style white runners seemed to curve up like a pair of elf slippers affecting her gait. Her hair was yanked into a messy ponytail by an oversized elastic and she wore the preoccupied expression of a mind absorbed. It appeared that this sad, almost comical vision may have been homeless.

As she crossed in front of us my embarrassment for her changed to,

Embarrassment for me.

And I turned to look at you,

Looking at me,

To see me,

See.

I asked the question before you could hide anything in your eyes.

"*I look like that don't I?*"

You nodded "Yes."

And your eyes shadowed,

With an embarrassed kind of pain,

For me,

And how I would take,

The revelation that:

We had both recognized,

The complete ensemble,

As one of mine.

For a second I thought,

Maybe I did bug you?...How could I not?

But then you released my hair from its ponytail and gently finger-brushed it until it shone. You removed my outdated runners and rainbow colored socks, kissed my feet and drawing me onto your lap brought my mouth to yours.

And I understood that your embarrassment was for me not you and that as far as you were concerned nothing about my behavior really mattered.

Unless it mattered to me.

And because it didn't matter to you,

It mattered to me.

And so I changed.

You have always helped me

Get over things.

Like my inability to endure malls.

I had balked at calling it a fear because, "*I wasn't afraid,*" I explained while recounting a story. "*I just felt panicked and couldn't stay.*"

I rationalized as if there were a difference between fear and panic.

We were in the States. You wanted to shop. I hated shopping. You wanted to take advantage of the low prices. I wanted to run. And the panic started to set in. I pulled back on your hand and explained that this was something I couldn't do.

I couldn't be around groups of people unless I was performing.

I hadn't been able to feel comfortable in such environments ever since my husband first filled me with the fear of his possessive retaliation. He viciously warned me against talking to men, or even women for that matter. I, he pointed out with a vengeance, was so disgusting that I couldn't even be allowed to have a friend that was a girl. I quivered and,

Told you about

My husband,

My fears,

My limitations.

You didn't make it into a big deal and you didn't make fun, you simply looked at me and said, "Maybe you should get over that."

Of course!

How simple. Maybe I should!

So, I got over it.

I no longer ran in panic, though I still didn't like to shop.

However, that probably had more to do with body image and finances than phobias and abuse.

Because, of course, money was always a struggle.

And, feeling beautiful was a feeling I'd seldom felt.

Except with you, always with you. Even when I knew you began to wish I was as thin as I'd been when we first met — before I quit smoking and you started feeding me — even then, I felt beautiful. But never again, never since then, because my body has only ever felt perfect next to your perfection,

Every time.

I suppose that's because your body *was* so perfect that I assumed myself the same.

But I think it was really because when you looked,

You looked to be pleased.

And so you were.

Pleased.

Which was enough to please me.

You always helped me.

Get over things.

And survive things.

Like my self-esteem,

And my cars.

At first it was hard for me to ask for help. Help in my world has too often come at too high a price.

That's why, when I broke down in the middle of the night I walked for miles and then hitchhiked home. It seemed strange too that, when I told you about it, instead of getting angry or being threatened by my independence, you were simply surprised and a little hurt. You didn't sulk or pout. You just seemed concerned that I hadn't thought of asking for your help.

Even so, the next time the car acted up again in the middle of the night I was still afraid to phone, to call out to you. I didn't want to hear you react in anger to my waking you up, instead of with caring for my situation. I knew you wanted me safe, that you had meant it when you asked me to give you a chance. But I also knew that people often meant their offers only at the time when they made them.

I was afraid you would refuse to help me, or worse, that you would help me but with annoyance.

It was the last time I was ever that way afraid. If I needed you, even now, I would call.

Except I've lost you and, like Mary, I don't know where to find you.

Though I doubt if leaving you alone is all it will take to bring you home.

Wagging your delicious behind in this tale of my wished for reunion.

Because I'm always too busy looking at the memory of the process,

Of losing you.

I remember feeling a little envious, of your success.

Because I was becoming less and less valuable as the catch of the day.

Because while your life got better and better and more and more stable as you accomplished each of your goals, mine continued to be interrupted by phone calls from schools and neighbors and police and such.

Yet still, my children blossomed.

And still you helped me at every single turn. Even as others came to stand between us.

Like Deja, my newest child, for whom you were a terrifying memory because you looked like an exact replica of her alleged childhood molester.

And the girl that had your baby,

And the one that had the abortion,

And the fiancée that eventually became your wife.

You helped me always.

Because we both knew that in a different life we'd be the ones in the foreground, though the background may be full,

Of others.

You never minded that I was a slut.

And neither did I,

Mind you,

Not minding,

Nor being the same.

Because you helped me survive things.

And you helped me learn things.

Like, how to hook up sound, and the difference between a male and a female RCA and how to troubleshoot with unfamiliar equipment. You never minded my techno-phobia but walked me through it all, showing me only what I needed, accepting that I had to understand the why of things. You talked me out of my pen and paper, took it lovingly from my hands and replaced it with a keyboard. For that I am eternally grateful.

It has become my tool.

And I have survived

Because you helped me

Create things.

You risked your job, sneaking professional-quality tapes, lights and cameras for me to use. Then you read the manual in order to learn how to edit so that you could help me to create a performance reel. Because you loved me enough to want me to succeed, though we were no longer the person in each other's life.

And you gave me a Visa, under your credit, with no strings attached and no guarantees asked.

And you co-signed as the primary purchaser on a house you saw only once.

And you helped me whenever I asked,

You to do things that no one else would do.

How is it that you loved me so much?

How is it that so much time has passed,

Even here in the present world.

Where it is the third day since "the happening."

My friend Ted is here now. He couldn't stay away. Instead he brought food, drink and a book, promising to read quietly while I work on the computer.

I'm not sure it's a good idea. I feel strange having him sit across from me while my eyes well with tears over the truths I am writing about you,

And us,

Knowing that he loves me too, unable to tell him what I'm saying.

I told him that I am writing a book. I couldn't say it was a letter. He knows too well at what moment I was inspired. It would frighten him. And he would expect the letter to be for him.

Besides, I think that if it is too much for me to tell you what happened in only a page or two then it is more than too much for me to tell him at all.

For he wasn't there,

Though he was.

I did tell him that I wasn't writing for money.

That I was inside this thing,

And that I had to get it out of me.

Perhaps I'll let him read it when I'm done. It depends on how the whole thing ends. Because, although I'm writing to tell you about something that already happened, I am also telling what is happening as each moment unfolds.

So, though "the happening" is what started this letter of memories and is the story I am moving towards telling, I have no idea what comes next, or what it is I need to say,

Because I haven't learned it yet.

That's why I don't know if I'll let him read it.

Because I don't know what "it" is.

I do know however,

That this odyssey seems to be buried, in the telling,

Of the very thing I do not know.

And so the journey goes and goes,

Ending only when I do,

Tell the mystery,

I have yet to solve.

And since "the happening" is the beginning of the story,

Which is unfolding as I write and live,

I don't know what telling "the happening" will bring me to,

Or how it will affect my life,

Or what it will mean,

Or how it will end,

Because it hasn't ended,

Yet.

Though we have.

Many times over.

Did I ever tell you how much it took,

For me to end you,

To function,

After you left my home?

It took vomit and hypnosis and dancing in diapers.

I'm not kidding and it wasn't funny.

I loved you too much.

For yours and my children's sake you needed to be gone.

But for mine?

Every once in a while, when thinking of you, I forgot that,

What's good for my children is what's good for me.

My mind just kept replaying and replaying every nuance of us.

As I seeked to discover how to let go.

And instead discovered that,

If ye seek with persistence,

Ye shall find,

The problem magnified.

I just couldn't let go. Though I filled the dance card with as many men and women as I could find,

And found them lacking. I closed my eyes and learned to picture something else,

During the act.

Of pretending love.

I returned to the techniques of before you, showed me that,

I didn't have to go away, during the act,

Of love never pretended.

Because,

You already were my fantasy.

So I thought of you,

Behind closed eyes.

And foolishly wondered why,

You never,

Went away.

You never left me alone,

After you left,

Though we tried to take the future out of the then.

We had sex at every opportunity. In the studio, in the truck, the hotel, your house, the station garage. It was dangerous but desperate makes dangerous and we knew we were losing. We couldn't stay away from each other, couldn't keep our hands to ourselves, lied to new people and searched each other out.

Whenever fate allowed us the opportunity we drove around in silence,

Just for the sheer pleasure of it.

But you were seeking to build a life, with someone, with whom you could move forward into tomorrow. And I couldn't hold onto you while you tried to break free of my grasp. So we attempted to turn love into sex as a means of transitioning away.

I think it worked for you.

But for me?

Even in those moments you created unmatchable memories.

Because you were never very good at not being a dream.

Do you remember that time, after we were no longer us, when you bathed me and fed me and shaved me and carried me; clean, young, fresh, pretty, onto the waterbed. I forgot that we were apart, though we were together.

Fell into the caress and drowned in the joy of your cool tongue as it traveled along the bottom of my foot. You always aroused, never tickled, though my foot has not been a G-spot for anyone else.

You stood between my legs and looked at me; an indelible imprint upon my

Mind, as I remember.....

The sun was fading, bringing the magic hour glow through the slats in your blinds,

And soft lighting my legs.

And your chest...

And arms...

And face.

I wish I could draw with words how beautiful you were.

How beautiful all these things were.

Even me.

You were blond, and tanned. Thin and taught. Your skin was soft and warm. Your gentle hands strong and rough. Your teeth were straight with small sexy little gaps between them and your nose was large enough to stand out and make a promise. Your stomach was perfectly packed and tightly ridged. Not even a speck of fuzz obliterated your beautifully defined chest but a treasure line of dark fine hairs mapped the way to your penis.

Which was glorious.

And then you knelt at the foot of the bed and though your body fell out of the light, your Nordic, intensely blue eyes, reflected the fading sun and threw what felt like rainbows,

Of color vibrations,

Upon my face,

And belly.

You opened my legs,

Bent my knees,

And gently spread my lips apart.

I felt my clit pop into view just as you covered it with your tongue.

Your cool hot tongue. I felt so clean and beautiful and happy to have forgotten that we were no longer one.

The pleasure was deep and intense and I wanted to force you onto me, make you part of me, keep you,

There!

I put my hands on the back of your head and held your face tight against my groin. Your hair was as soft as a woman's and your head as hard as a man's and I got lost inside the mixture as I took one last look into your eyes.

Arched my body,

Held my breath,

And pounding you to me,

Came.

And came,

And came,

AND CAME!

and relaxed.

I looked down at you, feeling girly and a little embarrassed to have gotten so lost inside my orgasm.

You looked up from between my thighs.

You raised your face,

Smiling that cute little Adam Sandler smile,

And, OH MY GOD!

Your teeth, were filled with blood, blood that had come oozing from your, pounded against my pelvis, bleeding nose. You laughed.

While I apologized, for getting so carried away,

With your head.

And then you held me,

While I remembered,

That you were no longer mine.

So I tried to get over you. Determined to reclaim my life I spent two thousand dollars on a dating service, that introduced me to friends,

And turned up the volume on my seeking to find,

Some one else.

But my head swirled with gentle images of your caress, everywhere I looked.

I couldn't escape, even into housework, without bumping into visions of you.

I couldn't even do the dishes alone because the minute I looked out the window into the backyard I saw us, sleeping naked, under the blankets by the fire, uncaring that we risked the possibility of discovery.

You just kept haunting me with the breath of love.

And my heart ached. For you had given me the ungiveable, you had given me acceptance,

Silently cared for my strangeness,

Made no judgments against me for my zombie like wanderings in parking lots and unknown places.

You simply helped me by walking along side and, holding the back of my shirt, subtly steered me from place to place, keeping me safe so that I wouldn't bump into things.

You listened, bemused and enraptured, to my ruminations about life. While I continually got lost,

Thinking great thoughts.

You never seemed to find it a burden,

To love, the artist in me.

So potent was the memory of what I believed you to be.

But if there was any hope of getting free from your affect on me,

I needed to stop being so bewitched by your acceptance.

So, I bought a book called, 'How To Fall Out Of Love' and began practicing all manner of insanities,

In an attempt to bury myself far enough into the sand to make you disappear.

The book told me to start by making long lists, which turned out to be short,

Of all your bad habits.

And then it told me to make more long lists, which turned out to be even shorter,

Of reasons not to love you.

I was wallowing in writer's block and not being very effective at helping myself.

So I got my kids to assist.

The lists got longer,

And crueler,

Though the effect was benign.

These were their lists, not mine.

Of what consequence was that?

When we looked at you we saw different people.

So how could their opinions matter any more than they already had mattered,

When I chose to allow the disintegration of us and let you move you out of the house?

Could my children's opinions matter enough to move you out of my heart as well?

No! Apparently not.

I was discounting the help that I was asking for.

And that's why the book didn't work.

That's why nothing worked,

Not self-hypnosis,

Not emotional transference to a safely unattainable film star,

Not even cutting and pasting pictures of you onto ridiculous images like pigs, and fat ladies.

Nothing,

Absolutely nothing,

Worked.

But some things helped,

Like the giraffe.

The book suggested that I imagine the least attractive part of your body and assign it a degrading symbol. I was then to replace the body part with the symbol whenever I thought of you. It was a dilemma: I liked all your parts. But the proportion was a little off on your long legs. So I tried imagining you as a giraffe in a pair of cowboy boots.

Actually it wasn't such a bad idea,

It at least made me laugh,

Which was a beginning.

Eventually I got to the end of the book.

The last chapter,

"THE MOST SERIOUS OF CASES SECTION,"

Came with a warning,

"THE NEXT CURATIVE APPROACH IS EMOTIONALLY VIOLENT
AND SHOULDN'T BE USED UNLESS ABSOLUTELY NECESSARY."

The book actually suggested that I not even read the chapter unless my situation was dire.

Which of course made me want to read the chapter.

As I'm sure the writer knew it would.

The book, the chapter, and all the ideas were ludicrous but, you know,

The situation was dire.

So I tried them, every idea, including the last one.

It told me to take a repulsive image like feces or vomit and plaster it on your imagined face....every time I found you in my fantasies."

The book pointed out that the important thing was to stop thinking about you. "So, make thinking about him unpleasant, use a little aversion, pick something gross and,

BREAK THE HABIT!"

I chose steaming chunks of freshly spewed vomit,

And that's how you looked:

My pukey git along little dogie giraffe.

I started to feel like a mental bulimic,

With a strong compulsion to go to the zoo.

I also started to feel like a shrinking violet,

No longer basking in the reflection of your beauty.

I felt choked for starlight,

Ugly,

And fond of puke.

But fond of,

Felt better than enraptured by,

And the crack in the damn that the giraffe had started,

Began to widen, relaxing your grip and easing my pain.

Till finally,

While desperately seeking an image that would crumble the wall and give me total freedom,

You supplied the inspiration.

We'd known each other for over two years and still you had never danced with me. Not ever! Not even to impress me on the night that we met when, foolish in your drunken stupor you had romantically serenaded me in an unabashed off key bellow.

I didn't mind our not dancing. I just wished for your company, when I danced. Because moving to the beat, was my greatest social pleasure and one that we had never been able to share,

At least not on the dance floor.

And I just knew that anyone who could make love like you had to be able to dance. It was simply a matter of letting your self feel it: the sex in the song.

"Look, Jeff, you don't need to be a good dancer. If you are having fun, you're good. Fun is the secret, fun is sexy."

At least that's what I told you,

Over and over again,

Until on that day when I said it for what seemed like the hundred and thirty-eleventh time, and you miraculously agreed.

We made our first dancing date and in spite of the fact that you and I were not each other's other, I spent two days cloud walking with anticipation. The night came, the music started and, since you were hedging, I swayed to a few with your roommate. He was always nice to me and didn't need too many beers to make it to the dance floor.

As usual once I found myself inside the music I didn't really need a partner, didn't really need you to dance, didn't even need you to get out of the chair. Dancing for me is a pretty singular activity anyway. I often close my eyes and fall into the rhythm, happy to spend an entire evening gyrating alone, with someone to talk to during the breaks and moments of recuperation. I just wanted that someone to be you.

But you'd promised to dance. So you did.

Several beers into the evening, you smiled and swaggered a John Wayne swagger onto the dance floor. Then, I swear to God you actually said, "Here you go, babe, your dream is about to come true."

Like you meant it.

You took a stance and prepared to join me in my gyrations.

Darling, I love you but no wonder you don't normally dance.

You're awful!

Absolutely, irrevocably, unbelievably, awful!

Your legs are too long, your rhythm isn't. And you just kind of bend from leg to leg like a strangely double jointed giraffe trying to kneel sideways and inward all at the same time,

Over and over again.

You one-step wonder you.

It turned me off. Finally.

So maybe it did matter whether or not you were any good,

Since having fun is what makes good,

And fun is the part of good that's sexy,

As opposed to your strained, unnatural smile,

Of trying to please me.

It occurred to me that you were right:

You didn't, even remotely, have fun dancing.

I supposed that was why you sucked.

To me it seemed an impossible thing to not enjoy the art of the dance.

Strangely, enough, watching you join in but not be absorbed by my favorite activity, not only gave me the space within which to analyze, your imperfections,

It gave me the space within which to begin,

To let go of your imperfect, perfection.

And that's when I became aware of my ability to choose:

To love or not to love,

And gained the freedom of goodbye.

Until my mind changed it's mind and began to recreate what it was seeing,

"But he's so sweet to try, look how almost adorable—"

"NO! NO! I WON'T THINK LIKE THAT!"

The scream in my head, my need to get on with my life, took control, and I began to begin again,

To analyze for letting go.

And then, the final necessary ingredient to my release came in the shape of you,

Drunk,

Which I hate.

You helped me separate,

Gave me the tools,

I chose to use.

And so over the weeks ahead whenever "the romance" threatened to embrace me in a cocoon of "remember whens" I imagined your long legs dancing ... over and over again.

But the image of you dancing wasn't enough of a turn-off to stay that way, so I began to falter, into love...and stopped myself. "NO! I need a way out!"

I added some things to the imagining and imagined you dancing in a huge diaper with enormous baby pins, and smelling like whiskey, and grinning that stupid John Wayne "bet you just can't get enough of me" grin. And when that wasn't enough I added vomit to your face.

Till slowly,

After many weeks,

The humor of it all,

Crumbled the wall,

And made a joke of us.

I was finally free, because,

For the first time in two years,

I had let myself see you do something you weren't good at.

❖ THREE ❖

My Darling, Jeff, another day has passed and I find myself feeling guilty for taking so much time away from my family. The end of the month is around the corner. I've been immersed in you and not working, and I have no idea how I am going to meet my mortgage "note" (as they say here in the States).

Funny how we both ended up living in America though we traveled completely different paths to get here. You followed your career, I followed a man. I was jealous when you moved. A year later I met Tod.

And followed you.

Sometimes I think I conjured Tod up.

Because, when he hugged me, my head landed on his chest, at the same spot as it had landed on yours.

He was tall and had long legs like you. And his balls! They were soft and clean like yours, no hair, just beautiful, warm, clean-smelling skin.

God! How I loved his balls.

Because they were like yours,

Made mine again.

So we fell in love with falling in love and got married.

Marriage!

What a bust that turned out to be.

For me.

How about you?

The last time we talked was so abrupt.

Always I've known how to reach you, always we were friends, so when my marriage fell apart and I found myself living on the streets with four disabled boys and a pregnant teenager,

Whom else would I call?

When you were days away from walking down the aisle, or, as in your case, walking down the beach, and you faltered in your fidelity, it was my phone that rang. You told me you had cheated, slept with somebody other than your future wife, whom you hadn't seen in months and who was miles away. We talked about how your engagement had had to flourish over the distance of two countries for more than a year. What did you expect?

Not to be yourself and want company?

Thank you.

For calling me.

When you needed someone to talk to,

Someone you could tell the truth to,

Without having to say too much.

What a compliment.

What a testament to our friendship.

How sadly sweet you sounded,

Adorable,

In your, "Please approve of me self chastisement."

Your unsure-ness was a new sound in our silence.

Oh sweet thing. So sorry. I missed a beat. When you wanted to know if you were bad and, not hearing your need for a straight out response, I talked about expectations, lies and promises. When I told you, *"not to worry, at the end of the day sex is just sex, not a crime, not a love killer, that's the province of guilt."*

I should have said, *"Of course not baby. How could you be bad?"*

But I didn't.

Instead I talked outside the silence.

Used the words of knowledge instead of the knowing.

Then,

I consoled,

And said what I thought you wanted to hear. *"Ah! Hon. What's the big deal? If you love her marry her."*

But I should have said, *"Don't!"*

I should have said, *"You're like me Jeff,*

You're not monogamous."

"And if, because of that, you lie,

Because she needs you to,

It will hurt,

Both of you.

As you seek to love,

Yourself."

Which is what happened, I think.

Because when I paged you,

Needing your voice,

It took you two pages to return my call.

Usually I didn't even have to page.

And when you did respond,

Hurt was all I could hear,

In the sound of the ring.

In the tears and embarrassment.

"Lynette?" your voice questioned the answerer of the phone,

ringing with a wrongness so obvious, as you used my name,

As if you didn't already know me,

By my voice.

"*Yes Jeff?*"

"I can't." I heard you swallow. "We can't," and swallow again, "talk to each oth—."

And your voice became inaudible air breathed in,

To me

"I can't," you cleared your throat, "call you anymore."

You seemed to be trying to explain as you lost the battle with the lump in your soul.

Your voice cracked and I could barely hear the last two desperate words.

"OK? Babe?" you seemed to beg.

"*OK.*" I love-whispered back.

I could feel you hanging up, could see your worn out stance, your heavy arms and though I wanted to leave you free to make your own choices I still had to try,

To fulfill mine.

I had to try, "*Are you OK? Baby! Are you OK?*" to reach out and stop it.

And as the phone came back to your ear because you had to answer, had to help me, to tell me you were OK, your wife began to scream, so angry at my Jeff.

"TELL HER WHY! GODDAM! IT! YOU TELL HER WHY!"

And as I heard you whisper,

"Please"

To her

Like a quiet prayer for compassion,

The phone went dead.

And you were gone.

No longer my friend.

Just an echoing pain,

Shared.

oh god!

❖ FOUR ❖

The more I write the more I remember-cry and remember-cry and remember-cry as if it is impossible to run out of reason,

For tears. It feels inescapable as if there will always be more, pain, calling,

One more drop of water to fall from my swollen eyes.

It leaves me feeling really funky, like a soul divided,

From itself.

My life keeps trying to intrude. The phone is ringing, customers calling, publishers leaving messages, kids asking for the meaning and definition of life, for concrete help with this and that, even the grown up ones like Dessa who wants me at jitterbug dance lessons so that when I play father to the bride we can dance with some flair,

And maybe just a little,

So we won't look peculiar or gay,

In front of her new relatives.

Which, except for how it would affect Dessa,

Would be OK with me.

Even though, well, you know how I feel about something as narrowly focused as lesbianism.

That it's a choice,

I didn't make.

Oh! Oh! Jeff!

Dessa! You're probably confused. You don't know about Dessa! She's getting married on April 3rd to a key grip, who runs a successful movie equipment rental company. He's a really nice guy. I just love him because I love her with him.

Can you believe Dessa's getting married?

And no cynicism about marriage you! Just because it's been hard for us doesn't mean it'll be hard for them.

She's done so well Jeff. She's just the most positive, caring, hard working, intelligent little woman I know. She's a registered massage therapist, an art director, and has chosen to put the horse before the cart by getting married before having children. I guess, in light of my (and my other daughters') choices, Dessa's still a bit of a rebel.

But she's definitely not the little drug abusing, house wrecking, police attention getting, condescending, liar that you had to deal with while I was in Europe.

Of course you never described her that way, never would have said those things, especially about Dessa, but I know how she treated you,

Knew it even then.

In fact what you did say was that the kids were great and everything went fine.

Please! Who were you kidding?

By now the girls have grown up enough to enjoy telling the stories of their youth, finally confirming what I already knew.

That when I was away and you were the caretaker, everyone misbehaved,

Even you.

And then you all helped each other hide it. The lot of you got together and making a plan, divvied up the responsibilities.

Your job in this crisis correction was to smooth over the ruffled feathers of the police and Children's Aid and to contain the authorities enough to keep me from knowing anything upon my return. The girls" job was to clean up the destruction that their party had caused and to not tell on you for being an absentee babysitter.

Thank you!

For caring enough to lie.

Silly,

All of you.

There was no need for ineffective secrets.

I knew my children and you,

Knew I'd been asking too much.

And had asked it anyway.

Nothing happened I couldn't have foreseen,

If I'd wanted to.

I wasn't about to judge any one of you,

Who met my hindsight seen expectations,

A failure.

You did the best you could.

All of you,

Did the best you could.

And so did I.

You know Jeff,

You never needed to hide from me,

Ever!

Though it seems you thought you did.

You never needed to, because you couldn't. I always knew.

It's the same with Ted. I always know.

At first that bothered me.

Especially when he found it so amazing

As if I don't always know with everyone.

It bugged me when he called us "connected."

I didn't want to believe in connected,

As special.

I was trying to remain separate, from any one person, but connected to all.

I was trying to be cynical, about romance.

And so,

At first,

I looked at the fact that I could read him so well,

And saw transparent.

But then I realized, it was only possible for him to be transparent to me, because I had learned to see him. Perhaps we were connected after-all.

It's always that way when you're talking to yourself,

And pretending there are two of you.

You learn things.

That you couldn't learn alone.

He's right.

We are connected.

All,

Three of us.

Because he and I are the same as what you and I used to be.

Sure he and I are more into articulating what it is that we know, than you and I were, so it's definitely different, but that doesn't mean it isn't just as good or maybe even better,

For long term growth,

And uncovered honesty.

But it does feel different,

It's not a silent,

Reality so great that there's nothing to discuss.

It's a seed,

Growing,

Seeking sunshine.

And this funky—with you and with him with no separation between the two—feeling, is probably clouding up the sky a little,

Leaving him lonely,

For total focus.

While I focus on you.

I'm with you, even though, ever since your wife decided to get her feelings hurt you are gone to me. And the fact is, I have no idea where to send this letter, even if I want to,

And yet I write.

Without an address.

While my new friend,

And all of my family,

Wait.

Because, as I told them,

And him,

I have to look at what's inside of me before I can ask myself if I wish to get it out.

And because,

At every possible ending,

I am afraid to stop.

So I guess I lied when I called myself whole,

Said that "the happening" had made me that way,

Because I am not.

What I should have said was that I had found all the pieces. But they are only pieces and everything has not come together yet.

So I write as a divided soul expressing itself,

Through you,

And through him,

And through itself.

That's why I asked him to go away, though he didn't go. He followed me instead. And for a brief second I worried that his behavior might be an indication of the future I was destining myself to live in, with him, in, side it. Solitude was what I wanted and solitude was why I had left my family behind to come here, so that I wouldn't have to function on so many levels at once.

I knew that if I diluted my focus with daily living I would remain unchanged by my own revelation.

And then I would continue to circle on the same spiraling zero that I had circled on for the past six years.

Around and around,

Around and around,

Circling,

Until I stopped avoiding being willing to look into myself to map out a new pathway,

And change the shape of things by putting the pieces together,

Which, if I chose it, could take forever.

Ideas like these,

Are the meanderings of my mind.

The meanderings that,

Used to take place in the silence,

Between us.

Remember? Listening to me? Think.

And just as you were able to, so too, has my new friend begun to hear my thoughts,

Or perhaps I have begun to let him.

As I told you he is, or at least he seems to be, a very nice man,

Perhaps it's time,

To let another nice man,

Be my someone,

Else.

But even if it is time,

It still feels strange to have him here,

While I type.

It feels like a breach in the solitude,

Counterfeiting the silence.

And it is weird to have him say nothing,

For he and I,

Talk.

But I am allowing the weirdness to become comfortable.

You know, Jeff, at first; I thought you and he had nothing in common and that that was what was making him special. But now I know you do. I think I've known it ever since "the happening." But perhaps, it is while I write around the truth, that I am discovering I know it. And as your presence fills the room and he tries you on and wears you well, the similarities grow.

He told me something last night, something beautiful.

It was around midnight when, eyes swollen from crying, I decided to stop writing and go to sleep. I shuffled into the other room. I was exhausted and ready to drop. I saw him sitting up in bed, arms loose at his sides, silent in the dark. It had been eerie writing to you while hearing him snore. I felt his half asleep smile and knew what had woken him: He was worrying about his place in my life. I wondered if he had heard my tears.

There wasn't much I could say.

Not yet,

Because I was worried too.

So, I ignored the unspoken reality. I tried to reassure him with a happy, loving, worn out woman, greeting. *"Hey, why aren't you sleeping?"* I snuggled up next to him and, kissing it, laid my head on his naked paunch of a belly. I explained nothing. It was too much for me at that moment.

We talked for a while,

But not about that,

I guess it was too much for him too.

Eventually we ended up on the subject of bisexuality. He was trying to become comfortable with it, imagining the day when I might say, "See you later honey. I'm going out with Mildred? Or Marg or maybe even Cill." He was inching his way towards clarity.

Slowly, one finger at a time, he was letting go of his previously held convictions.

He was letting go,

Like you did.

And like you,

He was trying to understand me. So we talked and I answered his questions with sensitive frankness. He was cute, making a problem out of nothing, knowing I wouldn't abide it, letting it go. I think I even stifled a giggle, wondering what he would look like in the bra and panties you once offered to wear.

Unlike you,

I doubted if he'd ever offer,

Though it would be safe.

For I would decline,

Again.

Because,

As you know,

I prefer truth to pretense,

Even when truth is pretense.

And so we talked truths.

And he told me his story, though I'd known some of it before.

And I laughed,

And laughed,

And laughed,

For the sheer joy of it:

Years ago, when he was in College and a little strapped for cash, Ted and a couple of his friends would go to the gay club to flirt and dance and get beer money.

This wasn't news. He had told me this abbreviated version before, in an attempt to empathize both with one of my job choices and my bisexual nuances.

And yes, since, I suppose your wondering what I mean by that, I did have to go back to being an escort.

But not for long.

Romance Therapy Work that's what I called it.

In fact that's what I did.

I taught people to love.

I turned it into a legitimate job and even claimed it on my taxes.

Like you, Ted understood my choosing the vocation. Unlike you, he didn't mind it because he had been a customer,

My first,

This go round.

Actually I kind of created him,

A friend made manifest.

To ease the re-entry process,

I made him up.

You know how that is,

When life gives you exactly what you ask for.

I'd needed money,

Again.

So I connected with an escort agency,

And began,

To answer men's phone calls,

Badly.

I put off the inevitable for weeks, not wanting to regress into a job I had already left behind me. But I was drowning in the money abyss, paying for everything with credit cards and rotating checking accounts.

My previous income had fallen away the minute I bought my piece of paradise, a house on 67 acres of wooded privacy. I was left scrambling to pay the mortgage and feed the kids, who needed the 67 acres of seclusion away from staring eyes, in which to thrive.

I had bought the house to solve problems for my family, not to create them.

Shame on me for being so addicted to moving,

That I saw it as a solution to all my children's growing pains, like bad friends and xenophobic neighbors. This time after driving for days following a path of small town papers we ended up here, on some, what I had thought was affordable acreage, in the middle of nowhere. Out of money, I applied for every available job in my new community and was hired at every interview. I would work for a couple of hours, then, part way through the day (because for some reason in that area of rural Texas my new bosses wouldn't tell me my wage until the day I started work), I would calculate my rate of pay times forty hours, plus overtime and double shifts.

But, in every case even at eighty hours a week, my paycheck after taxes, would only come to one third of my monthly bills.

No wonder my paradise was so cheap!

The locals made so little, that the people were starving.

I didn't want to be part of that group; my children were already thin enough. So I tried fundraising for two months after which I counted the profits of just over four hundred dollars: two days worth of living expenses.

I couldn't do it Jeff. I couldn't be normal while raising abnormal children. I couldn't come up with the solutions that others might find. I considered stripping but at the time I just didn't feel pretty enough. Besides, no pun intended, I didn't want to be so exposed. Also the job of tease seemed crass compared to the job of love.

So I got an escort agent,

Because I didn't want to never see my kids,

While I worked twelve hours a day for the local railroad.

I didn't want my babies staying home to starve alone,

At a slower pace,

Than they were doing already,

While we lost everything,

Yet again.

I chose *Romance Therapy*,

And became proud of my work.

But first,

I decided to meet the perfect client,

Who could connect me with an upper class world,

And end the "I can always do *Romance Therapy*" cycle,

That I was about to become proud of.

I wanted to belong to the world of social acceptability.

I wanted to become a different kind of proud, of myself,

For giving my children something to be proud of.

I wanted someone who wouldn't want to be only a client. Someone who could help me in some way and be my entrance ramp to the avenue of success. Someone, who had created me to fill his need, as much as I had created him to fill mine. And so, though I pretended to myself to have returned to work I answered the phone badly and backed away from making any bookings or any money at all for three weeks,

Looking for the on-road,

Waiting for his call.

When I would just know,

That he, my soon to be friend, was perfect for me.

Eventually, he called, thinking he was looking for someone else who, fortunately, wasn't available that night. Though he didn't yet know that he was actually looking for me, because I was also, perfect for him, he was easy to redirect.

I had manifested him into my world by building a man with the opposite/same need as I.

The minute I heard his voice,

I felt safe,

Right,

Like he was the one,

I'd been waiting for.

I cut off the competition and moved into position.

I never asked him a single question, didn't even give him a chance to think about his purchase or to quiz me or to decide whether or not he wanted to love me. As far as I was concerned that hand had already been played. My eyes were closed and my instincts were steering. I got his address and was on my way over to his place before I even hung up the phone. He opened the door and ushered me in, checking to ensure that the neighbors hadn't seen me, or my dilapidated car, which they might mistake as belonging to a friend of his, effectively spreading my poverty grown trashiness onto him.

Stay with me, Jeff, though you are gone.

Don't close the book, keep reading,

These words are not meant to hurt,

Or brag or pay you back in any way.

What would I pay you back for?

Your love?

I just need to tell you this before I can tell you that.

I have to explain what's been happening or "the happening" won't seem important enough to be worth the words. And I'm talking to you because I'm trying to talk to me and because, the time when I was with you was the only time I ever found myself,

Inside another.

If it helps, imagine you, when I tell you what happened to,

Him.

For in truth it is the same as you shall see.

He turned to me as the door closed and within the sweep of that motion I moved in and melted into his body. We kissed. Then broke away.

He was in the habit of hiring women of the night, had even fallen in love with some of them. When he felt the need to tell me of his history, his heart, his longings,

Within minutes of our meeting,

I knew that I'd been right.

We could be something,

To each other.

Because he, like you, came sexually unfettered by social morality and pre-conceived judgments,

And wouldn't find me putrid.

And because, he spoke gruffly, using anger as hard shell camouflage, like a peanut brittle outer shell which protected, I believed, a soft sweet center just waiting to be savored. I knew, I knew how to melt him down, using my mouth, to spew words and swallow his need.

I sent my energy to greet him. Laid my upbeat, disarmingly contrasting gentleness upon him, and felt his defenses rise to stop me. We were in his kitchen. He crossed his arms and leaned back against the counter, telling me of his latest love, warning me that he was fragile.

I respected his pain and stroked him with my empathy.

We went upstairs, to his bachelor's bedroom. For,.

Though he had a wife, he lived alone.

And we entered his boudoir.

I did what I always do.

I became you,

The lover of love.

I dipped my head into the drunken pool of sensuality,

And wore your skin,

Was you,

As you would be if you were a woman.

I looked in the mirror,

And saw me beautiful.

As beautiful as you,

Used to make me feel,

So the sex was good,

As it always is.

But something else happened,

Something outside the character of you that I play, when I play,

And I started to become myself.

Just a little,

Carefully.

For even though I had created this man, I hadn't realized that I had wanted the truth to be anything other than the pretense.

Till he stood naked, unprotected by other loves,

And showed me his scars waiting for my repulsion.

I knew that feeling,

Wanted to respect it,

Share in it.

So,

I began to disrobe,

You,

And listen to his mind.

I responded as me,

And noticed how easy he was to read.

I began to write, Braille upon his body.

We were in the Jacuzzi, lying opposite each other. As I stroked him with my hands I used the memory of the sensuality of yours. But I didn't re-become you. I remained myself. His orgasm drew from his throat a soft whimpering sound.

He smiled a kind of sad smile.

And the room filled with empty.

So, I re-felt your presence.

I turned off the whooshing jets to clear his vision, slid my hand beneath the water and discovered his foot. Drawing his toes to meet my mouth I licked them, teasing, playing, nibbling.

I flowed easily from one acted upon idea to the other,

And felt a sameness between us:

The sameness of you and I,

And you and he,

Without ever noticing the similarity,

Between the two of you,

Except for his Viking-blue eyes that promised to sparkle almost as bright as the sea.

If only all the shadows would grow quiet and the ghosts fly away,

Leaving the room full, of two,

Pieces, of everything,

He and I.

His mind, as I listened to it, was full of romance.

And that was the trade-off,

What I would have to give him to get what I was after.

And so I wondered:

Romantic singular focus,

Was I capable of that?

Did I even want to be?

I couldn't imagine why?

What does one gain,

From dissolving into some,

One person,

Instead of them all,

For more than an hour at a time?

There it is in my head again!

Hey?

Jeff?

And Ted?

There's a Def Leppard song:

When you make love,

Do you look in the mirror?

Who do you think of?
(That I can't stop hearing,)
Does she look like me?
(In my head,)
Do you tell lies?
And say that it's forever?
(Since Valentine's Day brought me to,)
Do you think twice?
Or just touch and see?
(The beginning of this letter,)
To us.
(On the day when I hit the deer.)
And the words began to loop and loop and loop inside my head.
So I'm writing down the lyrics to the chorus,
That repeats its points,
Within my mind.
Lyrics that whisper and beguile,
And come hither hints of lovers' truths.
I'm writing down the words,
Because their chant has,
Become part of my experience,
To shake.
And because,
Like "the happening,"
I want the words out of me so I can stop spiraling in this blur and see the signs,
That help me understand,
That I'm okay.
Like all the other clues to myself that have fallen into place, and told me
I was where I was supposed to be.
Refueling my sense of cosmic intention,
Giving me the strength to keep me going.
Like on that night with Ted,
Reminding me of you,
With me not listening,
To so much evidence,
That I cannot become less.
We are all,

One,

Person,

You and he and I.

We are all one,

Though we try to be many,

Even as we hold up markers,

To identify our unity:

Markers, signposts, coincidence,

A trail of trees, buried in the forest, showing us the way.

Like the branches of our names,

In the game of,

History played.

You and I and he,

All three,

Of us changed our names.

And became new people,

Of our own design.

All three of us,

Then protected that design,

By using aliases,

And became even newer people,

Of a transient kind.

All three of us,

Were the same person,

Lost far inside,

The people of our minds.

When we first met, I was Laurie-Anne; he was Mack, and you, in your drunken stupor,

Called yourself Scott.

In the beginning,

We were all, pretenders,

Seekers and inventors of personas,

Triplets, born under the skull roof, of self-creation,

In this world we call reality.

Then, that night at Ted's, as he and I discussed each other's other worlds, which led to our views and spiritual beliefs, life turned into possible truth.

And I began to be convinced of what I already knew,

That I had made Ted,

Out of a life's worth of wishes and wanted designs.

For, like me, he believed he,

Created his own reality,

At least a little.

Meeting a man who believed in this way was something I had recently decided I wanted.

So I came face to face with my own power and responsibility,

As all the mosaic pieces fell into place,

Teasing me with the knowledge that I had created finding him, in the midst of him creating finding me.

Thus it seemed, we created each other,

For ourselves.

And though all the soon to be discovered "coincidences" might have blown someone else's mind,

Spine-tingling the hairs on the back of their neck and sending them searching for the wish-fulfillment booze genie in a bottle,

I didn't drink,

Hocus-Pocus Horseshit,

About supernatural fingers of fate.

I inhaled, consumed and drank,

As Peter Pan from the imaginary quantum physics plate,

Creations of my own design.

Thus, getting what I ask for is not at all eerie and is, in fact, exactly what I expect.

So to have just been given my own radio show, on a small community station that would lead to nowhere and then immediately upon deciding I wanted it, to connect with someone who could place me at a higher level in a station that would lead to somewhere,

To discover the senior vice president and CFO for a nationwide radio and television news conglomerate,

Reaching to touch me,

Existing in my world,

Simply because I had asked him to,

Was, quite frankly, to be assumed.

And so, though it might have blown someone else's mind, it didn't blow mine.

It didn't shock and amaze me that Ted's job was, just like yours had been, Jeff, an uncanny complement to mine.

No surprise that when I needed to start at the bottom you were there to help me with the basics and now that I needed to start at the top he was here to help me with the rudiments,

Of high powered success.

It didn't shock me because I didn't believe that the Divine Plan,

Was drawn up by someone else.

I believed that, what was,

Was,

Because I decided it to be.

Ted, was like me,

Believing out loud,

What you and I had believed in the silence.

And when I walked away from Ted's that night it was with the almost conviction that I was in control, having created everything according to my own criteria. Ted would be a regular customer and more if I wanted. I knew that I had already gotten out of the romance industry exactly what I had gotten in it for, I had found someone looking for love,

With a new age attitude,

Who was intelligent and turned on by conversation,

Whose talents complemented mine,

Who knew more completely how to be a success in the concrete world around me than I did,

And who liked to share what he knew,

So that I might always be learning,

And never become bored.

And so that the time we would spend together would not feel like selfish time away from my kids but mind expansion time that would benefit the all of my family,

However indirectly.

A workaholic,

Who's dream it was to not live with his wife,

In case I became one.

Or maybe instead of a workaholic ignoring his wife,

A romanceaholic,

Who already had one,

To keep him busy,

Because romanceaholics always want too much time.

Ted was all of these,

A work/romanceaholic,

And a husband,

Who didn't live with the wife that kept him busy.

Perfect.

Ted's absentee wife lived thousands of miles away in a beach house full of family to keep her warm.

Ted was used to living out of two houses, probably even liked the freedom. He was busy and wouldn't require too much of the time and attention that belonged to my children.

Good! I didn't want a partner to absolve into but a sensual touchstone with whom I could spend short spurts of quality time. A gentle, lover of open sex, that was in charge of his erection,

And orgasms,

And needed not to possess me,

Or stick a flag of ownership inside my heart.

Someone who viewed escort work as socially valuable but would, without judgment, still understand my need to move away from it.

Someone whose career position could raise me up into that network at the top of the business portion of the media community so I could jettison my kids and myself off the bottom rung and into financial independence.

Someone I could borrow but wouldn't have to keep....Someone like Ted.

And as I walked away I knew that I could have everything as long as I continued to want it. How empowering that was.

And what a different headspace from when I met you. In those days, I had just begun to know that I was in control, was still, searching for an inkling, giving it a name.

Perhaps giving "it" a name,

Is the pilgrimage of this letter?

Which is meant to discover why "the happening" happened.

Because something doesn't jive.

If I am in control,

Why am I crying?

If crying is a choice,

Why do I chose it?

Have I really asked for this roller coaster ride of memories?

Am I talking to myself?

Okay! What am I saying?

What is the message?

That I have yet to remember?

Am I telling myself to let go of you?

To have him?

Or to have you,

To have anybody,

Including me?

Maybe that's it, Jeff, maybe it's about having, not letting go. Oh, I hope so, because I can't seem to let go of you?

Especially when I am just now,

Beginning to see,

That you,

And me,

And he,

Are the same,

Pattern.

Do you remember who I was when we met?

Someone trying to become respectable.

I was trying to evolve into a clean, acceptable, performer/mom,

Trying not to be pulled into the illusion of control that being a call-girl miraged, clearing my lungs of cigarette smoke, aching to be lovable.

You loved me.

And helped me,

Like myself,

With you.

And that's where I am now,

Liking myself with somebody else.

I am watching a man look within himself in order to understand,

Me,

What a compliment,

Again.

And in that willingness to see something,

You both wished to not know,

Each of you remembered your own bisexual nuances,

And more.

I just love confessions,

Those debilitating little made up problems are always so much bigger to the confessor than to the people they are hiding them from. Yes,

I love confessions because,

I love helping people,

See,

No crime,

In themselves.

So when I found Ted sitting up in bed last night pondering our relationship, unsure of what was going on, it was a delightful relief to not talk about us but to instead end up on the subject of his less-than-affluent college years. He had realized something and wanted to share it with me.

Those trips into the gay club had been for money: an easy way for the gang to get drinks paid for and throw a little cash in their pockets at the same time.

"*That makes you a dime-a-dance boy,*" I laughed with glee.

He raised an eyebrow, and looked at me...Something else...I saw something else.

"*Did you have sex?*" I prodded trying to catch him off guard.

He hesitated..."NOOOO." And began to blush.

"*Your mouth, Did you use your mouth?*" I guessed, smiling, full of child like excitement.

He thought for a moment, " NOOOO."

It was a guessing game now, like charades or Balderdash. "*Did he use his hand on you?*" I squealed.

"Well, no."

"*You! You used your hand!*" I laughed freely. "*More than once??*"

I saw his face admit something even he found funny.

And I laid on my back and laughed,

And laughed,

And laughed,

Even louder,

Then at some point he actually said, "Those guys like me. I don't know what it is about me? But those guys like me!" And, shook his head with a kind of complimented wonderment.

Unaware that they liked him,

Because, he was like them.

After I got myself under control and finished laughing I told him that even though the past was behind him (intended pun not intended) he still had that edge:

A kind of soft sensuality,

Which underlay the power frown and crossed arms,

Of his "this is me being a man" stance.

So, he had been telling me his story to relate to my story. He had begun with an awe-struck expression over the fact that he himself had once been a whore,

And discovered something even more amazing,

That whether he liked to admit it or not,

I wasn't the only bisexual in the room.

"No!" he shook his head adamantly. "That was just for the pleasure of cold hard cash."

"*Hard, being the operative word.*" I teased.

And again, I laughed and laughed and laughed and laughed,

Full of the joy of watching somebody become amused with himself.

Glad to be living,

Not just writing,

Computer screen words,

While I cry.

And the glad to be rid of you,

Reminded me of you.

And I remembered when you made a somewhat similar admission,

About men.

You were so cute; sitting on the couch in your living room, bare chest and worn jeans, full of boyish embarrassment. You seemed like a confessing ten-year-old who was looking at the dirt, kicking it and then glancing up every few minutes under the brim of his cap. You appeared every minute of those six years my junior, as you blushed and squirmed over being turned on by the telling of the story.

You told me that you had always wondered what it would feel like to put a penis in your mouth.

It was exciting to watch you,

Fight, to accept, the desire.

"Have you ever tried it?"

I asked,

Wordlessly,

In the titillating,

Silence,

Of your lust.

"I was asleep,"

I raised my eyebrow questioningly.

"All right, mostly asleep. Drunk! And I had an erection."

"From sleeping?" I wink smiled, soft and gentle.

"Ya! Probably!"

"So what happened?" I nudged.

"He undid my pants and started in on me."

I don't remember the rest of your words or exactly how the story went.

I just remember your face as you told me,

And my feelings as I listened.

You were so sensual,

So vulnerable,

So much a man-child.

So beautiful!

I remember that you said when he wanted you to reciprocate you got angry, surprised by your own previous reaction. I think you said that it grossed you out more because your head began to clear and you realized he could hurt your reputation. That, since you knew him, he knew not only you, but your friends as well. You had been worried that he might talk about it. And because of the danger you hated him, for something he hadn't even done.

I think these things but I'm not really sure. Perhaps I've added and changed the story, mixing interpretation with assumption.

It doesn't really matter because the story is not the point,

Or the reason I have always remembered you thinking about it.

It's because on that day and, on all days, through you, I discovered that such sensual openness in a man, especially one to another with kindness and love, is sexy to me.

And that the only part of your story that wasn't beautiful and manly,

Was the angry part the fists put in,

To illustrate the manly. that I could no longer see.

So, when Ted shared his sexual revelation, I looked for the loving part, the sweet unveiling,

And found it in the willingness to tell.

Because I already knew what he sometimes forgot.

That the only shame in sex is the shame of shame itself.

And, as I saw the beauty of you in him, I saw the ugly angry of him in you. And you both became more human, more perfect, more attainable. As he kissed my back and mounted me from behind.

❖ FIVE ❖

So Babe!...Are you starting to wonder what this letter's about? Well, I think I'm ready to tell you now. Though I'm not sure I have the ability to do it well...

My life, as always, has been interesting since we broke up. Some of it you know and some of it you don't. The part you don't know is what the letter's about.

I guess I did something to myself without even noticing. I began to stay separate during sex, to divide myself into pieces and compartmentalize my emotions. I suppose it was a safety valve or defense mechanism.

I probably didn't notice for a bunch of reasons. One; sex was still fun, though different. And two; it had been that way before I met you so it seemed natural to return to my previous habits.

Which meant that in order to climax during sex I had to imagine some scenario other than the one I was in.

I guess I just assumed that without you in the room there was no way to make love without fantasizing: at least not if I wanted to climax.

Besides, lots of people fantasize so I didn't see it as a problem so much as a solution. Which it was for a while, until I ran into some people that reminded me of you.

Like Ian: he was the cameraman for "Cross Country Cookin,'" the Canadian T.V. series I hosted. He was a techie, same as you: smooth, sexy, easy with machinery.

That show was hard on me. I frightened the producers who quickly began watching me for any evidence of insanity, of which, as you know, there is lots. And the more they found off camera crazy, the more they worried about my on-camera persona and seemed disgruntled with my work. The more they seemed disgruntled the more bruised my professional self-confidence became and the more my work became something to be disgruntled with.

Each day began as they would hem and haw and stare at me through the camera lens, changing the lighting and studying me from every angle, talking about my makeup and looking, I assumed, for the pretty spot.

Then, apparently unsuccessful, they would ask me to double the foundation, eye shadow, contour and blush. Till by the end of the seven weeks on the road, I was having trouble holding my head up under the weight of it all.

I was their chiseled creation,

Whom they treated like a child,

By chaperoning my every move.

I wasn't allowed to go out at night alone, which is my passion. I began to feel controlled and hated, like a prisoner the guards were attempting to rehabilitate, with a makeover program from the Stepford Wives in Pleasantville.

And the harder people tried to control me the harder it was to control myself, to stop myself,

From ripping off my clothes and walking naked in the wind.

I always felt that way whenever I was stopped from making decisions and told what to do because at that point I'd gotten used to being the one in charge.

I hadn't felt as if I were being robbed of my rights since the abusive marriage I got out of just before I met you. So since I was used to being my own boss, not being treated according to my version of mutual respect seemed worse now that I was independent than it had when I wasn't.

Those people — the producers and I — didn't mesh. They wanted their show to be buttoned-down and well-behaved. I wanted my show to be knee slapping, loose and zany. They wanted presentation and plastic smiles. I wanted fun, flighty, adventurous and loving, knowledgeable, concerned. They wanted dead. I wanted alive.

They wanted someone else. I wanted me.

We were working long days and getting little sleep. As we traveled we lived in tight quarters with each other, and I hadn't seen my kids for almost seven weeks. I felt guilty for leaving them and lonely for their love. I felt fragile. My director was wonderful, and fast becoming a dear friend, but he tried too hard to protect me, by trying to understand me, so that he could explain me to the others and get them to like me. He wanted to safeguard my feelings.

Or so he said,

As he relayed all the cruel opinions I needed to be safeguarded from.

Ouch!

And everyone was taking care of me,

As though I couldn't take care of myself.

So,

Of course,

I couldn't.

I was feeling unappreciated.

And so, of course, I wanted sex.

All the men were married and the only women traveling with us might as well have been. One was Lynette Jennings, the producer, and the other an adorable little German girl camera assistant with rippling muscles and a beautiful disposition. Both of them were completely immersed in the romance of the love between each and her man at home.

I seldom had call to look at the producer,

But I watched the little camera assistant with admiration.

And watching her love,

I felt alienated and was reminded of the belief in love,

And acceptance,

Which underscored my homesick separation anxiety with aloneness.

So when Ian asked me to sleep with him, I told him that his teasing was cruel in light of my naked nerves. That since he was married and shouldn't really be on the make and I was single and I was vulnerable, he should step lightly. He didn't.

Thus, since I had a fascination with his round tight butt, which looked like yours,

I answered the call,

And went to his room,

To touch my vulnerable,

With his lust.

To softly caress,

My cheek to his.

Perhaps,

"Fascination", with his butt,

Is too light a word.

Maybe infatuation?

Passion?

Or obsession?

I was fixated,

On his way,

His smoothness.

Which reminded me that,

I hadn't been fixated,

Since you.

So I was scared,

And hooked,

And mouthing on the bait.

After supper, with the crew, all hanging in the unexpected glory of a few hours off, he yawned, excused himself and headed for his room. I waited, told a few more jokes, laughed for a few more minutes, then said my goodnights and pretended to head for mine.

The door to his room was slightly ajar. So I slipped in and softly swung it closed, into darkness.

I stood motionless and without breath, letting my eyes adjust to the absence of light.

The room was dancing in the subtle shifts of graduating black,

Barely made visible by the scented candles that soft lit the moisture heavy air, that wafted through the hardly open door, straight ahead of me. I eased it wider, disturbing the mist, and leading the candle flames to waltz. I stood immobile in my jean shorts and loose fitting T-shirt,

And saw,

The slow dancing flames,

Fill the steam,

With shadows,

And brush upon the man,

Relaxing,

Near dream state,

Waiting in the tub.

Oh, Jeff, I realize how strange it must be for you to read, these images, how much it must seem that I am just trying to titillate you and give you regrets.

But remember me. I need no vengeance, for the loss I chose to have. I share the imagery, to share the feeling, and find a way out, holding onto your hand.

As you wash my hair,

And kiss my feet,

And make clean,

Water,

The most sensual,

Fountain of Youth.

Ian, exhaled and lay his head back onto the porcelain pillow of the tub, not looking at me, seeming relieved that I had come. I entered the room, heady with the smell of marijuana and, feeling droplets of steam gather on my face, closed the door to contain the mood.

Till that moment I had never even touched Ian's hand, never kissed his lips, never been held, never seen him naked. Yet there he was,

Soaking,

Everything,

Clean.

I dipped my head into the water and allowed the wetness to draw me in. I stepped into the tub, clothed and uncaring. The hot sank into me and saturated my jeans. We got drunk, on the intensity of wordless, fantasy sex. I heard him whisper, more to himself than to me, "I knew you'd be like this." I was home again, as I found a space in the silence, to become completely instinctual, like a panther in the night.

Oh sweet feline.

I had missed the you,

In me,

Jeff.

And the night would have lay there, isolated, in the recesses of magical memories, if he had expected me to slip out, as smoothly as I had slipped in.

But he didn't,

Instead he asked me to stay awhile, to wait while he went to the store. Making it normal, as though I was a trusted lover not an apparition of the night. He came back with chips and cheesies and soda pop and chocolate bars. And the past within that past made me feel loved,

Bathed and fed.

Still, I could have left it isolated from my life, stayed emotionally separate, if only he hadn't played the music station and danced naked, easily carrying me, with my legs wrapped around his waist, singing, "All I want to do is have some fun!"

And brought the playfulness, back into the room, of my heart.

And so,

I made him up,

Out of pieces of you.

Desiring,

To have him,

Care about me.

Though I tried not to,

Care,

If he did.

He didn't.

The next morning he handed me a book I had never heard of, "The Bridges Of Madison County," with an inscription on the opening page.

"To Lynette...Because our specialness is reflected within."

A small voice inside me wanted to scoff at the manipulation.

I knew he was a slut, like us, and I knew the game of trying to create romance out of air. But the longing tempted me still. He was smooth like you, and me, and my heart was,

Sore,

Beat up,

Wanting,

It's fix,

Of believing

He loved me.

I read the book. Knowing what it was doing to me, wondering how many copies he'd bought,

And inscribed,

For all the women who would have to let him go,

Back to his wife.

And even though I knew the truth, I believed the lie. I let myself drop anyway, into the crashing waves, of unrequited infatuation.

And, just as he had planned it, I imagined us both as the characters within the book.

We were intimate only two more times. And though I made a project out of him, taking fruit and yogurt and hot and cold liquid to the sexual playground, each time was less wonderful,

As he seemed less and less interested and I became more and more emotionally desperate,

Than the time before.

Till on the last penetration, I hid my face in the bed, as he took me from behind,

Aiming to please,

Himself.

I felt like a job quickly done.

No love.

That's the difference between the made-up ones and you.

They never love me.

Though I like to pretend they do,

As they like also to pretend,

So that I will forget it's pretend,

And think that I do too,

And that they just might,

Eventually.

I hurt,

When the show was over and the TV series ended,

Giving up the fantasy of Ian,

The smoothness,

Of sex,

So warm,

Like you,

And your sleep covered skin early in the morning,

On a languid summer day.

Mmmmm!!

I remember one lazy nap time afternoon, telling you how sexy I thought you were when you still had sleep on your skin, and loving the way you marveled over me, "You're so awesome. I love the way you talk, the way your mind works! You are the only person I ever met who can feel sleep on a person's skin." Your eyes melted into mine, adoring me.

Mmmmm!!

No, I didn't have to work quite as hard to forget Ian as I had to forget you, didn't have to imagine him a giraffe dancing in a diaper, but I did have to go to my computer and vomit,

Words!

Like now.

So I wrote "Dancing Naked In The Wind" and breathed deeply. I let my keyboard-flying-fingers, and the end-of-a-road-trip-return to my family's presence, make me real, and heal me,

Into breaking.

So, as my heart mended,

My mind came apart,

And the perversion of the images became more pronounced,

Till my;

"Now it's time to climax, so I'll close my eyes and dream"

Fantasies twisted into troublesome,

With a touch of romance.

Oh, Jeff, I just,

AHHH!!! Yuk!

OK, I'm going to say it.

Here's the thing.

Like I said, you are the only one I never had to fantasize with in order to climax.

No big deal right?

Wrong!

Because what I imagine is disgusting,

And one day I imagined that the person on top of me was imagining what I

was imagining.

It made me feel like the duo sex offenders,

Of Paul Bernardo and his fiancée

And it turned me on.

Which made me sick.

So I tried not to think gross thoughts,

But then I couldn't orgasm,

Ever.

So I justified it by trying not to see it as an illness or even a problem,

And went back to climaxing on command.

But there was this little echo,

Of agony,

That I kept having to shake away.

I never wanted to think about what it meant and got caught up in the justification that everybody fantasizes.

Sex is fun and I never wanted to risk thinking the pleasure gone. And even now, even after "the happening,"

I still don't,

Want to,

Think it's important.
Because then,
There will be no pleasure,
Without guilt,
Or shame,
Or judgments of sin,
Which I do not believe in.
Still,
Every once in a while,
I would remember,
Me with you,
And see the fantasies as a problem to be solved.
Every once in a while,
I would long to climax,
As one,
Body,
Mind,
And soul,
In time,
And space.
Every once in a while I would long for it.
Every once in a while I would feel ashamed,
Because I believed,
That all things start,
First as a thought,
Then as a belief,
Then as a reality.
And with that as the recipe,
I knew no way to not create,
Since I knew no way to not think.
Thus, I could not help but create,
What I thought about.
And that was the fear, and thus, the thing,
I couldn't stop considering.
The recipe,
Which, since I know it to be true,
Is:

My thoughts matter,

In the creation of me.

So though,

Loving your smooth way through Ian,

Should have been a grand,

Experience,

And it was,

It was only so,

Once,

When I closed my eyes,

And saw beautiful.

After that,

When it was over,

When it was almost,

Over,

I had to close my eyes,

And...

Be hateful.

Always.

For,

Ever,

Since I first discovered that my genitalia was a terrific, feel-good, stress-relieving toy I've been fascinated with sex.

I was sixteen and had been sexually active for several partners before I discovered that being touched felt good...

As long as I was dreaming.

In fact, my first orgasm came when I was asleep, dreaming dreams which had been strongly influenced by the Happy Hooker's sounds of sex porno album.

And that's how I first came to realize that fantasizing makes climaxing possible.

That's also probably when I first got turned on to women since the best part for me on the album was a scene between Xavier and another female. In fact it seemed that all my fantasies were affected by the information that went into my mind via books and television more strongly than the input created by my life.

Making my life reflect my mind,

Which reflected the influences of the time, seemed unavoidable.

However, even though women were my dream creatures when I played with them I still needed a fantasy in order to climax. It seemed I couldn't have an orgasm with men or women until I learned to focus away from my partner and into the playground of my media influenced mind.

So I read books with plenty of food for fodder and began to incorporate more and more the stories they presented. Each fantasy, once familiar, became uninteresting, too tame and lost its power. Variety and unacceptability became a necessity. And I widened the net from which I drew my ideas as the input to my dreams came from darker and darker, seeds.

So delicious did these fantasies seem that the temptation to act them out became irresistible.

So I lived out some of these scenarios and discovered that fact is not better than fiction.

Since most of these twisted dreams, when done for real, not only left me depressed and ashamed and were not as exciting as the thought had been,

They also no longer seemed twisted,

Which disabled the fantasy.

That's why, in order to get the same orgasmic thrill, I had to step up the level of gross or cruel elements to my imaginings,

Because, for some reason, disgusting was the only thing that brought me to orgasm,

Eventually though,

After a while of secret thinking,

The new idea would begin to seem so delicious that I would just have to try it out for real.

And every time,

It was a disappointment and the dream was disabled.

So, I traveled farther down the road to get the same results, like a sex addict cyclone-spinning deeper and deeper into the vat of social sin, until finally, I noticed the pattern.

And stopped acting upon the impulse,

Of temptation.

I halted the process,

Before the process halted me.

That's about when I got married,

Again,

For the third time.

At least that pattern (the pattern of merry-go-round marrying) could be done in public.

My husband was very controlling. Which suited me at first because I felt that I could not be trusted to choose how to control myself. And, since I believed that I couldn't be trusted, when my husband confirmed my suspicion by calling me derogatory names, I knew that he must be very smart indeed. I had found my other half, I thought.

He saw through my apparent kindness, kindness that even I'd been fooled into believing in, and found me disgusting and named me slut. Which also suited me as I figured he was probably right. Since that's what I had suspected, for years ever since my mother had first called me one, ever since I was younger than school, younger than any memories of,

Any other kind of pet name being attached to my person.

I counted on my husband to control me into respectability and teach me how to behave so that I could like myself and my family could be proud of me for finding someone who agreed with them. I hoped to change myself into their vision of good.

I guess that's why, when my husband molested my daughter which reminded me that my father had molested me, I felt my complicity in the fact that I had followed the family pattern for success.

And so finally I stopped listening to what others told me and began searching for my own truth,

And discovered that all the work is done in the mind.

I read script and transactional analysis, re-investigated the Bible, put it aside and re-read "Siddhartha." I adored "Bach's Illusions" and,

Felt, almost there, when finally, the cloudy sky of my confusion opened up to deliver,

"Seth" and "The Nature Of Personal Reality."

I learned that one gets what one expects,

That I cannot not exist,

And that I will not find a hell,

Unless I build it.

And wanting to build a heaven,

I tried to turn away from fantasies of spanking my mother and having sex with strangers in back alleys.

I indulged in the soft sensual kindness of women and, stepping up my spiritual search, tried to heal myself.

Until I met you,

And for the first,

And last time in my life,

Thus far,

I made love without pretending.

How about you, Jeff?

"When you made love,

Did you look in the mirror?

Who did you think of?

Did she look like me?"

It's OK, Jeff! I was just teasing.

You don't have to answer because I already know. I heard your thoughts.

You told me, both in the silences and with your words. You had no secrets, though you sometimes thought you did.

Do you remember that night, when my house was our house, and we were lying in bed, delighting in reading each other's mind? It was such a lark to try and play the silence like a parlor game. You would think of a color and I would try to see or hear your thought and tell you what color it had been. Then after three correct answers it was my turn.

We were both good at it,

At first.

Till we thought about it.

And decided not to be,

Just in case.

"**When we made love,**"

To others,

We could hear each other think.

So on that night of mind-reading games,

We fell asleep,

In our mental walls,

Afraid to think,

After, "**we made love,**"

Having barricaded the silence.

And that night,

Because of the fear of being listened to,

Of being caught thinking of someone else,

I had had to think of someone else,

In order to climax.

And that's when I noticed that I hadn't had to before.

I fell asleep with the question of "Why?" on my mind.

And Astral-projected.

We had been trying to follow the flight paths of Richard Bach and his wife, Lesley. We'd been trying to share the journey together, for the past few nights, and had had no real success at traveling the ethers in tandem. I had Astral projected alone before, during my childhood. And recently I had had astral projection dreams of hovering in the silence and communicating with Dar, my curious, non-verbal son. These experiences made me a professional compared to you. But I was still, am still, unable to project on command.

However, I had faith.

If Richard Bach and Shirley MacLaine and Jane Roberts could master it, I figured that, with a little practice so could I.

And since Lesley and Richard Bach pulled off flying together, I figured with a little practice, so could we. And so I talked to you about it. I was kind of embarrassed at first but you were so cool. You just grinned your little boy grin and agreed to try,

With no success.

So tonight, we had switched to mind reading,

Which had threatened our secrets,

And sent us scurrying into sleep,

To visit them,

You in your dreams,

And me in the air.

I found myself flying away from my body. That was not unusual. That was the point I always got to. But then the feeling of weightlessness would terrify me and the fear would suck me back to my original position. I would lay tingling all over, AWAKE!!! to the millionth degree, mad at myself for being afraid.

But this time I stopped the fear, coaxing myself through, telling myself to relax and, flying through the house and into the city, found myself hovering over Eli, who had been my lover before and occasionally during, you.

He'd fallen asleep reading. He lay naked, spread-eagle, face down on his bed. He was snoring. His left hand extended to the cloth covered box he used for a night table and was resting on the back of an open, dark blue, hard cover book.

I was afraid, coaxing myself, the entire time, just barely able to hover, terrified of falling. I tried to move position to see the title of the book, which appeared to be gibberish from that angle, and had the notion, "Wait till I tell Jeff!" Which sucked me back at the speed of thought.

Only this time while I was being sucked back in I knew why I was returning. So, I was able to redirect the energy without waking my body. And something amazing happened!!

Do you remember?

I woke you up and told you all about it?

It was like being a cartoon character. I was standing on nothing, with no backdrop or depth to my surroundings. It was an indistinct blue, like standing in the sky would be if there was nothing but sky, anywhere, while the sky continued to appear the way it appears when you look at it from earth on a absolutely clear but not very sunny day.

There was no light and no dark. There was no movement of air or temperature to register. Nothing was anything. It just was. There was a cloaked figure, air standing next to me, the figure resembled television's idea of what the Grim Reaper looks like, though only mature love emanated from his presence. I was filled with excitement and energy, immediately recognizing my freedom.

There were no boundaries and my body was my toy to shape and reshape at will. I stretched this way and that. Extending one arm six feet while shrinking the other to inches. I squished short and then tall, turned male and then female, became insect then bird, all the while firing questions at my happy reaper friend. Who almost exclusively answered with, "You already know." And he was right in every instance, I already did.

Though he carried no face outside the shadow of his hood I saw him smile at me. Loving who I was, he watched me with the same delighted maturity that a mother watches her child learn to walk, then smiles everywhere, with all of her being. I was loved. And the wonder of me flowed out of him as I shot my energy fire cracking in every direction.

"*It's tooo fun!!*" I spoke.

"I know." he mind answered back. "It always is."

This was not a dream.

After some no time had passed I stopped asking questions and simply Play-Dough-danced my body in the knowing,

The answer,

In the inkling,

Of the question.

When we discussed my going back, at first I didn't want to go but then, in a blink, the question caused the answer and,

I was,

Going.

However, before my return took the magic from me,

I chose to carry some proof with me into my future,

By correcting my teeth.

In the slow motion time space between shooting back,

And bolting awake,

I repositioned my two front teeth,

Straightening the overlap,

And my body felt the movement.

Do you remember when I woke you up that night trying to explain the feeling in my body?

It was as though I had been sitting on my foot for weeks and it had gone completely asleep, and then spread those fuzzy prickles densely through my whole body.

And it was as though each prickle was a shot of energized wide-awake oxygen,

Leaving me a million lives from sleep.

Do you remember?

Do you remember that the cloaked figure looked like you,

With no skin on, wearing my ex-husband's hooded housecoat,

That you had not yet worn?

And that my two front teeth stayed straight for five days,

Until you moved out,

And I no longer wanted,

To know,

That nothing happened against my will.

Knowing still.

I sat by the fire watching the flames, miserable over the knowing, knowing, knowing,

That you'd be gone, when I got home.

But that morning, was before the knowing,

So with straight teeth and a wide open mind,

I still liked what I knew,

Which was more than everything,

Until well after the sun had made it's morning jaunt,

Into the absolutely clear but not very sunny sky,

Until long after you had taken my son's to the zoo.

Until, dragged by an avalanche of warning, I grew stone heavy tired, and fell into dreaming only to awaken seconds after sleep. I was bleary eyed and drowsy and standing at the precipice of a choice. The precognitive vision had handed me two awarenesses. I had been given today's winning lottery numbers worth ten million dollars and the knowledge of our impending break up, which heavied my head. To wake up and write one down meant to become aware of the other.

In that moment, the imminent sadness of loss was heavier than the uplifting happiness of possibilities so I chose to forget and not believe and hid back into dreams of nothing.

Until your truck pulled up, too soon to be back from a day at the zoo.

Apparently as you pulled onto the zoo parking lot Rye jumped from the truck and ran, rapidly zig-zagging amidst the cars, immediately getting lost, at least to you. So your boys-in-tow-trip-to-the-zoo never even made it through the front gate. Because, by the time you found Rye while dragging three other crazy kids, your nerves were frazzled and the idea stank. You headed for home.

From what I could gather, you felt inept and resentful of your own inability to handle their disabilities.

And so,

I fell to the ground,

Just when I had begun to fly,

Free of the limitations of my life,

As you ran to be free from the demands,

Of my home.

And I let you,

Take with you,

My ability to make love to,

The one I am with.

Even though I knew,

That all experience follows the mind,

As it follows all experience.

I worked hard to get shuck of you,

Dancing you in diapers with vomit on your face,

Wanting to be rid of you,

So that I could keep you,

As a friend.

I tried so hard to get rid of you,

That the problem I've been avoiding giving words to,

Was given birth.

OK, Jeff,

I'm gonna say it:

in my mind I became a child molester.

There! **WAIT!**

Just listen,

Let me explain!

It's like the suggestions from that image of your four years younger than me smooth skin in a diaper and my need for you mixed with all the messed up ideas and memories in my head: like my dad molesting me until I was old enough for school,

And created a mental monster in me.

And so to orgasm, I dreamed, explicit dreams, of one little child who looked like me.

Oh, I had another fantasy but it was beautiful, romantic and full of kindness and though it often flirted on the edges of my mind, it never got enough of a hold to take me with it,

Except on four occasions:

Like that first night with Ian,

And then Michael,

And Mitch,

And finally,

Ted.

Except for on one night with each of them, whether I was sleeping with a man or a woman the only way I could have an orgasm was to close my eyes and imagine a child, someone just barely out of diapers. Eventually, the child became a little girl named Bonnie,

Is that your wife's name Jeff?

I can't remember.

But I think it is.

Anyway, Bonnie comes in the room and, depending on who I'm with and what we are doing the scenario changes. For example if a beautiful woman is giving me attention then I simply superimpose her image with Bonnie's. The fantasies are usually this benign and this gross. Sometimes she stands over me, sometimes she sits across from me, sometimes out of fear, sometimes out of love, sometimes out of a rather robot-like response system, but always she does what she is told.

Just like I used to,

With my father,

And my husband.

And yet,

The sin is mine,

And feels not at all related to them.

Because it stays in my head, not theirs.

I have gone through a variety of reactions to this pedophilic fantasizing. I have tried allowing it so that it would lose its power and go away,

But it never did.

I have tried using it to maintain separateness, analyzing it to gain understanding, celebrating it to give it honor, being ashamed of it to respect it's danger and always whether I think I am willing to or not, at the point in the throes of sex when I want to have an orgasm,

I make the choice,

Close my eyes and call her forth.

I make the choice,

Believing that sex with a,

Young,

Person,

Is bad,

Even in my mind.

And since I believe,

Though I try not to,

It is so.

I miss you, Jeff.

You were my only natural lover.

And you left your mark.

Though I had fantasies before you,

They were just cruel,

And cruel was better than this,

Because it was so divorced from anything I knew to be true.

And the only pedophilia,

Before you,

Was me,

As the victim,

Of my dad and all the other older men who seemed like him.

Before you,

Because I never wanted to be what they were,

I slept only with,

Much much older men,

Than me.

Which kept me innocent but made the men in my life,

Exactly what I thought they were.

Men unlike you,

The younger than,

Me,

Taking my position,

And giving me theirs.

I was the older woman,

Knowing that,

Loving,

Younger,

Is bad,

Always.

Because it hurt,

When you stopped,

Loving back.

So, since it is bad and therefore matches me, younger, is all I ever want anymore...in my head.

And in the years that have passed since you and I broke up, 'til on the night of "the happening," just before writing this letter, there have only been three occasions when I came to orgasm without that unacceptable image in my head.

However, on all three of those occasions I was still imagining.

And though this other image took my breath away and brought me to tears.

It has not become a vision I can use at will.

But seems to come upon me,

When the need is strong,

And the similarities,

Between you and my partner,

Intense.

Like the first time,

I ever witnessed,

The vision,

Of sensual beauty,

There,

In the tub,

With smooth,

Like you,

Ian.

As I closed my eyes, and threw my head back, and saw:

Me, thin, void of body fat, like in my twenties, and early thirties, like when we first met. I was dancing in the air, no steps really, just a rhythmic floating with a tall soft haired faceless man, whom I've always believed represented the actor Jeff Goldblum, and whom I only now, as I write this begin to realize represented you.

Jesus! I just remembered, just this second, that he was the actor I chose when the book about falling out of love told me to replace you with someone else, someone unattainable, as a first step to walking away. Jeff! I also just realized I chose him because in the movie "The Fly" when my kids and I were on set waiting for our cue, I saw him. He was standing behind us and when Rye threw his hat on the ground Jeff Goldblum picked it up and handed it back to me.

And his hands were the same as yours.

Oh my God! I never remembered that till just now.

His sensitive, gentle, enormous hands, were the same as yours. No wonder I found him sexy.

Jesus! I just realized he has the same first name as you. Christ, Jeff what are you doing in my head, shaping my thoughts, making me crazy. It's like I never got rid of you, just camouflaged you, dressed you up as somebody else.

What made you so beautiful,

To me?

When you make love,

Do you look in the mirror?

Who do you think of?

Does she look like me?

When I made love that first night,

With Ian,

I thought of me,

Dancing in the air, with a faceless man, in a suit. I was wearing a long, almost transparent simple gown. My perfect body was a black silhouette beneath the gauze like material that waved in the breezeless air. The man was all shadow and darkness, all perfect.

He undid my gown by releasing a single shoulder snap and let it drop off my body and fall, beneath my feet, which stood on nothing. He lovingly backed me up till my calves nudged against the hardness of a coffee table-sized rectangular marble block, and eased me into a sitting position. He placed his hands with a patient urgency on the inside of my knees and spread my legs.

He slowly removed his suit, which disappeared as it fell away.

He never for a second took his eyes off me.

I never for a minute felt naked as I basked in wearing nothing.

Once he was exposed he knelt in front of me and caressed me,

With his beautiful hands,

As though he were me,

Doing what my own palms wished to do.

Then he reached one arm under each of my legs and lifted me,

Effortlessly,

Without ever leaving his knees.

He picked me up,

And then dropped me down,

Onto him. And brought me back,

Mind,

And body,
Into the room.
With Ian.
The dream lover,
Dream,
Was over.
It never worked,
With the same guy twice,
Or with me alone.
And it usually,
Didn't work at all.
Though I kept wanting it too,
Believing that when it did,
When I became able to make beauty,
Appreciation,
And mutual desire,
My turn on,
I would be sexually,
Healthy,
Nutritiously fulfilled.
And that's why when the dream lover dream,
Swept over me for the second time,
I thought I had made it,
Into the arms of romance.

❖ SIX ❖

His name was Michael.

I had been working in a strip club in Toronto for almost a week. I was trying to gather up the funds I owed the United States immigration department and had only fourteen days to do it in. My friend Fred – you remember Fred? The one who produced the film I did in North Bay? He suggested that I go to work with his wife. She was a stripper for one of the classier clubs in town. She had started working there instead of at the local daycare when her husband and kids found themselves facing bankruptcy. The job had saved their situation, so he thought it might save mine.

As I said before I have always stayed away from stripping even though one of my childhood idols was Gypsy Rose Lee. It's just that the job is so brazen, so high profile. I have never wanted my reputation to adversely affect my children. And my reputation was likely to be sullied enough to adversely affect my children if I made the stripping choice because my series was running on National TV at the moment rendering at least my face recognizable. However, I was cornered. The kids and I had no home, as I had already given up my house in the expectation that we were headed for the states. So with no where to go back to there were very few choices left. Besides I wanted to live in America. I just knew things would be better for my children there.

My situation seemed desperate and as I listened to Fred I reasoned with myself that, actually, if I was recognized it wouldn't really matter, wouldn't really affect my children since I wouldn't even be living in this country anymore. I was leaving.

And not a moment too soon.

I wanted out of Toronto, needed to get away from living this life of being constantly harassed by 'pop in' visits from Children's Aid. I wanted to live in America. I was hoping to live with my new husband Tod— the one with height and legs and balls like you. But I couldn't ask him for help paying this last minute unexpected immigration bill because I was trying to prove that the kids and I were not the burden I knew we were. The marriage had already suffered enough of a tumultuous adjustment to disabled kids and pregnant teenager needs. I didn't want to add financial ruin to the load.

I wasn't worried about Tod having any serious moral issues with the idea — his last wife had been a stripper — and I told myself I was only protecting him from the strain of too much problem solving. Because the truth is, I guess I knew he wouldn't come through and so to avoid disappointment, I didn't ask.

So I wasn't worried about him having a moral issue, I was worried about me.

I decided to close my eyes to the social repercussions, strip for a few weeks, offer satisfaction for a fee and pray not to be seen, by anyone of note. It worked! I must have had an overblown sense of my own public popularity. You know Canada; no one's a star, so only two people (friends) recognized me. And they'd seen it all before.

About a week after I started working in this unexpectedly hilarious environment Michael and a bunch of his co-workers came in. They were all drunk, and very playful. Fred's wife and I did "doubles," giving the guys a little "girly" show, playing, laughing, letting the money roll in, till the lights came on and the night was over. It had been fun for all. But Michael, who hadn't had his turn for personalized, two-person lap service, wanted more. Time had cheated him.

I'd been sitting on his lap waiting for the next song when the unforgiving glare of the lights, which signaled the evenings end, burst on. He moaned his disappointment. I whispered in his ear.

He whispered back, conspiratorially, grinning with boyish excitement, "Could we do that?"

"*Sure.*" I smiled; open, friendly, liking the idea.

He looked around, then pulling me even closer, mouthed the words, "How much?"

I had no idea what to charge but I knew how much I still needed, "*Three hundred and sixteen dollars and seventy five cents.*"

Michael was a romantic, a single man with a fair amount of money, who hadn't had sex in a year. When we got to his place I took a shower while he prepared the setting. So when I emerged clean and fresh and wrapped in a towel the room danced with the sensual breath of candle flames and a roaring fire. There was a thick snuggly quilt laid out in front of the fire while Celine Dionne serenaded us from every room in the house. I floated into his arms and we moved together dancing just long enough to feel the connection.

He sat me down on the quilt and excused himself, saying that vanity and the desire to see all of me forced him to exchange glasses for contacts.

He had prepared a glass of wine and a plate of fruit and cheese and placed them close to the fire. He left me for a moment as all my sensories salivated and fell into the swirl.

I heard the toilet flush, the shower spray and the sink shut off. Then there he was, standing naked in front of me, wearing the twin to my ex-husband's robe that you once wore. My breath caught in my throat as he melted into the quilt beside me. Our eyes looked into each other's and we saw something more than sex and having not tasted even a sip of the wine I felt drunker than he, lost in the moment.

Of you.

Michael was short and wore glasses so I hadn't noticed it before but there he was, inches from me, unwrapping my towel,

Resembling you.

As his hand cupped my breast with such gentle reverence I stared at the ghost of you in his face. He had the same blue, bird like eyes, the same nose, the same hair, the same clean water kiss. I leaned back on my knees; he spread them apart and looked at me. He understood the candles and the silence. The spell was cast as he let his robe fall to expose himself.

Even though,

Unlike your clean hairlessness, he was covered in a feathery forest of fur from shoulder blade to toe,

Because,

The other similarities between dreams and memories and hoped-for fantasies all melded into me,

Before we,

When we,

And after we,

Made love.

And I looked in the mirror,

And I thought of,

Yes, he looked like you,

He told me stories of who he was, taking care to take the time, to become a person and the one with whom I had connected.

He was smooth,

Like you,

And Ian.

He talked and caressed and kissed, all the while using a gentle deliberateness to keep the sexual sensuality alive in the room,

While he undressed his life with confessions.

He had been a drug addict and achieved very little until recently. He called it a wasted ten years but he was clean now and quickly heading towards financial independence. He had never been married and was involved with no one. I started to believe that maybe, just maybe he could be real,

For me,

And wanted it,

In spite of my husband.

Isn't it ironic?

Don't you think?

To finally find the chemistry,

With someone who wasn't already married,

Who might want to marry me,

After I'd already married?

It was the irony that gave the story a hook to hang my heart on.

I'd gotten used to saying that I liked my men married because then they wouldn't want to see me too much. But now that I was going to be living a country away and I was the married one, it seemed I liked my men single.

Because, it felt better not to have to worry about hurting some man's wife. And it felt better to think that he wanted more from me than sex.

I hoped I wanted more from him.

Tod wasn't an issue. I knew he would remain unscathed, knew he wouldn't really care. So I was in the perfect playground for wanting more because there was no reason not to. Especially since, even if Michael also wanted me and began wanting to see me too much, he couldn't.

Maybe that's what made "the wanting" ok.

It's not that I'm a bitch it's just that, you know how it is, Jeff, with so many needy kids, and so little money, and my work singing at night in the bars, I just don't have a lot of time to date. And that problem is what caused me to develop the pattern of wanting my men married. That way it's perfect for both of us. Because he's working during the day and busy with his wife at night and neither one of us wants the burden of spending time with each other.

So it made sense and felt good,

To believe my own excuses.

Until I noticed that,

I never wanted the burden of spending time with,

Any one,

Not even my husbands.

No one,

But my children,

And you,

The lover,

I was trying to recreate.

Because,

When I was with you,

I couldn't get enough,

Time in your presence.

I brought you home,

To my bed, that had always otherwise been,

My sanctuary from men.

I brought you home,

Often.

For you were the exception,

I was trying to re-accept.

You had all the qualities,

That I was afraid,

Too much time in their company, would show me they hadn't.

So I believed my own excuses.

Even though,

It had been different with you.

I began to hope it might be different with Michael.

And in hoping realized that I had always wanted this. But that I had been afraid.

That saying, *"I like my men married and unable to move in"* was easier than saying, *"I'm afraid he'll reject my children and that'll force me to reject him."*

Which was pretty much the story,

Of what was already happening between Tod and I.

I needed a place to put my heart.

And Michael looked like a good location.

Since we had enough chemistry,

To fibrillate,

My deadened feelings,

And shorten the miles apart.

It was easy to let myself love,

You,

Again.

Until Michael and I spent enough time together,

To fibrillate,

And give life to,

The missing parts that weren't quite you,

Which shorted out the chemistry,

And flatlined all the love.

It happened quickly as it always does.

Like when, two weeks after moving in with my husband, Tod stopped pretending to be able to share in my children's lives.

And when Michael called,

To say that,

He thought we should find out,

If what we thought we'd found,

Was actually what was there.

He flew me from Houston to Toronto to spend a few days with him to examine the possibilities. It looked promising at first, when he told me stories of his past escapades: the bisexual experiences during his drug days and the desire to be paid for sex.

We'd begun with him paying me, so his fantasies felt like a relief,

Freeing me of the fear of moral judgments.

He cooked wonderful gourmet meals and took me to deliciously expensive restaurants.

But then the apparent sameness slid away as he,

Revealed that he wasn't clean with the erotic smell of soap,

But anal with the uptight need for clean.

He wasn't, as he had at first appeared, a classy man indulging in the richness of his surroundings,

But a class-conscious etiquette convict-chained to appearances and the need for presentation.

I imagined my children swimming in the accouterments of his home,

And revisited the fear, of the hurt, of their rejection.

I doubted that my screaming, jumping, finger-flicking, paper-ripping hyperactive mentally challenged teenage boys would meld even remotely into this environment.

I looked at Michael,

And ached to hang onto,

The smoothness.

My addiction to "Smoothness,"

Appeared to be the decoy,

That was drawing me into the blind,

Exposing me to the hunters,

Who were aiming down the barrel,

Of their well-worn guns,

Forgetting to care,

If the explosion caused me pain.

My addiction to "Smooth,"

Was my Achilles heal.

And that made me like a cat in heat,

Seeking the scent, that disconnected my brain,

And drew my bodies flame.

My addiction to "Smooth" put smoke in my eyes,

And blinded me from the truth,

Making it difficult to tell the real in you, from the counterfeit,

Which turned out to be the synthetic smooth, in both Ian and Michael.

Theirs was the manufactured liquidity, of pot and alcohol,

And not smooth,

Which is, the music of self-confidence and open-minded sensuality.

My mental meanderings away from the project at hand evaporated.

You know, Jeff, I think the reason I didn't see it honestly is because I wanted,

To not,

Realize that I may have been in love with you because you were movie star sexy,

Rather than finding you movie star sexy because I was in love.

And the harder I tried to find in Michael the you that I had thought was there, the more out of sync he seemed to feel and the harder he pulled away.

Till on my second visit to see him, he shut me out completely.

It was an unusual visit. I had gone to his house for the quiet of no children, seeking a place where I could be alone at least during the day, to work on my book, "Freak TV." The writing had gone fairly well but the solitude left me longing for companionship. Thus, for the most part, I was happy to turn my attention to him when he would come home at night. Then, as the relationship got funkier and funkier I became more and more tempted to write the story of what was happening around me, rather than tip tap typing autobiographical whinings about problems I'd already solved. It was tempting to write off track because for me, writing is about achieving resolution, though I often pretend its intention is to get remuneration.

I wanted to fold the past in with the present to write about both at the same time, to analyze, to understand, where I had come from and how I had gotten to today.

Until, when, the stress of rejection induced a disconnectedness that I mistook for a Zen-like state. I wrote as though I was merely a conduit for the knowing that moved inside the fingers of my soul. I wrote and learned things that I hadn't already known, and suddenly, for no reason, I believed that my half-finished story of self would end on a rich note, with me winning millions of dollars on the lottery,

Though I hadn't yet.

And I guess at that moment precognition seemed pretty,

Stupid,

I stopped wanting to write about truths from then and before then and someday when.

I started fantasizing about ways for my hurt, romantic pride, to get even.

I felt a child like,

Finger wagging,

Na na na na na na,

Need for revenge.

I was becoming petty watching Michael turn away. I wanted him to regret it. I imagined him reading about my winnings in the paper, frustrated over all the brand name sunglasses he could've bought.

I remembered how I had felt when my last husband won the lottery, and then kept all the money to himself leaving me and the kids with no way to pay rent. I recalled how ugly it looked when he, sneered in my face said, "You blew it" while waving his winnings in front of me. His behavior, his seemingly smug happiness over being able to stand back and watch his family suffer, had made me feel sorry for him, relieved to no longer be a part of his life. And yet, even though I knew from experience that it wouldn't work, I was sneering inside now too, just like my ex-husband had done, hoping to create regret for rejection through financial one-upmanship.

Except I wasn't one up.

I hadn't won anything and the whole thing was just a load of petty make-believe.

My thoughts were rambling,

With wishes that don't come true,

I was losing my perspective, fast.

I lay down for a nap. When I woke up I knew I should leave, that Michael had shut me out to wish me gone. He had rejected only me, having never even met my kids. It had been about me, no other excuses, no one else to blame. It was time to go.

And in the freedom of letting go I heard a voice tell me that Michael did not belong in this book I would never finish. But that there would come another story in a year or two which would follow the precognitive vision of flowing past into present and writing about men. (I suppose that book could be this letter!)

And also in the freedom of letting go I knew, since I had never for one second, regretted leaving my abusive husband; not even when he held $100,000 in his hands, money cannot buy regret and Michael would probably not miss me,

No matter what the future held.

So I packed up and went to stay with Fred the film producer and his wonderful stripper wife.

Well, Jeff, since it's possible that the book I imagined during my nap, the one that Michael belongs in, is the letter I am writing now. And since that would mean that that imagining was future sight,

What do you figure? Could my imagined lottery bonanza have been more than just stress petty dreaming? Is it possible that I might win, when I finish writing? Is there any way to know the difference between future sight and wishful thinking? Or are those precognitive visions like versions of tawdry daytime talk shows wherein truth and fiction are blended so completely together that they become impossible to separate.

Are they like that, making it impossible to hear, the real story?

Of what is yet to be?

The pot is thirty million. True, it's not the ten million I dreamt of when, the you and I part, of you and I died. Still, I guess there's no harm in buying a ticket, or two,

If I can dig up enough change.

That's what I did the day I left Michael's:

Dug up enough change and bought a lottery ticket.

Not coincidentally, that is also what I did, the day I let you ...leave me.

I wish I could honestly say that I was ten degrees cool that day, wish I could say that I walked away with frigid ease, but I didn't.

I pined,

And wrote,

And wanted,

Your sexy smooth,

Back,

In whatever guise.

And that's what lead up to finding,

And leaving Michael,

Wanting your sexy smooth,

Back.

It had felt icky desperate,

Not from the loss of love,

But from the low self-esteem the lack of tender visions caused,

As I puked up my dreams of a future in his arms,

And replaced them with dreams of Bonnie.

I pretended to myself that no dreams affected me that not even my horribly putrid pornographic mind had any bearing on the reality of who I was.

Meanwhile I tried and tried in vain to re-experience during sex the fantasy of that first night together with Michael,

That I had first experienced during my first experience, with Ian.

Because those dreams were representations of my wishes and beliefs, they did affect me. They affected me as all inspirations that create the need to quest after,

Do.

But the vision of dancing lovers never came back according to my will, no matter how hard I willed it. Even when I closed my eyes and started the scenario according to beautiful memory, instead it twisted and warped and reworked itself into the pedophile dream. Every time.

And I be,

Came,

Ashamed.

As sex be,

Came,

A frustrating, search for sensual truth,

That I would abandon, in order to come close to orgasm.

And because I believed I needed it I would regress and call forth,

Bonnie,

And feel dirty,

Enough to achieve,

Pleasure.

Till eventually,

I didn't want to be what I was.

I took a nap, to hide in my dreams and get away from myself,

To erase, for however long, the knowledge of my own existence.

And remembered,

The way to not be,

Is to not be,

Where you are.

I left,

Every one that came along,

And returned,

To my original preference for married men who,

Left me alone.

But in addition now I preferred them, thousands of miles away.

So when I met Mitch Hedberg, a stand-up comedian common-law husband from Los Angeles, I was interested. It was a strange situation. I had been quasi-dating Marv, the owner of the Laugh Spot for about a week. The relationship had no chance at a future, though we were still checking it out unsure of how to stop. There was no real attraction between us and his head was still mind-buried in the past of some other girl. So he couldn't get very hard for very long. It seemed that in Marv's world, tender sex wasn't nasty enough to be exciting.

I could understand.

We had the same problem in reverse.

I liked it tender and sweet with nasty thoughts inside my head.

He liked it nasty and impersonal with tender(?) thoughts,

Of someone other than me?

Inside his head.

Marv could only have an orgasm if I lay with my face in the pillow while he pleasured himself on my backside. As you can imagine, this was not exactly a real drawing card for me.

I was trying to figure out how to stop seeing him without losing work, (As you probably also remember, the last time I broke up with an important figure in the comedy world my standup career dried up for two years.) when Marv supplied me with the answer: Mitch!

Marv invited me to the strip bars. He loved to hire a girl to table dance for me and then sit back and watch me get excited. So to be a good sport, I did...get excited. He also seemed to see it as his duty to entertain the comedians from out of town, especially Mitch, his protege, whom he had brought along tonight intent on sharing me.

Mitch was cute and young with blond blunt-cut jaw length hair that fell in his face, for he tended to tilt it downward. He had a shyness that was belied by his mannerisms and was constantly reaching to touch me, my arm, my back, my hair. As I checked with Marv to see how he felt about the situation it became more and more obvious that he liked to share and that maybe, he was hoping for a threesome.

I hate threesomes!

Though I do them for friends sometimes.

I hate them because there is no intensity of focus,

No intimacy,

No way to lapse into fantasy and climax.

I made my distaste for the idea clear,

Repeatedly,

While the night got weirder and weirder.

Eventually we ended up at my friend's mansion,

Where I was house-sitting while I worked on the never-ending book I'd begun at Michael's house.

We were in the game room playing pool. Marv kept trying to push me towards Mitch and even suggested that Mitch watch while he (Marv and I) had sex. A coupling which obviously would have turned into Mitch and I, since Marv and I had never had sex cause, like I said, Marv wasn't very into intercourse,

With me,

He wasn't very good..

Or perhaps I was the one who wasn't very good at it,

With him.

Fact is, Mitch was cute and Marv's persistence had kind of pissed me off, especially when he drunkenly started suggesting —in response to my distaste for threesomes — that I invite one of my daughters over to sleep with him while I slept with Mitch, making it two twosomes instead of one threesome (a disgusting request I got surprisingly often though I generally just say 'NO' and don't usually bother to experience disgust).

I told Marv to go to bed and leave us alone. I even tucked him in, and, with Marv's blessing, took Mitch onto the trampoline for the aphrodisiac of acrobatic love.

I guess Marv was kind of ending us with a bang, which got me burning mad. And I guess, we were both using Mitch, though he didn't seem to mind. And truthfully neither did I. I mean, what the heck! It was fun, frolicking, fornication that brought your laugh to my ears. Though it was too silly, to get under my skin.

Mitch had all the danger qualities: blond hair, little boy grin, smooth style.

That's why I didn't expect him to actually like me,

Because, I always feel like those guys like you, are out of my reach...to grab on to.... and hold.

Besides he was young and I felt old, enough for him to laugh at.

Until,

As I slept,

He didn't,

Laugh,

And,

Couldn't keep his hands off me,

Like I was a drug,

That he couldn't get enough of,

No matter how many times I pushed him away.

That always weirds me out.

I can never understand it when someone,

I like,

Becomes too excited to let me sleep,

And likes me back.

Some how being near my body kept him awake.

It was alarming enough,

To make me feel vulnerable.

So the next time he came to town,

I stayed away.

But the time after that,

Well,

I'd been thinking about him,

And I guess,

I just happened to be in the club.

I think I knew it would happen with him. His comedy was so fresh and different, his persona so vulnerable, little boy cute, that I think I knew I only had to set the stage.

To see the vision.

And I was right.

This time, what had failed to rekindle the pureness with Ian, created it with Mitch!

I took control and,

Having ordered a cornucopia of delight from room service,

Placed the tray beside the bed.

Mitch was stoned...Smooth...Languid...I dipped into his mood,

And swam in the drunkenness of sex.

I sat straddling his naked body,

Exposing body part,

After body part,

Pushing his hands down,

Not letting him touch me,

Plucking food items from my tray,

Nibbling,

Licking,

And eating them off,

First me,

And then him,

And then both of us.

He strained to touch me.

I eased away,

"*Let me!*" I whispered.

He did,

Let me,

Float off,

Into the fantasy of the dance,

Which took me away and brought me back again,

Into the recognition,

Of the pattern.

I knew that if I tried to have this experience with Mitch again,

It would elude me and tease me to frustration,

Because I'd feel insecure,

Unsure,

Of whether,

He liked me,

Or just my smooth.

And unsure of whether,

There was anything to like.

So I haven't seen him since.

Though I often call the club to see when he's in town.

That's all of them Jeff,

The almost-only people this heavenly dream happening ever happened with.

Though that is not "the happening" happening I'm leading up to telling you about. All my fantasies whether dark or feather-light are merely background stories to the truth I have yet to tell. So, except for the night when "the happening" happened,

That's everyone,

With whom I have ever danced.

Though I'm sure I could have,

With Bill,

Whom I never dated,

Nor would date,

Because I loved his wife.

They appeared to be a devoutly religious Mormon couple. They owned and operated a children's entertainment company. I worked for them, first as a show assistant to Barney the Dinosaur and then as a solo performer, imitating Cinderella, Pocahontas, Esmeralda, Arial, Snow White, Mini Mouse, Baby Bop and any other children's character I could convince them I was capable of.

With them I did storytelling for the physically disabled, the mentally challenged and the normally made. I created a clown character that was neither a very good juggler nor much of a magician but who could improvise comedy out of nothing at all.

Because of them I made enough money to survive another divorce and learn the ins and outs of Houston. Helen, Bill's wife, knew how much money I made, knew it wasn't enough to live comfortably on and tried to help out in whatever way she could.

It was Helen that gave me extra work, extra food, extra Christmas decorations, extra clothes. It was Helen that watched my behavior and for whom I had to create a diversion.

Because it was being around Bill that made me talk stupid.

It was ridiculous really. Bill and I had nothing in common and he showed no real interest in me. In fact, truth be told, he seemed more interested in my daughter Deja, (The same daughter who had been afraid of you, because, as I've said, you look almost exactly like her stepfather and alleged childhood molester).

You remember Deja. You were there when she first came to live with me.

Your reaction was overt. You looked at that brand-new thirteen-year old daughter and whistled in appreciation, "WOW! She is going to be incredible when she grows up. Take off the braces and you've got instant beauty."

No wonder she was afraid of you.

And no wonder I let you move out.

And no wonder Bill was interested more in her than in me.

Because, you were right she is beautiful, with or without braces.

She is also brilliant, strong and the mother of Dakota — the first grandson I ever hand-delivered — in the first, of several, most awe-inspiring moments of my life.

A moment, which came about because,

Deja didn't want to be prodded and pried at. She didn't want to lose control of the choices made over what was happening to her body. That's why she left the hospital when the doctors treated her as though she was too young to have any say: no part to play in the role of giving birth to her son.

We agreed that she would bear down and deliver her baby at home. It was the most incredible thing I have ever witnessed and the greatest compliment any of my children could ever give me.

She drank castor oil and lay down to wait.

We dimmed the lights to near blackness.

Dessa and I hunched unobtrusively in the corner, waiting,

Watching,

While,

Deja;

The lioness woman child,

Paced,

Naked,

On all fours,

Back and forth,

Upon the bed.

Deja controlled her labor, turned it off and turned it on,

Staying in charge of her body.

Till finally,

Deciding,

To let go,

She leapt to the edge of the bed, calling, "NOW!" and pushed,

A beautiful baby boy from her seventeen-year-old womb. Not quite done, this remarkable young lady delivered the after birth, stood up and took a shower.

No wonder I see myself in her,

She is an amazing force to behold.

It makes me proud,

To think,

I may be like her.

And so,

To support her son,

Deja worked with me,

And Bill,

Who liked her better,

Because she was,

Younger,

At the very least.

I trembled near him anyway...since I didn't know how to not.

For he was tall and blond and handsome and well-built and his hands were like Jeff Goldblum's, whose hands were like yours. He was young, smelled clean, and had a boyish childishness. He was good at everything he did and better than me at almost everything I did.

So when I stopped by for costumes,

And Helen was out of town,

And he fed me as a social gesture,

I became tongue tied and stupid,

And clumsied my way out of there.

And as the situation got worse,

Each time I neared the house,

I dropped a few more I.Q. points,

And an extra prop or two. So,

I created some pretended infatuations,

With other staff members,

And even Helen herself,

To mask my behavior,

And divert them from knowing.

It was my crush on Bill,

That turned me into the Mrs. Magoo of children's comedy.

But it was my crush on you,

That gave me the crush on Bill.

So Jeff that's it.

That's the effect you had on my life.

I have been eternally searching,

To find you again,

Victim to the young,

Tall,

Blond,

Sleek,

Silent,

Strong handed,

Intelligent,

Slutty,

Amoral,

Boyish,

Talented,

Sensuous,

Caring,

Smooth,

Clean water kissing,

Promise of men.

And the funny part is,

That even with all these clues,

Of all these yous,

I had no idea,

That I hadn't let you go,

No idea at all.

I thought I was just fickle.

Thought I was just lost in the lust of new beginnings.

I had no idea that,

With every beat of my heart,

And every fluttering breath of life,

I was unremittingly,

Loving,

You.

I had no knowledge of the obvious, no awareness that, I was seeking to not love you, whenever I brought forth,

Bonnie,

Hoping to climax,

As the person in charge,

Alone,

And free of needing you.

I was love-hating your youth.

So I allowed the little girl Bonnie to bring me pleasure, not caring that, all the work is done in the mind.

❖ SEVEN ❖

When you make love,

Do you look in the mirror?

Who do you think of?

Does she look like me?

Do you tell lies?

And say that it's forever?

Do you think twice?

Or just touch and see?

Def Leppard is in my head.

Jeff's letter is in my head.

Ted's wife is in my head.

The needs of my children are in my head.

The sound of my soul is in my head.

The events as I live them before during and after they happen are in my head.

My head is a very crowded place.

No wonder I used to love our silence.

There was no room for conversation.

Wink, wink, nudge, nudge, say no more!

Just kidding, babe,...well… sort of.

You know how I am, always searching to understand, thinking on several different levels at once, amusing myself in the playground of my mind. So I guess it's not really any wonder that I built a fantasy life to orgasm with. The surprising part was more the meaning of the fantasies than the existence of them.

Usually I thought people made too big a deal out of these little connectors in the mind, giving them power, making them ominous. Usually I scoffed at such psychiatric mumbo jumbo. But I wasn't usual anymore.

Things had changed, become different.

I could stand away from it, finally.

And you know what Jeff?

Standing back, gaining perspective and seeing it all made it easy to

Brush away the extraneous bullshit.

You know why you left such a big effect on me?

Because you loved me so much.

And for no other reason than that.

Thank you!

So, babe, it's March 1, 1999. Two weeks has passed since I started writing this letter, and a lot has happened. In fact, in my life, I've reached the ending to this letter, even before I've finished telling you about the beginning, "the happening,"

The impetus for the odyssey that gave me all my pieces,

That eventually brought me back together.

And as this odyssey brought me to it's end I have remained busy, my life, as always, is full, of all the happenings that happen, every single day. I've surprised Dessa by flying her to Toronto for an unexpected wedding shower, taken a week off from writing to be with my kids and run errands. I've babysat for Tsara to give her a break from babysitting for me, and to let her get out for a bit of fresh experience. I've edited a personal performance tape for Ted's company to present when attempting to place me in a new job.

I dealt with the resort personnel when my grandson got a knife and sliced up all the furniture because my son had gotten him fixated on knives and his overtired mother had fallen asleep. I gently calmed the two old people that nearly shot my oldest boy because he came upon them unexpectedly in the dark. And they, knowing nothing of autism, assumed he was a strung out drug addict screaming with rage rather than a simple little crazy boy screaming to scream.

I've driven into town and picked up Dessa from the airport. I've run to comfort Ted whose wife, after threatening suicide, disappeared when she found out about us. And then finally, culminating the two weeks, I took a three-hour drive to Dessa's Houston bridal shower, which was wonderful. Though it was a little uncomfortable because I was meeting her perfectly, properly attired, future in-laws while dressed in inappropriately suggestive clothing having never made it home the night before.

So as usual I've been busy, trying to keep it together. Not as usual, I've been spending, sending money out, with nothing coming in:

Last night I arrived at the cabin, intent on finishing this letter before turning my focus to the bills of life with less than three dollars in my wallet, none in the bank and very little remaining credit to play with.

Even though, when you knew me, this sort of money pressure would have been extremely stressful, and even though, as of last night, all the bills were overdue by five thousand dollars, strangely, I didn't feel worried. In fact, despite the appearance of my financial situation I consistently turned down offers from people wanting me to return to my work as a "*Romance Therapist*" because I was intent on making the highest possible choices for myself from last night to forever, despite my inability to see what those choices might be. And so, though I should have been worried, I was not ...worried... much.

Because I believed in magic,

Because, I believed that, at this point it would be impossible not to.

Jeff, do you remember that time after you had moved to the states when you flew me all the way to, where was it? Florida? No actually I think it was Dallas. Anyway, wherever it was, did you ever wonder why that trip went the way it did? Why I turned around and left as quickly as I had arrived?

Oh sure Tsara was in an accident, but I had talked with her, I knew she was OK. I didn't have to leave. So why did I? And why did that accident happen then, at that time?

And how completely did the choices of that day affect the future?

Did you ever wonder about it?

It was one of those trips for which looking into the future would have meant recognizing my own design and that didn't match with my plans.

You and Bonnie (Her name is Bonnie isn't it?) had just begun to talk seriously, had just begun to contemplate monogamy. I think you were feeling a little hemmed in and wanted to hash it out with me, see if we were still as good as we'd been, decide whether or not to go the path of falling in love,

With someone else.

Your job had you traveling all over the place and you sounded lonely a lot of the time. I guess that weekend you wanted to fill the void with the warm company of someone who wouldn't ask for a future. When you asked me to come visit I was complimented, surprised, that you had asked me instead of her. I was oh so happy at the thought of several undisturbed days in your company. But even as I packed my bags and prepared the kids for my absence it didn't feel as though I was going to be with you.

Tsara was going through a rough time. That damn Ken had dumped her, disappeared right after she got pregnant, some engagement that was. It hurt so much to watch her dreams crumble. I can't express clearly enough to help you comprehend how it feels to observe your children's pain.

Though, I guess, by now you may have learned it yourself.

And if you have, then you know, that it's just hard.

And sometimes you can't find the way to separate yourself from how you feel.

My Tsara! The thought of something threatening her life is.......... unthinkable.

She had gotten her license only days before. There was a slight morning mist as I drove to the airport, while Tsara came along to drive the car home. We rode in relative silence for her and I. I felt weird the whole time, like something ominous was coming. I felt fuzzy, dazed like a person in shock.

I tried to understand my funk. Tried to put it off to the fact that I was uneasy leaving the kids, that I didn't really want to go because I was afraid I hadn't set things up well enough, hadn't covered for all the possible emergencies. Worried, that my little men would be taken into custody again for thinking and looking different from the boy next door. Worried, about, you know, the usual stuff.

But it felt different than usual, more important than the norm, more edgy, more...intangibly frightening, enough to build a brain full of numb. I just didn't know why.

When Tsara and I parted at the airport I sat down and put my head into my hands, trembling without cause. "Too much coffee?" I hadn't had any yet. I just felt clammy and disconnected. I got on the plane and made the trip. I kept wondering if my discontent was a product of guilt over getting in the way of your new and blooming relationship and wondered if maybe you were wondering that too.

I got off the plane and thought that perhaps something had happened to you and that that's what my feeling was about. You were late, increasing the probability. I tried to read but couldn't focus. I tried to phone home but nobody was answering.

I tried to write but couldn't think.

I tried to call you but —

Then suddenly there you were.

Bright and sunny and tanned and smiling happy to see me.

The truck roared up beside me and I vaulted inside desperate for your sweet water kiss. We pried ourselves away from each other and you took off just ahead of the officer who was yelling at us to stop blocking traffic. You whizzed over to the nearest La Quinta, explaining that you had snuck away from work — which was running long — and that you would be back as soon as you could. One more kiss and you were gone. I was alone in the room. I decided to run a bath and instead found myself calling home to check on things.

Tsara, my first-born, had been in a five-car pile up. She had completely totaled my new station wagon. She was still pregnant and though she'd taken a blow to the head, she was otherwise fine. Physically. When I talked to her I asked if she needed me to come home. Her teeny tiny little-girl, "no" was the loudest yes I'd ever heard.

And that was it.

I left.

Suddenly, I understood why, when I'd looked into the future, I hadn't been able to envision us languishing together in a weekend of love.

Because we weren't going to be, the future I designed hadn't written that in.

I didn't know how to get a hold of you so I left you a note, called a cab, and went back to the airport, having unknowingly tasted our very last kiss.

We were never together again after that.

Though that trip was the path that led me to move closer to you,

By moving me to the states.

Because on the way home I met a man that gave me a business card that connected me to a producer in Nashville that made me feel I could succeed in the U.S. Then when, a year later, I arrived in Nashville, he connected me with Sandy who became my friend and introduced me toTod, who was tall with balls like you and whom I married a month after meeting.

And that's when, me and mine uprooted and headed for the states.

Oh baby, I bet you had no idea: the power of your balls.

Do you ever wonder what would have happened if I'd stayed in your hotel room that day?

How much we would have ...

Laughed?

I've sometimes wondered if my leaving paved the path that led you to marry Bonnie.

Who knows what that weekend would have brought?

Neither of us I suppose.

Though I think I knew the whole time that, that weekend wasn't going to happen, for us,

Because my future lay somewhere without you in it.

I think I knew that seeing you would only have made letting you be separate from me more difficult. That I still wouldn't have gotten you back, or have chosen to be with you.

Unlike Ted,

The new you,

Who I not only chose,

But created:

He was a "trick,"

Of mine.

Not the only "trick" mind you,

At least, not for very long.

We met in September of '98. Just after another one of those periods when my financial life had whirlpooled away and left me drained of all resources. I'd already lived off my credit cards for as long as possible. There were no high budget commercials or movies coming and the one and only film job I was offered, I turned down, due to its content, extreme nudity and my flabby rounded belly. The magazine I had been writing for went bankrupt. My main sponsor — the one who had largely supported the home-schooling program I was doing with Cash, Chance, Rye and Dar — turned out to be a drug dealer and got arrested. And all of this happened just after we moved into our freshly purchased, brand-new (to us), '70s home.

So, I went to all the local service groups asking for help. I wrote for the local newspaper, and was given a local radio show of my own. It felt as though I was moving towards celebrity status in this little town near Mexia, Texas. I was looking successful, though, there was still no way to cover my bills.

So as I told you before, I created Ted to ensure that my return to work as a "*Romance Therapist*"—which at least paid enough to keep food on the table—would be short-lived. It wasn't that I resented the idea of having a lot of sex with a variety of men, that's fun. It's just that it wasn't the kind of fun I was wanting to have.

I wanted to be with my kids working on normalizing their behaviors. I had come across a book called "A Miracle to Believe In" by Barry Neil Kaufman detailing the journey of a little boy's emergence from autism.

I'd gotten hooked.

And since the Kaufmans had created The Option Institute where they taught their "emerged from autism" approach to families with special children, I bought all the books and tapes and began taking courses. It's an amazing place and my life and my attitudes have changed immensely from their input. In fact I'm taking Rye there in April. At least I think I am. I haven't finished paying the bill yet (Three thousand dollars due yesterday).

You know how school always was for my children. I should have started schooling at home a long time ago. Then, maybe Dar's teaching assistant wouldn't have molested him. But home schooling is so unheard of in Canada. It's looked upon with suspicion, feels like a crime and would have increased the neighborhood awareness of my children's difference. So I couldn't do it there, not without creating more problems and putting my guys in greater risk of apprehension by Children's Aid.

And that's why moving to the States has been both, my financial downfall and my greatest blessing. Because in Texas, they let me home school, no questions asked. Thus my kids have begun to grow, clearer, brighter, happier while I luxuriated in the blessed burden of being their teacher. The solution though was also the problem. For, the only way to home school was to stay at home and do the work of cheerleader to learning. And the only way to stay at home, was to not go out to make any money: money that I would have been making, so that I could stay at home and not go out to work.

Just another little ironic hook to hang the story on.

I don't care though.

Chance has learned to read. It's amazing! Considering that, after seven years of standardized education he hadn't even mastered all the sounds of the alphabet. Now after one year of home, sometimes phone, schooling, he has begun reading at the grade five level. And Cash, sure he is still a slow learner but he's emerged from retardation and his autistic-like mannerisms have decreased enough to become a mere quirk of personality.

Which, if you think about it, probably means he's traveled a greater distance in one year than most of us will cover in a lifetime. And best of all he's still going. He's become curious! He is learning to ask questions and expect more of himself, to believe in success and to contemplate dreams. Of course there's still Rye and Dar, the autistic ones that take longer to change. Even so, though Dar still appears to most people to be mute he has actually begun talking well enough so that at least I can understand. And Rye, well, Rye has pulled all his crazy pieces together. He is no longer so "out there," and seems to have left the autism behind. He is reading, doing math, not hurting himself or others.

So as you can see when the money ran out I was faced with a choice: teach them or feed them. I chose both,

Somehow.

Home schooling was working. I finally knew how to help my kids learn. I just couldn't give up and take a full-time job,

Or two.

I had to stay home.

But the family was getting hungry and I wasn't eligible for any government programs that could solve our immediate problem. So it was up to me, I had to solve them. That's when I decided to find a line of work that would pay me enough per hour to let me stay home, if not all of the time, at least most of it.

I called it *"Romance Therapy"* charged by the hour and actually helped people with sexual self-acceptance issues. Which is interesting since they say you teach what you need most to learn. I re-packaged the oldest profession in a way that would make it legal and allow me to claim it on my income tax. I had found my niche, my solution, my way to still teach, everyone. But my brain began to segment into a thousand little pieces. Ted called it compartmentalizing. He advised me to get good at it and professed to have no problem with what I did for a living.

Except he did,

Have a problem.

That was obvious the second time we were together.

We'd been together over an hour. And though I had attempted to stick to my schedule and take control of when the orgasm happened Ted was a great lover and he slowed down the action enough to maintain the romance he was buying. "Shshshhh." He held my head gently and kissed me while we rocked. My heart felt warm. There was something similar to you in him. So we made love for money and the inching of truth continued to burrow into me.

Then, I mentioned that time was up. I had to go see someone else and his face seemed to fall in, his eyes grew angry and he flopped his right forearm onto his forehead. He was obviously bothered. So, I used my personality to control the situation; a technique I had learned years ago when being threatened by the hands of an angry husband. I maintained my safety by countering the ugliness of his mood with an apparent un-awareness of its shadow and then I lit it away in the cheeriness of my disposition. He regained his facial composure quickly. But his mood remained low.

So, I listened to his mood, and his mind; a skill I have become good at as long as the other person isn't trying to stop me.

He'd just been acting bothered, albeit convincingly enough to fool himself, and that was his problem. He didn't really mind my working, in fact he admired it. He was used to calling escorts, had been doing it for years, had even loved a few and he relished the "good" ones for their easy attitude and availability on demand.

He and his wife had been without sex for years, long enough that he felt completely justified. I heard no guilt over his infidelities, only noticed a slight shimmering of un-easiness where finances were concerned.

It was a small measuring of discomfort that swept effortlessly under the belief rug of "I'm the one that makes the money." There was a lot more emotional garbage there but I chose not to hear the echoes of their fights. And moved to listen to his feelings about me.

He liked me, mostly though because I seemed to like him. Also he believed we had so much more in common than the simple fact that I had knocked his socks off. I contin-ued to weave my way through the workings of his mind. He found me overwhelming and somewhat unbelievable, my stories were suspect, it was his nature to be cautiously suspicious, negative about the likelihood of relationship success while he jumped in without hesitation. He still believed in "romance" and ah! There it was: the reason he felt disgruntled by my leaving him for someone else.

He was a romantic in the purest sense of the word.

He believed that love was something that "happened" to you, something you had no control over. He also believed that the way to feel like the most desirable of men, the best catch out there, was if an escort, someone who was used to and could have any-body on her terms, for a high fee, set aside her work and stopped asking for money. This to him meant that he had sexual value and was also his ultimate proof that she really cared.

He was a skeptic wanting to find that special woman who could erase his skepticism.

There were a lot of other little beliefs flying around like "women go after men like him for money, better to start with the money and go after the love" but I had begun to contaminate the process by making conclusions about what I heard and was no longer clearly listening. So I moved to real conversion and slid into my hippie-style long dress.

We kissed and held and made plans to meet again the following Sunday. He hinted that perhaps I should schedule only him that day.

He didn't set the money out where it was easy to get nor did he bring it with him when he walked me to the door. He put me in the position where I would have to ask for it and then, when I did, he pretended to have been so carried away that he had forgotten. This was obviously his technique with women of the night, for whom he felt there could be a future. He was trying to begin the process of being special. Though his technique was more common than he probably realized.

He muttered something about forgetting the money part whenever it feels personal in the exact same verbiage that two of my other clients used when they played the same 'you take my head away' game.

And though Ted was acting to make it real I had heard his thoughts and felt his desperation, and knew that making it real was really what he wanted.

He got the money, gave it to me and I left.

I went home.

I hadn't really had another customer.

I just wanted to leave.

Being real was not what I wanted.

I didn't believe in romance,

Anymore.

I believed in love,

Friendship,

Focus,

And intensity,

Which is often perceived as romance.

But I didn't believe in romance,

If romance meant it happened to you,

Without your control.

I believed we did it to ourselves,

Decided to jump in love,

Though sometimes we couldn't see how,

Or why.

And sometimes,

Once we jumped in,

We forgot how to swim.

With you, I forgot how to swim,

And drowned. Because,

With you I couldn't get enough,

Couldn't be with you enough,

Taste you enough,

Feel you enough.

With you I couldn't think,

Couldn't work,

Couldn't eat,

Couldn't drive,

Without dreaming of you,

And feeling the butterflies,

Of naked nerves.

It wasn't like that with Ted.

Neither for me,

For him,

Nor for him,

For me.

I listened to him think about it the next time we were together.

He had many pasts with many women but Lisa was the one he had told me the most about, the one he was always comparing me to, both in and out of his head.

When he had purchased her time she had come over to give him a massage.

According to his memory of her, her rules were that there was no intercourse allowed.

So when she gave him her number and said that next time, with him, she would do more, he was hooked, by the hooker that wouldn't hook.

Or maybe, from the sounds of his mind, he was hooked before that.

I thought it was an interesting method for making the client feel special and getting rid of the agency fee. I suggested that she may have planned it that way, watching his eyes in case he chose to make my comment hurt. He squirmed, hiding something, seemingly feeling caught at gullible. She had been on her period that night, it took him months to find out,

That maybe he was a typical piece of work for her heartbreak collection, and that saying the right thing to make a man feel special was her job.

"Of course you silly, sweet man." I thought. "She was an escort."

Because where escorts are concerned I was the skeptic,

After all I was one.

And when I told a man he was special,

I meant it,

Every single time.

It felt good to make people feel good,

Efficient to make a living during my social time.

It was joyous to watch a man,

Or woman,

Or couple,

Discover their sexual being.

It was a very loving experience,

To be able to accept any,

Quirk,

Or aberrant behavior,

As honorable.

To play at love,

Snuggle,

Care,

Explore,

Create,

Perfect.

Perfect,

To be,

In the moment.

But with Lisa had it been the same?

Did she love her customers? Had Ted really mattered?

I felt protective, concerned that he had been fooled, though I knew that we only fool ourselves and that what was real was always and only our own perception of the truth. Still, even though I knew that what he believed was true was true,

I wondered what was true,

According to what I believed.

I didn't know Lisa but I knew Patsy and so as I tried to piece together who Ted was and how who he was affected me, I used the pieces of his conversations, my experiences working with Patsy, and the fluttering of images that passed across his mind to gain understanding about the man in my arms.

Patsy was an "angel" he'd said, "and the dearest of friends." He met her after Lisa dumped him during the time when he was trying to recuperate. With Lisa everything had been out of control. He had been ready to leave his wife, willing to raise and support Lisa's kids as his own, "Put them through college. The whole nine yards," Ted announced, with his arms folded in front of his chest to stay protected and keep me at bay.

I ignored the body English. I moved into him, melding my form into his, easily melting him into opening his heart,

Which still hurt and bleated out cries of unrequited love.

Lisa hadn't worked as an escort out of necessity, she didn't have to pay bills, her husband—who had introduced her to the business and occasionally drove her to see clients—took care of that part of their lives. Lisa, worked for extra money and pretty things. Her being married allowed Ted the imagined safety net within which to fall in love because married people don't ask you to marry them. And hence you can fall completely in love without completely disrupting your life.

And then, there it was again, another catch-22 in Ted's thinking:

Ted also believed that because of his hard business exterior he needed a woman with whom to be soft. And if he found that woman, the "right" woman, the one with whom it was real, nothing, not even spouses could barricade them from being together.

And he wanted real,

And he wanted romance,

And his wife was closed off,

Had been for the past seven years of celibacy.

And Lisa was an actress, alive and creative,

Like me.

And so Ted began to talk, telling me the story of his lost Lisa love,

Trying,

Undaunted by my differences,

To recreate her,

In me.

He had gotten a new job that moved him to Houston from the east coast where both his wife and his lover remained behind.

That's when Lisa ended it. And Ted met Patsy. Who helped him put one foot in front of the other,

Immersed in despair.

Ted was desperate to understand. Had Lisa loved him? Had she been real or was he a game to her? Why wouldn't she talk to him? What had gone wrong? So he confided in a friend and asked that friend to please call Lisa.

"Approach her as a customer, that way she'll give you some time, then you can talk to her and tell her about me, ask her if she cares." Ted's friend understood the pain, had observed Ted's marriage for several years, he was happy to oblige.

"Yes, she loves you." He reported.

And Ted was proud of that,

Still is.

They might not be together,

But at least they were real.

His friend had said so.

"And I don't know if she will or not but she said she'd call you next week." his friend informed him.

She did.

She called him at work,

Just as she had done on the day when she broke up with him.

On that awful day when she told him that there was no point in continuing the relationship. She had said, "You live there and I live here and it just won't work." She then reiterated everything she had said the last time they were together. "You don't know me. You don't know who I am." and told him not to call her anymore. This would be their last conversation, she insisted.

A week later when he tried to call her the number had been changed.

And every time he told that story I heard his mind splintering from the pain of the memory.

And every time he told the story he remembered his trip to New York.

"I went to a play, and I hadn't called her even though I'd gotten the number. I'd been a good boy. I stayed away. But then I kept thinking, "Maybe I should have invited her? Maybe, if she knew I was here she'd—" his voice trailed off and he sat in silence for a moment, thinking, re-seeing, the events of that night. "So when I got back to the hotel I called ..."

Ted called the escort service. He wanted to talk to her but he didn't want to call her house and risk getting her into trouble. So he asked the service that had originally hooked them up, to call her for him. They recognized Ted immediately, "Hey, it's you! Ya! She really likes you! Didn't you move away or something?"

"Yes but I'm here now. Could you get her to call me?"

"Sure, she doesn't do much escorting anymore, just massage, but I'll get her to call."

Ted told the story with a lot of gaps in his speech, still, quiet moments while he remembers how he felt,

And his face rearranged itself into tender expressions as his mind brushes over memories of her.

"She didn't call...I waited for hours...I was in pretty bad shape...at midnight I called back,"

They were surprised that she hadn't called him. She'd said she would.

They called her again.

And Ted waited.

"Till 1:30, when the phone rang. You know what she was doing?" He began to justify, " I know what she was doing. She was agonizing over calling. That's why it took her so long. She told me never to call her again. That she didn't like me, had never liked me. She was as hard as a prostitute. That wasn't her. I know what was going on. She was just doing that for her husband."

Ted must have felt that night the way I felt the night I sat by the fire, listening to it's admonitions that I had set you up to leave me, that I could have helped you more with the kids if I'd really wanted you to stay. The fire told me you'd be gone when I got home and laughed at me for suffering.

I think Ted must have felt,

Wrong,

Laughed at,

Dying,

Till, at two thirty, when she called again:

"She said she was sorry. She said, "Look, I'm sorry that you're hurting. I never meant to lead you on or hurt you. I know your suffering and I wish I could help you with that. But I can't. I love you but I just can't."" And Ted, finger-pointing into the air insisted; "Now that was her. That was who she was. She really was loving and kind."

But loving or not she was gone,

He realized,

He needed,

Help.

He called,

And talked to Patsy,

Who helped him to let go,

One painstaking visit at a time.

She'd been there for him,

Making him laugh,

Being crazy,

Full of antics,

When he needed her,

And he loved her for it.

But he didn't wear her the way he wore Lisa.

She didn't exude out of his pores and cross his arms over his chest.

He didn't seep in the memory of the last time they were together,

Or the last time they weren't.

Like on his other business trip to New York.

After the phone call she'd made to his office,

After Ted's friend had fooled her into meeting with him,

By pretending to be a client,

Then telling her he was a friend.

He had convinced her to call Ted.

And Ted had waited for the call.

Anxious, Hopeful, Uncertain,

Every day…...Till it came.

"Lisa said," Ted reported, ""Look, this has got to go real slow, I mean real slow. If we're gonna do this. We'll have to get to actually know each other, for real. I don't want you to just make me up this time."

Ted said Lisa said then said "I said, "We can do that. I come to New York every other month. We can go slow.""

I asked Ted what made her so special.

His face became all tenderness,

His countenance,

Gratitude,

"She had a way of taking care of me without patronizing."

And I thought of you Jeff,

Helping me to make it easier,

Not because I couldn't do it myself.

Just because you loved me.

And I loved Lisa,

Ted's,

Jeff.

Lisa gave Ted a post office box number to contact her with. He sent her at least eight cards with optional dates for getting together. She never called or wrote him back. Perhaps after she hung up that day she realized the futility in explanations. Knew that he hadn't really listened, ever, hadn't heard her cry to be loved for who she was, rather than who he made her up to be, out of the pretense from which they'd begun. (Something I'm probably guilty of doing with you, Jeff, right now.)

Perhaps after she hung up she realized that the only way to have something else is to look somewhere else. (Something I'm pretending to be trying to do. Look away from you.)

And so she quit on him without taking the time to talk to him about it because she knew: a man that doesn't listen, doesn't listen.

Perhaps.

Or perhaps she just knew that yearning for her was his path to walk. So she got out of the way and let him walk it.

Till finally he found himself back in New York sitting in the same restaurant that Lisa had met with his friend in,

Waiting: He had dropped her a card asking her to meet him,

And waiting: He had given her his cell phone number,

And waiting: And two dates to choose from,

And waiting: Monday or Wednesday?

He ordered dinner, and ate alone.

The restaurant closed, on that Monday,

When he made it to the end of the path and sat down, giving up, and ceasing to walk.

He didn't go back on the Wednesday. He knew she wouldn't be there and by not going back he could always imagine that she had,

And ease the rejection just a little.

Instead of returning to her he called Patsy,

And she talked him through,

To the next day,

And the next,

And the next,

Until Patsy moved,

And he called me,

A year after his last trip to New York.

On the day we first met Ted told me about Lisa his love, and Patsy his angel. I told him

I knew Patsy and he asked me not to mention that he and I had been together.

"I don't think she'd mind but, you know, no point in worrying her."

AHH! Another monogamy pretender.

This business is full of them,

Especially the romantics.

I explained that he shouldn't worry, that I knew her from the recent past and that I had no contact with her now.

I remembered what Patsy's boss had said in describing her.

"Michelle—that's Patsy's real name—is the most professional girl I've ever hired. She keeps her books so organized that the lists of who to say what to and when are always up to date. And Michelle can get the men to pay the most for the longest. If you work together, let her do the negotiating."

I never used her real name, because we never really got beyond a professional relationship.

So she was Patsy and I was Laurie-Anne.

I told him that we had done doubles together. His face registered surprise and he asked me what I meant. I explained that I had met Patsy on the job and that, though she wasn't into women as much as I was, she had been a real trip. He seemed shocked, saying, "She never told me that!" while rubbing his chin.

I wondered whom she had pretended to be and what made him think that their relationship had been sincere and complete enough that he should know everything.

At first I was worried for him, afraid he had been duped,

By all of them.

Especially when he told me the name story: Customers are always so funny about trying to feel special by getting to know your real name.

Meanwhile, most escorts, and most strippers, give out their actual names in two or three meetings. I would do it in less. Of course none of the girls admit that, that would ruin the game.

Sometimes it seemed as though the fake name was just there so that we had something to give away.

However, sometimes the fake identity is part of the fun, and then you keep it. There are no hard and fast rules; it's an instinctual kind of job.

Point is, when Ted bragged that, "I'm going to get your real name. I got Lisa's after a couple of visits, of course Patsy, nobody can get her name. Don't look at me like that, I know, everybody thinks her name is Michelle."

I thought, "That's because it is."

While Ted smiled smugly at me as though he were the one and only educated consumer escort truth-knower.

Ted continued to regale me with the order of events.

"I took her to New York. I figured I had her. She needed to tell me her name for the ticket. So I said Pats what name do you want me to put on the ticket? 'Oh, you can use Michelle,' she says. But what are you going to do? You need ID." I said, 'Don't worry about that I have lots of I.D,' she says. She is such a pistol. I mean you just can't nail her down."

He seemed so proud of his tough little mystery girl.

Which is obviously what she decided to be.

I have to admit though; her trench coat and sunglasses persona was a good choice.

It is infinitely more exciting to be with a sleek, expensive, quicksilver, Mystery Mercedes,

Than me, the funny, furry, fat fannied, ford,

Escort.

I stifled a giggle at the imagery.

Because, though I might not have been all that fat, I was funny and it had been a long time since I'd seen the sight of your razor.

Obviously I was inwardly competing and comparing myself to Patsy.

I wondered if she was sincere about caring,

Since for most girls duping clients is the name of the game, that sometimes I was afraid even I had begun to play.

It was a weird headspace, Jeff. I mean, you know me, I think about EVERYTHING.

That's a problem that gets in my way all the time. Because since I understand why things happen, or what someone else will feel after I do a thing, it makes me afraid that I am manipulating simply because I am seeing the connectors. Then sometimes I don't do what I would have naturally done simply because I know that it will get me the desired response and that makes it feel like a manipulation.

So in fact I end up manipulated,

By my ability to manipulate,

And confuse myself into thinking,

That the game is the truth,

And the truth is the game.

So even though I was myself with Ted,

The ease with which I could read his thoughts,

And give him the right reaction,

Made me feel unsure of what was real.

It made him feel connected,

To me,

It made him seem transparent,

To me,

It made me feel unsure,

Of me,

And Patsy,

And Lisa,

Who had also been able to read his mind.

Like the night they were lying together in the after glow of passion.

And Ted said, "I'm thinking about the weirdest thing."

And according to Ted, Lisa said, "I know. New Orleans."

And there'd been no precursor,

No reason for her to think that,

Yet she'd been right.

"Weird!?" she'd said.

And as Ted told me this story during my break from writing, having brought me lunch, I saw it again.

The samenesses between Lisa and I: his two dear deer-crashers,

And knew for certain that she was his you.

And I chuckle to myself,

Wondering how often the four of us had been in the room together,

Touching,

Hearts,

And I remembered my third night with Ted.

We laughed and giggled and combined sex with conversation.

We talked about dealing with transition and loss. Both of us had suffered through financial ruin, though he had never had to declare bankruptcy, and we shared our stories, enjoying the empathy, agreeing that with bankruptcy, like divorce, the suffering was over by the time it got to court.

Then Ted returned to a conversation we'd had the last time we were together.

"You know, I think you were right. I think I did want my job to fall away. There were so many reasons why it was OK with me to let my world blow up." And he discovered as he spoke just a little more of what I'd been talking about, taking ownership for creating his own reality. Because until that moment he'd always told the story of his fall from power in order to tell what he used to be, could have been, might again become,

In order to gain sympathy for the cruelty of the past and value for the possibilities of the future.

But now he was slowly coming to understand that it might all have been according to plan,

His.

And as I ran my fingers lightly over his penis he told me about a book he was going to give me to read.

"You'll love it." he promised,

While I pumped.

His eyes got that faraway look, "It's called 'Conversations with God.'"

He whimpered as I once again competing for control proved my supremacy as the queen of when, in the orgasms department.

I had been a little put off by the title of the book he suggested, because, the word "God," was no longer a part of my vocabulary. At least, not as the name of a deity I don't believe in. And so that wee bit of put-off-idness separated me enough from the act of love that I found myself left reading the pictures of his thoughts.

His face clouded in sadness as he came to climax,

Inside memories of having and losing Lisa.

When you make love?

Do you look in the mirror?

Lisa.

Such a simple name.

So close to mine.

Who do you think of?

Does she look like me?

And she did,

Look like me,

Do you tell lies?

And say that it's forever?

I closed my eyes,

And called forth Bonnie.

Do you think twice?

Or just touch and see?

But it didn't work.

There was too much truth in the room.

To completely leave it.

So I worked with what was there.

I thought of Patsy and Ted and reached a peak of acceptable release.

I thought of Patsy. The first time I met her was the first time I ever worked a job with another girl. In fact Patsy was the only girl I'd ever done escort doubles with. Patsy was a complete professional, she bought outfits and wigs and toys and whipped cream.

She was unlike me, who wore no panties as a turn on, simply because I couldn't afford to buy panties. I had solved the "sexy outfit" problem by creating a natural "love child" style to belie my financial situation. I had refused to invest in costuming and had no desire to encourage toys because it was important to me not to make a career of this work.

Unlike me, Patsy, did exactly that.

And that's what made her so cool. She was a consummate professional who loved her work and got the best out of it. Near as I could tell she had no children and battled with an on again off again personal relationship.

And on the first day I met her she was a blond.

Patsy had been lost for hours. I'd already given up waiting and gone inside. The fellows were young, probably college kids, football players from the looks of them. I checked with my instincts, no tingles, no warnings. I felt safe.

Patsy had been the one to set this up. The fellows wanted one blond and one brunette in order to realize their dreams. Patsy, needing a second girl, had called my agency and arranged for a brunette.

The pay was better than usual,

Patsy definitely was a good negotiator.

At any rate I didn't want to be there forever so I suggested that we all get in the tub and start the festivities, so that my time could come and go, with no dependency on her reliability. Patsy kept phoning for new directions, and I kept washing and playing with my new friends. It was enjoyable in a benign sort of way. Nothing special.

Until the doorbell rang and in trotted this southern slang slingin, boofed up hair sproutin, little white lingerie wearin, teeny tiny titty totin, chickie of the night, "Why, hallo thar boys! Ahm sarry! Lordie Ah,jes couldn fin ma way to beat the bell fries. Look at me. Ahm still shakin. Yall'll jes haf to give me a minit har ta pull maself together!"

I was in the bathtub at the time. I stuck my head in the water so nobody would see me laughing.

We were a little out of sync. I'd been doing open and intense when Annie Oakley with the hairdo, came in totin toys and whip cream in a can, for a little comic relief.

It wasn't my,

YEE! HAW!

Style.

BUT IT WAS A MEMORY.

And where I was always the same,

Me,

Patsy was always different.

The next and last time I worked with her she appeared stylish with bobbed red hair. This was her real hair and in it she was beautiful and classy and a compliment to my earthy, natural style.

We talked on the phone a bit, she wasn't feeling well on occasion, got beat up once, treated me like a respected colleague and asked me to cover the phones while she recuperated.

Patsy declared her trust in me. I gave her name to some of my clients, as I got out of the business, while she stayed in.

Patsy was a pistol and she played the game well. So when Ted referred to his relationship with her my antennae went up. Patsy would be whatever she needed to be to keep him as a client and make him feel special. When he told me that she had insisted on keeping the relationship a paid professional one because she had to be very careful, if she let her barrier down even a crack she would just melt and lose herself she was so vulnerable, that she said she didn't usually do this caring thing, that he was starting to matter, that she was really starting to like him, I recognized the sound of a woman keeping the money rolling in.

He seemed so naive, so impressed with being special, I didn't know whether to laugh at him or love him for it.

And I didn't want to be too cynical about Patsy because after all I was beginning to say all the same things. And though I tried to pretend to myself that I was pretending, I knew that something deeper was going on.

This man seemed kind.

And wanting to be lovable.

Being an acceptance seeker myself,

I wanted to love.

So if I was human,

I guessed Patsy might be too.

I talked to a few people,

Asked a few questions,

And discovered that Ted,

Really was one of her exceptions.

So I stopped hemming and hawing when he brought up her name and started enjoying his stories about their peculiar friendship and the psychic they had seen together.

Right about the time I stopped rolling my eyes, he asked me what I was alluding to every time he brought up her name?

So apparently he couldn't read my mind,

But he had noticed my nuance.

I explained that the distrust was gone but that I had doubted her sincerity. I told him that I knew he had called her recently because she bragged about it to a mutual acquaintance. It was obvious by her comments that as well as caring about the money, she had cared about him. I tried to explain that though I knew she was a good person I also knew that she was a professional and didn't want him to be fooled. I knew, because I knew some of her other clients, and they said that she said all the same things to them that she said to him.

Though that didn't mean she meant them any less it did mean that I wanted to help him be careful if he needed to be. I tried to explain that I knew for another reason as well. I knew because I was doing the same thing, using him to get money, though I cared for his well-being, it was after all my job.

I tried to tell him because I was still trying to believe that about myself and because I wanted him to love me with his eyes open. Because I had already decided to love him.

It had been a wonderful evening. We had gone to a restaurant to eat and he had put the money straight into my purse as he got in the car. This meant he listened to me. And my heart took an extra beat.

Being listened to is a gift that few people besides you have given me.

Let me explain:

I had e-mailed him about his 'hesitant-to-pay-me' money issue.

I had explained with painstaking honesty that with so many kids and a home schooling program to run I had very little time. So though it was true that he was becoming important in my life, if he didn't pay me I couldn't afford to see him.

I also explained that his pattern of forgetting the money and making me ask for it, knowing that I was feeling awkward because he was becoming a friend, made me feel manipulated at the end of our past two evenings together. So, if he wanted to see me again I would need him to give me the money the second I arrived. That way we could avoid the problem, forget about the money and enjoy ourselves.

He listened.

And stuck it in my purse saying, "There, I don't want you to feel awkward."

No muss, no fuss.

How could my company be worth that?

And how was it that I was able to be so honest with this man.

What made you,

And he,

Enough the same,

To let me,

Be me?

We sat in the restaurant eating sushi, my new passion, and one that Ted said I shared with Patsy. It was our first time out as a couple and I found myself saying things I hadn't known I would.

Trying not to mean them,

Hoping he'd believe me,

So I could,

Mean,

"*I just want to be yours.*"

Them.

When we returned to his place,

We made love, soft and sweet,

With you in the bed,

Though I didn't see you there.

Then, because I was acting silly and mimicking Patsy the subject of her came up, bringing other escorts into the room.

I tried to explain without shedding distrust on my own feelings that being an escort is like being an actress. When you take on a character you are still you. You just use those parts of you that match the character, repress the parts that don't, and let the process of realigning the characters beliefs create a new perspective on the truth about who you are and hence what you feel. We are all actors, in the beginning, performing as the perfect mate, in our search of looking to put new people in our lives.

And as I explained myself via the world of acting all the actors in Ted's life flickered in and out of the room as he lost touch with my words, which were buried in the sounds of his memories.

Visions and moments and flickers in time.

His mother turned actress late in life, his performer, writer, son turned friend and confidante, his son's confidant comedienne, director, common law wife. His very own actress,

Ex-lover Lisa,

That looked like me.

And as the mother and son faded away, Patsy took a step back and Lisa filled the room.

And this time,

When we made love,

I looked in the mirror,

Of his eyes,

And forgot to think of,

His strokes,

Cause she looked like me.

So when he crawled inside,

It felt like lies,

I'd been telling forever,

Though I wanted to believe,

He was having sex with me.

Without a condom?!?! Oh my God! He'd slipped it in and climaxed immediately!

I couldn't believe I'd gotten so lost that I'd let it happen.

For a split second he basked in the pleasure of her and I as one.

"*What are you doing?*" I was aghast. " *You can't release in me!*"

"Why? I thought we...I mean, I thought..." he stammered.

And my mind swept full of all the women he must have indulged in unprotected.

"*I'm an escort.*" I whispered.

Disappointed to find this man,

Who could treat his health and hence mine with such frivolity.

He jumped from the bed. And threw his hands on his hips.

He was a naked, half bald, paunchy, fifty-five year old man prancing around angry, with ejaculate dripping off the end of his penis.

His face was steeped in anger, which was hiding his fear and he paced back and forth. "What is that supposed to mean? Don't tell me I did this again?" But he looked so ridiculous and despite all the emotions that were flying in the room it was hard

Not to giggle.

Even though,

It was such a big issue for me.

How could I explain it to a man that was too busy hurting to hear? He stood, afraid to crumble, ready to explode interpreting my words as meaning that it had all been a paid-for fantasy,

Terrified that I was like Lisa,

Just another heart collector.

And I was,

Not,

Sure.

Everything I felt about this issue came at me in an avalanche of awareness; I was an escort. He had paid me to give him a certain kind of attention and focus, the same kind of attention any therapist would give only without the limitations. The perfect date, someone who listens, to all of you, and becomes, like the experienced virgin, everything you want.

Many men forget the deal just as many people fall in love with their psychiatrist. It's easy to get lost inside the intimacy even sometimes for the psychiatrist who falls in love with the patient.

With me the game is never exactly the way it should be. Because I don't want to evolve into someone I don't like. So I am who I would be if I had the time to give my date my total attention. Hence I created "*Romance Therapy.*" I do my job with love and I seek the customers who need, what I already am. And within that huge horizon of me-ness I vary

the mood to suit the person.

So was it a fantasy? Had I tricked him?

Well no.

And yes.

In my real life the cell phone stays on, the kids call, work pages, my worries intrude, my needs exist and I am me,

With baggage.

And my baggage is always too much for men.

Or women.

Even though,

I occasionally,

Try to believe,

Otherwise,

Like now.

And that's when,

I realized,

That,

I hadn't lied!

OH!

I hadn't lied!

I hadn't known,

That.

So,

Was it a fantasy?

Perhaps,

The fantasy was mine.

After all he was a married escort-purchaser. What made *me* think *I* was important? That *I* was special?

What made *me* believe that *I* could read *his* mind?

That what *I* perceived was true, *was* true?

And for a second I lost my footing. And my body hit me with, too heavy to stay awake, fight avoidance. I wanted sleep.

He stood naked with his hands on his hips,

Looking old,

Pale,

And taken.

And I remembered that he was a romantic,

That no one is special unless you make them so,

And that he was aching to find me,

Willing to be set apart.

Was he lying?

To himself?

Well yes,

I wasn't everything he thought I was,

But I would be.

And I had all these thoughts in less time than it took to raise my eyes and rest them upon his face. All these thoughts and more, dumped down on me and buried me in an avalanche of understanding.

He was pacing still...Wanting me to explain what I had meant...Begging me to give him a reason to still believe. In the fantasy.

He wanted to be different than all the other men I slept with.

He found that difference in the lack of a condom.

I found his not using a condom a multi-layered insult that wrapped around itself too many times to unravel. But I tried anyway to explain my logic and insert it into his emotional state.

"You met me as an escort, that means I sleep with lots of other men, the minute I let you not use a condom it should mean to you that I might let someone else not use a condom and so you should never want to risk discovering that I would agree to that, as it could mean your life. Also the men who believe that not using a condom makes them special believe that with everyone. So if you try to have sex with me without a condom that means you have sex with other women without a condom. And most of them are escorts who, if they let you not use a condom because you are special, then they let other special guys have sex with them without a condom. So to me, the one who can be trusted, the one who loves you the most, is the one who is always careful. And maybe that's why I find condoms sexy."

They leave me feeling clean,

So to me, no condom,

Means I'm not real,

And that the man doesn't care,

And that makes me want to leave.

Do you remember, Jeff? How all this condom love started? It was after you got that girl pregnant (actually now that I think about it maybe **her** name was Bonnie) and we became more honest on our views about monogamy?

You had moved out of the house already but we had been unable to stay separate. I could have been happy living and loving that way but I knew, maybe even more than you did, that you were too young to be satisfied never having your own children, though if my body could have done it I'd have jumped at the chance. So we stayed together, though apart, while we drifted away.

Then one day the phone rang, the same day I gave you a bleeding nose, and I realized that it hadn't been ringing lately, that you'd been turning the phone off whenever I came over.

And I knew.

Though you lied about it,

For a week or two.

Until,

Grinning, with fear and shame,

You told me.

Oh baby! Why did you need to hide it?

Why did you want me to believe you were someone you weren't?

I loved you just fine the way you were,

Slut and all.

Since when does acceptance only run in one direction?

So we talked about it: My views on vows of monogamy,

And this time you listened to all my words,

That I had only just come to understand myself.

"I want you to choose to be with me every time you are. I never want duty, or guilt, or shame, to enter my body, through you. So I never want you to mind my behavior, or yours, when you're with me. You can't cheat on me, except by layering guilt in the way of our being. Cheating happens in your head. It's something you do to yourself, not me. I don't care."

Unless you do.

"Sex is just an activity. It's great for your body. It's great for stress. And sometimes it's easier to love yourself through someone else. Asking someone as beautiful and sensual as you not to have sex, at least some of the time the opportunity presents itself, would be like asking you not to masturbate."

And you know how I love to watch you do that.

"The real reason you lied was because you wanted to have both of us until you could figure out which one was better."

I remember looking at you with shining eyes, *"Jeff, we both know you're walking away from me, I'm just trying to squeeze out every drop before you go."*

And we made love.

Till I recognized that if she was pregnant,

You hadn't been careful with any of us,

So I got out of bed,

And I looked in the mirror.
And it looked like me.
Guilty in the silence.
I riffled through my desk,
And found a condom,
In case we tell lies.
And say that it is never.
I took you into myself.
Knowing that love means handle yourself care.
Forever.
I miss you, Jeff.
Do you remember how it felt, to lay awake that night, in the silence of our understanding?
I do.
I remember.
Every day.
As I seek it in Ted.
Who has become,
The only other man with whom,
I ever truly liked myself.
And it began that evening,
Because, though I didn't explain myself as graphically to him that night as I did in these pages,
I did speak clearly.
Despite his furiousity,
I was never sucked in,
To pretending,
He had misunderstood.
And I was proud of myself,
For being me,
In the face of an angry man,
Who could hurt me.
And because I was,
Me,
He,
Was he.
And rose,
Above his fear,

To risk to trust.

And did his best,

To engage his intellect,

And hear me,

And understand.

And *that* made him special,

Like you...And me.

And I thought,

Perhaps his transparency, the fact that he is so easy to read, isn't something to scoff at.

In fact perhaps his transparency is his treasure to be bared.

And so I felt safe, in spite of the hands on the hips behavior. I even giggled at how silly he looked tirading about with his semi erect penis pointing slightly downward like a diving rod. And when he asked me what was so funny, I had no fear. I simply chuckled.

And then said, "*Well look at you!*" while telling him how ridiculous he looked.

And he softened,

Because my laughter was loving,

And I knew that with Ted,

I got to be the parts of me I liked the most.

So I discovered that night,

That I liked him,

And that this romance might just be real,

Therapy,

For me.

So I did something wonderful:

I enjoyed my ability to understand and know,

Without using it to manipulate the end result,

Ever.

When I left that night both of us were still a little bit bruised emotionally. We articulated it, and felt it:

The carefulness with which we treated each other.

Ted seemed to be searching for a way to remind me of the inner connection we had together.

I had been talking about creating your own reality and all its repercussions in regards to condoms and monogamy so he pulled out the book that according to my senses seemed to have some relationship to Lisa and brought her presence front and center where it had been almost all evening.

And as he walked me to the door, swearing that I would love the book that his wife had hated, he told me the story of the time Lisa totaled her car,

Twice,

On the way to his place,

By hitting a deer.

And for no reason that I could understand,

Yet,

I felt lost in a kind of unreachable deja vu.

As I drove home that night, knowing I would never read any book that had "God" in the title, I was cut off by someone driving a high-performance silver-bullet BMW...very fast. It was the exact same kind of BMW Ted drove. So, when it forced me off the road I stopped the truck Ted had just helped me to buy and sat,

Motionless,

Feeling for a second that the driver had been Ted,

Knowing that that was impossible,

And understood,

For no reason that I could relate to the preceding events,

That this book,

"Conversations with God,"

Had helped him to get over Lisa.

It was a strange awareness that mingled with my belief that I should always read any book that comes to me through a friend. Then clashed with my egotistical belief that I had the answers already and didn't expect anything but shortsightedness from his silly little "God" book.

So when I got home I read a few pages, and put it down, thinking, "Well, I'm sure it helped him, he was grasping at straws. But it's too spiritually regressive for me."

I kind of chuckled to myself,

Full of Conceit,

As I fell asleep,

And dreamed of you,

Singing that damned Def Leppard song,

At the Player's Lounge,

Where we met,

Sure that there was no one for whom I carried a torch.

❖ EIGHT ❖

You know, Jeff, if there's one thing you and Ted have in common it's that you both liked to feed me,

Caring,

With food.

I was afraid I was about to get a healthy dose of both.

Ted and I were sitting in the Denny's right next to the Fairfield Inn where I was staying. I was between customers and had agreed to meet Ted for a bite.

It had been a strange day. I had been staying at Deja's and answering pages from men when Ted and I decided to meet for lunch. I knew that there was something on his mind and I was sure I knew exactly what it was. So of course I got lost on the way to our rendezvous point. I gave up looking for him, putting off, procrastinating, a discussion,

That I was also sure, I wasn't ready to have.

It felt accidentally on purpose, this not being able to find him. I was frazzled.

My pager kept buzzing and I was missing out on work trying to connect with him. He wasn't answering his cell phone and I guess neither of us was sure that we really wanted to put our issues on the lunch table.

That's the point at which I gave up.

I went to Eatzies, a deli near Ted's house, and left a message on his voice mail re: my location.

I bought a small order of cranberry rice and sat down in the sun to let the day sort itself out. I was wondering whether or not I should just forget the whole thing with Ted who I had started calling SMack. After all, I knew what he was going to ask. He was going to ask for special treatment, to be able to see me without paying. I didn't know if I could do that. So I asked myself, "Could I?" and pondered the possible answers. Just then, handsome Bill, from the children's entertainment company happened by.

Luckily, I was feeling beautiful and somewhat affluent, sitting all dressed up in the ritzier part of town, being smiled at by all the la dee da deli patrons, so Bill didn't have the usual effect on me. In the past I would have dropped something or bumped into something but this time, even though or maybe because, he was no longer forbidden married fruit, I just felt happy to see him.

It was a nice glow, nothing special though. I suppose because there was no heat shared, no reflected fire from thoughts of you.

Perhaps, Jeff, I had begun to put down your torch to make way for someone new.

And perhaps without recognizing the sign,

I was answering my own question of "Could I,"

By manifesting this "chance" meeting with a man from whom, it appeared, I could no longer feel your heat. Had my need to drink the magic of you through someone else died?

Perhaps.

Considering that I never before in my life,

Ran into Bill unexpectedly.

So maybe the extinguished torch is why I allowed Persistent SMack to meet up with me between appointments later that night.

We were in the restaurant next to the hotel where I had been seeing other men and I remember thinking that the setting was a kind of sweet justice, appropriate to the conversation I suspected we were about to have.

He took my hand and looked at me, having just explained that though he had tried to slow down the speeding runaway train of his emotions for me, he had failed. He sputtered, cleared his throat, paused, looked at me, paused again. He was struggling. I didn't make him say the words. He'd been vulnerable enough. He had already told me that he loved me and that even though jumping in so intensely, so quickly, had hurt him before and scared away Lisa, it was how he felt,

It was who he was,

And he wanted to be that,

Way,

Successful,

In love,

As himself.

So when he cleared his throat and averted his eyes saying, "There's one more thing."

I reached across the table and cupping his face in my hand saved him the agony.

"It's OK. You don't have to pay."

I felt safe. I had no doubt in my mind that he was generous enough to help me whenever he could; something he promised to do as quickly as I thought the thought. He reassured me. But it hadn't been necessary. His actions had spoken to me in advance of his words. This was the man who, after only our second time together, having seen my trash can of a car, had unasked for mailed me, two thousand dollars for the purchase of a new truck. No strings attached.

Of course I realized that his generosity was born out of embarrassment and self-interest. He just didn't want such an awful car drawing attention and being associated with him by being parked near his home.

However, knowing why someone does something for me doesn't discount the benefits I receive from the act. It only shapes the style of the ones I might receive,

In the future. And since I was not the type of person to live with my eyes on the future this was a realization I chose not to have.

I did recognize one problem though. However, it was not with his helping me to help himself.

To the best of my knowledge that's what everyone does when they behave in an altruistic manner because altruism is just a more beautiful type, of selfish act.

My problem was with the catch-22 of our perspective, situations and beliefs.

I hadn't really been seeing many customers, just him, and a couple of safe regulars. I had set it up that way, managing to avoid contact with too many eager beavers yearning to be touched,

Mostly, because he paid me.

And now there'd be many more men,

Mostly because, he wanted to be free,

In order to be special, and was about to become, just one of the lot.

It was a hard choice for me to make.

I had liked it the way it was.

Not so much because of my morals as because I didn't want to be at risk of disease or jail or injury. Fate had been kind I had received an insurance settlement against my car—the 1981 embarrassment for SMack—which had been smashed by a semi truck effectively turning it into a moving compost heap and allotting me enough money to pay my house note. Between that and some new credit card cash advances, my bills were caught up.

Whether SMack realized it or not, I had pretty much been his girl,

From the beginning.

The catch-22 came into play because in order for me to not charge him money so that he could feel like I was his and he was mine, I would have to step up my work schedule and sleep with more men. Kind of ironic considering the fact that SMack was the one who believed in monogamy, albeit not with an escort.

It seemed ridiculous really, because though emotions always follow logical paths to their destinations, they seldom follow logical paths that I can see. Still, I knew he needed this gesture in order to feel important.

I thought of the only two customers I was seeing. One wanted to do my nails and hair and give me massages and the other arrived with his eyes closed asking to be blind - folded. He wanted a mystery girl that teased him by staying just out of reach while she talked about other men. He wanted each hour with me to last all day, every day, by extending the curiosity. He wanted to feel a sense of troubled longing: Thus, the mystery. Which left him sniffing the perfume of strangers, and wondering after my identity every time a longhaired girl walked by. Both clients were, rich, handsome, perfectly built and harmless. The latter of the two would be expecting me in half an hour.

I told Ted about my clients and explained that he had pretty much been my sole source of support, that I had pretty much been setting myself up to fail as an escort, and that losing him meant working more.

I talked about how difficult it was to separate myself into different emotional pieces for a variety of people wanting sex and then do the exact same thing with him without feeling the bleed through. I told him that I didn't want to be a financial burden and that this bleed through was my problem to cope with. But that, on the other hand, I just didn't know how my dealing with it would affect us.

He talked about compartmentalizing emotions and compared it to bringing your work home. I joked that perhaps he needed to be a gynecologist to understand my situation. He accepted the joke but then returned to the reference and held fast on his advice.

I let the lack of caring escape me because the fact was, we had the same problem,

I probably couldn't really love him as long as he was paying me either.

On the other hand, inside this business, there was a good chance I'd resent him if he didn't.

I tried to express the danger to our relationship. I wanted to honor the problem enough to give us a chance to work through it.

I told him not to worry about falling in love with me too quickly. "*With me*," I explained, "*If we're going to do it, quickly is the way it will go. I'm a busy little doer*," I joked, "*I don't have enough time to go slow*."

"*Besides*," I winked, "*I hate it when it takes too long*."

"Ha Ha Ha " he singsong teased back.

I told him that the problem wasn't so much in working and being with him, as in running the business when I was.

He took my hands and said, "How about if I promise to never get in the way? I promise I will never mind if you have to see a customer instead of me, or answer your pager, or make a phone call."

I had my doubts, considering that he already minded, and it must have registered on my face.

"Look I know the whole drill. Patsy used to answer calls from my place, go on a job, then come back and spend the night."

I thought she probably did that on the slow evenings, tricking him so that he would ante-up and become the trick. That was the scenario that seemed the most likely to me since she never allowed Ted to talk her into sex without pay. For a second I envied Patsy's toughness. And said, "*SMack! You hated it when she did that. You made her turn off her phone. Hell! You even hid her phone*."

"YAAAA!" He singsonged again, this time with embarrassment, ducking his head, and grinning, like a little boy caught in a lie.

Wearing the same expression you used to wear,

Jeff,

Every time I caught you telling me something that wasn't true.

"OK, maybe I did that, once." Ted lied. I raised an eyebrow. "OK. Twice." he confessed.

I decided that that was close enough to true. Besides, it was time to go to work. The conversation was over.

So both the half of me that was trying to sabotage the relationship and the half of me that wanted to make it work,

Agreed,

To stop charging,

And went to work,

To run away from a blind man.

And went to work,

To not run away,

From this new man,

Who was also blind.

And went to work,

A lot more often.

And the things inside my head began to divide and divide and divide into little pieces of satanic mosaic art.

As I called forth Bonnie,

And called forth Bonnie,

And called forth Bonnie.

While I worked,

And worked,

And worked,

As I saw Ted,

And took care of my children,

And did my radio show,

And substitute taught,

And did caretaking with retarded adults,

And wrote articles for magazines,

And did voice-overs for commercials,

And helped Deja,

Survive a bad relationship,

While she helped me,

To edit a new tape,

So that I could get the new job,

That Ted was helping me get.

All so I wouldn't have to work.

Because it was dangerous,

While I drove,

And got no sleep,

And drove,

And got no sleep,

And drove,

And got no sleep,

And my children suffered,

My raw nerves,

As Ted complained,

When my eyes got heavy.

And I lost all sense of sequential awareness.

As happenings,

Fell upon memories,

Upon memories,

Upon truth.

Truths like:

That his promises were crap.

He didn't handle it well.

He pouted when I had to work,

Which left me feeling resentful,

As I moved into the arms of a kind, and gentle, desperately lonely, brand-new, soon to be a regular, man called John.

I knew Ted was hurting himself by believing himself rejected, even though he had set himself up for it.

So I called him and called him and tried to assuage his pain. I tried to reach out for him because I understood,

The confusion.

I'd set myself up too.

But though I was calling I couldn't get through,

On that evening when our relationship was threatening to snap.

His phone was turned off, which turned out to be, a blessing. He worked through the mental gymnastics himself and at four in the morning he e-mailed me to let me know that he knew what I knew,

That this Hell,

Was of his own making,

And didn't have to burn.

I read the e-mail with bleary eyes that barely survived the three hour trip home as I swerved across the highway,

Relieved, to still be lovable,

Whole.

I was exhausted,

Like when I used to visit you,

And couldn't get enough,

Sleep,

Because I couldn't,

Get enough.

But this time I was exhausted because I couldn't get enough,

Of his amazement over the coincidences that convinced him,

Of our complicity,

In the creation,

Of our world.

Couldn't get enough,

As we talked and talked and talked,

About the mysteries,

Of being the mystery.

And so, on that email night, when I was too tired to sleep,

I picked Ted's book- the one he'd handed me months before- up again.

This time I found it, right.

And "Conversations With God" changed me while I was getting to know Ted, the way "Seth and The Nature Of Personal Reality" had changed me while I was getting to know you.

And I understood why SMack had given me the book. He wanted to make us the same, to imprint me with the same changes that had been imprinted on him,

While reading it when,

He was letting go of Lisa.

Though he'd never really noticed,

That, that was true,

Because he was still enough of a romantic,

To not realize, that he was so much of a romantic.

Thus the number of women had climbed,

While he blew like a leaf in the wind,

Looking for romance,

Till finding me,

The Romance Therapist.

Four days after that email, SMack decided to give uniqueness and substance to our love, by coming to meet my kids, and see my home, and know my world.

I was nervously trying to finish an article that I had been hired to write and for which I was six hours behind on my deadline. Ted was due to arrive and I wanted to be able to give him some attention when he got to my house rather than send him off to play with the kids while I raced against the clock. My armpits started to smell like a skunk, which, as I'm sure you'll remember, they always do when I'm nervous. Which of course makes me more nervous which enhances the stink, which enhances the nervous which enhances the stink which enhances the nervous which,

MMM Lucky! Sexy me! He? We?

SMack would be driving up any minute. And me? I was still, a thousand words from finished. Since I had interviewed him for the story I needed to be done so that he could read the way I had paraphrased him and approve the content.

Rye, who had already met SMack, considered him enough of an old chum to not be trying to impress, and incited the grandkids to make noise and mess the house in an attempt to break my concentration, which as I'm sure you'll also remember, can be formidable.

Chance, who's fifteen now and, by the way, completely anal about, no let me rephrase that, completely in love with vacuuming, was tapping his toes wanting to clean the floors because he hadn't as yet met Ted and was always very concerned with first impressions. I, however, refused to let him turn the machine on, as the noise would interrupt my concentration, which was not formidable enough to withstand my distaste for the sound of vacuums.

My fingers were whizzing, my mind was racing and as the kids yelled, "He's here." I put the last words in the computer and jumped up from the table a victorious, disheveled, no sleep all night, nervous wreck.

He entered the house too tall for its low ceiling and surveyed the surroundings. He told me that the house had potential. The unasked-for opinion bothered me but I knew we were both nervous so I looked beyond the comment to the man who was trying to fit in. Smelled my armpits and ran to change my clothes.

He liked the article, seemed OK with the kids, took us to an all-you-can-eat restaurant, didn't eat a thing and started to yawn, exhausted by the stress of us, every noisy one. It was more than obvious that he'd done what he could do and needed a break from the troop. So I gathered all nine of us together and split us between, my truck, which Tsara was driving and his wife's jeep, with him at the wheel. We headed for home.

Ted backed into a car on the way out of the parking lot.

Oops!

This could be hard to explain to his wife,

Not the backing into someone part but the doing it here:

In the small town of Corsicana Texas, half an hour from his secret lover's home and nowhere near any business he might have been able to pretend he was on.

We looked at each other, and simultaneously thought-said, "Val!"

Ted jumped out of the jeep.

When he got back in he was exuberant with relief. He rubbed his hands together with glee, "That was easy. Twenty bucks and we're out of here."

We accelerated away.

I looked back at the Mexican family that was as large as mine in a beater car that now had a broken headlight and thought, 'I would have given them a couple hundred.'

"No insurance for them, no damage for me. Whew! That would have been hard to explain!" Ted laughed with relief.

For a second I joined him in the joking that somehow felt harsh.

And wondered why I had introduced my kids,

To this bad example of, another woman's man.

When I first met Ted his marriage had been irrelevant. After all, he had hired me. Most of the men who call escorts are married. Besides I liked married men. His being busy with work and women meant I was insulated against his expecting too much of my time. Better yet, if we did become a "thing" he wouldn't mind not moving in with me because he already had a wife.

So I was safe,

From having him reject us,

And move out.

Then when I got to know his situation and the fact that his wife lived at the beach house on the east coast while he lived in Houston I thought, "Great! They're not really together. Even better he's used to two households so if it works out, Wow! A dream come true."

I contemplated a stress-free life where he lived in one house and the kid's and I lived in another.

And I began to imagine, a little at a time, the possibility of the two of us having a future together. We talked more and more of creating one world out of all this mess and the closer we got to each other, the more his wife suddenly began to flex her muscles.

According to Ted, he and his wife had not had sex with each for over seven years. According to his wife whom I would eventually meet, it had been nine. Ted's stories claimed that he had had extramarital sex, for just as many years as his wife had been celibate. Yet, in all his dealings and with all that was lacking between them, she had never questioned him about anything. Initially she had seemed to prefer to not know. Eventually she had asked for a divorce.

SMack had avoided the transition of a terminated marriage by avoiding the discussions. Now suddenly, as he began to welcome the change, she became the one that was afraid and began to want him back. She started asking questions.

I told him time and again in as many ways as I knew how that I didn't want to hurt his wife, didn't want to be the cause of pain, for anyone, especially him. He could leave her and, if he was describing his unhappiness honestly, probably should. Something I believed because, as I explained to him, though I have always regretted marriage I have never regretted divorce. But I insisted, *"If you leave do it for you, not for me. I am not a guarantee."*

And I meant it.

He saw a divorce lawyer,

For me,

Anyway.

I suppose his obvious intention to make his future out of us was why I had introduced him to my children.

SMack checked into the Holiday Inn. I took the kids home, congratulated them—especially Dar who hadn't jumped up screaming in the restaurant once—for their superb behavior. I spent a few hours reassuring them that SMack had liked them, and that they had been terrific, before leaving Tsara to baby-sit. I joined Ted intent on spending the night in a nearby hotel.

My kids had a hard time understanding why adults would need time alone. They felt rejected when people came to visit and then chose to sleep somewhere else. So I helped them understand by answering their questions with frank honesty. Thus, when Chance asked why SMack wasn't staying with us I told him that SMack and I were old enough to want to have sex and that we didn't want to do that at home and risk embarrassing the family. My concise reporting on the possible happenings, between me and a man he had just met, embarrassed Chance who was perplexed why anyone would want to sleep with his mom.

But the honesty satisfied Rye, amused Dar and inspired Cash to pretend his version of grown-up cool.

Best of all it rejected none of them.

And left me free of the need to fabricate.

However, I too felt a little disgruntled to not be working and to have the time to stay at home while still ending up sleeping away from my kids. I never seemed to see them anymore and I was lonely for the sight of their slumbering innocence. While at the same time I had no desire to ask SMack to stay overnight on the second hand pull-out couch that I shared with Dar.

Ted's home was white and austere, so new that they were still doing the finishing touches. And while his felt like an Ajax commercial with Mr.Clean at the helm, my home felt like a cottage in the woods with catchall furniture and mismatched rugs. I didn't want him sleeping at my house because I was afraid he would feel like he was sleeping in the slums.

I was having a little difficulty dealing with the fact that he had money and I didn't. Oh sure, I was paying my bills, but only just, especially since I kept blowing off clients to spend time with him. And when I wasn't spending time with him, I was prioritizing the future by staying up all night while Deja, who was just learning how, tried to help me edit a promotional reel on equipment that couldn't do the job, not because the equipment wasn't good enough but because it was overloaded with all the other jobs she was having to ignore in order to help me. I tried to return the favor by not sleeping some more, and helped her with the medical video she was learning her way through. So I wasn't making enough money or getting enough sleep, which was going to make me worth less money. I was sinking deeper and deeper into debt, which left me feeling more and more like a bad catch for the eligible man,

Or even the not eligible,

Ted.

I was exhausted as my life kept calling me to action. But that's my life, one thing follows and overlaps another, from second to second, from child to child, from,

So many things,

Always.

OH!

OH!

JEFF!

There is a new discovery in autism, a hormone that seems to almost cure the kids. It's so exciting but it's still too new to get my hands on. Well, actually it's old, it was the first hormone ever discovered, and it's even F.D.A.-approved but for short term diagnostic use, not for autism. I did however manage to get one dose for Dar before all the distributors ran out. It was amazing!

It was like he was motivated to learn for the first time in his life. He just ran around the house, excited to try new things, and Jeff, he copied me! Can you believe it? He copied me! Over and over again! For two whole weeks!

OH! And his bowels he'd been having so much trouble with them. We were giving him stool softeners and Metamucil, every day. He would hold his bowels for five day stretches leaving the feces so densely packed into his intestines that it would squeeze all the moisture out. Dehydrated enough to suck all the water out of the toilet bowl, this poop that had to pass through his anus couldn't be flushed without cutting it to little pieces first. It had achieved the same diameter as the trunk to a ten-foot tree. It must have hurt like hell to evacuate a trunk with such very dry bark. He bled profusely as it scraped tissue all the way out of his bowels. So, of course, he avoided it. Every time. Elongating the duration between movements and increasing the problem. Resulting in him avoiding it, even more.

Whenever he did finally get the courage to go, watching his ordeal was more challenging than watching any of my daughters engaged in the act of natural child birth.

The poor dear would break into a sweat and shake his head NO! NO! NO! and then try to jump away from the poo in an effort to avoid the pain.

Tsara and I would take turns cheering him on. We were practically living in the bathroom with him.

Eventually the whole family was chanting cheerleader style shouts of,

"You can do it! Go to it!" encouragement.

I lost count of the number of times I stayed in the bathroom with him for ten and fifteen hours at a stretch. The other kids would come in to do their reading; their science, their math and we'd all try to convince Dar to release his bowels. There were so many nights when Dar and I reached the point of no return. So, too tired to even pull his pants up from around his ankles, this great big man and I would fall asleep on the bathroom floor.

And one infusion of Secretin later Dar is still passing his bowels even though we haven't been able to get our hands on the stuff for seven months.

But I will get it and I don't care how long it takes. I'll wait! I could wait forever now.

Because I know it works. And my son has a future.

Can you believe that? Dar has a future,

As long as I can afford it.

Because,

Of course it's expensive.

What good drug isn't?

And of course money is a problem not only due to the cost of the hormone but, because, if the drug is going to give it's full effect, I have to stay home to help Dar learn and assimilate the changes in his perceptions. But that's life, money, money, money, everything, comes down to,

Money.

Which is what I was worrying about on my way to the hotel.

Compared to me, SMack lived rich. He traveled in the kind of circles where women did their makeup, and their hair, and their nails, on a daily basis. The kind of circles filled with woman who like to shop at Macy's and Saks, and give their two-week-old dresses away to people like me, with children like mine.

Ted's romanticism led him to dreams of Julia Roberts in "Pretty Woman" where he was Richard Gere and I was, a little girl delighted, thrilled to be treated to a no holds barred shopping spree.

And I know you're laughing right now at the thought that anyone would expect me to be thrilled by a shopping spree, especially for clothes.

And of course I wasn't.

Though I was thinking,

About learning how,

To learn to like it.

So we went shopping. Apparently I needed an outfit to wear to the interview that SMack had arranged. It was for the position of T.V. news anchor. SMack had extended himself, pulled some strings and put me in line for a placement meeting with his company's program manager. It was a big deal and I needed to make a good impression. So he took me shopping for clothes having turned his nose up at the outfits he had thus far seen me in. "Smooch!" that was his nickname for me, "You can't wear a tie-dye dress with sandals."

I was a little insulted; of course I had access to other outfits. I'd been in the industry long enough to know how to dress, and if I needed to I could borrow from Deja, she was about my size and most of her clothes were expensive. But when I protested, he just looked at me in disbelief and I became too uncertain to force the issue. "C'mon Smooch! Let me do this. I want to do this."

So he took me shopping and though I appreciated the effort, I hated the activity. Especially since Deja came along to help, and tried to protect me from him, as though I needed it and couldn't do it myself.

So when SMack picked up on her cue, and the two of them began to handle me as though my ego was fragile, it was. And I felt like I was back on that damn TV show.

Being taken care of as if I didn't know how.

I took comfort in the knowledge that Deja's motive for over helping me was love,

And the desire to know more about me than SMack did.

But I was less than comforted by Ted. He seemed to be motivated by the desire to show off the fact that he was able to show me off.

Though I'm sure he called that love,

Even as he made fun of me,

And my aversion to buying myself clothes.

Which reminded me even more of my aversion to buying myself clothes, and, of my last job in television.

Oh how I hated being primped and preened and perfectly made prissy,

By somebody else's idea of what marketable might be.

Oh how I hated,

Not having a character to hide behind, and smiling into the camera, as

Lyne Louise, as if to say, "*This is my idea of me.*"

And as I remembered hating it I also remembered that, though I have always wanted to work in film and television, I have never wanted it to be as myself. I'm an actress not a host.

Besides, if I am going to host a show, for groceries or rent or whatever the motivation, it has to have some flair, some reason for being ...

Not boring.

Like, add a touch of zany with a little bit of fun, anything really, anything but milquetoast,

Which my show was,

To me.

And even more than hosting an un-offensive show filled with tedium,

Even more than that,

The one thing I have never wanted is:

I HAVE NEVER WANTED A JOB IN THE NEWS!

In fact, if you recall, I often said while watching my friend Ziggy Lawrenc do man-on-the-street interviews, when she first started working for CITY TV "*MAN, I WOULD HATE A JOB LIKE THAT!*"

Because I didn't watch the news, didn't trust the news, I thought it was slanted, inaccurate and emotionally unhealthy. The only job I desired less than a news position was a career in service TV, which is what I had gotten last time.

But desire it or not, these were the jobs that were offered to me because, these were the jobs I didn't want bad enough to get nervous for. Besides, as they say, "You have to start somewhere, pay your dues, work your way up in the world."

Even though everyone continued to announce that I should have what I continued to want:

A talk show wherein the expert opinion of Ms. or Mr. Mom guest—in so far as the story relates to their particular child—is considered of equal or greater value to the guest professional from whatever field the day's story is centered around. In other words: a "Parents Knows Best" kind of approach that applauds the heroism in inspirational stories of parental love: Stories like "Lorenzo's Oil," "The Woman Who Willed A Miracle" and "Son Rise; The Miracle Continues."

I wanted a program that pointed out the pride of parents and the heroism of their determination.

A television show that would mirror my already existing radio program, but that would pay, a lot more money.

However, as always seemed to be the case, what everyone said I should have didn't appear to be what I was about to get.

And I still needed a respectable job with a good income, so I could pay bills and refinance my debts. And this job was the only one I was being offered a shot at.

I swallowed my objections and let Ted spend too much money on a so-so dress and a beautiful jacket and got the hell out of Saks. But it left an impression, a scary one.

If I was going to be with SMack I was going to have to learn how to shop, in stores, instead of hand-me-down garbage bags from family and friends.

As I slowly drove to the hotel, just miles from my house, I mused over memories of the presents between us. I remembered the "Pretty Woman" video I had bought Ted for Xmas, only to discover that his wife had bought him the same video some time before; two identical gifts for two different reasons. His wife bought it because Ted liked Julia Roberts, and I bought it because he liked the whore,

In me.

"Now that," I thought, "is funny!"

I found the idea amusing and was chuckling to myself, when he opened the door to his hotel room,

Pulled me into his arms and said, "Well? What did they think?"

It took me a minute to realize that he'd been worrying, waiting for a report on my children's reaction to him?

You know. I don't think anybody has ever cared before!

Not even you.

SMack, listening for an answer, threw on a jacket so that we could go out for dinner. I restated any little comments about him that I could remember my children making. Then I explained that they hadn't said too much about him. I explained that my guys were too preoccupied with their fear of rejection and his opinion of them to even realize their own right to have an opinion of him.

"Mostly they asked me if I thought you'd come back."

"Ahh!" he nodded, "They're OK. I like your kids. I do! I really connected with Chance. He seems normal, not disabled at all. He's going to do just fine. Dar's harder, he's going to be tough. Cash I don't know about. He didn't say too much." Ted rambled through them quickly having done surprisingly well with all the names.

I assumed that was probably because I had given him two documentaries that visually described me via my kids, and my unusual approach to parenting. I had given him the documentaries mostly to warn him of what he was getting into but also to help him feel more comfortable with who they were and where the names fit.

"And Rye! Whoa! You are really tough on that kid!! I mean tough!" He pointed his finger at me and raised his eyebrow as though I were a child that he was teaching a lesson.

That was definitely not a good idea.

And I'm sure you are laughing right now,

In remembrance,

Of how I must have reacted.

Ted had just run his nails down the chalkboard of my soul,

And committed the gravest sin,

Of emotional abuse,

In my opinion,

By giving me an unasked for negative opinion, about, not just me, but my parenting.

And when it looked as though,

He was about to follow it up,

With the final sin,

Of unasked for advice.

I deflected him before he could really piss me off.

I changed the subject and stepped out the door, guiding him to follow suit. Thus, I was able to avoid looking at him, while I tried not to react out of habit.

How many times had my family been hurt by assumptions from the onlooker?

Probably thousands. I mean sure Rye was autistic, but he talked and related well, he did all his own self-help, some of his homework unprompted, was motivated to fit in. Rye was a miracle of love and whether I was the perfect parent to him or not I was ALWAYS doing my best to respond to his need.

Ted knew nothing about Rye that the documentary hadn't told him. Well, nothing other than to see this slightly disabled child, be told by his mother that he couldn't come to the restaurant, because he hadn't minded his manners. I reminded myself that just because other people had worn me out on the "make her defend her parenting issue" didn't mean Ted didn't deserve an explanation.

So I waited till we found a place to eat and decided to clear away the pebbles before we built an alter of misunderstanding.

I carefully dissected for Ted the altercation between my son and myself, exposing all the exciting accomplishments that had taken place. I noticed something new about me, a subtle difference in my ability to convey:

I wasn't at all defensive.

And I knew some of the reason for that was Ted,

And some of it was me.

"*That was mean.*" I spoke simply

"What?!" He immediately grabbed my hand across the table, and searched my eyes for what he could have possibly done that was cruel.

"*The thing you said about my being tough with Rye! That was mean!*" I tried to soften my tone to an almost little girl sweetness. I wanted him to hear what I was about to say and not default into emotional self-protection. I didn't want him to feel attacked, as though I, in any way wanted to fight.

I wanted him to understand because if he didn't I would have to go home.

I would not ever again let anyone cause me to waste time second-guessing myself with my children. We had been through enough, been damaged enough, by judgments and attacks on my parental motivations. My children had suffered. They had been subjected to many educational horrors in the name of telling me what to do until eventually we had been coerced into being easily coerced out of our own country.

Thank Goodness! Because it was only after I had the perspective of a new country with new laws that I was able to completely understand the slow-draining damage that was being done to my family by all the prying into our business.

It was only after I moved home to the United States that my children and I began to make progress. And so now, for the forever that I'm a mom, I refuse to be hurt by the judgments of any prying,

One.

You know Jeff,

You never did that to me,

That thing that every one does,

You never once opinionated on my parenting.

Thank you!

In fact, more exceptional than that, you were never fooled by my kids.

You knew instinctively the difference between the ones like Jady and Chance, who were so busy pretending to be nice that they didn't know how to actually be, and the ones who were so naturally nice like Cash and Tsara that they didn't know how to pretend. I loved that about you. It's one of the things that made me want to keep you. Unfortunately, since your eyes were open, you also understood them well enough to know that, they were more than you could handle.

So did I.

That night, trying to teach Ted something you knew without learning I missed you. Though at the time I didn't remember why.

SMack and I spent that evening in the restaurant, dodging conversation with the waitress, who had just recently been a guest on my radio show.

Sandwiched, in between her visits and the overzealous continuous flow of coffee refills, I explained the psychology behind attempting to cure a house full of weirdoes.

I told him with great pride what an awesome moment he had witnessed,

"You have no idea what kind of self control it took for Rye to not freak out when I said he couldn't ride in your car, or worse, when I said he couldn't come with us at all. He was amazing. And so was I by the way. It would be a lot easier for me to just ignore his behavior and smooth out the wrinkles till you left and then punish him. But he can't maintain the thread of his behavior that long and I would have missed a great opportunity. You were the only tool I had to motivate him with. Well, not you so much as Val's 99 Jeep S.U.V. For Rye that's where the power lies."

"He is totally fixated on brand-new vehicles."

"So I jumped on his acting out, the minute it happened. Then I used the fact that we were all going out and that some of the kids were riding in the jeep, to punish him with, knowing full well that if he got control of his behavior I'd reward him by rescinding the punishment. And he did!

He gained control of himself, in spite of everything he thought he was about to lose out on! And so he got to come. But I still had to punish the original outburst, so I stuck to the first punishment and made him ride with Tsara in the truck instead of with us in the jeep. Which could have prompted a new tantrum but it didn't. He handled it! If you had known what was going on you'd have realized what an incredible moment in Rye's history that was."

"And you'd have admired me for the fact that I was willing to take the time to stand strong in the face of my son's needs"

"Especially since at that moment all I really wanted to do was impress you. So, having my autistic sixteen-year old ruin the outing by throwing a four-year-old's temper tantrum, could have caused me to cave. Especially since, giving in and getting him to shut up was exactly what I wanted to do. Instead I did my job and stayed a parent."

Ted began to apologize and explain that he hadn't understood.

I cut him off, gently,

"I never expected you would. That's why I am explaining now. But I need you to know me, to know that I can be trusted to be kind,

That there is never a moment when I am not doing the best I can for my kids,

So next time if you're not sure,

Don't tell me what I am,

Doing,

Ask me."

So he did.

And I did my best to help him understand,

Without ever minding that he didn't already know.

And it seemed as though he grasped the concepts,

Though they were at odds with his own child-rearing techniques,

Because,

I hoped,

He was a very smart man.

Though he had a bit of a temper,

That I didn't like,

And refused to ignite.

Something I noticed as, the waitress over serviced us in an attempt to be helpful. I made a mental note of SMack's constant air-expelling, eye-rolling, body-shifting annoyance with her for trying to talk with me. I considered saying something but we'd had enough psychology for one night.

"All in due time." I thought, "All in due time."

"After-all, Ted probably has classy fast-paced non-intrusive New York restaurant expectations of the waitstaff and needs some time to adjust to my town of eleven and its galley of eateries designed with the farmer in mind." I pondered without hearing myself.

"However," I worried, " He also does the same thing whenever we are together and my children call." But I had been putting that off to his difficulty dealing with, dealing with my work, and the subconscious connection he had made to customers and the ringing of my cell phone. I assumed that for him, my ringing phone was synonymous with my having sex with other men,

Right in front of him.

Which for him would be an insult,

For, though I know many high-class, well-placed men who would be titillated and would love watching their lovers and or wives, play with their friends.

Ted was not one of them.

Despite Ted's desire to have his behavior toward me be consistent with the moral outlook he held for himself, in regards to his approach to me, he was still a man who had been socially trained. He'd been a willing student to the lessons of hypocrisy gleaned both from his youth and his previous "banker's" career. He'd been taught that though men behaved in whatever manner they chose "good men" proved their "goodness" by becoming consumed with the guilt of moral dilemma afterwards, while "good women" never behaved that way at all. Moreover good "smart" men had one woman for loving and at least one more for loving the sex he felt guilty for.

So in light of those beliefs, if Ted were to consider truly loving me, not only would I be judged wrong for role-playing with other men, Ted would have to find himself guilty of letting me. And eventually I would have to become the one he didn't actually screw.

And so sometimes he behaved in a way that had more to do with training than soul.

And though he usually saw escort work as benign and unthreatening,

He still sometimes wished,

In spite of the money,

That I wasn't doing it so he could stop feeling threatened by his own lack of concern.

He seemed to feel as though such a change in my life,

Would make him better somehow,

In my eyes.

And it probably would have.

It, would,

Have.

In spite of the fact that,

As I told him,

With me,

Monogamy,

Is never a promise,

Though he still squirmed when I said it.

Inside Ted's beliefs there were still a lot of mixed messages that left him reactive to ideas he didn't know he had.

And watching him react with the waitress, and the phone calls and my children, and all my other various commitments, was making it increasingly obvious that SMack, like most escort clients, was focus-selfish.

SMack, it was beginning to appear, was not good at sharing my attention.

But that, I knew, could be a function of low self-esteem and seemed to be common in men whose wives were always busy except when they were preoccupied with changing their husbands. Regardless of the origins of his need for my uninterrupted attention, it was something we were going to have to cope with and I had no doubt that with my family, the problem would come up again. We could deal with it then.

And if it didn't come up again, well, then I had misread the situation and it wasn't a problem.

At any rate at that moment,

I didn't want to be the teacher anymore.

It was time to go back to the room.

As we changed environments the subject moved from my family to his and we talked about Val.

She was becoming real. She had become the wife who discovered that she wanted her husband after all.

Ted seemed to receive it as a confusing compliment that his wife was suddenly interested in him.

I saw it as a testament to the lack of desperation in his stance and mannerisms, the new gentleness that was being born of renewed self-confidence and a fulfilling sex life. He was becoming a magnet and his wife was attracted.

I listened to the stories.

I watched his defenses,

Laid myself open to his mind,

And tried to discover my role.

Lover? Therapist? Friend?

Did he want to bridge the gap at home?

Or keep it in focus?

I tried to help him feel comfortable,

So that he could relax,

And go with his instincts,

And know that I would be happy,

Regardless of the outcome.

I knew what I wanted,

A man who was himself,

Whether he stayed with me,

Or walked away.

So,

He told the stories:

Val had surprised him by asking bluntly and without preamble whether or not he was having an affair. Perhaps, he surmised, she had used that tactic so that he would be shocked into answering truthfully. However, she had asked him at a most inopportune time—they were in the car about to join their entire extended family for Xmas dinner—so maybe she had only wanted to appear to want him to answer,

So that she would not appear stupid for not knowing,

Just in case,

He was.

As SMack said, "Now was not the time to be honest!"

I suggested that her timing might mean that she did want to know the answer,

The answer, "*No.*"

"Exactly! You're right. Yes. She doesn't really want to know. I mean, look Smooch, she never asked me that before, not even when I was such a mess over Lisa. Of course Val and I weren't living together she didn't really have to notice, but I did see her every other weekend. I was completely consumed with Lisa, totally preoccupied. And then when we broke up, I was dying. If Val wanted to know the truth she would have known then. In fact not knowing took work. I looked awful."

"*Maybe you weren't attractive enough to her then to notice, maybe she had her own stuff going on and didn't have enough left over to pay attention to you.*" And as I said it I knew it was true.

She'd had her own stuff going on,

And he was much better looking now.

Because he was happier.

I liked to think that I had something to do with that.

And as he paced a little and shook his head and messed with his half head of hair I got the rest of the story, the metamorphosis that was going on at home.

Val had begun to seek his approval, investigate his fidelity and try to reconnect. Where before she had been headed toward divorce and constantly dissatisfied with him, now she was reconsidering the marriage and finding his charm. They had things in common, went out for dinner and talked about politics, often. Meals were their mating grounds because in restaurants Val seemed less inclined to try to make him over.

When eating out they would commune their intellects, when at home Val was annoyed at his every move, or lack there of.

It sounded like the marriage of my grandparents and parents and of all the customers I had ever seen, wherein at least one partner wishes the other partner were someone else.

And the other partner, the one who calls me, simply wants to be accepted.

Of course after enough time together the lines of behavior between two people get fuzzy and the victim becomes the abuser and nobody can tell who wants what anymore.

Besides a victim is an abuser,

Of themselves. Something it took me a long time to learn.

But suddenly Ted was becoming neither. He was feeling good about himself, sexually satisfied, emotionally appreciated, and it was changing him to the point where, Val was being attracted to me,

The Lynette in Ted.

"Well if she's being turned on to my reflection in his eyes it's a good thing I'm bisexual. Cause, you know, I couldn't sleep with a woman every night and not want to touch." I chuckled to myself.

SMack caught me and when I told him what was so funny we both laughed freely and snuggled on the bed. "Not Val. There is enough Catholic in Val that that would just kill her. But you'd probably like her. Val hasn't looked this good in years. She'd probably turn you on."

I kissed him and got up to run a bath.

"And she's making me dinners!" he shuddered, "Weird!"

I brushed my teeth,

With his tooth brush,

Because I love to brush my teeth,

But never remember to bring my brush.

"And Oh Ya!" SMack smacked himself on the forehead, "I almost forgot. She wants to go to Colorado."

I spit, washed out the toothbrush and turned to face him.

"Don't worry. I'm not going to let her come."

It occurred to me that it was her place to go if she wanted to.

SMack explained, "I told her no spouses were allowed. And do you know what she did? I couldn't believe it. She checked."

It occurred to me that Ted should be more careful with her and stop taking so many chances like hiding in the kitchen pantry closet to call me on the cell phone whenever she was around.

She was only around for about two months a year, how tough could waiting be?

"I think it was my secretary who told her about one of the other spouses going along. I'm going to have to have a talk with her. That isn't cool; secretaries have to keep their mouths shut. But," He held my face in his hands, "I'm getting dangerous, Smooch! I think I want to get caught."

"I know, but please. Don't use me to hurt your wife. I don't need to go to Colorado. There'll be other trips." I got in the tub. *"It's OK with me. Everything's OK. Even if you don't want to see me for a while."*

I no longer had any desire to learn how to ski.

"Smooch!" He got down on his haunches and took my face back into his hands, "That's our trip. We need it. I don't want her to come."

He began looking through his shaving kit with the bar of soap in his hand. "I thought about staying away from you until I sort all this out, but I don't want to do that. She never wants to come to this stuff. Now all of a sudden she's pushing for it, asking me who I'm taking, why I don't want her to come along. She keeps telling me she knows I'm lying about the spouses, and that she knows I'm trying to be alone with somebody else."

"What do you tell her?"

I got out of the tub and searched for lotion.

He put the soap down, stripped his clothes off and hopped in behind me.

" Well," He looked a little sheepish. "I told her that" he dragged his words out in a long sing song, "I don't want" Then quickly ran all of the rest of the words together with a little boy's "don't-tell-me-that-I'm-wrong countenance. "her to come!"

He dried himself off and looked to me for approval.

I thought of how difficult it would be for me to go on this trip. All the organizing, all the leaving Tsara to do the home schooling, all the feeling like I never see my kids, now that I just spend all my time making the money to pay for the place, that I bought so that I could spend all my time with my kids. I thought of all the extra being away to cover the bills while I'm away, and knew that I didn't want to do all that for a guilt-ridden vacation.

Sure I wanted to start adding "Sports-styled skill acquisition" to my list of activities but I wanted that because I wanted "fun."

And pushing Val out of what should have been her option to attend was about to take the fun away.

Besides ever since this trip had first come up, when I looked into the future to check on my choices I couldn't see me skiing.

We got under the covers and snuggled trying to get warm.

And very gently,

Between kisses,

And strokes of loving,

Caresses,

I convinced him to give his wife the option instead of me. We joked about writing her name on my ticket and he connived to let her check into the airfare, feeling that she would probably not come since the ticket would be exorbitantly priced now that the date was less than two weeks away.

And I thought of how hurtfully we treat people once our agenda is to keep them at bay. I whispered that maybe he should give her a chance, see if there was anything besides politics still left between them.

He put himself inside me and, using his most favorite expression of sincerity, he placed my head in his hands to look in my face.

"I don't want her there. We fight all the time. I want you. I want us to have four days with no kids, and no customers, and nothing to do but see if we're compatible."

I repositioned my torso and allowed myself the vision of afternoons spent warming up in the company of handsome ski instructors. I considered the glory of evenings buried thick in conversation with Ted, talking, loving with our minds, deep into the late hours of the night.

I would go.

Colorado would be beautiful and I missed the,

Mountains,

The peaks,

And Valleys,

Of my youth.

Then, with his head between my thighs,

I helped him get to know me.

To see if we were compatible.

I closed my eyes and focused,

On the dance of finding the rhythm.

Then as my frustration grew,

And his patience waned,

I gave up and switched positions.

I called forth,

Bonnie,

To accomplish the mission,

Easily done.

We caught our breath for a minute, thinking, letting our separate worlds fall away. I felt the tired sweep over me and he began to talk,

About how connected we were,

In an attempt to keep me awake.

I could feel him get annoyed by the stickiness between us. I got out of bed to get a cloth to clean us off.

I was smiling to myself remembering that one of my ex-boyfriends used to say, "Ain't sex mahhvelus when it's dirty?" just at the moment when SMack commented on how completely wonderful it was to know each other's feelings, like the way I was smiling just then full of the after glow of,

Us.?

My smile grew bigger as I remembered that a customer of mine had said the exact same thing the day before.

"I love your smile, Smooch!"

I laughed outright at the misinformation appearances give. I jumped on the bed to tickle him and heard him think,

Which made me think,

Of Patsy.

Thus, the tumbling blocks of spirituality and Val and Patsy all came crashing into the room.

I had gotten over my egotistical reaction to Ted's favorite book, "Conversation's with God" and given it another chance. This time instead of expecting the book to either affirm my beliefs or be deemed unacceptable, I took my beliefs with me while reading the pages and found some amazing revelations buried inside.

In fact my so-called psychic awareness had been enhanced and was doing triple time as a result of the unfolding the book had brought me to. So if there was one thing Ted and I had in common in a really big way it was our appreciation for, "Conversations With God" and our melding understanding of the shaping of the world.

Val had gotten angry about the book. According to Ted she found it an insult to her sensibilities as a moral woman with a background in Christianity. Ted and I could relate to her fear, having both at one time contemplated with a good degree of sincerity, lives in the ministry. With a belief system such as that to fall back on, "Conversations With God" could easily be perceived as the tool of the devil, and lead you to fear for your after life.

Ted said that Val had been really angered by the chapter on fornication.

Considering that the two of them never had sex, together, her attitudes weren't surprising. Especially in light of the fact that she and SMack viewed the world through individually chosen psychiatric gobbled-y-gook, which reinforced their respective viewpoints about whatever they wished to believe was true and vindicated them from the need to understand each others needs.

So (according to SMack) Val, as a result of her past in which she had "stuff" to deal with, was weak. SMack made excuses for her, encouraged her, to shut herself off instead of facing the issues. As Ted continued to analyze her to me, he explained that he felt she needed to justify her very thick emotional barriers where sex was concerned, and that "Conversations With God," wherein sexual organs are referred to as terrific toys meant to be played with, just wasn't going to support her in doing that.

If SMack knew his wife as well as he thought he did then, I would have to agree; this kind of flippancy must have seriously jerked at the remnants of her Catholic origins.

It was a real source of difficulty between him and Val and in many ways mirrored the problems that Patsy faced with her boyfriend, Jim. That sameness was one of the things Patsy and Ted had in common. Patsy was into palm reading and demons and hocus pocus spiritual sittings. She had introduced Ted to a lot of experiences that her boyfriend just wouldn't abide. In fact he didn't even allow her to talk about it. According to Ted the problem left Patsy feeling lonely, though she put on a good 'Forget About Him' face for the rest of the world.

I myself no longer believed in the ghost and goblins of spirituality.

However, having once honored the conjuring up of ethereal astral bodies as other-world friends, I could remember the spiritual climate. And I definitely understood her passionate addiction for following the path.

The subject of Patsy led my mind and our conversation to the visit Ted had had with her a few days before.

It was the second time he'd seen her since we met, though he pretended that it was the first.

I find it interesting to watch someone lie,

Because I used to lie,

So much,

Until, when I was about twenty-two, I realized that everyone knew,

No one had been fooled,

Though many had been confused,

And given me a wide berth.

Lies are a funny thing that none of us can completely avoid.

Like lying about having sex with someone else.

Remember, Jeff??

Lying as if you had committed a crime by sleeping with her instead of me.

Sweetie, I wasn't there! Though my vagina is an amazing toy I still haven't figured out how to stick it in my lovers pocket to be brought out on those rare occasions when he, she, you, might be in the mood without me. The closest you could probably come would be to sleep with someone else and pretend it's me.

Which, when you think about it, is still a lie.

Yes, lies are a funny thing.

Especially when they are about sex,

And how much you've had of it.

Like the lies that are caused by the person being lied to, as in, when someone insists on monogamy, from someone who finds that difficult to give.

Did I do that to you,

Through inference,

Or did you and Ted,

Do that to yourselves?

Were the two of you like that person who wants one-sided monogamy, and pretends to be monogamous in order to set up a moral standard for their mate to live by,

The person who wants to do as they please without worrying that their partner is do-ing the same,

Because it is wrong,

For their partners,

To do,

According to them?

Sometimes I feel as though the world is chock-full of these lying pretenders whose own behavior curtails their freedom by making them distrustful and jealous of their mates ("If I am doing it he/she could be doing it!") creating the need to spy and control, and building a prison out of nothing at all.

Which shackles them to their believed-to-be-undeserving partners, an ironic situation which the lie was meant to avoid.

Funny! **Don't ya think**?

But those aren't the only kind of lying cheaters.

Sometimes cheaters are simply social liars focused on reputation.

Like the ones that believe they are good people in fulfilling relationships and want to be perceived as such. So, since socially a good person in a happy relationship is usually viewed as monogamous, they lie and pretend they are.

But this social acceptance is a man made structure of pretense, built upon the shifting sands of societal approval, which leans upon the illusory influences of economic class, religion, political empowerment, citizenship, era, location, weather, style, appearance etc. etc. etc. and crumbles into a pile of rubbish at the slightest possible threat that the time has come for the waves of any number of truths to crash down upon it.

So, since the parameters for social acceptance constantly shift and wiggle and redesign their assumptions,

Then the creator of this illusion inside the illusions is often lost like a rat in a maze with repositioning walls. He becomes intrinsically uncertain whether or not the virtuousness of "The Moral Deciders Club" isn't maybe, omnipotently, impotent,

And nothing more than a house full of mirrors,

Feeding him his own bullshit.

But, still worried that those mirrors of social acceptance, might know more about him and his relationship than he does,

And that, just possibly, they might punish him for what they know,

He becomes consumed with the need to hide, himself, in lies.

Because the need to fabricate screams loudest in the person with the need,

To be attached to the results,

Of being stamped, moral.

Until they notice, that need,

And then the need to decoy society becomes proof that their need was created by the knowledge that they had something to hide from themselves, standing testament to the fact that the moralizers were right "their relationship is and always was bad."

Sometimes the problem is complicated even more,

Because this proof becomes increasingly more beguiling to believe,

If the camouflage they used from themselves was used against their partner as well.

A problem, which is made worse, if the partner was fooled.

Because,

Ironically,

The liar may resent the partner for not seeing through the lie.

Because,

That means, the person their partner is in love with is the fraud,

That they see in the mirror.

Which means that, the love belongs to the socially-influenced made-up character they have pretended to be,

Which means that, the liar, as a liar is unloved,

Never accepted,

Or even befriended,

Because of the lie,

Caught,

On their own hook,

Afraid to reveal themselves with the unveiling of truth,

And face the possible rejection of the character they never really were,

Happy with,

Or they would have been not lying,

In the first place.

Thus, since they are never themselves they never chance to meet the people, who might have loved them for them,

If only they'd been visible enough to find.

And so I don't believe in vows of monogamy,

Because of games we've all played,

Being the people we've all not been.

You.

And Ted.

And I.

But though you both may be,

I am not,

Those people now.

Nor was I,

When you and I were together.

I have stopped playing the games by not believing in monogamy as anything more than happenstance, the result of choices enhanced by timing, selectivity and a busy life.

And in addition, since people lie to me whether I put them on the defensive or they put themselves there, I have ceased to have a problem with being lied to.

Fact is, I have to deal with the truth a person presents to me whether it's true or not. So since I can deal with it as a detective or an acceptive I choose the reality with the least amount of work,

And deal with the results that effect me of another's behavior. I leave it up to them to deal with the intent.

Their lies, I have decided, are just another way of communicating, who they wish they were,

And how well they know themselves,

Next to me.

You lied,

All the time,

Even though you knew,

I didn't care.

And you lied even though I knew,

As much as you suspected I did.

And Ted lied, sitting across from me talking about Patsy,

Even though he knew too.

Because with Ted, no one has ever needed a PI's license to hear the truth.

Because Ted thinks in pictures that are easy to see,

For all of his women,

When they choose to look.

I wonder, whatever made him think that I would prefer the impostor he pretended to be to the person he was?

What made you think it?

What made neither of you know,

That I could take pleasure in your pleasure?

That life,

Can be,

As simple,

As that.

I had already told Ted that I loved his wife,

Because he loved her,

And because she loved him.

Why would it be any different with Patsy?

He was her friend,

So she was mine.

Why is that so hard,

To believe?

If she was a stranger,

Who had just saved his life,

Or your life,

Would you,

And he,

Not expect my gratitude and love,

To flow freely to this unknown person?

Would you not find me foolish to be jealous,

Of not having been the one to save you,

Missing the opportunity to celebrate,

In your aliveness?

And if I should love a stranger,

Who merely shapes your life once,

Should I not love a friend?

Who has helped to make you the man I love?

Even as the friends of the man,

And the man himself,

Recreate,

Who they are.

Can my love,

Not reflect that to?

Is it so fragile,

As to shatter,

At the slightest touch of change?

Or sex?

Or meetings of the heart?

Or lies,

And secrets,

And feelings of guilt?

You and Ted are a lot alike.

Both too transparent to lie,

Though that didn't stop either one of you from trying.

You about your baby,

And Ted about Patsy.

Ted had been keeping me a secret from Patsy. At first it seemed to be because he didn't want her to feel that her position as the "Special whore" was at all in jeopardy. Later though I guess he was no longer sure which one of us held the title "Special." In time I think, he just didn't want to hurt her by rejecting her as the one who wasn't. Mostly, it seemed, he didn't choose to hear her warn him against loving me, by labeling him naive, for doing it again, for loving another escort.

Eventually though not telling her became silly, especially since he had always paid her and she had never actually gone beyond friendly professional. At the most they were very good buddies. So, on his last trip to Dallas he had taken her out to dinner in order to,

Tell her about me...sort of.

He sat on the bed telling me about the evening,

Pretending.

Nothing about my way with him had ever asked him to do that.

I could see all the images of the lies in his head.

He had slept with her.

What was the big deal?

It's not as if I didn't sleep with other men.

I had done everything I knew how to do to make him feel comfortable with the truth.
If he wanted to lie to me and make himself a fraud that was his choice.

And if I didn't like the man,

He would create with enough pretending to be,

Then he could hate me,

For not loving his suit of armor,

And that was his risk.

But if I did like the man,

He would create with enough pretending to be,

Then he could hate himself,

For not being he.

And that was the diversion,

He used to keep from learning to fly.

I hoped he would discard the counterfeiting and learn to freely swing through the ethers by my side.

So I let him lie,

For now.

While he made love,

To me,

And thought of her,

Afraid I would know.

And so his fear,

Made him unable to stop,

Remembering.

And we made love to her together.

Though I didn't have an orgasm,

And he didn't notice,

That I had heard his thoughts,

And gotten lost in the deception,

As he slipped the condom off,

Because he,

Needed to feel special,

By making me dirty.

And suddenly I felt so tired I wanted to die.

"No, Smooch!! Don't go to sleep."

" C'mon it's early!"

" It's only 1:00."

Why would he never embrace my desire for condoms?

Why? When I was so often willing to creatively embrace his desire for none?

I tried not to feel angry, but the more he nudged me awake the more I resented his presence.

And as I pushed myself to sleep I could feel his hands all over my body, all night long, taking him away from me and gifting me with dreams of Mitch.

His hands,

Kept me from resting in my slumber,

Or recuperating in my dreams.

I was getting tired,

Annoyed with needy men,

Trying to keep me awake and making my sleep shallow.

I wanted to scream at this man who was so inconsiderate with his secretions.

I tried not to hate him by remembering how hard it is for some people to sleep when they are away from home, when they have too much coffee, when they are so happy to see you they can't get enough. Tried to remember how hard it is for some people to care at all about any one else's health.

And I tried to forgive him for hurting my children by exhausting their mom,

Every time we got together.

However, the next morning, after an entire night of not mattering, of being exhausted by my constant losing on the "No rest for the weary, please just let me sleep" battle-ground with SMack, I sat in the easy chair, fuming.

And when he asked me what the matter was.

I said very simply, *"You have got to quit this or I won't sleep with you."*

He apologized and,

When we went out for breakfast he allowed me to talk about low self-esteem, and how easy it is to become an undertow when you are trying to build yourself up on the strength of someone else,

And I insisted he stop.

Because he was towing me down and wearing me out.

And I was starting to feel like I did when I was with you,

Just before I tried to send you away,

Afraid that you were abusive.

Till you fell to your knees,
And begged me not to leave you.
And so,
I didn't,
Leave you,
Until,
Long after,
You left me.

❖ NINE ❖

Oh, Jeff, it had been such a wonderful evening.

SMack had been right!

We needed this vacation,

Away from the worlds,

Of our making.

And, as we returned to our very ugly, $350-a-night room, nestled in the middle of the Colorado Mountains, I breathed a sigh of absolute contentment,

Dropped onto the gaudy bedspread,

And stretched my over-full body,

Lengthwise across the first of two,

King-size beds.

I let the too-small shoes I had borrowed from Brandessa drop to the floor,

And SMack came over to rub my aching feet.

I had done it,

I had found all the "sexy" he'd been hiding,

Beneath that eggshell exterior of low self-esteem.

This was the thing I tried to do for all my customers:

Draw them out of their cocoon and show them their beautiful.

My mind swept over all the things,

The customers, the meetings,

The secrecies and schemings,

The many kids and no kids,

The prophecies and notions,

The work that is play,

And the play that is work,

The stress I created and the duties I shirked,

And all the different choices and options along the way,

And all the preparations that had led me to today.

I was self amused and giggled,

And tried to stop thinking in rhyme,

Because sometimes it could last all day,

And make me a lousy conversationalist.

Ted stopped massaging my feet. I wished he wouldn't.

I was tired.

I heard him run the bath.

And thought, "God, this tired is good!"

It had been dreamlike really, wandering around amongst the yuppie-rich ski bunnies and ski bunners. We'd been looking for a private haven amongst the milieu of patterns and people and found it by the fire. We curled up facing each other. Our features were softened and brought alive by the dancing of the flames which blended the clash of colors on the pillow covered overstuffed flower patterned couch. We were surrounded by calming ancient libraries of wood, while thousands of doily-sized feather-like drifting flakes of snow, melted as they touched down upon the fifteen by twenty, picture framed pane of glass.

The scene outside the window was Carolesque,

And timeless.

We were two stories up, staring in each other's eyes, against a backdrop of shops and chalets, bellhops and valets, skaters and skiers and fire warming feeters—oops there I go again—

And we laughed,

And talked,

And played,

"Show Off Your Mind."

And I discovered that his,

Which was formidable,

And a match for mine,

Complemented me,

Because it was filled with,

The knowledge and information,

I hadn't yet acquired.

I fired business question after business question in his direction and gloried in the pleasure of watching him be something he is very good at. I was turned on at the head, which, as I had told him in my e-mail after we decided he would not pay me anymore, "is for me the ultimate G-spot."

I thought of that day and the letter I had sent him upon returning home in an attempt to create a contract of acceptability in our relationship.

In it I explained that my problem with getting together just because we want to instead of for a fee is that, "I have a hard time justifying being away from my very needy kids unless I can see it as somehow helping them, however indirectly. Thus my idea:. If we take a few moments each time we are together for you to teach me about finances, especially investing, then I will feel as though my children are going to benefit somehow somewhere down the road."

"And you will keep me interested, as long as I am learning."

Because,

Though I am a non-curious,

TV-avoiding,

News-disdaining,

Magazine-not-reading,

Anachronism of information,

I want to know,

Everything,

About people,

And their passions.

SMack must enjoy teaching, because he answered all of my questions that night with the thorough simplicity that is the providence of the confidently well-informed, which made it easy,

Fun,

Enervating,

And very very sexy:

As it always is,

To learn from a master.

It reminded me a lot of how I used to feel when you would teach me how to handle my sound equipment, or,

Wear orange coveralls,

Underneath my car,

Holding a wrench,

Greasy,

Teaching,

And handling your tools,

Like they were a sensual,

Extension of you,

Good at something,

I didn't already know.

You were my hand over hand.

And Ted was my mind over matter.

I was beginning to see him as a part of my life.

And knowing these things about me, and my attention span, which is driven by a thirst to know more, and often turns away from someone, with nothing left to teach,

I knew it about him.

So as we moved into the restaurant,

I asked him questions,

That would keep me knowledgeable enough,

To keep him interested,

In my own,

Formidable mind.

We ordered sushi,

Because ever since Deja,

Reminded me of it,

I have become a fanatic,

Even more so,

Than Patsy,

With whom I seemed to have more in common all the time.

And here in the middle of the Colorado Mountains of all places,

Was the most incredible sushi,

I have ever,

Or could ever,

Eat in my life.

Hence the feeling of overstuffed bliss.

I was full to overflowing with an insane desire to run around the hotel room singing "I Could Have Danced All Night" in my second-soprano paper-thin head tones. Fortunately for Ted he kissed me and redirected my joy.

We ended up in the bath. And as we washed each other in all the intimate places, every customer I had ever seen entered through the doorway in my mind and passed their hands upon our bodies. I wasn't good at pretending to myself I could compartmentalize,

As if any experience,

Can leave a person,

Untouched.

So I melded,

Drew them in,

And allowed him,

And me,

And them,

To become,

One.

And as I washed him my mind passed over the past few months, of working to work and working to not work. And I thought of Clint. The man who hadn't made love to his wife in thirteen years and just wanted to hold me, and love me and feel like a man. Like many of the customers who tried to stand out from the crowd by making me feel adored so that they could feel adoring. The spark in Clint's marriage had begun to return after only two visits as I taught him to use us to enable them. By visit three the guilt he felt obliged to experience had begun to set in. Soon it would be time to stop.

He was a nice man,

And I watched him,

Them,

Feel wanted,

In my hands,

Because they,

Were:

Dark and handsome Edward who cared more about talking, seeking acceptance for the lack of lust towards his wife, getting solace from suffering for days before and after each visit, flogging himself with guilt.

Tall and gorgeous Steve who needed to idolize and adore for an hour every two weeks. So that when he ordered and bossed and controlled the staff beneath him, he could remember he was kind.

Tom who looked for forgiveness ever since Vietnam and John who was every woman's dream date but didn't stay in one town long enough to build towards intimacy, with no strings attached.

And sweet precious Jerry who turned out the lights and pretended I was his "ill-with-lupus wife." He couldn't make love to her as she would bruise from the slightest touch. So he caressed her sick body through my healthy one, whispering in the darkness, silently, her name.

Curtis, Mario and Brian who were physically disabled and required a great deal of care, from catheters to carrying while radiantly gifting me with their smiles of divine physical beauty. In fact most of my clients were beautiful.

Inside,

And out.

Except for Edmond who wanted to role-play and humiliate his mother. And Sam who wanted to marry his. And Bert who never touched, who always only talked, letting me teach him how to relax and deal with women. And the doctor and the trucker who wanted me to just not notice that they were fat.

All of them were kind,

And if they weren't,

I knew instinctively before meeting them,

And didn't.

I was proud of the me,

In this job,

That others just, took for granted.

But still I avoided the job.

Especially as I discovered,

That I could be totally accepting,

Because I was afraid that such an attitude could be used up,

And because I wanted to give that totally accepting part of me,

To my kids, all the time. Thinking,

As though such an attitude was limited to eight hours a day. As though I couldn't be that person, every minute, in every walk of life.

I returned my attention to the ablutions of teeth brushing and lotioning as Ted reiterated the details of getting me here instead of Val. And wondered at the fact that I always seemed to be cleaning myself when we talked of Val.

She had checked into the price of a ticket after Ted had finally said, "Fine, if you want to come, come!" And then done nothing to help her to make the purchase. It would have cost her over a thousand dollars, an amount he already knew she wasn't about to spend. So she didn't join him in Colorado, but she did start reading "Conversations With God Book Three,"

In an attempt to join him somewhere else.

"It was pretty frosty when I left this morning." SMack shuddered, "So I kind of waved and snuck out the door while she was on the phone."

I felt sorry for Val.

"BYE!" He mimicked his wife's off-the-handset response.

And I thought, "If I was her and I wanted to catch him cheating, I'd get in the jeep the minute he left the house and drive to Colorado, just to see who the hell he was sleeping with." I suggested the possibility.

"Nah! She wouldn't do that. Oh, by the way I talked to my secretary. She's not the one that told Val about the spouses. In fact she told me this great story about having to field a wife and two girlfriends for her last boss. I don't think we have to worry about her."

"She flirted with you didn't she?" I teased; proud of the way he was emerging from his shell.

"Smooch, would you stop being so psychic!"

"Sorry" I laughed as I thought that she had probably lied about not telling Val.

"Oh! Oh!" He bounced up and down, an excited boy, " I almost forgot. Val changed the dates for her trip. She's going to be gone on Valentine's Day."

"Whoa, that sounds like a setup to me. God, SMack, if I was like Val and I wasn't sure whether or not you were fooling around, or even worse I was sure and wanted to be proven right, and I had as much money as you guys do, I'd hire a private investigator so fast it would make the yellow pages burn."

"You would?" *"Yes!"*

"Nah!" *"Absolutely!"*

"Seriously?" *"Without a doubt."*

"OK, I'm living dangerously, maybe I want to get caught." *"No kidding."*

"Look, SMooch, I want to be with you." I opened up my towel, "*What are you waiting for?*"

And invited him in.

I loved sex with Ted.

He was sincere and void of fetishes and paid close attention to my body.

And I never, never, never felt like I couldn't tell him what I wanted.

But then as he maneuvered me into getting on top,

I felt insecure and did this weird kind of mental flip from Lynette into:

"Laurie-Anne: *The Romance Therapist.*"

Who is bright and kind and very loving,

And doesn't ever feel,

Fat,

Or ugly,

Or old,

Or that her tits are like empty sacks,

Too long and thin,

When she gets on top and leans over.

And along with Laurie-Anne came all her customers,

With all their fetishes and all their insecurities,

And when SMack touched my breasts,

Clint touched Laurie-Anne's,

And as SMack kissed my neck,

Edward breathed in her ear.

And SMack sucked on my fingers,

While John massaged my feet against his groin, and Patsy sucked on my toe.

And as Ted's world mingled with mine,

Val asked for hugs and Lisa,

Gave instructions,

Explaining that she'd love to show me how to really make SMack happy, but she could only give massages.

SMack began to whimper, so I called forth Bonnie, who kissed Lisa and refused to lift her dress.

And it was over,

For SMack,

When I realized that once again we had gone without a condom, while my eyes were closed.

Though I'd placed one on the nightstand and had even warned him on our last condomless sexual encounter that there'd be no more sex if he didn't protect us.

As the room cleared, and SMack panted, I decided not to climax.

It just,

Didn't seem important,

Anymore.

I lay on my back feeling icky.

I felt itchy and uncomfortable and considered dumping myself off the edge of con-sciousness to avoid thinking about how icky and resentful I was feeling. Because I just didn't want to talk about condoms anymore. Normally, after sex and as drained of sleep as I was, I wouldn't have had any say in the matter, but then normally I would have drifted,

Into the sleep of the sedated.

Fact is, I'd been tired ever since we arrived at four that afternoon and it wasn't until around ten or eleven that I found myself laying next to him, on my back.

So I'd done pretty good at staying awake.

But I knew SMack wasn't ready for sleep,

And wouldn't be happy if I was.

And though I should have been seething with anger over our condomless sex I was too tired to be angry and too angry to be anything but tired.

I remembered how cute he'd been when we first arrived, snuggling me, teasing me, playing at playing with me, until I said, "*I didn't get to bed last night. If we have sex I'll pass out.*"

SMack shook his head sweetly, "Oh no no no."

And eased me off the bed.

"*Maybe just a little nap.*" I suggested.

"Uh-uh, come on, let's go."

He marched us out the door,

In search of memories,

Which we found.

Wonderful memories!

Until now.

I wanted to be done.

However, SMack was obviously still energized,

And we had come to Colorado to be together,

So, I figured I could stay awake just a little while longer,

While not thinking about the repercussions to my no condom, no sex threat.

I would deal with that tomorrow, I intended.

Besides I had to fart,

And not wanting to do that laying next to him was keeping me from relaxing my muscles enough to fall asleep, anyway.

Controlling the problem was taking all my focus.

Neither my mood nor,

My flatulent preoccupations matched at all,

The glow on SMack's loving face.

Which reminded me of the time I slept over at his place,

Before his wife decided to get him back,

And made it their place again.

I had told him how much I loved early morning sex, whenever I was half asleep with my body feeling all sleek and hot. And he'd remembered,

Like any good lover would do,

Like you did, after,

Every time you woke us up together.

But on this remembered occasion, with SMack, I'd had a problem.

I needed to poop.

And the toilet was too close to the bedroom for me to relax and go. How could I maintain the sexy in my persona, as I grunted and pushed and smelled up such a clean white house,

In a relationship so young?

I know what you're thinking,

Since when did I care about such silly things?

Well, quite frankly,

Since my bowels got old enough to be the one in control!

Now I know it's funny, but that doesn't change the fact that it was a serious problem. I mean I got diarrhea all the time. Who knew what might happen. So every time he touched me or put any pressure anywhere on my body I was in a panic, tensing my muscles to hold my sphincter closed while still trying to appear languid, as though I was too tired to play.

I'm sure I didn't handle it well because I could sense him feeling more and more rejected as he tried to hang out, entwined in loving closeness.

He had wanted to remain in bed and go in late to work. His leanings stood in stark contrast to mine. I was avoiding his touches, using apparent tiredness to keep him from squeezing me, and my feces out. The emergency grew more and more imminent,

Which gave me a sudden burst of energy with which I began bum-rushing us for the door, making my pretense of tiredness all the more evident.

I no longer gave a crap.

I needed to find a public restroom full of strangers that also didn't give a crap,

About my crap.

And even if they did, I didn't give a crap if they did give a crap when I crapped.

Because,

Who gives a crap,

About a strangers opinion of,

Crap?

The tension between us increased as I anxiously scoured the streets for the nearest restaurant, wanting nothing more than to be rid of him, so that:

Fruity or flatulent,

My fears could be dispelled.

He looked sadder and sadder while I became more and more,

Terrified.

Till finally, we pulled into the parking lot to eat breakfast at the local, soda fountain-style, been-there-forever pharmacy. In that moment when we walked through the door I felt certain I could smell a foul odor oozing out of the thin beads of sweat lining up on my forehead. My stomach turned over preparing to dump. I nudged him aside and ran to the bathroom.

Where I sat, realizing,

That if I didn't tell him what had been going on,

He would go to work feeling upset,

Knowing I'd been hiding,

Something,

Wondering what,

And wondering why.

And eventually all that crap would be piled so high, that it would be the relationship that got flushed, instead of my very loose stool.

And though this may seem like a joke,

It was actually a very serious situation,

To me.

So I joined him at the table,

Hid my face behind my hands,

And confessed,

My predicament.

He was so cool.

Trying not to embarrass me further he suggested that next time,

I brave the reality check, use the bathroom downstairs and,

Go.

Oh,

Of course,

He had a bathroom downstairs!

And of course as I lay in Colorado the memory made me want to,

Chuckle,

But my rectum began to spasm as the gas pushed against the muscles of my sphincter rendering laughter dangerous because,

I just wasn't ready for,

Furious,

Flatulent familiarity,

Yet.

So, knowing,

Because of his comfortable reaction to that morning's poo incident,

He would understand,

I asked him to turn on the TV,

And make it loud!

Then grinning with embarrassment,

I shuffled into the bathroom,

Like a Chinese lady running.

When I emerged from the bathroom SMack muted the TV just long enough to point out that the Rolling Stones were on. I dipped into my suitcase and grabbed an absorbent pair of Winnie The Pooh pajamas.

"What are you doing?" SMack seemed bothered.

"*They're cute!*" I protested.

And as I lifted my leg to put them on,

An innocent little remnant of my already released fart,

Burped out!

But before I could laugh,

Ted muttered, "Geez! I might as well be at home."

And, flicking the button on the converter,

Brought Val,

And Mick Jagger back in the room.

I crawled into bed beside him,

And lay still,

Feeling,

Empty,

And sad.

SMack wiggled his toes and bounced his knees to the beat.

"He's great!"

I heard more music.

Ted elbowed me, "Don't you think he's great."

I answered quietly, "*Sure, of course. It's The Rolling Stones*"

And heard more music.

"I mean look at him." Ted pointed at the TV, sounding incredulous, "The guy's still nuts." His voice sounded annoyed,

With me.

I heard more music.

"You're not getting into this." His tone grew more brittle, "How can you keep still?" As he air tapped to the music.

Which I couldn't hear anymore.

"*I don't know. I like him though.*" I tried to reassure Ted.

Who flipped off the TV,

With a "Forget it, then" air.

Then throwing back the blankets,

He stormed into the washroom for a piss.

'Pissing' seemed appropriate considering how pissy he was acting.

I curled up on my side with my back to the washroom and contemplated sleep.

Which annoyed the hell out of SMack!

"Smooch, NO! It's early. Don't do this to me."

Every nerve ending in my body went dead as I fell into emotional numbness.

"*I am not doing anything to you.*" I responded with a robot like cadence.

"Smooch??!! I want to talk to you, that's why you're here."

Without moving even a breath I spoke, "*Really?*" Then said, "*I didn't know I had a purpose.*" And, "*We'll be here for four days.*" Monotone with tiredness, "*We can talk tomorrow.*"I promise explained.

"UGH!" He exhaled in exasperation, "I might as well be at home!"

He carelessly complained, for the second time in two minutes.

I could feel his anger building.

"What is it?" I wondered, "That makes him see my needs as subservient to his? That makes him see sleep as something I can do without? What is it that he sees when he looks at me?"

"Does he see me as his prisoner thousands of miles from home?"

That was certainly how I was beginning to feel,

Like a prisoner.

Even though he'd promised me I could go home, leave at any point during the trip if I wanted to.

And it was a promise he'd had to make to get me here in the first place because,

Despite the fact that I had made the decision to be a *Romance Therapist* in order to spend more time with my children than any regular job would have allowed, it hadn't been working out very well.

And my kids were falling apart from neglect.

Even though, just as I had expected, I didn't work many hours, I was many hours away,

From home,

Waiting for work,

To call and place an order,

For me,

To work.

That's why, the day before the trip I called Ted to say that I didn't want to go because, as I explained, Tsara had virtually been raising my children. She had three young babies of her own and was too overworked for me to justify giving a holiday to anyone but her. Even more relevant was the fact that Tsara's having too many children and too much to do meant she was unable to integrate my children's needs well enough to prevent their regressing,

Into a pile-up of angry fists and shouts,

While Dar jumped and screamed,

Like a possessed jack in the box forgotten in the corner.

So Chance, the second youngest, shouted orders, inciting rebellion as though he were an exhausted, disillusioned, hate-filled father. Which pushed his brothers into screaming "You're not my Dad!" as they displaced their anger onto each other.

Tsara hid in her room, hating the example they were setting,

For her own youngsters,

Wanting to move out,

Trying to put her world to bed.

Rye called me, partly to tell on his brothers but mostly to reach for my attention,

Which he,

And they got.

I lost my perspective of understanding and of caring for my other son's various needs, as Chance the "stirrer-upper" refused to come to the phone to listen to my anger,

Teach him that anger was good.

Feeling unable to bridge the 150-mile gap between my children and me,

I steamed with rage,

And refused to be ignored.

I vaulted into my truck.

And headed for home,

Immediately after telling whoever was listening on the answering machine that I was on my way to beat the shit out of all of them.

I put an exclamation point on my anger by hanging up on my, "We're being good now. Please don't come home!" children, each time they phoned.

About ten miles down the road I saw myself in the rear view mirror,

And pulled into Taco Bell to get fat.

What was happening to me? Why did I feel like racing home and getting a baseball bat to beat my children into nice quiet submissive little pancakes of flesh? Where had my unbelievably persistent patience gone?

I ordered two more soft tacos and a Mexican pizza,

And wondered why I was asking myself questions that I already knew the answer to.

I hadn't felt like this since taking the kids out of school and eliminating the bureaucratic finger pointing that seemed to assume I had caused my children's special needs,

Even though they'd come (been adopted) with labels intact,

Even though the teachers' passive-aggressive behavior and their behavior modification techniques were what reinforced each of my babies' particular learning dysfunctions.

Anger had consumed me at every turn as these finger pointers blamed me for all of my children's developmental differences, even going so far as to require a doctors note of proof declaring me innocent of any responsibility for Cash, Chance and Rye's gene pool created lack of physical height,

As though being short was a disability, caused by me, the adoptive mother,

Rather than a "cuteness," caused by my children's heredity of origin.

So here I was, once again doing anger. But this time I was the only teacher they had for me to yell at.

The anger felt as though it was being caused by my inability to be in direct control of what happened to my children. After-all direct control was what home schooling designed to create.

Because my children needed help with how they dealt with life's happenings as they happened. Or so it seemed,

It seemed to me.

But actually I knew the anger was because of what I believed these happenings and my children's ability to deal with them,

Meant about me, And my ability to teach,

Any of us.

So I tried to check in on myself to see how I believed my babies' problems reflected on me and why I had chosen anger as an expression of that belief. I tried to look closely enough to understand my own flaws but I needed sleep and couldn't think.

I remembered that sleep deprivation is a form of torture,

Used by governments,

Religious groups,

And un-understanding boyfriends.

Exhaustion, I realized, could be partially responsible for my overwrought nerves. While the rest of the blame went to guilt and resentment over the fact that,

Nobody but me,

Could do the job,

Of mothering my children,

And their very peculiar needs,

Even though, everybody but me, seemed to be doing it.

Then I remembered that I hadn't been able to see myself skiing as I looked into the future and assumed that I wasn't meant to go.

I thought of you, something I had been doing a lot of. I thought of how overworked trying to fit you into my life had made me when we first got together until I grew willing to let you come,

Into my world,

Amongst my children,

And see my load,

Of rough-cut diamonds.

I remembered that trip to see you in the States when, like at our beginning, I had had to leave my children in order to be in your company. And leaving them had placed Tsara, who crashed the car that I had asked her to drive home, at risk. I shivered. If I hadn't put you ahead of my children, she never would have been driving.

That's when I called SMack and told him that I didn't think I should go to Colorado, though I wanted to: especially in light of what he,

And Val,

Had gone through to get me there.

I explained and explained and gave him my reasons. He said, "Look, Smooch, maybe you just need the rest."

Ya! Maybe I did.

I explained that being away from the kids would be stressful right now and might turn out to be less restful than taking care of them would be.

"I tell you what, if they need you, get back on the plane and go home." he reasoned.

"*Yesterday, right after I left, Cash went after Rye with an axe.*" I tried to shock him into grasping the seriousness of my situation.

"You don't have to stay the whole time, babe."

I wondered how long it takes to kill your frantic little brother with an axe?

Then I considered what a huge statement it would be to my guys if I had to come home from a vacation in Colorado because they couldn't behave.

And how much more effective than going home now that would be.

If it turned out that a statement was indeed needed.

"It only costs seventy-five dollars to change your return." Ted pleaded.

And suddenly my fear of being imprisoned in the mountains dissipated and going seemed like a good parental choice.

"*OK*" I agreed, to the audible sound of SMack, sighing his relief.

I had chosen to be an escort so that I might meet an upper-level intelligent man who would help me to not be an escort so that I could pay my bills without having to be away from my kids while at the same time maintaining some semblance of pride.

I had ended up getting everything I was trying to avoid.

Because being with SMack had begun to mean being more of an escort and less of a mom than I'd ever been before. It was a strange kind of role for a girlfriend to have.

I had been sucked in,

To thinking that actually working at *Romance Therapy* would help me to pay the bills without being away from my children 24 hours a day. Instead I had ended up away, for days upon days, as the job turned into me and my geriatric G-spot, sitting in parking lots waiting for my phone to ring, piling up hours away from my country home to be near the city where the customers resided, feeling like a man who works his whole life so that his wife and kids can stay home and have fun spending the money.

Only they weren't having fun,

And I kept missing the work to drive back-and-forth while I exhausted my resources.

And my teeth had just cost me four thousand dollars,

Of debt,

To stop hurting.

And my daughter deserved to have help paying for her wedding, but I couldn't even pay her back the money I'd borrowed, to buy my gas, so that I could make money, to buy my gas, so that I could make money, to pay her back.

And I was staying with Deja,

Who let me sleep on her couch,

As long as I didn't sleep,

Since she couldn't sleep,

Because she was lovingly staying up all night,

Working on my promotional reel,

So I wouldn't have to be an escort.

However, even though I was trying to stop doing it,

When I did do the job I liked it,

Because within it, I chose to feel kind,

As I gave myself orgasms,

Though it interfered with SMack,

Whom I was trying to fit in.

I hoped that separating me from my situation by going on a vacation might help me to think more clearly about how I had set up my life and why I was having so many efficiency problems,

In an industry that was so completely efficient: combining sex, money and social opportunities, in one-hour increments.

Besides I wanted to ski.

Back in Colorado,

With SMack,

Who was rifling through his suitcase,

In as loud and as angry a manner as was humanly possible,

For a very tidy man,

Who had a tendency to hang up my clothes,

Every time we were in a hotel.

He found some pajama bottoms, forced his legs into the appropriate spots and snapped the waistband. TOUCHE!! His anger shouted.

I didn't move,

At all,

Trying to shrink up,

Really small,

Thinking in rhymes,

And wanting to call,

My new friends,

To have a bawl.

I thought of the two guys I had met on the plane.

The one I was sitting beside was a pediatrician,

For whom I had turned on my charm,

Trying to befriend him,

Hoping for help,

In acquiring,

Secretin,

The hard-to-get hormone,

For Dar.

While SMack sat in the seat behind me,

Forgetting that I am kind,

Becoming jealous,

Angry that I would be so rude,

As to pick some man up from the distance of only a seat away,

In an airplane,

On a vacation,

For which he had paid.

I snuck my hand behind me,

To touch his,

And reassure him.

That I would do no such thing.

It was gay week in Aspen, which was, only minutes from Vale.

My new "flaming" doctor friend and his partner had invited me to come,

To their chalet and meet a few girls.

At this point in the vacation, for which he paid, I was beginning to

think that picking up a woman might be a thing, I would definitely do.

So, while SMack tossed and turned,

I considered asking them to come and get me,

To put a fun-filled roof over my head,

Till I could leave in the morning.

And get away from SMack.

The baby, bully, boar.

Because I just had to,

Get away.

Because,

I was.. ..

Just.. .

So..

Sad.

SMack plopped himself onto the bed beside me.

PLOPPED!

Onto the bed I wasn't in,

As if to say,

"Well then, I just won't sleep with you!! So there!!!"

Which was a relief.

And suddenly the childish ludicrousness of his behavior hit me.

And the weight of the last few months lifted off my shoulders.

It occurred to me that I was watching a dress rehearsal of us together,

Or a reenactment of him and Val,

As he Huffed and Hawed,

And Hemmed and Puffed.

Tossed the covers off,

Turned,

And threw the covers on.

And instead of choosing to hate him,

I started to laugh,

In a tiny unthreatening voice,

Free of malice,

So free of him.

I was amused,

By the comedy.

"WHAT IS SO FUNNY?!"

"Well………*you actually.*"

I giggled, "*Look at you.*"

And since nothing in me,

Or the energy I sent him,

Seemed bitchy enough to fight with,

He was incited to riot,

Against himself.

He punched the pillow, and stuffed the pillow,

And punched the pillow, and stuffed the pillow,

And head banged the pillow, and bit the pillow, and stuffed the pillow,
Over his face,
He grum-mumbled, "Fine! I'll go to sleep."
And the room froze quiet.
While I lay within, the beautiful calm.
I was,
Emotionally separate,
From everyone,
Even me.
And a remarkable thing,
Happened. I saw,
The invisible nothing,
Of his problem.
And then I saw,
The absolutely self-created,
Invisible nothing,
Of every problem,
Of every person,
In all of existence,
Even me.
Finally,
I had seen,
The truth.
Finally I had seen,
That what applied to him,
Applied to,
Even me.
So finally I moved forward into freedom by granting my own wish,
And going home.
I let go.
And, what had promised to be a wonderful evening,
Became a wonderful learning,
And,
Was,
Wonderful!

❖ TEN ❖

The next day I made a huge statement to my children. I went home early from my skiing vacation,

Having never skied.

But this time, on this trip, I didn't go home because they were so bad that no one besides me could handle them, nor because they had gotten in trouble,

Nor out of guilt,

Nor out of pity.

This time I wasn't angry,

Wasn't sad,

Was,

Just in love,

With them,

And me.

I made a lot of decisions that changed me internally that night. I decided things that I'd been telling myself I was trying to decide for most of my parental life.

And having decided them easily,

Discovered that deciding, had never been hard.

It reminded me of when I finally quit smoking, just two weeks before I met you. I had worked so hard at it, suffered so much for the quitting cause, and in the end when I no longer needed to work hard at it, it was easy.

It had taken me over ten years to complete the "breaking of the lung pollution stick habit" process that I had begun in 1979. And yet, as I said, after so many years of failed attempts, in the end, it was easy and took nothing more than a single decision, the very same decision I had thought I'd made, so many times before.

I,

However,

Had not,

Been truly motivated,

Enough to discover a new self-image.

Though I had been extremely motivated,

Enough,

To busy myself with trying to.

And though I had believed I already understood this to be the problem and the reason I couldn't quit I hadn't known what to do about it.

The "Colorado" decision,

As with the smoke-ending decision, when I made it for the first, one-hundred and fifty eleventh time,

Was all it took to turn the suffering of working at it,

Into the easiness of change.

Until finally,

Nothing was difficult,

Because there were no problems.

Life,

Love, And following my wishes,

Was easy!

And the decision began the process,

Of putting my broken personality pieces,

Back together again.

I reconstructed myself right there,

Under the hard-to-look-at bedspread,

In the ornate ugly,

$300 a night,

Colorado hotel room.

I discovered the easiness with which I could melt into calm,

SMOOTH,

As I lay in the dark of the deep part of night,

Listening to SMack fuss.

I looked at my life,

Of that moment,

Of the moments preceding that moment,

And of the various versions of the moments to come.

I mentally followed the path of some of my choices:

I could stay and baby-sit SMack's fragile ego,

Ski and pretend I was having fun.

Or I could go to Aspen,

Pick up women, ski and create carefree avoidance style fun,

Swirling in the sheer diversion of it.

I could Fight? Cry? Run Amuck?

What to choose?

I looked at my patterns,

And asked myself who I was,

And who I wanted to be.

And the answer came easy.

I wanted to be a mom.

And like the day when Tsara had the car accident,

I made a choice,

That had the potential to kill my relationship.

I went home,

To heal my relationships.

I decided many things while I looked at my life that night. And as I examined the patterns I drew an end to all the circles I was running around in, getting nothing done,

By erasing the need for the approval of others.

I didn't want to be a news anchor, or write trite articles for fashion magazines, or put on a radio show for a station in so much upheaval that the equipment and staff turn over were so bad the program seldom made it to air.

And I didn't want to be a *Romance Therapist*.

Because, I didn't want to spread myself so thin,

That my children never saw me.

I didn't want to give myself up to seeing clients and boyfriends and future bosses and chasing down auditions and sharing the most loving and accepting, patient and be-friending, energetic and focused part of myself to every one,

But me,

And them.

So I decided,

That the money,

Would come,

With no strings attached,

From somewhere,

And quit,

Everything,

But loving,

Myself

Through,

My children.

When I got on the plane I chuckled to myself thinking of Deja my, private, living room, stairwell-ski-instructor, preparing me for Colorado. I enjoyed the anecdotal memory of learning on the foothills of her second floor stairwell for a moment and then moved to the realization that, in spite of all our work together, she would be relieved to find out that my precognitive awareness of not skiing, had turned out to be correct.

Because, even though Deja, whose excitement over my learning to ski had set her to talking incessantly, full of reminisces, advice, warnings and the loan of all her ski equipment,

Even though she wanted a family member ski buddy,

She wanted something else,

More.

She wanted to believe in my ability to know.

So that as she bravely faced the dichotomies in her life,

I could be her compass.

When she turned to me for vision she wanted to have faith in my answers.

So since I had said, "When I look into the future I don't see myself skiing."

Making not skiing, a prophesied event, that she wanted to believe in,

My not skiing would make me someone she could,

Believe in.

And since, Deja and I were, in so many ways, the same person,

Believing in me meant believing in herself.

As the plane touched down I thought about the fact that, since I had told no one I was coming home meant that nobody would be there to pick me up. I also thought about the fact that I didn't have enough money to get home, and no remaining credit with which to rent a car,

But, surprisingly, I wasn't worried.

I knew the answer would surface.

And knowing it would, it did,

Surface—in the form of a no-nonsense little green neon. I drove it home while Deja and I talked on the cell phone. I smiled as she told me how relieved she was that I hadn't skied, how reaffirming for her and her belief in my gift of fore sight, which reaffirmed for me,

Her belief in me as her mother,

With the all-knowing eye,

Zooming, smooth as a magic carpet in flight.

There is something to be said for being psychically connected to the universe,

For being able to reach out and touch knowledge with your hands,

And grab onto the answers with fists of love.

There is more to be said for problem-solving magic.

And it was this magic that was taking me home,

In a car rented on a saturated credit card that had just, hours before, "coincidentally" upped my limit: Nothing surprised me anymore, for I had discovered the no problem part, of all the problems, that we choose to solve.

And I was content in the knowledge that Colorado had given me,

The minute I made the decision, which caused the crazy cacophony I called my life,

To break into small particles of dust,

That dissipated into the invisible,

While one clear picture of family love emerged.

I was happy in a worry-free,

Spiritually-connected way,

That was joyously unfamiliar,

Though I felt as though I'd experienced it before.

It was because of that feeling that; when SMack threw off the covers, came to my bed and said, "That's it. I can't sleep. We have to talk."

I could speak clearly and concisely, with all the concern in the world for his feelings, yet still, never once consider, not going home.

It was beautiful to feel so caring yet strong.

I asked him:

Why his need to have me awake, should be more important than my need to sleep?

And asked him,

Why his reasoning that a few glasses of wine makes him morose, should excuse his self-induced emotional-pit-of-despair behavior that led him to dump misery on me, in order to cheer himself up, when he knew in advance the effect of the drink?

Why, when he'd left his first wife largely as a result of her not letting him sleep, preferring to "discuss" all night her dissatisfactions, why, having experienced it himself with such suffering, would he believe it was OK to treat me in the same manner,

And not expect me to leave,

As he had done?

I asked him these things and more,

Gently,

Lovingly,

And waited while he answered,

Listening to his patterns.

The whole evening reminded me a little of the time I broke up with you, only stronger, clearer, more completely void of the fear,

Of losing.

By insisting,

On not being,

Abused.

I realized something and shared it with him,

"There must be something right between us, because I like who I am when I'm with you." And then wondered if I was missing the point, of his being made manifest and wondered if I shouldn't have said "I like who I am in spite of you…. So there must be something…. right ….. in …. Me?"

Do you remember those 'I like who I am when I'm with you' words, Jeff?

You are the only person, outside of my children, I ever truly felt like that with.

His, "Where does that leave us?" response was different from your, "Me too" love.

I placed my palm gently on the side of his cheek,

Feeling his fear,

Loving him,

And said, *"I don't know. That's up to you. But for now I'm going home."*

"So, you know where I'll be. I'll be a tree."

Sheltering my saplings, and beseeching them to grow,

Greater,

Than me.

As I sat on the plane I wondered,

Unattached to the results,

What this strength in me would create in him,

If anything?

And,

I began to suspect,

The thing that I have now come to know,

With the aid of retrospect:

If that trip hadn't happened,

Neither would,

"The happening,"

Have.

For over the next two weeks I smiled in calm abeyance to my instincts and parented my children from day-to-day immersed in wonder, love, adventure and patience.

I created fun without expense as we camped on our property, invented the fifteen mile family walk-along in an attempt to be actively together, visited the cabin, played pool, basketball, tennis, swam, picnicked and danced in the living room.

I read to them,

Talked with them,

And was,

No longer diluted,

From all the men dancing in my head.

And so I,

Outlasted Chance's six-hour outbursts of "I hate you, you bitch!!!"

With clarity,

Strength,

And love,

In spite of the laundry and broken pipes and shrinking funds,

That seemed never to completely disappear.

And as Ted began to turn around and look at himself,

We spent time together with my children nearby.

He instead of me,

Did the driving back and forth.

He used a condom,

And made his visit to my home memorably,

Funny;

We were in the local hotel (because where sex was concerned I still insisted we take it out of the house) . We'd already made love when I noticed two distinct poop stains on Ted's side of the bed. They were obvious, lying, as they were at the head, too low to be covered by the pillows and two high to be covered by the sheets. This had happened once before at the cabin, also on SMack's side of the bed. However he hadn't realized it as I had managed to maneuver the blankets and prevent his detection and pursuant embarrassment. What to do? With the poo,

Markings of territorial bliss??

How to keep our stool in our stomachs, put a plug in the problem and keep the problem out of our relationship????

What can I say, Jeff? SMack and I are a lot older than you and I were.

Feces has become a way of life,

And a concern.

The sight of SMack's stain made my own bowels rumble so I got up to go to the bathroom. I used the privacy of the throne to ruminate, wonder and analyze how we were going to deal with this unintentional marking of territory. I thought about the scene from "Kiss Of A Spider Woman" wherein the prisoner voided his bowels all over himself. He was, in spite of his extreme illness, devastated with embarrassment.

His darling lover—played by William Hurt—made the event seem commonplace and just pooh-poohed away any comments to the contrary.

In the film, William cleaned up the object of his affection's eliminations with the gentlest of love. So beautiful was the scene, so powerful the impact it made on me that, having the opportunity to prove my gentle kindness through the cleaning up of my lover's bowel babies, seemed, at that moment, the most perfect of possibilities.

Not wanting to give SMack the same option, to do for me what I was about to do for him, I wiped my own bottom with a newly inspired rigorous attention to detail. I prepared to return to the bedroom area of the hotel room, and remembered,

And thought of,

The time I found my father, helplessly lying in his own trail of diarrhea, on the floor of the hospital, surrounded by an audience of onlookers, deep in the throes of his first grand mal seizure,

A few years before the diagnosis of brain cancer,

That led to his death.

Even then, at that unexpected moment of stress, I had recalled "Kiss Of The Spider Woman," and wished that the doctors and nurses would back off, so I could do for my dad what William Hurt had done for his lover.

In an offbeat way this unimportant little stain on the sheets was offering me up a second chance,

To be William Hurt and,

Prevent humiliation in the face of embarrassment.

I reentered the sleeping area, aware of the sensitivity of the moment, which was magnified by the fact that SMack, who had pulled up the blankets to hide the smears, was in on the predicament.

I remembered his, "I might as well be at home" comments in Colorado and wondered if he was ready to handle so much unsexy familiarity.

Not pulling the covers down to get under their warmth would have made it obvious that I knew.

So I pulled the sheet down,

And pretended I didn't,

Notice.

I got in,

And maintained the pretense.

I laid my pillow (noticing that it had also been decorated with the e-coli medal of feces) and consequently my head almost on top of "it;"

The poop de jour so thinly spread and drying up upon the bed.

I had gone ahead and laid my head almost, but not quite, on top of "it,"

So that he would see me looking at him,

And not worry about me looking at "it":

His elimination.

I started to converse,

About stuff.

We talked and talked and his eyes kept moving passed my head to the spot just beside my pillow.

Every time I would move to adjust my position his eyes filled with alarm, and then relief, as I settled in, having become comfortable and unsoiled for a few minutes more.

Until the next moment when his eyes would once again fill with alarm as, needing to change position because I knew I shouldn't, I would just have to squirm a little more.

Then when because of the look in his eyes, I became unwanting of movement. My neck and back started to scream at me in discomfort till finally, in need of an out, to relieve the merry-go-round tension of his horror, I made a suggestion,

Sound like insistence,

That we get dressed and go for a diet Coke.

Because, being a long-time parent, if there's one thing I've learned about human behavior, it's that all problems are easier to solve with a change of environment.

Leaving, allows you to put it behind you, by removing the emotion, from the place you
leave behind. So we left, because, I was hoping to do exactly that: erase our personal
attachment, with the stuff, from his behind.

When we returned from our Coke quest, I walked in the door, and headed straight for
the bed. I grabbed the blanket, no muss no fuss, and matter-of-factly said *"I'll just turn
this sheet over."*

He mumbled, "Good, because I soiled."

Embarrassment blushed across his face as he averted my eyes and looked toward the
ground.

I responded with my "this sort of thing happens every day" voice and said, *"No big deal.
Let's just turn it around so you won't have to keep looking at it."*

I felt perfectly light-hearted and kind.

And he became comfortable enough to be the one to start the jokes about his fears that
I might lie in the remnants of him.

I was so completely impressed with my handling of the situation that, well, I just
thought I was wonderful.

And thought that, "He is lucky to have someone with as much class as me."

I felt like the goddess of love and sex and kindness to humanity.

And in that mindset, steeped in my own impenetrably high self-esteem, we made
love,

He like a lover,

Me like a lover possessed. Me the,

Passionately,

Perfect,

Pretender,

That I pretended,

Myself to be. Pretty,

As he grabbed my buttocks, and,

My anus belched,

A loud,

Long lasting,

Flatulent,

Emission.

Of gas!

What class!?!

The fart returned my humility and dropped us into spasms of laughter that sustained
my orgasm for an unprecedented length of time and took my,

Climaxing to a new and glorious height,

Of class "A" love.

Farting, with me, was apparently no longer just like being at home and had become,

More like being at home,

I suppose because, we were now on equal footing. After all if soiling was OK for him to do with me, that earth-shattering balloon belching release from my bottom must have rung, like the music of equality, in his ears...And surprisingly, he was tickled by the sound.….. WOW! What a change!

But it wasn't just his new gas attitude that impressed me,

It was his whole attitude,

That had become a gas,

Which I expressed!

Even as I expressed,

My appreciation.

And buried in the guffaws of open acceptance I warned him that,

With me there are no secrets because there can't be.

Because, in my house, with my children, we are all too connected to not share,

The joy of a joke.

I chose that moment to tell him how naked he would be loving me, how exposed the lover of a writer is, especially if that writer is me. And I warned him that with my family the secrets come out even before they have a chance to become secrets. Because we tell stories and because, even when we don't, our minds do.

For we are psychically connected and in fact I believed,

That Tsara already knew, all that I knew, about poor SMack's poo.

When Ted took me home, Tsara, the home-front helper angel, with whom I have witnessed many miraculous things, said: "Last night I had this weird dream that I went poo in the bed and then this guy I was with, just cleaned it up, as if it were a normal everyday occurrence."

SMack and I looked at each other, smiled and shrugged.

Apparently, I was right, we had already,

Shared,

The story,

And the lesson,

And the laugh.

And the wonderful part was,

He was OK with the lack of privacy that most men cannot bear.

He was OK, even as much as you were.

Though I think you were better at ignoring the farts, since with you,

I never made any.

Because,

You and I loved in the silent ethers of romance where no sound exists.

Whereas SMack and I romanced on the building blocks of life.

And as the base elements improved upon the real,

Real improved upon the sexy.

And Ted admitted having succumbed to the delightful pursuit of sleeping with Patsy.

He removed both the lie that stood between us,

And his assumption that, even though I hadn't admitted it yet, somewhere deep inside me it would actually matter.

Of course,

His assumption had been wrong,

Only the lie affected me,

The act did not,

Except in that,

I was happy for his pleasure.

And, as real,

And honest,

And direct,

Turned SMack,

From the Dream Lover Dream,

Into the Lover Dream Lover,

I decided to see the handsome,

In us both.

While he turned,

And turned and turned and turned in my direction.

The new SMack,

Made it easy,

To speak out.

And so I did.

I pointed out that he "hmmphed" whenever my children interrupted our private time,

He said, "I didn't know I did that." And stopped,

Completely, even with waitresses.

And I began to believe,

That people change.

And every day,

His acceptance of me,

And of himself,

Reminded me,

More and more,

Of you.

And that's when it, "the happening" happened,

On Valentine's morning,

While we were making love,

It was during our second go-round,

After he'd fallen asleep on the couch that we'd already had sex on,

While I watched movies,

And occasionally pondered his handsome face,

Even as he snored.

The movies ended and,

I shook him tenderly,

Not wanting to disturb,

Yet not wanting to abandon,

Yet needing the bed.

I whispered, "*Hey, Sweet thing. Want to sleep here or come upstairs?*"

He reached for me,

All soft covered with sleep,

Smiled through tired eyes,

And kissed me.

Then he pulled himself up from the couch,

Put on his bifocals, which I find sexy,

And pushed the buttons on his VCR.

On the way to the stairs,

He took me in his arms,

And humming,

Waltzed with me,

On the dance floor,

Of the empty dining room in his home.

We mounted the stairs.

A strange ethereal quality filled the house,

And I found my eyes crying,

Un-surprised,

And un-understanding,

That Bonnie had died.

We found his bed.

He kissed my neck,

And penetrated,

My heart.

I closed my eyes,

And,

Floated,

Air waltzing,

In a transparent nightgown,

With a tall,

Thin,

Man,

Almost,

As perfect,

As this fantasy me.

I still couldn't see his face,

But as he kissed my neck,

And undid the shoulder button,

On the gown,

I recognized,

A familiarity,

In his hands.

As always I stood naked,

Perfect,

Young,

Beautiful,

Clean.

In his arms,

That smelled like,

Soap,

Tears flowed from my eyes,

As SMack made love to my body,

And the man,

Placed me gently on the smooth,

Rectangular,

Marble,

Slab.

I leaned back on my arms,

Not quite knowing,

Yet,

What I already knew.

I tilted my chin back,
As he spread my legs.
My hair dangled behind me,
Tickling the marble,
As I not quite recognized,
His touch.
SMack moved into the new,
Favorite position,
I had taught him.
The one where he is on his side,
And I am on my back,
And our faces are nowhere near each other.
We made love lying eons apart,
While tears tracked,
From my dreams,
Onto my pillow.
I was lost in a world of my own making.
I watched the scene in my head,
Girl and onlooker in one,
We both saw.
The man,
Knelt between my knees,
On too long legs,
Naked,
Hairless,
Perfect,
Chest,
Tanned,
Tight,
Belly,
Packed,
Bal---
Oh my God!
It was,
YOU!!!!
I turned my onlooker head,
And looked behind me,

Into my past. And saw,
All my unrequited infatuations,
As morbid fascinations,
Fixated on the need,
To recreate you. And saw,
Gasping with surprise,
The obvious,
Something,
That I had believed was buried,
Too deep too see:
YOU!
You!
You!
You!
You!
You!
You!
you.
I had been carrying,
A glow in the dark,
Brightly lit torch,
Burning,
Hot,
For the believed in,
Love,
Of you;
My savior,
Sex messiah.
Don't you think it's rather funny,
I should be in this position,
I'm the one,
Who's always been,
So calm,
So cool.
No lovers fool.
Running every show.
I loved you so.

I love you so.
You were the original Lover Dream Lover,
Of my Dream Lover Dream. You!
Finding me pretty.
Sensually,
Stroking,
Caressing,
Loving,
With the marvelousness,
Of the, hugeness,
Of your,
Unforgettable,
Hands.
Those amazingly gentle,
Terrifically strong,
Hands;
Yours,
Mine.
You reached your long sinewy arms under my legs and lifted me,
Easily.
I wrapped my legs around you,
And held on for dear life.
And finally,
For the first time,
In forever,
I saw your face!
And felt,
Dizzy, lost, distant, alone, happy, gone, crying, crying, crying.
The onlooker and the girl looked behind themselves to see into my creation of me,
And of Bonnie.
They tried to comfort me with understanding:
I had laid blanket upon blanket of lies over my love in order to distort it into something I wouldn't want and ended up wanting the distortion.
I had tried to hate the youth, the beauty, the feminine.
And in hating it had created,
Lust,
For a young beautiful feminine creature,
That carried your wife's name and brought you closer to me,

As we both made love to Bonnie.

Till unbelievably,

No longer needing a conduit,

I saw your face!

And you kissed me,

With your sweet freshwater kisses.

For the first time,

In,

Ever.

And finally,

I came,

Back, into the room, with SMack.

Still tasting you,

I brought you with me,

To let you,

Become,

Gone.

How is it that I hadn't known?

That it was you,

That I was seeking,

To dream?

That I had done so much damage,

To me,

In the making of me?

My morals,

My ideas,

Running,

From everyone,

With you in my pocket.

How is it that I didn't know.

I?

The one who knows?

The onlooker and the girl had become me now so this time I looked behind myself through the blurry vision of eyes that wouldn't stop crying and saw it all: The truth about me and you and Ted. Strange how much easier it had been to see through the two of you than to see into myself. Jeff, you were my sensual panther of silence. A twilight creature that thrived on the salivating pleasure you derived from the sensations of your own muscles, rippling, as you leapt and stalked and crawled and cleaned and chewed and drank your mate, which, wasn't always me, the feline in heat.

While Ted was my horned owl in flight, seeking the evening air for a partner in the hunt. Seeking a woman with whom to swoop and kill and feast and unite, into as one, someone with whom he could saturate the darkness of the night, with hootings of greatness, observations and sight.

And I, it turned out, was a unicorn. A fantasy creature that never existed,

Me?

An illusion created for the romantic-at-heart.

I pranced and reared and neighed my way into the beds of men.

Forever looking,

Because I believed without believing I believed,

In the perfect complement, to my very sensual soul.

Me,

I was the one who had carried a torch and hidden its glow behind cynicism and disdain.

I was the romantic realist searching for you,

Never listening to myself when I tried to speak the truth of my own self-deception.

Jeff?

When you make love,

Do you look in the mirror?

Who do you think of?

Does she look like me?

Do you tell lies?

And say that it's forever?

Do you think twice?

Or just touch,

Me?

I miss you.

Even now.

And that night,

As SMack reached his pleasure,

Wistfully,

Emitting that low whining sound,

That always makes me think of Lisa,

He opened his eyes, and saw my tears, and saw me.

I felt like a whole person,

But I guess I looked the same,

To him.

Because he wasn't,

Yet,

Whole,

And couldn't see,

Behind himself,

As me.

So all of his women flowed into me,

Though I tried to keep Val out,

To respect her privacy,

As a wife.

And because she was present tense, having her flow into me meant identifying, empathizing, becoming,

Her sorrow,

For it was louder than her joy.

I tried to keep her out, but she surrounded me,

Everywhere I looked.

Her books, her pictures, her decorations, her creams, her cloths,

Her smell, her touch,

Her,

Everything.

And now with you back inside me,

Returned,

The silence,

And the knowing, of,

Also everything,

I had selectively refused to know.

And the only way to kill the process,

Was to return you to the grave,

Of my avoidance.

And that,

I just...couldn't...do.

Any consequence of truth was worth having you back again.

And besides what was the point of guilt?

A whore doesn't refuse to sleep with men just because they're married.

She picks and chooses on the basis of,

Finances and fetishes,

Mileage, cleanliness and physical safety.

I'd behaved appropriately,

According to my lifestyle.

So, though from the pre-beginning I felt like more than a call girl with SMack, my escort moral code had bled through enough to make me not feel guilty over the existence of his absentee wife.

Until now,

That she was an in house wife.

And you had given me back my heart to love her husband with.

Now that I felt wholly connected to that part of me that falls in love with truth rather than fantasy I wanted that love to be good and pure,

And not hurt another woman,

Into burying the torch that she carried for the man I was with.

Because, the torch burns,

The carrier.

And because I knew what it was,

To be the wife and feel violated.

And I didn't want to do that,

To anyone.

Though I had wanted to be the other woman rather than the wife,

Because, the other woman knows all the truths,

The other woman has the insight.

Because the other woman knows,

Everything,

The wife could never guess.

And that's why being the other woman has always seemed better, because there are fewer lies as long as one doesn't expect to become the wife, which is what happens when there isn't one already.

And the other woman doesn't just know everything, about the husband, she also knows everything, about everything, including the wife.

I shuddered at how awful it would be to have another woman know more about me than I did about myself.

I didn't want to be painted by the brush of such intrusive coloring,

Neither as the victim,

Nor as the perpetrator.

Her pain became mine as the room breathed her into me.

When I smelled the pillow:

I saw her life in that room.

I saw her sleeping,

I saw her crying,

Saw her curled up in the fetal position,

Saw her standing by the bed.

I saw her showering.

I saw her changing her clothes.

I saw her,

Tickling her husbands back.

And I saw,

That I was an intruder,

In her home,

And that that,

Was going to hurt her.

I looked into the futures,

All of them,

And saw no options,

No way for me to keep the reality wherein I face my truth,

Without also gaining the reality, wherein she faced hers.

She would know,

Almost as much as I did,

Soon.

Unless I chose,

Again,

To not,

Know,

What I knew.

I touched the book beside their bed,

Hating that I had opened it,

Hours before.

Reading her underlines,

I had peeked at her soul.

I tried to push it,

The knowing,

Away,

Without losing you,

But,

They came together,

Fused as one,

And to have you,

I got her,

Pain.

I just wanted to leave, just wanted to leave, just wanted to leave, just wanted to leave, just wanted to leave, just wanted,

To leave.

Just,

Wanted,

To ....

leave.

I did not want to know her thoughts,

Or inhale,

Her black hole,

Her despair,

Her desire to die,

Her humiliating past.

I was in her room,

Lying on her side of the bed.

I'd used her toothbrush for God sake!

What the hell was I doing here?

How dare I know my way around her home, with, him. I knew everything, where they kept their chopsticks, their bowls, their cutlery, her shoes, her lotions.

My God! I had used her lotions!!

That's what hurts, that's what hurts, knowing that someone else has touched your things, and your husband encouraged it, offered it up, like you were nothing,

I didn't want to be that someone else,

Treating her like nothing.

I just wanted to leave.

And I saw her picture.

I didn't want to see her picture.

I had been here so many times and never looked,

Out of respect,

For her,

Or lies,

To myself.

And she looked like me,

When you make love,

Do you look in the mirror?

Who do you think of?

Does she look like me?

Do you tell lies?

And say that it's forever?

Do you think twice?

Or just touch and see?

I didn't want to just touch and see anymore,

Since,
Seeing you,
Meant seeing everything.
I JUST WANTED TO GET OUT OF THERE!!
With you in my arms and her in her bed.
I just wanted to go home and hold on to you for awhile,
To write and write and write until I could understand.
This.
To cry because I missed you,
And because I had you back,
Though you were gone.
I just wanted to,
Hold on to you,
Till,
I could finally say good-bye,
Because,
I never got to do that.
And the tears,
And the tears,
And the tears,
Flowed,
And flowed,
And flowed,
Unassisted,
By me,
Releasing themselves,
And washing my world clean.
And SMack,
My darling SMack,
Who had opened the door that let you in,
To release my tears that cleansed me clean.
Who had loved me enough to let me feel safe enough,
To be brave enough to unveil the mirror,
And see the affectedness of my affection.
To see my fakeness,
For him,
Because of you,
And for you,
Because of,

The smooth;
That special something,
That was nothing more,
Than your affectation.
And with SMack's help I looked in the mirror of my dreams.
And looking gave me the freedom that gave my soul a voice.
SMack asked me if I was OK?
"*Too much emotion.*" I whispered.
He held me,
Understanding,
Something.
So SMack is why, I couldn't get up to write,
The words that suddenly blanketed my being,
With the love,
So newly,
Rediscovered.
SMack,
Is why,
I couldn't,
Get up,
To leave,
And go,
Home,
With,
You.
Right then,
Because,
He didn't deserve to have me always leaving him,
For other men.

❖ ELEVEN ❖

Well, Jeff, I ran away to the lake again, to be alone. Needing the security, I locked the doors, to keep Smack out. And,

Making sure that no one was getting in,

Side the cabin to be my distraction.

Though as my obsession you were in,

Side my mind. I was immersed,

In the loving, of you,

And the memory of your hands,

Everywhere, In,

And on,

Me.

"I love you.

Even now,

Even as,

I realize

That the person I am in love with is probably nothing like the person you are today or maybe even the person you ever were."

A truth that, when thinking it, reminds me of the movie "Message In a Bottle,"

That movie that SMack tried to use as a tool to romance me with, hoping that it's sensuous scenes of love would,

Screwdriver,

Screw,

My heart,

Into loving him. For,

In that cinematic story, (just as in yours and mine) one out of the two true forever loves must become a ghost, frozen in time. One must die, or disappear gone because, the loss of love at its peak improves a movie (even if the movie was made within my mind) by freeze-framing all the feelings.

Statued still,

So that the partner left behind can be protected from living with the agony of watching the object of their heart's desire become tarnished by everyday loving.

That way, all those formaldehyde feelings, can be permanently preserved, into a petri-fied vision,

Of what I and all the other torch carriers wish to remember as the truth,

Of what our true forever loves—who are never at risk of becoming other than imag-ined—will always be.

And that, rather than being screwed into falling in love with Smack, though love him I did, is exactly what I had done: I'd preserved you and made you a ghost.

Even though, as far as I knew,

You lived,

For someone else.

And that's why I was there in the cabin again,

Trying to conjure you up:

To be with you,

To get my fill,

To send you away,

I needed you,

To stop,

Haunting me.

And, in order to blow your shadow from my mind I looked about me in the physical,

Seeking direction, from the world beyond my world, asking how?

To cast a spell,

To call the wind,

To do my bidding,

And scatter you to the ethers.

The answer came as my eyes were ripped towards the muted television flickering a commercial for the upcoming movie "Poltergeist:" The story of a haunting!?

And because I knew that all who seek answers find them, though often subtly blended into ordinary things,

I listened, to the clues, in the world without,

And all around, me.

As I opened my ears,

To the whispers, from the world within.

And saw,

Myself,

Think,

About You,

My smell-able taste-able touchable apparition.

And saw,

Myself,

Watch, You, Reflect, Me.

It had to stop.

I could accept that now.

So I used what I knew about hauntings, from movies and books and instincts and beliefs, and understood that you were here for a reason.

Understood,

That if you were to be exorcised from me and dispelled from my life, I must help you complete your tasks still left undone.

And then,

That epiphany, that had been knocking on the door of my consciousness since the journey began, found its voice inside my head. "Of course! You are my ghost! And if you are my ghost, the ghost of my making, then,

I created you!

So, the business still left undone,

Must be mine.

Mine! It's me wandering around in my made up world refusing to go into the light. Me, wanting, something completed before letting go."

"Great! What do I do about that? How do I finish up what I've left undone if I don't know what it is? And how do I find what it is when I'm hiding it from myself? I mean the part of me that's hiding it, will know when the part of me that's looking for it is getting close enough to find it. I'll probably just divert my other half into thinking in the wrong direction." And because I believed in a mind that was divided into two, mine was.

I held to the concept, afraid to be diverted, even as my thoughts began to turn into thoughts of not turning. "It's like trying to hide something from God. In fact that's exactly what I'm trying to do. Maybe, in a way, for me at least, that is who I am. God!"

I shivered, thinking, in another direction. "Maybe these two separated parts of me are tired of being apart, divided by the game. Maybe I will just change it and decide not to separate, decide not to play anymore."

And, I thought-birthed, what seemed to be, a brand-new concept, at the fork in the road.

"I guess this not deciding to play would only be a new game. But maybe in the not playing game of life I get to win, by not creating a side to me that loses. Or maybe, by becoming one, the word "win" would be lost from my vocabulary. Let me think," I thought, "Let me try it. Let me think as one, as yet undivided soul."

And I saw that the clues, to what this business I had left undone must be, were grounded in the fact that I chose you, to be my visionary messenger superimposing images upon images that I was seeking to understand,

Through you.

About you,

Inside of me,

Inside of,

You.

"*So, Jeff,*" I opened my arms and whispered, "*tell me, teach me, play your images upon the screen of my soul and show me what I need you, to need me to know.*"

"*As I lay my being into your hands, possess me, write for—NO!—write with me.*

Use my hands as yours,

To caress,

The keyboard,

And let me feel,

Your feather-light touch,

Everywhere."

I listened to your whisperings,

As they wrote with me,

From within.

I was openly yours and laid no limitations between us. I called you "*Spirit of my own Design,*" as I begged you, "*Take me where I need most to go.*"

And together we played this letter like a piano,

Letting the notes follow each other,

Deciding themselves to be,

Limitless,

Free.

For days upon days,

Alone in the cabin,

Playing our music,

Until the volume receded,

Into the crescendo,

Of silence.

During those days,

While you continued to haunt me,

With the same soft sweet melody of memories,

That had been serenading across my mind for the past three weeks,

I slow-danced inside.

Your ethereal notes,

That could have,

Given a different mood, intent or curiosity,

Been a child's lullaby,

Full of the sounds of my family.

But instead, as we danced,

What I heard was the sexual dissonance,

Of the otherworldly beautiful,

Lyrically brazen,

Perverted refrains,

Of love,

Unrequited and floating out of reach.

And that's when I knew that the dissonance,

And the perversion,

Was merely judgment,

That I had judged,

As unharmonious, with me.

This letter,

Us,

Truth,

Could have been shared,

While being something entirely different, than what it is.

But this time, this telling, it is,

This,

View,

Through semen-covered glasses,

That I have,

Come,

To wear,

Often.

Though that will change,

Upon each reading.

Change and rearrange and be,

Come,

Some other pictured past of wishes unfulfilled and,

Fulfilled and,

Left to live or die in accordance,

With my innermost beliefs at the time that I read it.

And so I began to see everything about myself in this light, making truth a choice colored by the singularity of my perspective vision. My brain kicked into the gear within which it most often drives: "ANALYZE," and my innocence fell away as my sarcasm returned.

I questioned all I believed I knew and everything I saw. I wondered, why I was forever thinking it important to put words to paper, as if it would help me, somehow? I wondered, what made me so deluded, as to believe such powerful poppycock about my pen. Where did I get the idea that writing was clean honest therapy and why had I believed it?

And how had I believed it when, I already knew that writing is never an act of true, writing-for-writings-sake, purity? How, when I already knew that, no matter how skillfully I tried to trick myself, the truth was, whenever I wrote, even in a diary, somewhere in my mind lies the awareness that the words might someday have an audience,

Of at least,

One,

At a time?

And so I would write with that one, like you, in mind.

And finally, I stopped hiding from myself, and admitted that,

I wrote this love letter song to teach myself with,

As the one,

You,

In me,

Reads it.

So that I might be inspired to croon,

Out my lyrics of pleasured plurality.

And also so, I might be able to serenade you,

Because I want to be heard by you, in the now.

And then, you, having heard, might be caused to feel,

Me, caressing on your tomb of enshrined sensuality.

And I guessed that the way to do that was to call this letter a book and get it published.

In truth I suppose I knew all along that publishing this book length letter of yearning for answers was my intention. And, in truth, I suppose I knew why!

Because,

I repeatedly imagined you seeing me on a talk show, or noticing my picture on the back cover of this poetic story, as some stranger in an airplane sits across from you and reads it. Most often I imagine the discovery as a television moment with me holding our book in my hands.

While the camera zooms in, the screen fills and the title, calls,

Your name,

And you audience me flying,

On the wings of your heart.

Recognizing my own thoughts I noticed the possibility of that reality, I wondered,

"What are the odds, that,

We would even like each other,

Alive,

In the physical?

And needing clarity,

I wished for the answer,

To dispel your ghost and maybe, just maybe,

Raise your body from the dead,

Of gone,

To make you human.

Perhaps that's what this letter is: an incantation to raise the dead and materialize the ghost,

Into a man,

Called mine,

No more.

So I prayed a witches' wish; that my thoughts might find their way home to you,

By delivering this verbose child of ours,

Unto your hands,

And into your mind,

From the notes within mine.

I thought the thought,

"I hope it finds you."

But then realized that,

Maybe I didn't,

Want to risk being public.

For a few minutes I wavered,

Unsure of my decision,

Uncertain of the world I'd find in coming out of the closet of my mind, naked.

Certain, uncertain, certain, uncertain,

Certain,

That no matter what the consequences were; I would still be able to hear the harmonics of life even, while withstanding the discord of public scrutiny.

Uncertain,

Because, while taking a break from my writing, I un-muted the TV and saw Monica Lewinsky—President Clinton's forbidden fruit-trying to do exactly that.

And because of the obvious sameness between the question I asked myself and the scene being played out on the screen in front of me, I turned my attention to the world at large, listening to the message in the happenings, seeking the certainty I wavered upon.

Monica Lewinsky was emoting humanness and trying to be a real person dealing with the real issues of her, and her family's,

Life.

Monica Lewinsky was trying to befriend the public, even as she was being a cinder, (Ella),

In the public eye.

She looked smutty girl-next-door-beautiful; this Monica Lewinsky trying for miracles,

Was brave.

She looked steadfastly into the eyes of renowned journalist Barbara Walters who seemed to me, to be treating the young woman with superiority and disdain.

Sadly, the on-camera chat fast became a media circus of other networks via the ones without the right to air the actual interview cashing in by creating whole programs centered around debates over the believed sincerity of the woman Barbara Walters questioned, in order to entertain.

CHA CHING! CHA CHING! CHA CHING!

And so all the character defaming and opinionating led me to form my own media made opinions. The way I viewed it, it was the interviewer not the interviewee that seemed insincere. I raised an eyebrow of distrust towards Barbara Walters herself.

And suddenly saw,

Every one of us,

Even me,

Sitting,

In judgment,

As we sat,

On the right hand,

Of CNN.

And as we sat,

We sat as,

Imposters: Pretenders to be,

Casting the first and subsequent stones,

Together.

And I remembered, what it had felt like, in my years as a high-focus Toronto single parent standup comedienne actress mom of special needs kids, with an unorthodox lifestyle and a heaping helping of "if you're not with me (in other words, the same as me) you're agin (in other words against) me" attitude.

To be front and center, of other peoples need to opinionate.

And I remembered,

Traveling with my children all over North America performing in prisons.

It had been a great idea—showing my kids what it's like on the inside—that would, I hoped; keep them from wanting to live there. It was expensive (Prison seldom pays) but worth every bankrupt cent. Because, it was such a wonderfully unique adventure, that, I believed, lightened the hearts of some very burdened convicts. And that, I discovered, brought my makeshift family together, into a closer tighter bond.

I remembered thinking I was kind and being told I was exploitative.

I remembered, finding that hurtful,

Which I painfully enjoyed,

As I pushed on my emotional bruises,

Until I didn't anymore.

And I remembered, appreciating the press,

Only as long as,

They appreciated me.

And then, I thought about publishing this recipe for how to make love out of nothing at all, and knew that such an act could re-create that same malicious need of the media driven masses,

To play the vengeful God and lay judgments of sin,

On me,

And all those who came into my arms,

Including my children, who'd already been blamed enough for being my children.

I thought about having my affection

Be it for "peanut-butter-mommy-make-it-better" kisses,

Or a banana split fun-day with Halls Mentho-Lyptos on top,

Of the penis,

Turned against me,

And balked at the possibility,

Of having everything painted with the same wrong brush.

I took a deep breath and scrutinized my life, as I remembered it, over the past few years.

I had been enjoying my anonymity. And I wasn't sure I was ready to have big fat cigars and public persecution become the most reputed bond of commonality between Monica and I, though I knew it to be a possibility. Not because I had ever done any thing sexual with a cigar but because the world is full of the tragedies the media has made for the sake of something to say.

I thought that Lady Di's recent reporter driven demise, underlined my point and illustrated the possible dire results reporters cause when blinded by their need to stalk and peek and intrude into people's lives with extreme insensitivity,

In order to create stories of people running away.

Stories,

Of people,

Running away,

In fast-moving cars,

That crash into walls!

Like Lady Di,

Who thusly gave them,

The biggest story,

They ever chased.

And then I wondered if writing with such intimate honesty about myself,

Might not possibly destroy all those who loved me?

And thinking about that, brought me to the awareness that the coincidence of the controversy over Monica's televised talk airing at the precise moment when I asked the universe to answer my 'to publish or not to publish' questions meant; I was using her to warn myself about the future.

And though I wouldn't run, I was afraid that my children might,

Crash and burn.

Especially Chance,

Who could barely handle the attention of a mother's advice, let alone a reporters opinion.

So I waited,

And stalled,

The books publication,

Till I thought Chance had grown up enough,

To handle,

The publicized intimacy of my revelations.

And all the subsequent revelations,

That others might invent,

Out of nothing at all.

Because after-all a good reporter knows how to mercilessly create through juxtaposition,

And so he does,

Cause unwarranted opinions that make me angry,

While still he is,

A necessary component,

To my success,

If I want to be heard.

In fact it was that "mercilessly creating" part that turned me off the idea of being a news anchor, when the opportunity, with annual salary and health benefits for the family almost presented itself.

The thought of accepting such a job made my back quiver with revulsion, for the me, that I would then be, because, I just didn't want to have any connection whatsoever with the sensationalism and methods of news acquisition: That's also why I sucked as a journalist,

Even though I was a good writer,

Who didn't want to leave the feelings out.

I also sucked when freelancing for magazines, that told me what to say and how to slant the piece, in order to represent the publisher's opinion while signing my name. So, even though it was my goal to teach, to bring knowledge to the world, to unearth and display previously hard to observe truths, I was specific on how and why I wanted to do that.

And that's why even though I wanted to be a talk show host, which is like being an anchor in that they both engage in information-sharing, I wanted to be more than a font of misery. I wanted to be personable, kind and as friendly as Oprah.

I was adamantly determined not to be the sort that seeked to entertain by gaining ratings on the backs of other people's humiliation because,

I didn't want to live the life of a person perpetrating cruelty upon others.

And that is one of the reasons why, even though I saw this book's value in its ability to be scathingly honest, I hid the identities of those who might be hurt by my tattle-tellings of terrific tail: because tattle tellings always perpetrate, upon someone. So I began to change, some of the names in order to not hurt others, though, I continued to fear, that continuing to consider publishing might hurt me.

Wanting it anyway I decided to believe that I could continue to move forward and risk the bruises. I supposed it was worth it because, I believed I had something important to teach,

Myself,

By teaching others.

I believed I was right.

At any rate it seemed like a noble goal to desire to teach the world my ever—changing vision of what we are and how best to go about enjoying that until it occurred to me that, in this, I wasn't alone, or special and that I might actually share this noble goal,

In some form or another,

With everyone,

Even,

Talk Show hosts,

Of the Jerry Springer, Rickie Lake, Jenny Jones variety.

I squirmed at the thought of any possible sameness between us and searched for the difference instead. For though, upon thinking of it, I did believe that those hosts, also believed, they had something important to teach the world. I also believed that even if they did, have something grand to impart, they probably wouldn't, because their jobs were in the way. Their method of belief dispersion, I believed, was dangerous because it got jumbled up with the need for effectiveness based on sensationalism instead of compassion and they were in the position to teach millions of people from that standpoint, a lot of very contagious blame throwing.

I, I was certain, was more enlightened, more entitled to my non-ratings concerned opinions than they were to their popularity contest ones. I, in my self proclaimed superiority, refused to create, even through observation, an existence wherein their kind of trash could be as good as my kind of garbage. The way I concocted it, I was the one with the credibility, for all the things I surmised, about whatever talk show host I was surmising,

Because,

I had done the research,

And worked both sides of the talk show circuit, bent on revenge.

When,

While I was on location shooting the Canadian Television series "Cross Country Cookin" my friend, and sometimes director, Dana Danvil, took advantage of my absence from home and invited my daughters Deja and Brandessa, onto the one and only 1994 Canadian show for trashy talk. It was called, "The Shirley Show" and, Dana Danvil had just been hired on as a producer.

She offered my daughters money to perform on the show. She promised to pay them as actresses and they, thrilled to be working, agreed.

According to my children, Dana set them up to compete against each other in much the same way that a television cop from a show like "Law and Order" might create distrust between partners-in-corporate-or-any-other-crime, by talking to them one at a time and then lying to each, about what the other had said. Dana, it seemed, was using our friendship and its implied faith in my judgment, to gain my children's trust. Then, she abused that trust, for her own personal gain.

Part way through the manipulative process of prepping them for the program Dana explained to my girls that Deja, who was an ACTRA union member, would be paid more than nonunion Brandessa, who was simply to receive something from petty cash.

This increased the competition between my daughters. And Brandessa, who no longer wanted to do the show, phoned me to report what was happening.

"But Mom, I can't back out now, Dana keeps crying and saying she'll lose her job if we don't help her. Besides, Deja really wants the money. If I don't do the show she'll be mad at me. And the last thing I need is to cause more trouble between the two of us. Dana's done a good enough job of that already. Like, she keeps trying to dig up dirt and to get us to call each other names and you know, stuff. It's bad, mom."

"*Then don't do the show. Dana's job is not your responsibility.*" I told her. "*And from the sounds of things, Deja will be better off if you don't do it, than if you do.*"

However, despite my hours of support and convincing arguments, since I was out of town shooting on location, the power of my influence dissipated over the miles. Meanwhile Dana talked to them and talked to them and talked to them, planting ideas, twisting beliefs and marveling aloud at how much they must hate each other, and how horrible it must have been to become sisters during the beginning of their teenage years.

And so, since she was right, since it truly had been hard for them, she was able to make it hard again. Remember Jeff? Remember what a challenge it was for my daughters to find their sister-ship? My girls,

Innocents who, like me, the mother they adored, wanted to make a difference. My,

Girls who, were excited at the prospect of sharing their story on television because— also like their mother—they thought they had something to teach.

My girls, innocents who,

Expected their mother's friend to take good care of them.

And that was just the kind of vulnerability, mingled with just the kind of altruistic motivation that Dana needed to coerce them onto the show.

However, unbeknownst to Dana, the girls had made a pact between themselves. They had, on-their-oath promised, not to abandon each other but to stand together as sister-friends and tell the truth, no matter what, because, according to most, everyone, they knew,

Their story was worth hearing.

Even you said it was Jeff? Do you remember? How it was as you just barely moved out of my house before Deja moved in.

Remember what I told you, (as we pretended to be together though we were apart), about feeling an audible "click" when Deja walked through the door. As though now that she'd arrived I could close the porthole of invitation I'd left open for all the children of the world because the one I'd been waiting for had finally entered in. Somehow I knew that the vision was complete. I had finally found all the daughters and sons I was going to mother. Though it felt as though I may still raise – or possibly father— four to five more. That's when I knew that Deja, was meant to be with us, just as, with the same kind of instinctiveness, I knew, you, were not.

Interestingly my children came to live with me, in the way that, as a child, I had predicted they would. A self-fulfilling prophecy? Hmmm I wonder.

And the question brings me to the memory: of a time when I was around eight or nine and hiding in the bathroom to escape my mother's rage. I promised myself that I would remember how that fear of retribution felt, and swore never to cause any of my little ones to run away trembling and hide from the justice of my hand. And then I asked myself how many children I would someday have. The answer then heard, came in bunches: first two, then six, then eight, then twelve, and finally thirteen.

Did I ever tell you about that Jeff? About how my children came – Tsara and Brandessa (born to me) Dar, Cash, Chance, Rye, (adopted) Jady, Deja, (guardianship) Jory, Tyran, Shay, Declyn (the grandsons I father)—in bunches, exactly as I had predicted? So far, according to me,

I have one yet to go.

But I was telling about Deja, the last daughter, and how she and Dessa became new best friends, having known each other for only a few months.

It was during this beginning, during the infatuation period of their friendship, that Deja's biological mother, kicked her thirteen-year-old daughter out of the house, in an over-the-top screaming, irrational act. That irretrievable act turned out to be a blessing for Deja who was finally able to escape the anger and sexual dysfunction of her environment, for me, who was granted one more beautiful child to love, and eventually for Dessa whose position as blond-haired, blue-eyed, brilliantly creative daughter was first challenged, then usurped, and finally, ultimately, shared.

But, first,

Brandessa's transition was a scary one,

For me, as the mother of my second-born.

I watched, breath held, paralyzed with foreboding, as my baby girl fluttered like a panicked sparrow, her teeny little heart racing with fear, as she came crashing headfirst into that plate of glass called the illusion of freedom and known as, "flirting with death."

Do you remember any of this Jeff? You were there, but were you watching, me, watch her,

Fall off the cliff of sanity into the oblivion of drugs and Russian Roulette-playing friends.

Until,

From each member of the family,

An outstretched hand was clung onto,

And Dessa emerged,

A sister,

To all,

And someone,

For all,

To admire.

My girls were proud, of what they'd become, because it was right to be.

Dessa and Deja were young women to behold. They loved the idea of sharing their story.

But the daytime talk show wanted sensationalism not sensational. So my children were separated from each other backstage and prepared for battle. Brandessa was set up as the sister who caused all the problems while Deja was there to "have it out with her." That's when the first argument of the day ensued.

Dana instructed Deja to become reactive, to fight with Brandessa convincingly enough to appear to need to be physically restrained. Deja refused.

Dana insisted that the show needed the girls to enter the stage from opposite sides and come out fighting "Or else," Dana cried, "You'll get me fired! I'm sure your mother wouldn't want you to do that."

Which was an assumption on her part since I quite honestly really wish they had.

When Brandessa joined Deja on stage, a few of the audience members having been set up to hate her in advance, booed her as she made her grand entrance. The sound of judgments avalanching in her direction saddened, heavily, her teenage heart. In an effort to gain strength and feel impenetrable, the two girls held hands. And since neither the subtitles placed under their close-ups nor the host's pre-written questions matched my daughters' behavior, Shirley—who was beginning to look very uninformed—began to insult my children, "The two of you are just a couple of spoiled teenagers who lied to my staff in order to get on television." And then, as Shirley's voice went up a pitch she, either out of frustration or as a means of covering herself for her own lack of awareness, continued to throw unverified blame at her two young guests, "Look we didn't seek you out. You called our show. You told our producers that you had an issue with your sister. You—"

And according to Dessa, Deja, who couldn't take another second of this pretense, threw herself out of her chair shouting."YOUR PRODUCER, DANA DANVIL, IS MY MOM'S FRIEND. SHE BEGGED US TO COME ON THE SHOW BECAUSE THERE WEREN'T ENOUGH GUESTS. SHE TOLD US WHAT TO SAY AND THEN TWISTED EVERYTHING AROUND. SHE'S THE ONE THAT TOLD US TO LIE. WE'RE THE ONES THAT WON'T!"

The audience booed and shouted and Deja's words got lost in the din.

Shirley insisted that, "the girls made that up." and her fans believed, her.

At least I think they did. Just as I think that's how it went, though I can't be sure,

Since, I only have Dana's and my children's word, mingled with the evidence of,

Deja and Brandessa's resultant, pain, humiliation and breaking apart, of the bonds of sisterhood, so recently built,

To go on.

And Dana, "my friend," who was getting paid to create controversy, never got the axe, despite her, commercial-break-in-my-daughters'-ears-hissing-proclamations that "You just got me fired."

In fact it was I who got the axe to grind with her.

And once the show was edited Deja's shouted "truth" disappeared while Shirley's did not. Thus my children were made to look like, "spoiled teenagers (which they definitely weren't) trying to get on television (which of course they were—albeit with a little more class)."

And Shirley?

Why, she looked like the hostess with the mostess,

Keen nose for ferreting out the deceptions of fame-hungry adolescents.

At least that's how it seemed to me,

When I watched the Shirley Show version of my daughters' humiliation.

Watching the show had taken some doing too. I was still on the road the first time the episode ran. I asked my fellow crewmembers to take a few minutes out of our driving schedule, (We were traveling from one location to another). They, happy to help me, agreed. So we pulled over and watched the infamous program on a panel of TVs, in an electronics store, in a mall, on the day that Ian bought me the book, "Bridges In Madison County."

They joined in my disgust, over the people in our industry, who use their position to benefit themselves, with so little concern for the results of their actions or the pain that they might potentially cause,

My children,

Media folks, who behave like pimps, pimping, the naive that they then tarnish, to the public; people who sell and solicit scripted dramas of bullshit truth in order to make their deadline and achieve popularity;

People that primp and pimp, stroking egos and pretending to care, for the people in their crib in order to serve themselves a heaping helping of other people's pain.

Which is how I saw it.

When I saw red.

On the faces of my friends.

I was filled with a slow seething anger. I wanted to methodically crush what Dana stood for and every aspect of the Talk on Trash Show industry. My hatred against this perverted form of television that was founded on rumors and gossip and dangerously gained credibility by sandwiching real stories inside of fictitious ones in order to re-write truth, was passionate.

I feared for the people who believed in the reality that these talkies presented and who watched them religiously, rewarding the producers, with high enough ratings to keep that shit on the streets. I feared for these talk-show junkies as they shot up the shows' belief system diarrhea through their eyes and into their brains. I feared for the me, who might live by the neighbors, that built themselves out of this knowledge born of lies masquerading as gospel.

I feared for a society populated with pea-brained pretzeled people, moving about like walking packages of piled up poop.

I feared,

Enough,

To want to stop it because,

I hated these shows,

Even before,

They hated me.

Uncharacteristically for me I wanted to get even, wanted, revenge,

For my children's pain. Wanted it,

Bad.

As if there were such a thing, as even.

I wanted it, with an axe to grind,

Held tightly, in my hand,

Obliterating reason,

And chanting out my need.

I wanted, to be even,

With the virus,

That I invited home.

The virus,

That disfigured societies idea of the beauty of my children. I wanted it,

As if I'd had no hand in carrying the disease, up close, to their hearts,

And as if there were, ever,

Such a thing,

As innocence, for me; the girl who could see.

I wanted even, as though I already weren't,

And believed I wasn't, because I wanted to,

Avoid self-analysis.

I wanted to avoid self-analysis,

Because, I felt guilty, of poor judgment, and of being too passive,

To actually be angry, enough to do anything,

Which made me angry, enough, with myself, to at least seethe,

And finally seek, revenge, on everyone else.

And so, put "seeking revenge" in the lenses of my eyes and distorted my vision enough to safely pretend to myself that I was trying to self-analyze,

When in truth I was too busy looking out to look in,

And, unwilling to discover my own blame, I was thus unable,

To understand why my friends, and my husbands so often hurt my babies.

And since I was too busy blaming the world to be willing to blame myself.

I set my soul to simmer on the slow burn of seductive,

Seething,

And waited,

A Year,

For the opportunity,

That came.

When,

Dana Danvil,

My "friend?"

Called again.

She was producing yet another talk program. "This time," she boasted, "The show is being shot in New York."

"*MMMM!*" I responded, waiting for the part that would show me,

What Dana wanted me to do,

To benefit her.

The part, that went like this; "The host is Carni Wilson, Brian Wilson's daughter." For a second, I wondered if she meant that Brian Wilson from the Bare Naked Ladies song. And then I wondered, as I did every time I heard that song, who Brian Wilson was and why he warranted having a song written about him? As a result of my wondering, I just barely caught the rest of what Dana had to say. "Guess how she got the job! She was on a different talk show as the guest when these producers, who were looking for a host, saw her. She was so lively and funny they gave her, her own show. You know Lynette, that's how it is in the states. Hey, if you come on our show, maybe that'll happen to you."

And there it was:

The hook.

I was in an unemployed bind and I knew Dana knew it, because I had just told her. My husband had very quickly changed his mind about having so many weird, neighbor-attention-grabbing children, in a house he called his. He had asked us to leave and to keep going, all the way back to Canada,

Which we did.

Till our fellow Canadians—disappointed to have those weirdoes living next door again—yelled, "GO BACK TO TEXAS" at my kids,

Which we did,

When my husband said he'd changed his mind,

And missed us,

Until we got there,

And he reiterated that he was kicking us out,

With nothing,

Not even a home,

Which was less than what we'd had when we arrived, the first time.

"Maybe then you could stop living with your daughter." Dana pointedly suggested.

Ouch! Hook, followed by humiliation, nice touch.

My son's and I were living in Deja's apartment. She was an eighteen year-old single mom with a brand-new baby and just enough money from cashing in her ACTRA Insurance fund to survive on her own for a month or two when Tod kicked us out for the second, and last time. So we went to her, just as, she had come to us, once upon a time. It was her turn to extend a hand of welcome. Two months later, it was my turn again. And that's how my children and I survived the next three years of American life, teeter-totter helping each other stay financially and emotionally balanced.

It was a wonderful, awe-inspiring experience, however, at the moment when Dana called, I was at the beginning of this cooperative journey and completely unaware of all the beauty it would eventually bring. For the moment Deja was the one doing all the teeter-totter balancing while I looked furtively about me for an opportunity to re-become the financial head. It felt parentally shameful to be leaning on my daughter for help and I wasn't about to let it stay that way. But what to do, I was still awaiting my immigration status. I had no social security card so I couldn't work and had no system to fall back on? . . And then,

Dana called.

It occurred to me that I needed her, after all. I'd lost everything, even my reputation, everything, but my responsibilities, called children.

It had been a rough couple of years, especially on my finances. Between the prison tour which used up my resources, Cross Country Cookin' which gave me back a small portion of what I'd lost but then, because it changed my persona in the casting directors' eyes by making me a host, dried up my acting, singing, improv and stand-up comedy jobs, and ended up costing me more than what I had managed to make, I was in a pretty tough spot.

However I'd been in worse situations than this, I figured I could probably work it out. Until a bunch of college students decided to ride my comet's tail of success by trashing me in a documentary made from some stolen footage: mine.

I had shot that footage which was intended to become a docu-drama on crime and responsibility with them holding the camera. It was my intention to wrap fiction with fact in an effort to illustrate the truth about our inability to know the truth. But when, looking back on it, I mingled that with my—had not yet happened—talk show experiences and then noticed that the talk shows did exactly the same thing though for opposite purposes, I found some new ironies in the patterns of my own creations.

And wondered if maybe I wasn't just a one-note wonder God playing the same song over and over and over again looking for different nuances,

Circling circling forever circling,

In the ironies of life.

Until it occurred to me that perhaps my one-note song was for the purpose of discovering that it is in the nuances of life that the differences lie.

For even though I was conjuring up a here-to-for unused feature film format style that appeared to be the same technique the talk shows used mine, was for a different end.

I wanted to illuminate and challenge the viewer to bring their intellect with them when they watched. While Talk on Trash used the technique to confuse truth and increase ratings holding no regard for the long-term effect this twisting of truth might have on the audience, or even,

The participants.

Just as those nasty little college students in question,

Had no concern,

In my opinion,

For me, mine, or anyone else, they touched, with their lies. Whereas I did,

Not treat people with such disregard, most of the time.

In the students' doctored piece of cinema they called me many things, I did not want to be called.

And Dana was about to offer me an opportunity to set the record straight,

And bring out the truth,

As long as I lied,

With my manner and style,

Which would, through inference and attitude, make me like the people I was trying to hurt.

This was something I refused to do.

Besides, I didn't want to reward those fraudulent filmmakers by granting their dream come true wish for national coverage, on a subject I didn't want to advertise. They had taken the footage on my prison tour play about Turning Something Bad Into Something Good then mixed in an interview with Deja's natural mother and a couple of unknown strangers spouting sour grapes against me. It was and is my belief that Deja's mother was lying, heedless of the effect of hurting our daughter, in an effort to protect herself from any future allegations—for which she knew herself to be guilty—that Deja or I, might decide to sling, in her direction. The strangers, I supposed, were just repeating gossip as though it were fact in the hopes of doing something important.

Deja's mother apparently encouraged the students to mix her words with some of my acted-out, purposely created, dramatized, intended to appear like documentary-shooting footage. The end result turned the observers opinion of my desire to raise needy children, from Something Good into Something Bad. How unfortunate!

It must have been an exciting project for the lot of them. They were sure to get attention. Not only had they illegally incorporated Man-Alive footage (a respectable CBC show that had aired an episode of myself and my kids making the best out of life and entertaining prisoners) into their foul film but; when I got my new TV series I suppose they thought they'd hit the big one: I was a sweet little star on the rise and they had a trashy documentary about me. I can still hear the imagined sound of their hands rubbing together in glee.

They hoped to use my spotlight to bask in the glory of success. And for a glimmering second as their plan unfolded I believe they almost got what they were looking for. But, sadly, I was just the host of a cooking show and my star status wasn't anything more than the dim luminescence of a battery-deadened glowworm.

Perhaps next time they want to profit by shining in someone else's limelight they'll choose a star with some limes,

And a glimmer of light.

Perhaps not.

Some people never learn,

To choose the successful path,

Or person to follow. Some people,

Like me.

At any rate, right about that time, I was prime for any marriage that would take me far away from all this mess. Thus, when my infatuated, soon-to-be husband proposed, I allowed my head to be story-spun and said "yes," two months after meeting him. Then my new husband, Tod, vowed to be financially responsible as he coaxed and encouraged me to drop everything I owned and run into his arms,

Just before dropping me.

I was bankrupt. And living with my children in tow. So, since we were homeless I bought a tent and called it camping. The irony here is that, my sons—who never knew they were living on the streets—recall that terrifying time as some of the most wonderful carefree days of their childhood. They were hanging out with their mom! They loved it because while we rotated from tent, to van, to Deja's apartment, they had my attention 24 hours a day.

And I had theirs,

And though they weren't going hungry yet, I wasn't quite sure how I was going to prevent them from getting there,

While we lived with my daughter who was running out of funds.

Until Dana called, prepared to solve my immediate problems, as long as I was willing, to create some long term new ones.

"Look, I know you want to do other shows." she said, reminding me that ever since Phil Donahue first went on the air I had dreamed and deemed, myself a worthy guest with something to say. However, what we both forgot to remember was, I didn't feel that way anymore, about daytime talk, and hadn't, since all the copycat shows had created a cruel mockery of the trend Phil had begun.

Dana had my attention though because, as I said, I'd forgotten I didn't feel that way anymore, "Well, you can't get on any other shows unless you get in the talk show registry first: It's a holding bin of information on people who might be interesting as guests. All the talkies use it. I could show you how to get in on it. But I can't do that for you unless you do this for me." Dana explained. "Really! That's just how it works. You have to do a show to prove you're television-worthy before anyone else will take a chance on you."

This turned out to be a complete lie and an absolute reversal of the truth: doing one actually meant you've already done one and nobody else will touch you, that is, unless you don't tell them you already did one or unless you're famous.

However, Dana, who didn't seem to care a hoot for honesty, was looking for the buttons she had to push in order to motivate me into doing what she wanted. While I was looking, as usual, for too many things at once: revenge, money, work, a plane ticket home for Dessa who was visiting Deja and had run out of funds with no way back, to her brand-new independent life.

I was looking for a lot of things, that were really only one, thing, called,

A future,

Which, if I did it, this would likely destroy.

I agreed to do the show.

We settled on a performance fee, hotel, transportation issues, and the show's story line: Which, just as I thought she might, Dana perverted from the truth we'd based it on.

Apparently she had not yet learned the lesson, that life had recently, finally, taught me: **The truth is always, just as interesting as a lie**.

Dana wanted the subject of the show to be gossip. I wanted to talk about being an escort, because I'd been one and because it was interesting, and also because I wanted to say it out loud before some journalist pointed their finger in my direction and said it for me. I hoped to prevent any college student types in my future from gaining credibility by using my own happily disclosed truths against me, again.

I didn't want anyone else getting away with pretending they had been undercover geniuses and discovered things about me that they labeled: my shameful secrets. I wanted to talk about "things" to prevent the tabloids from ever being able to talk about them first and also because I am a, driven to teach whatever lesson I have been fortunate enough to learn from whatever happening I have been fortunate enough to have, person.

Which turns out to be a good thing since I've had a lot of happenings, happening,

That would have otherwise inhibited rather than enhanced me.

However, though happenings happen, so far, none of them have been as cloud bursting with mental clarity, as the one that led me to this book,

Which led me to remember all those foggy, thought-condensing periods in my life,

Before my finally recognized tears, of longing for you, began to wash away the soupy mist of murdered memories and show me love.

Dana and I argued, politely. I wanted to express myself as myself. She didn't believe the audience would accept me unless I displayed shame.

"You have no idea how mean they can be." She implored, with a statement that made her, appear to be concerned, for my well-being. I suspected however, that she was merely trying to manipulate me into doing it the way she wanted it done. I believed she was simply trying to create the scenario she'd had in mind, even before placing her call. In hindsight, I even more than believe it, I feel vindicated for suspecting it, because at the very last minute Dana twisted the script into a gossip-based presentation remarkably similar to her originally shared intentions. I remember it as mean, heartless even, because she didn't hesitate for a second to fulfill her desire of putting my daughter in that very hated-by-audience seat she had protectively refused to let me sit in.

Appeared-to-be-concerned-for-my-well-being-Dana didn't hesitate as she exposed my child to the angry throng, that she had warned me could be so mean.

It's a dangerous thing to do to a mother: hurt her, by hurting her child.

A dangerous thing that, made me want to get even, with Dana,

For making me think I could get even, with Dana,

Because the thinking I could get even had created in me a feeling (which I will soon tell you about) of superior intellect, which caused my intellect to shrink,

And left me vulnerable, enough to be manipulated, which manipulated my children,

Into my stupidity,

For which, as you can see, I blamed Dana.

Dana was good at her job: good at lying with an innocent face, good at warmly, generously, offering, an information gathering shoulder to lean on. I told her, "*I'm afraid that if I perform on the Carnie show, without the audience knowing it's fake, I'll damage my reputation even more than that trashy documentary did. I mean, Jesus! If that stupid thing can cost me work, just imagine what this'll do.*"

She insisted that the show was on a limited feed and not on a channel that could reach Canada. For the flickering second of a firefly's mating call the words "Satellite TV" tried to take purchase inside my head. But I rejected the intercourse.

Dana's truth, was truth that I knew to be a lie,

But chose to believe anyway,

Hoping I was wrong.

I needed to allow this illogical answer to be honest, because though you were still my married telephone friend, Jeff, you were the only friend I felt I had. And I couldn't ask you for anything because you were only my married telephone friend. I needed a friend who could give me real help, like money or food, housing or clothes, anything with enough substance to help me begin to change my life.

Dana was being that kind of friend.

So I closed my eyes, held my breath, and prepared to do the show.

Dana's scripts, it seemed, were limited to only a few ideas. Once again, she wanted to pretend that two of my daughters had been estranged and had not talked to each other for years, as a result of the harm that gossip had done. She said that the gossip could be about my having been an escort. And that way I could get the subject I wanted and she could get the subject she wanted. It seemed ridiculous to me since, if she absolutely had to have the show be about gossip there were plenty of true stories in my life that we could pull from. I refused to go along with her puke-enticing suggestions of, "Let's say Brandessa was angry so she made up some lies like, that you were having sex with guys in front of her while trying to get her to give oral."

"We could say that she was telling people that her brothers have so many men around them that they think the word "uncle" means "mom's friend.""

We could pretend you got kicked out of your neighborhood because of the gossip. So you all disowned her, sick of the trouble she was causing." I said "*No*" for millions of disgusted reasons.

But I still needed her help, so,

We continued to negotiate.

As I refused and rewrote every script she faxed me.

Until, after a while it just felt rude to be so inflexible.

And after awhile, she came to know what was important to me; like that I was only truly motivated to do the show when it served my long range goals by allowing me to confess the things I was afraid I'd be discovered for.

She used that knowledge, to get us on the show by continuing to insert the escort angle into the scripts, in order to keep me interested, enough, to make some money, which I couldn't do, if I flat-out refused.

So, slowly, incrementally, Dana wiggled me towards the goal she'd had in mind all along. Till, in the end, when Dana got her gossip and I got my escorting, nobody got the truth,

Which would have been far more valid and a lot more interesting.

But Dana was a director, with a limited field of vision, and since, directors can only direct with confidence that for which they have an understanding, Dana directed crass,

Which I could be,

Every time she directed me,

From film to T.V.

However, maybe, I was wrong, as is often the case. Maybe Dana's ideas weren't limited at all. Maybe she just had trouble letting go of the concepts that turned into catastrophes, until she proved them worthy by making them work, and so, tried again, and again, and again, to succeed, until the moment when, she could feel good about it all. Maybe so.

At any rate, recycling ideas is common in Talk TV, and for that matter in life: Because

It seems so much easier than creating oneself anew.

So Dana was repeating herself.

So? So were we.

"But at least this time," I consoled myself, "the remuneration will be fairly distributed and no sisters will end up turned against each other.

Because the relationship between Dessa and Tsara is unflappable and this time I'm in charge of the money." So, everyone was supposed to be getting paid...a goodly amount,

Even Deja, who wasn't scheduled as a guest, because Dana was afraid of her,

Own inability to control my newest child.

Deja it turned out was intimidating enough that Dana eventually promised to have the show pay Deja for babysitting my boys. And thus I was able to do the show.

Deja's check was to be invoiced for and then paid after the fact. No surprise then, that once the job was done and we were no longer needed, the money seemed to have trouble surfing its way through the mail and into Deja's hands. HMMM!

Coincidentally, the family counseling that Carnie Wilson looked good on air promising to set me and my children up with, must have been riding the same never-made-it-to-our-house wave.

And after we did such a good job for them too,

Despite our trepidation:

On the evening before the show was to shoot, I missed the plane and Dana spent the night with Tsara and Brandessa in a hotel room in New York, rehearsing them and re-scripting the next day's events, blasting away at the story line Dana and I had agreed upon. I was still in Houston, miles away from my children when Dessa called to complain about what Dana had been telling her to say.

Deja

Vu.

"Mom it's happening again. I just don't want to be the one the audience hates. I don't want to hear them boo me again. It's awful!" And suddenly my primary concern moved from money, plane tickets and self-exposition to my daughter's fears and concerns.

"Don't go along with it. When you get on stage, say it's not true. Or, actually, just don't do it. You're in New York. We can probably find a way to get you home from there. Anyway even if you refuse, the show still has to send you home, they can't leave you stranded there. That would be way bad for their image."

But Dessa was unable, to cause that kind of last-minute trouble, for anyone, even if they were causing that kind of last-minute trouble for her.

Besides she was already rolling down the hill. And she, like me, followed the path she was on once she was on it. This is not always a good idea and reminded me of the words John Heard's character shouted in the movie "Deceived" when, while attempting to kill his wife, played by Goldie Hawn, he repeated over and over again, "I always do whatever comes next no matter how difficult it may be."

I remembered how much I identified with those words that reminded me of me, and most of my unstoppable children.

Scary, the places we find our likenesses in.

I consoled myself with the realization that a similar theme could also be found,

In Newton's First law of motion, which states that: a body remains at rest or in motion with a constant velocity unless an external force acts on the body.

And since I much prefer to be associated with a scientist than a fictional killer I re-chose to see my likeness there.

But then I guess even Newton's Law could be used as a weapon, against oneself, or someone else. After all, every law is good, except when it isn't. In this case, the belief in needing an external force, was the weapon, Brandessa used, to not be able to stop herself with.

Because the only external force acting on Dessa was not one that was about to change the velocity of her "doing whatever comes next" attitude, since that external force was the one that got her moving down the talk show path in the first place. And though as someone on the outside I could have grabbed her and held her in place, I was too busy dancing to consider breaking the rhythm.

Dessa was probably thinking in Jim Carry screams of, "**SOMEBODY STOP ME!**" but since we couldn't hear her feelings over the sound of our own justifications, none of us did.

So Dessa didn't refuse to do the show. She walked one foot in front of the other down the road that Dana and I had paved for her. And maybe, now that I think about it, it wasn't that Dessa couldn't stop moving, so much as that she couldn't stop, stopping herself from moving, and so allowed herself to be moved, by those who wrote the script within which she played. Or even maybier: maybe it was none, of those things.

Maybe it was not inertia, nor an identifying trait with a murderous cinematic character but fear of being abandoned that set the stage upon which she pranced.

In fact, I suspect that, since Dana adeptly told Brandessa the story of another trouble-some guest who, having broken her contract with the show, was left stranded on the streets of New York, fear, was the true driver of what appeared to be Dessa's compliance.

So, since it seemed we were all going with the flow, I switched to Plan B and told my girls to just appear to be in agreement with Dana while behind the scenes but then, once on camera, to drop the facade as much as possible without blowing the episode and causing a scandal. We could, I explained—thinking I knew what I was talking about—make the situation work to our advantage. They'd keep our footage in, regardless of what we said, as long as we stayed interesting and didn't make the host look inept. "*However,*" I warned, "*if we make Carnie look bad, the same thing will happen this time as last time when you were on the Shirley Show. They'll edit us enough to make themselves look good while we look ridiculous.*" as if we weren't about to look ridiculous any way.

After I hung up, I called Dana and left a phone message telling her that, though I wouldn't contradict my children on air, I was not about to lie. I made that call, without even seeing the glowing green, of the green light I just gave the woman, who felt certain she could make my children do her bidding.

I thought I was being brilliant, though a queasiness in the pit of my stomach, tried to throw up a greater truth as Dana, who must have been thrilled to have such a pliable yet seemingly crusty marshmallow melting in the heat of her hands, prepared for curtain up.

My whole body went numb with don't do it dread as I caught the morning flight, knowing I shouldn't.

And as I headed for New York, it occurred to me that this, my emerging plan, to do as I pleased had, like Dana's, been my intention all along.

I just hadn't known, that I was as calculating as she, though a little less skilled.

I believe now, that I believed then, that making this show about gossip, unexpectedly be about truth instead, was how my family could get the revenge, that only I appeared to want. I thought that if my girls and I were classy enough, and clever enough to make it so that only the people behind the scenes would know that the show was going against their expectations, then when we told the absolutely should be heard story the way it really was, the other producers would serve themselves and their desire for success by wanting to keep us, that wonderful, engaging, family, on the air. I expected them to choose ratings and sacrifice Dana instead of us,

When we told them that she'd lied.

So, Jeff, are you laughing yet?

Do you remember how you used to call me the most jaded naive person you ever met?

I think it fits.

And I guess it's pretty telling that you chose to label me with an oxymoron,

That I enjoyed wearing.

Funny! Don't ya think? I mean, somewhere along the way I actually started thinking I could make a difference and teach people something, by representing my story with honesty the minute the cameras started to roll. I was thinking, as if I'd learned nothing from Deja and Dessa's ordeal, thinking, as the mark, the fish or the fool and thinking I was not. I closed my eyes to the truth because I thought I knew what it looked like already, and because, I thought that what I had to say, was important enough, to risk saying it (especially if I got to hear my own voice put it to words) and wasn't willing to risk finding out that it was not.

Laughing now?

I thought you might be.

I guess I'm still not a very good learner from other people's mistakes,

Or maybe I just like to live life, from every, possible angle,

Like a ball of refracted glass-spraying rainbows, of all the colors that are,

Upon my experience.

Yes that's probably true.

And this time I was experiencing it,

As the stupid one.

After all, Dana was the one who was sequestered in a hotel room, acting like a calculating mistress, planting ideas and manipulating minds: in this case my children's. She, Dana, was obviously, the one in control. She knew what she was up to, and how I would probably react to her plans (protect my children and not make a scene) whereas I only thought I knew, the breadth of the things she had in store for us. And just like a mistress who has the inside track on the cheating husband because he's cheating with her, Dana was the one with the overview who was privy to all the secrets. Whereas I was more like a wife, blinded by assumptions of qualified trust. Dana saw the whole story, in advance, which gave her the tools with which to connect the dots while I, the one with Polly-Anna eyes, was missing the half of it.

So Dana laid the traps and prepared to set me in them.

And it was all arranged, exactly as, she'd originally planned: Again, despite my desire to the contrary, Dana chose Brandessa as the one to draw the audience anger. I've never understood that.

Brandessa was to pretend to have told all those disgusting, gossip-causing-lies, about me and my profession as an escort. According to the story, Tsara and I had apparently disowned her and the two sisters (who just took a plane together and spent the night in the same hotel room) were to act as though they hadn't talked in years. Dessa was supposed to enter the stage after Tsara told her version of the story.

Which, if done properly, should set the audience up to hate Brandessa.

Why? When all Dana had to do to keep my daughter safe, was reverse the order,

And put me or my other daughter in the line of riot.

Tsara would enjoy inciting the crowd, because she never did.

Brandessa though, had a tendency to talk out loud in the faces of her enemies. All that schoolroom and schoolyard opinionating had left her bruised, because she was my child who needed to stamp the world with her positive influence by stamping out the negative influences, that came to hate her, and she was my child who worried and fretted if one person out of a hundred didn't like her, because she was my child who cared the most about popularity.

Looking at it now I wonder if maybe she wasn't drawing this bad girl talk show role to her, like some self-created, universe-requested, skin-thickening exercise gone awry. But then I think, maybe it was all merely low self-esteem made manifest in the actions of others. Maybe.

Maybe not.

It's easy to philosophize now that enough time has elapsed to drop away the daily grind and illuminate the highlights in my memory, but it wasn't easy then.

At that moment, desperation was blind and I had no sight from my hind.

I arrived in New York the next day with little knowledge of the new script. I was whisked directly from airport to green room, where I kept all the other producers from asking me questions by appearing emotionally raw when talking about my situation.

I searched for a few moments alone with Tsara. I needed to know what was going on. Dessa had been shut away from us in, THE SECRET ROOM while Tsara and I were never left unsupervised long enough to converse. So we tried to communicate through code talking, signing and whispers. And that's when I sort of came to understand, what was about to happen, and decided against it. We needed to take control, to find a way, to direct the action.

Somehow between Tsara and I, an idea was born. Tsara would confess on camera to having been responsible for the gossip. She would say that it was her, who had told the lies and then blamed it on her sister. Tsara didn't mind at all the idea of being the bad gal, perhaps, because she never had been. We were excited at the thought that Dessa could be colored clean, and felt as if we were somehow exonerating her for the mass opinions created on the Shirley Show. Brandessa would be the good one after all.

And for some reason we thought that meant we would be one up on Dana.

And there it was; we were so sucked into the story and the situation, that we thought ourselves the winners and the originators of the script, even as we spoke the lines Dana authored us into. We believed ourselves in control even as we marionette danced on the strings in Dana's play. We believed we were in control because that's how we were trying to gain it, by pretending we already had it, kind of like the lover who breaks up with you after you've already broken up with him. He does what you've done, albeit a little louder and with a little more flair: a sort of, "You can't fire me I quit." scenario.

So, we thought we were in charge because we changed the ending having never even noticed that it was the beginning and the middle that set the scene and called the shots. Thus I danced, as Dana's puppet on the invisible strings of Newton's law even as I got on stage and watched the audience boo my adorable daughter with vehemence and lust.

Dessa came out crying.

Her crying to soften the audience's mood, was a smart, defensive maneuver, because as most wives and girlfriends know, crying on purpose makes it not hurt for real. However, she was a convincing crier, which made me most tempted to stop the whole farce just in case her tears were actually genuine. I didn't though. Because, shouting proclamations of truth, would merely have caused a confusing scene that revisited an old hell upon Brandessa and turned her probably pretend tears into a river of reality.

So I held back moment to moment, even though I was worried about the pretense, if that's what it was, because I knew that anything I have ever pretended has in some way become true, implying that faking it might mean her tears were destined to eventually fall in earnest over this in-earnest display. And I worried because she has often told me that for her, and for me I must admit, being embarrassed is one of the hardest things to get over.

But then maybe I was the only one who was being embarrassed.

Which was a brand-new thought,

Freezing me in place.

I took no action and helped no one though I felt on guard, as though I might and in pain as though injured, because seeing my daughter cry hurts me,

When I suspect she's acting to protect herself from crying the tears that my inability to find a better way instilled.

But then I wondered if maybe my pain weren't the only real pain on the stage?

I considered, these, my un-spilt tears of mortification, and wondered if it wasn't maybe my salt-water drops that were destined to fall, crystallize, and become,

Genuine, rock,

Payback,

Valued at nothing.

Maybe it was me, not Dessa,

Who would see the results of this pretense.

In fact it had to be,

Because even if it was she, she,

Was just another part,

Of me, the me, that could already,

Cry.

I continued to play along. I tried to purify myself by not actually telling any lies. Though, allowing the scripted fantasy, I knew, lied all on its own,

With me inside.

And I found myself portraying the pathetic mother that Dana had wanted me to be as I defended my seldom acted on choice of working with men, to the disapproving audience who seemed to hate me because I had used, just enough shame to make them.

Even I didn't believe my justifications.

Dana had managed to manipulate, to use being wrong about the audience reaction as the correct technique for getting us, her guests, to do what she wanted done. It was easy for her. She merely lied about the psychology of the crowd, whenever that worked best, with the psychology of the guest. And just in case more than mind-fucking was required, due to the variable of stage fright or stage zeal,

Because pre-show preparations of the amateur behavioral scientists called producers of the talk show circus, might have missed a beat,

And because at no time was any guest left to fly solo, without instruction,

They used signs, professionally known as really big poster board cue cards.

I lifted my head to look out at the studio audience and saw, Dana holding up one of those poster board size, quickly made signs. "TSARA! CALL DESSA A BITCH!" I almost laughed, as Tsara, pointing to me, shouted the words, "This woman is a saint!" Dana began jumping up and down and waving her sign trying to get Tsara's attention. Dessa cried, "It wasn't me! I never said anything!" and my eyes were drawn to yet another producer holding up a sign, this time for the audience. They were being instructed to boo and yell insults, at my darling actress child. And, the audience members, hoping to attract the camera, play a part, be discovered, acted their role with enthusiastic hatred. As the show progressed and the audience asked questions other producers held up other signs to other scripted guests. It was like the battle of the bands, with a multitude of conductors, directing the symphony of sin, until the whole show reached a crescendo over Tsara's confession of being the source of all the evil that had befallen our home.

She apologized profusely to her sister for the deflected blame and our little group made up, in the warm embrace of each other's arms, while Carnie, taking the focus shouted, "We Care!" and promised to arrange for a year's worth of family counseling. I looked about me as the credits rolled (or rather would role when the editing was done) and wondered how many of the guests had been paid and who had been hurt, if anybody wasn't.

The show, of full circle story telling under Dana's finally finished direction, was over,

But the farce had just begun.

We were a hit.

If there is such a thing in the world of talk show trash.

It was hard though, to be proud of "being a hit" in such an arena.

After all Talk Shows are like the layman's A.W.A.

"WHERE FAMILIES AND FRIENDS FIGHT TO THE END"

Possibly of there lives.

Because, when a person is rattled and confused into showing himself as himself, in a most vulnerable yet misrepresented fashion, expecting to gather supporters and gathering enemies instead, the lack of popularity and ensuing ridicule, of national proportions, just might be the external force he acts upon to move himself to suicide.

Especially, after being on the Jenny Jones, Carnie Wilson or anybody's show.

Yes, it was hard to be proud of such an accomplishment, at least, not without feeling like the talk show version of an Amazonian bleached blond, muscle-flexing, G-string wearing, mentally challenged, gruff-voiced, face-sneering, steroid-using, wrestling woe-man; a role I'd only had once before.

Well not really. I mean I didn't bleach my hair blond.

I just wore it long straight and dark, like always. I looked like me, without a disguise and wearing a two-piece bathing suit rather than a crusty old, up-the-bum G-string panty. But even so, it was still, extremely tacky, to perform on a wrestling video. However, it was a step above the Carnie experience because at least it was an obvious piece of fictional entertainment that only, people who knew what they were buying, watched.

Did I ever show it to you Jeff?

I can't remember. I hope so. It was really quite a hoot. Though not as prestigious as the film on manners you dropped in to see me shoot, or rather, host.

In the wrestling video I used a lot of bad acting and four letter words while twirling my overage, mask wearing male student, above my head. I beat him into submission, till the tape ran out, which seemed to take forever. It was a two hundred dollar gig, shot with a camcorder quality camera. It looked grainy and ridiculous and was the most hilarious acting job I'd ever had, though nothing at all to be proud of.

Still, I did think of it as, something to laugh at, and tried to use that attitude as inspiration for how I could handle my humiliating memory of being a guest performer on the Carnie Wilson show because suicide was probably not a good idea, in light of the children.

Except, I couldn't, just laugh off the Carnie Show experience as a badly scripted piece of crap, because, they had a national audience of viewers that never even knew there was a script.

And that's what made it worse than tacky.

And so, for me, the wrestling tape was better.

Because, though some people suffer from the same confused lack of performance awareness in regards to the A.W.A., proved out by the fact that they break into brawls and/or tears while defending the authenticity of their favorite sport(?) filled with stars made out of stunt men,

In my can't-even-see-the-viewer-appeal wrestling tape, I doubted if any of the seventy-five dollar per video buyers, would find my acting so convincing that they would be afflicted by that same particular delusional state and think me really, "The Terrifying Tutor."

Though, as far as the talk show goes, I guess we were pretty convincing.

After all our little part-to-play made it onto Talk Soup to be laughed at. And then, proving that we couldn't erase the evidence and act like it never happened, the network used an excerpt of Tsara as the show's commercial.

So like I said, we were a hit,

Because, my children and maybe even I, had let our actor's ego drag us into attempting to be convincing, even though we would have preferred not to have convinced.

It was a horrible mess. That of course everyone in Canada, especially my agent who stopped representing me, saw.

I have to admit though, my daughters were marvelous actors and convoluted as it was, I was proud of their talent, even as I watched what was left of my career get caught in the P-trap as it flushed down the toilet.

And of course the minute the show was over the Carnie producers, who were concentrating on the next episode, washed their hands of us. Though Dana would have had us believe otherwise.

As she hustled us into a private behind the scenes room she, in spy like whispers explained, "First of all, you guys were great and Lynette, thumbs up, that was probably the best acting you've ever done." I guessed that meant she'd thought "pitiful" was beyond my range. I found it hard to feel complimented.

Dana turned her attention to my girls, "Now, the other producers are a little worried. They think the confession Tsara did was too pat and that you guys might be running a sting to catch us doing something wrong. See, this whole hiring people thing is kind of a game we play while pretending we don't."

"That's why I had to put most of the money in your mom's name and then label it replacement income for lost time at work. That's so nobody can ever prove it was a paycheck. It's up to your mom to spread it out evenly between you. Of course Deja's different, we can mark her down as a babysitter. Anyway, I told them that I would check to make sure you were the real thing. Which is no problem but, Tsara you really did get them worried, so they said they won't give me the check or plane tickets for you guys, unless you sign these papers." She slid them forward.

And the papers that Dana cornered us into signing were declarations of no fraud or fakery. "Good! Now you will never be able to admit that this was a set up unless you are willing to go to jail." Dana patted the papers into a pile and stood up to leave. I suggested she sign some as well. She laughed and left the room, finished.

We vacated the building listening to the murmurs of other guests discussing the money they'd made and competing over the amounts,

We squirmed in discomfort,

As a woman cried over the sadness she felt,

About the treatment she and her children had received,

At the hands of who, we could not hear.

I spent the following week at Dana's apartment as a visitor (A week in New York had been one of the perks Dana bribed me with). The majority of our time was taken up by Dana, who regaled me for hours, telling horror stories of all the coercion and cruelty that she and Shirley had committed, in the name of getting it to air. Dana said that she was much happier to be working for someone as nice as Carnie and that she thought Carnie would be a good host since she seemed to believe the scenarios were real. Dana wasn't sure but she said she doubted Carnie had any idea of the ruthlessness of her people. It was all one great big sneaky secret she laughed, as she bragged, about how she'd manipulated me and mine, and laughed, at how she got us to sign the fraud papers, as if that were unusual, cause every talk show makes everybody sign them, one way or another.

"So if you go on any other shows watch out for that or they'll sue you." She said.

A little idea glimmered and called me to attend,

As the stories she told, combined with the behind the scenes insights she gave and gave me the notion that, using this experience to make "Something good out of something bad" by writing a book designed to expose the trashy truth about Talk Show Trash, if indeed the truth turned out to be trashy, might be where my future lay. The point of the book would be to find out,

Whether or not,

Our experiences thus far had simply been because of Dana. And if so was Dana the way she was, as a result of her experiences, in her chosen vocation inside the talk industry, or (as was more my suspicion) was Dana hired and therefore able to cause our experiences, because she was already the kind of person that the talk shows needed her to be? Had she done the work all on her own and therefore created herself to be the perfect producer with no moral dilemma over behaving so insensitively?

And if so was there a whole nest of other producers just like her?

Actually there was another possibility. Maybe she was just a renegade making up the rules as she went along and putting the show at risk, unacceptable even to them.

So the question that I thought would be interesting to the public at large was: Did all the producers in all the talk shows treat their guests this way?

I realized if I wanted to write a book that would expose the industry for what it was, I would need to go on some more shows, undetected. So I decided to create a variety of different characters living a variety of different scenarios, custom-fit for talk show topics. I would need some good disguises and a group of people to help me, finally, a tangible something to ask my friends and family for. I was even considering asking for your help, until you called with your wife in the background.

Suddenly, you,

Weren't my friend!

And,

I dropped,

The project,

Everything,

For awhile,

Until,

Glenn, my "fetishy friend," called me from Toronto, where everyone loved the idea of the book and was proud to be part of the process. Glenn's aliveness contrasted my deadness and reminded me to live, without you.

I hoped to get the scoop on all the Shirleys and Danas of the world, partly because I hoped that that, would make the scoop on me, the Dana done it stupie dupe, look more like part of the expose plan and a little less like a stoop and scoop, scoop, full of made up poop: called Lynette's behavior circles like a loop oop de loop. Which is more honestly what it was since I really had been Dana's stupie dupe dupe.

The first thing I did was to sign up for the Talk Show registry that Dana had given me the number to. Our first call came from Oprah's producer, who quickly changed her mind about booking us when she learned that we'd already been on The Carnie Wilson Show. In fact any Talk Show that found us through the Talk Show Registry refused to book us for the very same reason. (As you may recall, Jeff, this is exactly opposite to what Dana had told me would happen.)

So, there it was, no Talk Shows wanted non-talk-show-virgins. However, Mark Schone, a reporter for "Spin" magazine, thought we were just right for him and his Talk Show exposing articles. It seemed that he too, was looking for the scoop oop idoop, which he found, when he found me screeching Dana songs out of key. Mark, the reporter, for whom I trilled like a Dana exposing bird, had located me, ironically enough, through the talk show registry that Dana had lined me up with,

Making it so that she,

Helped me,

Get even,

After all.

Because even,

It turns out,

Can be got,

If you call it closure.

And, though the rest of my plan didn't go so well, the exposing Dana through the press part, worked out beautifully.

In spite of the fact that I had no idea what affect, if any, the article had on her,

I knew what it did for me. It created an end point. Which reminded me of the last and only other time, I remembered, ever needing closure, on anything:

When my twenty-two year old brother was beaten to death and thrown off a balcony.

I remember being in a fog that never lifted until the murderer died, by his own hand, a year and a half after taking my brother's life. I remember being angry, so angry,

There was, is, no word.

His killer got a sentence of one year due to plea bargaining and ineptitude. And though I wrote letters, talked on the radio and made phone calls in an effort to fight for his memory, making a difference mattered too much. I blubbered and rambled and spoke in a hard to understand moaning croak because, I made little sense with raging sobs in my throat. So I moved no mountains and made no difference to the crime of getting away with the crime, of erasing my brother, my sibling, my friend.

I was relieved when his killer died.

Because it released me from the fantasies of vengeful murder that consumed me every time my lungs pulled air and reminded me that Henry's didn't, which reminded me that Floyd's did. And I hated that, that Floyd, who had punched and punched and punched my brother, could breathe.

Hated that.

Hated my mother for being gracious and hoping that the law would go easy on Floyd, "It could have gone either way." She said. And I hated her for not knowing my brother better than that.

Hated officer Bell for sitting with an open file and pictures of my beautiful beaten brothers face, face up in my peripheries. I could just barely see the last ever image of Henry's unrecognizable features on the edges of things, where my pupils refused to focus. So I looked directly into the officer's eyes and, pouring through the iris, tried to grab a hold of his soul. I needed answers. He spoke, "We have an eyewitness that says your brother begged for his life before Floyd threw him off the balcony. She says his words were, "Floyd, please! Why are you doing this to me? I am your friend." But I don't think we'll get her to testify. She's too afraid!"

Which brought the fog.

I couldn't see or think or be, anything more than a disassociated robot, though I lived my life from day to day, cared for my children and renovated my house. I was numb.

Except when in the company of strangers.

Then I would burst into tears and tell my story of loss to anyone: ticket agents, parking attendants, crossing guards, passersby. I would blurt and blubber my un-requested tale in a momentary thunderstorm of flurry until the quiet of the fog returned and I went on my way, to the next moment when, a bus would pass or a door would shut and I would have a second or two of soothing comfort imagining it to be my brother, heading somewhere, missing, seeing me; imagining it well enough to loose sight of the truth and believe, for just one blessed fraction of time, that he was alive.

Till the day I got the news that his killer was dead.

And breathed, looking into the future, as I buried my brother, from the nightmares of my mind.

Closure is different for everyone, for me it just means there's nothing left to wish you could do.

With my brother that moment was easy to recognize, with my children and Dana it was not.

In both cases when I tried to make a difference I made a mess, because my emotions were in the way, unlike the people I had to deal with who felt nothing. I needed to think more clearly than them in order to affect a result. Impossible then, for me to work with they, who were cool about the task at hand because,

They were only doing their job, while I was imprinting on my life.

And because the theys, like Dana, were only doing their jobs, their cognitive abilities were kept clear of pain and desperation and made available for calculating and collusion.

So, yes, the moment when the job was done was hard to recognize,

Until it came.

In the form of an eye for an eye,

The "Spin" article about Dana's antics brought me,

Public exposure for public exposure,

Like a life for a life.

But unlike the ending of Floyd Houle's life, in regards to the talk shows: until that article came out I had no idea what it was, that would gift me with the moment when I would be able to exhale, and breath, into the future as I buried the axe.

So, I just kept flailing about looking for the end point. While I walked the path, of thinking I was creating a career by writing an autobiographical look at daytime talk, and snuck onto a few more shows.

Two months after the Carnie experience we'd managed to book ourselves onto every national talk show, other than Oprah, that was being aired in the fall of 1995.

In each case, bar none, I found myself on the phone with a producer who was digging for the dirt on me, and everyone I knew. She (because, according to my experience, most talk show producers were women. I don't even want to think about what kind of statement a statistic like that makes.) would pump me for stories and push my emotions in whatever direction drastically contrasted with the other member of my team's attitude and personality. In other words, all the producers did their best to whip tender trusts and fragile friendships into a froth of frenzied competition, effectively creating corrosive combatants out of uncomfortable comrades. (I just love that sentence.)

I must admit however that, though always in evidence, the degree of this emotional smacking about, fluctuated from show to show. And regardless of the fact that, the reason for this variance is something I cannot provably pin point, I do have some suppositions, like:

That on occasion the producer herself was into S&M and enjoyed whipping.

That some hosts were demanding bosses who forced whipping.

That Jerry Springer style shows attracted the M part of S&M and were tacky enough to attract those who just love to be the object of on-air whipping.

That it depended on the kind of character I was pretending to be i.e.: A shy person requires more whipping than an obnoxious one does.

That it depended on whether or not the producer was trying to set me up to be the one they dumped on: *[I think this because it seemed that whenever I was not the one who originally phoned in and displayed an interest in being on their show (making my willingness to perform the unknown element) if the producer wanted to set me up as the bad guy, she would gently stroke my ego and soothingly convince me that I was the innocent party in her eyes and that she was certain the studio audience would feel the same way, and besides, "Don't you want to stop those awful people from saying those terrible things about you?" Stroking, stroking, forever stroking, to get me to declare war.]*

Probably though, that variance I originally referred to, was due to a mixture of all of the above.

The good news was that since our stories were total fabrication, nothing any producer said to us—about us—hurt. In fact, it was fun. It was also easy to notice the manipulating this time because we were void of concern over the outcome. So much so that I found myself almost constantly aware of the level of expertise these producers, as a whole, seemed to possess. And quite frankly I was impressed. You know Jeff I just kept wishing that my sons' schools would have hired from the producer pool. I mean, what if my boys' teachers were half as good at behavior modification as these, mostly young women were?

I suspected that if the Dana's of the world taught Dar he wouldn't even need Secretin.

He'd be talking, clearly, already. At least that's what I believed at the time since, I believed that, it was only because Dar's teachers couldn't understand what needed to be done that he was constantly halting his progress. If I wanted him to talk to someone other than me, then someone other than me, had to be as good at teaching him, to want what I wanted him to want—namely talk—as I was. And so far nobody was. I considered the possibility that maybe I'd been looking for help in all the wrong places. And then I scratch-that-realized that maybe the problem wasn't that the teachers didn't know how to manipulate Dar, just that they didn't know where to manipulate him to. They wanted compliant, I wanted bursting with language, and Dar, just wanted to be left alone. So, because no one but me believed in normal, for him, even he, Dar, receded a little farther into crazy, the longer he stayed in school.

Regardless of what might've worked none of it did, and these producers peopling the talk shows weren't applying for jobs to help my son, they were working the job of manipulating his mom, because I'd asked them to,

However indirectly.

So, we manipulated them into manipulating us, because I wanted to write a book exposing them for being so manipulative,

Without even noticing,

That I was wearing their clothes.

I guess that's what happens when you're in disguise, undercover, playing games.

And, because my identities were fake, I was insulated, from the pain I was about to inflict,

And not at all worried about being recognized because, even if my disguise wasn't good enough to prevent discovery, the discovery of the disguise was good enough to create an awareness of the fiction, which should prevent anyone from confusing me with the farce being presented as fact. I find it funny to note that it was only when there was nothing to fear in being recognized by the audience, that I found myself hiding in camouflage,

From the enemy I was fighting,

To turn myself into,

In order to be able to destroy.

But I was negatively affected, by becoming the same, confused, and uncertain of who to kill if not me.

So, for these reasons and as a result of some of the things that happened during the process I began to wonder if now that I had turned the whole thing into a harmless feel-good lark it wasn't even more dangerous to me,

Than when I had chosen to hold an opinion about it as a bevy of buzzards dining on the dreams of their dead.

Because now that nothing mattered and I didn't care about how they hurt me I also didn't care about how I hurt them, or even realize I would.

Which is why I say I became the same as they were. Because that seemed to be the state of their minds when they looked at me, as unaware souls who knew not the reason, they had to be so crafty, while being crafty still. We were the same, forgetting the truth while playing the game, even to the similar point of all of us thinking we cared about how we were treating the genuine guests and what we were teaching the naïve ones at home.

So what was I teaching? I suppose, in my case, the lesson would be: It's ok to become one of them, if that's what it takes, to teach them to not.

But I'm not sure it is OK, to forget, that there is no they, and we are all one.

Though I do it all the time.

Rather like the way that, from the moment I wake up I begin to head towards sleep until the moment I sleep and begin to head towards awakening, filling me always, always, with somewhere to go, in a world without end, forever, amen.

And so, when I am inside the game it is as though I am asleep, separated from all that I know to be true, letting this, new set of rules, become my reality, just as it should, in order to get a restful, new perspective, breath of change.

Before my remembering though, came my Technicolor feelings, as the pain of others convinced me that this made-up job of mine was worth doing. Pain that moved me into making it my mission to eradicate, the ache, of being publicly attacked, pain, like what I saw on the face of the hysterical crying woman backstage at the Carnie Show. She was the first one, the one that seeing, her, tripped my heart, into turning my vision outward and becoming more global. Because what I overheard broke my empathy bone and inflicted her pain upon me, without my even noticing, that I'd chosen for it to: She was screaming and ranting and cursing at the producers for treating her two daughters with such insensitivity, for humiliating them.

I fell into my own, memory gone sour, and: believing that because of it I had learned to traverse the waters, I began to seek to save, to build a bridge, for others to hold on to, in order to earn, the license for; lifeguard of life.

And I asked questions, of everyone, in search of the overwhelmed. And I got answers, from everyone, on the sidelines of the shows, like the talk show drivers that carried the guests to and from each episode, who heard all the dirt and just loved to spread it around. I heard stories like the one about two drag queens that tried to go on as sisters and who were, figuratively and literally exposed according to what the chauffeur supposed, because though he wasn't sure just how the gender was invalidated he did say that he heard a rumor about the fellow (?) being caught taking a leak standing up. And the thing that really struck me as commonplace strange was how completely in love men must be with the very idea that they can pee from the vertical, since that's how every man in drag you ever hear of getting caught, gets caught, especially in the movies.

Of course that's not true in every movie, in the more creative ones like "To Wong Foo, Thanks for everything, Julie Newmar" it's the Adam's apple that gives it away. Still, I guess, whether on the throat or the groin, it's the same thing when you think about it. Since in both cases it's a gender-identifying sticky outy body part that exposes them, by becoming exposed. So, for you guys wanting very badly to get on the talk show circuit in disguise, as your mother, I suggest gaining enough weight to hide the Adam's apple, and though that won't completely hide your penis since nobody's supposed to be looking there anyway if you just relent and crouch to release everything should go smoothly, as long as the makeup lady doesn't get too close to your beard.

"Though that seems like a really long way to go just to get on a talk show," I remember thinking, as I shaved a widow's peak into my hair while creating the character I called Lenny Cyr, who, try as he might, never quite made it onto the talk shows but did a great job performing his way out of getting into trouble when he was caught trying to get a state ID at the Drivers Licensing bureau. (So I guess, when I'm Lenny I call myself "he" rather than "it," interesting to note.) I also do an awesome in-drag comedy routine, whenever there's enough time between dates, to re-grow my hair.

And the memory of being in drag reminds me of another story about being in drag: She was a different drag queen than either of the sisters. She didn't get caught. And though the driver did tell me why she was on the show and what the subject of that day was—I can't remember the details and didn't write them down—because, the rest of his story was too funny to not obliterate my focus on anything else. The chauffeur swore that "it" swore him to secrecy while showing off "it's" dingle in the car on the way to the airport. It occurred to me that, unless that drag queen who—like me, may not refer to herself as an it—told the driver not to trust anyone but Lynette Louise then the driver was not a very good secret keeper.

Which implied that he couldn't be trusted, to not tell, or maybe even, to tell...truth? So I didn't. Trust him. Though, true or not, I remember the story,

And have told it you.

And there in lies the danger of every lie ever told.

Because once a thing that you find interesting enough to attend to, is said, if it caused you to react at all, in all likelihood, it has just been given life, inside yourself, where it shall take root and grow, to be eaten by another.

And then I remember the head shaking apparent sincerity of the driver from the Gordon Elliot Show "They's lots a folks cheatin and pretendin on this here show. But the sad ones is the ones who think theys gonna be hepped."

And I thought of the lady we had seen as we left the Richard Bey show.

She was crying, though her sobs were contained, which gave them to me, because I always ached intensely for the people who couldn't ache for themselves. So she contained herself. And everyone around her, who chose to feel, hurt, hurt, more than if she'd been throwing her pain about in an effort to release her frustration. She breathed, ragged, overlarge breaths emoting, deeply bruised dignity and refused to ride in the car they had sent to take her home. She said she was done trusting them. We watched her walk, I don't know where, in inappropriate walking shoes, with head down and no winter coat. She looked heavier than her oversized body could be.

But I'm getting ahead of myself,

As I often do.

Sorry, Jeff, I'll try and tell the story with some semblance of linear thought.

When it eventually came time to actually do the shows I realized I had a problem. I needed some first-rate disguises. I may not have been a star but I was enough of a television personality to be at risk of being recognized, especially in New York where many of the Canadian channels where able to be seen. And even if that were not true the Man Alive documentary episode on the kids and I had aired nationally in the states on the Christian Channel, several times over the past few months. Which is really kind of funny when you think about my anti-Bible and organized religion views. Any way I needed a makeup artist, which I didn't have. I would have to do it myself. I looked at my stick of mascara, vial of lipstick and handful of felt pens and realized that my odds of success were being seriously compromised. I didn't even own the normal woman's full complement of makeup.

So I made tattoos out of ink, borrowed makeup from my friends and placed my jaw in a bottom over top teeth position. I looked like me, only dumber.

Perfect.

Because,

First up was Richard Bey, on which I was intending to play, a very dumb bully.

The Richard Bey Show had advertised that they were looking for childhood horror stories of being bullied. The concept was to corner the bully, have everyone dump on him/her in the hopes of inciting absolute chaos and out-of-control fist throwing. Once that was contained, the victims were to lord it over the bullies by bragging about the various positions that each of them had achieved in society. Needless to say only failure ex-bullies were welcome to attend. The concept was a valuable one, for a movie, where the point of "good will win out" is made, without any crimes of humiliation or abuse being committed against the performers. However, Talk Shows, though scripted and performed like sketch comedy masquerading as improvisational theater, aren't movies, where everyone's in on the pretense.

I suppose everyone's life has some bullies in it somewhere. I know Dessa could have brought in grade school archenemies Todd and Marnie while I could have pulled from my past and come up with Marilyn Hunt, who loved to spit on me every time I walked past the special ed class. But we didn't. We invented from among us in order to not be hurt, and to not hurt, others. And that's how we ended up needing a high school bully the same age as my, twenty years younger than me, daughters. A role I thought I could fill. Because, I tend to look young, and besides, I figured, who knows, maybe I had a hard life. So I pushed it, or rather, I guess I pulled it back, by subtracting ten from the truth. Brandessa and Deja adjusted their ages upward by three while I told stories alluding to my having been a several times flunked out special-ed senior during their junior years. We put it all together and came up with a match.

Thus, since I was now the age-inappropriate bully and Deja and Dessa were my victims, we had a show.

Deja called into the Richard Bey talk line, and talked. Two days later the producer called the bully, me. She introduced herself, explained her purpose and then tried, very carefully, to reel me onto the show. I made it only slightly difficult. Once she thought she had me convinced by swaying me with her suggestion that I should set the record straight and tell my side of the story she informed me, the girls would be on air talking to millions about me whether or not I was there. (A statement I took to have no relationship with the truth.) She stirred me up, whipped me into that froth of frenzied competition, effectively creating corrosive combatants out of uncomfortable comrades. (That's not nearly as cool a sentence when I put it in this paragraph.)

She stirred me up by saying things, intended to stir. Things like "But she deserved it right? I talked to them. I could tell they were just a couple of uppity little bitches! Don't let them get away with all the lies they're telling about you. You come on the show and let them have it."

And I, the bully, acted "*Ya That's right Ya*" nervous and unsure of the show. "Are you a dyke?" she stirred. "*Hell NO!*" I frothed. "Cause one of the girls called you that." She whipped. "*They're the dykes.*" I sneered "*couple o dirty little cunnilingus queens*" I fumed, turning a pleasant activity into a lifestyle of unclean throne-sitters licking. "No kidding! Really! You'll have to tell us that on the show." She tried to make solid this beat-up mess of emotional whipped cream. "*Well, no, I don't wanna get in any trouble. I got a good job now. Well...I failed a couple o times. Yeah, well...I can't read. You're not just calling me on there to laugh at me are ya. Cause ya know that wouldn't be safe. I just don't want nobody sayin nuttin about me being dumb.*" I backed off. "Oh of course not. Nobody wants to embarrass you."

She lied?

When I arrived at the show it was in too much makeup bad clothes and no stockings.

The producers offered me pantyhose. I acted offended. I emoted; smoldering keg, of suspicious, slow learner, who knows what kind of behavior. I think if I would have been loud or obnoxious, which is more show-worthy than quiet, the outcome would have been different. But I wasn't. I was a very densely contained pressurized person full of stupid and scary.

My daughters were good to go, acting snippy and excited, blabbing, blabbing, blabbing, in another room, their inconsistent stories of Ms. Intimidating, me. "You have no idea what this chick is like....almost broke my arm...special ed flunky....soooooo stupid...not special ed, just a failed idiot. started on freshie day....middle of junior year...she was such a creep."

Meanwhile I overheard the producers say that David Letterman's people were stalking the halls, setting up their cameras and preparing to get footage for Letterman's Top Ten. My stomach flipped over. And the minute I emotionally balked at the idea of being caught on Letterman at the beginning of this project the producers began worrying about having me on the show. Suddenly, it appeared that I was a threat. And since coincidences always pique my interest, I thought about it. "Perhaps this Richard Bey, who just gave me the cold shoulder the minute he was introduced to me, doesn't want to look like a retard reactionary, by abusing a dummy on his first and probably only Letterman debut." And it occurred to me that for Richard Bey, this day could be a very important day.

After all people watch Letterman. I mean, Jeff, have you ever heard of Richard Bey? Imagine what that kind of exposure could do for,

Or against,

Him ...or me.

And the anxiety the two of us were probably sharing over the idea of being recognized for what we truly were, right there, on The Late Show with David Letterman reminded me of the first time I was ever on the Letterman Show. Did you see me on it, Jeff? It was two years before I lost you, two years before I found myself on the Richard Bey casting list, when The Late Show cameras first found me,

As an audience member in extreme close-up, that Glen Ottaway, one of my extremely well-endowed (He begged me to say that.) comedian friends just happened to catch on tape.

It was two years before, the Richard Bey/Letterman opportunity, when I found myself wondering if being in the audience was as close as I'd ever get.

The entire event miracled in one of those weird moments of manifested making: Deja had won a local beauty pageant and one of the prizes was a trip to New York. She took me and we went to see David Letterman.

The studio was EXTREMELY COLD!! Keeping the audience cold is a technique that many comedy clubs use (though David really takes it to the freezer level) which encourages people to laugh if for no other reason than to warm up. So I sent energy zipping through my veins, in an attempt to thaw my Renaud's disease-affected extremities, by playing a little game with the camera. I called it to me. And as I did that I was aware of the knowledge that someone at home was watching the camera come, find me, upon command. I love those moments of clarity, of knowing everything, while at the same time having words, for none of what I know.

I warmed up, basking in the feel of the camera's attention. And even though, I know that, that sounds self-absorbed I also know it isn't, about recognition. Letting the weather conditions fall away and be re-decided by the scene I am playing and then experiencing that belief as my new reality the minute the camera starts to roll, is just an actor's trick, that I used, to increase the temperature by telling myself I had been cast as the "audience member laughing with zeal," which worked beautifully because if you think about it, laughing, has a very warm feel. And calling the camera to me was just something I had to do to make the scene feel real. AHHH sweet poetry: the music of making the story surreal.

And I suppose the reason I manifested having Glenn catch it on tape is because it was the only way to know that my manifesting had really worked, and I hadn't just been deluding myself and merely assuming that I felt the camera's ability to heal.

It occurred to me that I should use a similar kind of energy in reverse, like a push instead of pull, repel instead of attract, send the partner fleeing, zip iddy do da dance, in order to get out of this show, that was beginning to feel very uncomfortable, especially if I ended up on David Letterman, where my amateurish disguise was sure to get me recognized, sooner than I wanted to be, and way before I'd gathered enough research for the book. Within minutes of that decision the producer came to me and said she was afraid the show would make me look bad so they weren't going to use me. She tremble-seemed very afraid of my reaction. *"Oh, OK"* was all she got.

The story she gave my daughters was entirely different. She told them, that she was afraid of what I might do, to them. So, to protect Deja and Dessa, she was subtracting our role from the show. As a consolation prize she invited them to participate from the studio audience where they saw audience members being passed notes with scripted questions to ask. Questions, that these plants asked, with apparent spontaneity.

I tried to believe that the producer's worry for my girls had been honestly motivated. It made me happy, pleased, to think of them as concerned, at least a little, for their guests well being because, I like to watch people care. Besides, this niceness would give the story some dimension. My book was meant to be an investigation, not necessarily a lot of tongue clucking about bad people talking.

However, when Deja and I ended up in the same airport at the same time taking the same plane back to Houston, I must admit, my tongue began to cluck. Where had all the sincerity, for what I might do to this poor snippity little girl gone snotty, gone? Had it indeed, ever even been sincere? Perhaps the show staff only minded my killing Deja, if there were national witnesses linking them to the crime or worse if we bloodied up the station property. Maybe that's why they had whisked me so quickly away, in the Bey Show car that drove me to the airport. I traveled separate from Deja, only while traveling in anything belonging to them.

"PHEW!" I suppose they thought, "Out of property, out of mind."

In light of Deja and her bully sharing a plane,

I suspect they didn't care too much, for our little lives once, we were a long arm away.

I suspect they just didn't want to look so bad on David Letterman day.

I understood. I didn't want to look so bad either.

When I arrived home there were five messages waiting for me from various talk shows. It was dizzying trying to remember who I was and what type of voice to use in each of the various cases. I wanted to be slow and methodical in my approach to this alias driven undercover work but my daughter, whose job it was to make most of the initial phone calls, wanted to go-go-go, driven by the hormonal rush of an impatient teenager. So we went, went, went while I stayed dizzily balancing, on the catalogue of character breakdowns beside the phone.

And told myself we were doing it to expose the truth and rescue the, would-be victims, though I sure didn't mind the prospect of gaining riches and notoriety in the process. Still the fact that I was aware of just such a possibility and thought it delightful did not deter me from sincerely believing in my cause. The way I saw it, nobody does anything for no reason, we just happened to have more reasons than one: some of them selfish and some of them not. So we felt good about tricking and bamboozling the people who were tricking and bamboozling us because we felt justified by these monsters of media mayhem's original provocation in warring against my children and in knowing that their casualties were not limited to me and mine.

And that's the way I was beginning to talk and think and feel, with passion bordering on fanaticism. And just as all the fanatics who have historically killed, maimed and tortured in the name of the rules of God, Allah, Jesus or a good spot in heaven, we felt righteously on the side of eradicating evil.

Until, while on the Gordon Elliot show,

Someone recognized me, from the Carnie Wilson Show,

And someone else, from my cooking show,

And someone else, from Man Alive,

And someone else, thought I was a B-movie actress, which of course I was.

And the first thing I thought when all this recognizing came to light was "WOW"

"If my face is so familiar, why doesn't anybody ever ask me for my autograph?"

I wondered, mildly complimented. "At least it's over." I thought, thinking of all the problems I'd had with makeup, fake ID and the invention of verifiable bogus jobs that the producers could check up on.

I was relieved, to be me, again because it finally felt, like the dizzying worry had stopped rearing up and threatening to trample us.

It was over,

We were caught,

During commercial break.

The show staff stood in a circle around us searching for truth. I admitted the deception, in the same sentence that I instinctively threw the words "Spin Magazine" around as a subterfuge to gain undercover credibility and prevent fraud charges. Gordon—quick to respond to the news of being duped—took the hands of Deja and I, and pranced us onto the stage to confess. While Glenn—who was invisible because he'd only been a phone in guest—hung up and ran away. I found myself claiming to the studio audience that this show, The Gordon Elliot Show, had treated us with kindness and consideration, and had been blameless in comparison to the others, at least in respect to the cruelties perpetrated by talk shows of that nature.

I swore it to be true,

And meant it,

Though it wasn't.

Because by the time we got to Gordon Elliot,

I'd been blinded by the game,

And by the, I'm your best friend, loving co-operative-ness that Gordon mingled into his hypnotic technique of gentle smiles mouthing words in tones of lyrical softness my mental acuity had been lulled, by him, them, the game, and by the character created freedom from fear of being hurt, lulled, into not thinking, thinking, there was no pain.

When all the finger-pointing and worry over being charged with fraud stopped, and since I accepted that the Gordon Elliot portion of the game was over, my nerves relaxed and the clouds dissipated from my vision.

And that's when I recognized the Gordon Elliot cruelty and the producer-director's culpability. And that's when I realized that I had distracted myself and forgotten my purpose, out of nervous guilt, over trying to trap foxes with a net of lies. And thus I had become self-confused and replaced the book focus of investigating truth, with the personal focus of, desiring to get away with the lie.

My vision had blurred and become distorted, by me, becoming them.

And I couldn't see the cruel,

Which of course it was,

Cruel,

To be exposed,

By them,

Or me,

Piggyback-riding into our future on somebody else's back.

Both Gordon and his staff had seemed so nice, so genuine. They had been inquisitive and looking for angles, true. But after all they had a show to do. Sorry there's that rhyming thing again. Anyway, I think they did try to handle us with tact and consideration.

The agreed-upon money they expected to give us was just babysitter reimbursement and since our story was trumped-up and not at all personal, nothing made us sensitive. Thus, everything they did, appeared thoughtful and kind. And that was the illusion I bought into, even as I watched them publicly humiliate my daughter. Forgetting,

That nice people doing mean things are by my definition, not nice.

After being contacted by Deja, the show contacted her mother (played by me) and her very old, apparently-used-to-be-her-mother's lover, lover, (played by the amazing Glenn Ottaway). They talked the two of us into coming on the show, though Glenn appeared to need more convincing than I did. "I can't take that kind of risk," he told them, "I'm married." At which point he pretended to realize that the cat was out of the bag and he should tell Deja, before they did. The producer convinced him to wait for the show date. She had an idea. Glenn could be a phone in guest; that way he would be protected from his wife's catching-him-wrath and the show would benefit because he would be telling Deja the truth on air, which is always good for ratings.

So that's what he did. He told Deja he was married, live on tape, with Gordon Elliot, emoting kindness, right by her side. The, in front of an audience portion of the show, started with me as I was brought on stage and exposed—with a studio full of eyes upon me—to my daughter's recorded pain. Which, if our story were true, would have been my pain as well, since I also, apparently, didn't know Glenn was married, which definitely would have been embarrassing since he was supposed to have been my lover too. Deja stood backstage and watched me watch her quiet humiliation,

Which tore me up, and I cried, without trying to not,

Because I was acting, which is fun, and not at all like real life,

Where you hold back your tears. And besides,

I was too busy being convinced by Deja's talent to add the element of restraint.

And it was thinking things like that, that made me notice that, I was wrong. In fact acting is exactly like real life. There actually is no difference between real and not, in regards to emotions. Because, even when I'm acting, my feelings, feel. I create them from what I choose to believe to be true for the character, and though, emotionally exhausting, like in life, it is often also exhilarating to be miserable, while immersed in a role. Acting, especially on a shallow level, is a lark. Something the talk show guests would discover if only they weren't talking about themselves. It's a lark, because though the character may suffer, I do not. I have fun. I get to feel real feelings without any of the usual repercussions reaching the real me. I get to play. And it occurs to me that my description of the art of acting is a great analogy, for the truth, about choosing to live, outside the spiritual realm, here, in a three dimensional world.

It's a lark,

To be a character on earth.

Except when I'm focused into the art of adding layers and constraints to the feelings of the character, called the real me, in order to more closely reflect the every day life I am choosing to build. So if there is a difference, a way to tell whether art copies life or life copies art, it lies in the number of layers I choose to put on top of things, because as Lynette I have lost count and been buried alive, whereas in the temporary character of a momentary role, I'm aware of most of my choices so newly made. Which means to me that the only difference between acting and living is the part I choose to play.

In life I am the character on the stage lost in the role, whereas on the stage I am the actor, acting as the character on the stage lost in the role. As the actor I get to remember that I'm acting as the character, whether here or on the stage, I seldom do.

I have these awakenings all the time but trying to hold onto them is like trying to hold on to every dream I ever dreamt. Still, this time I wanted a touchstone, a way to remain aware. So I tried turning my thoughts into a simple statement in order to solidify and make graspable these intangible ideas. But the best I could do was to come up with something, obvious and already known. Something that I'm sure, someone else, previously said:

Absolutely nothing really matters, unless I think it does.

Still, original or not, it spoke to me of the concepts that were glittering in my consciousness, concepts, that I knew I should never take too lightly because, if I think it does, it does. And that was the day that I realized, it's the "thinking it does" that makes it feel as though my feelings are forced upon me. Because I can't "think it does" unless I come to a decision about what I believe, and in believing in whatever I came to a decision about, I make another decision about how that should feel, and believe that, and so feel. Then, since my brain never quits, whether I'm paying attention to it or not, and since at that point I have already, thought, believed and felt, and know not where else to go I start the cycle over, finding that it is time to think again.

And so since I had noticed the cycle I began to think how I felt about it. And found that thinking about how I felt verified the validity of my feelings and caused me to believe in them even more. It was as if in this circle of activity, I lost sight of the choice to believe, even when I knew it was there. Thus, I concluded, feelings often feel forced upon me because, though I felt it only because I thought I should, most of the time I thought I should without even knowing that I thought anything at all about it.

So in effect I tricked myself into feeling,

Felt upon.

Then, accepting that as true—if I only felt feelings as a result of the beliefs I held about how I should feel (which I buried in those same feelings and seldom unearthed)—then the immense differences I experienced around me in the laws and traditions of cultures and religions, wherein the cost of questioning the ideologies, for each member of the group that buys into the doctrines, of these or any organized belief system requiring loyalty, and having hellish recriminations of un-understandable proportions for the breaking of that trust, could create such a chasm amongst variant ideologists that it becomes a deadly difference indeed.

And the part in all of this, that has always amused ,except when it frightened—me, is the part where both the fire and brimstone threatened cost of rebellious disbelief and the winged reward of blind allegiance are based solely on the ability of some raconteur and all his minstrels to convince me to have faith in the concept that they know more than I do about what is going to happen to me after I die, even though they too are still alive. And since there was a time in my youth when I believed that if someone says it's so it is, even though I knew I sometimes lied and said it was so when it wasn't and should therefore have known it could be not when others said it was, I didn't. Occasionally, since I had believed it was my destiny to burn in hell, the more I wanted to not believe, the more, in order to justify the life I'd already lived in accordance with the believing, I did. And so, in fact, my behavior and it's pursuant repercussions had nothing to do with God and everything to do with what I believed about him.

Thinking like this while living in the Bible belt of Texas is a savvy sacrilege,

Which I find scrump-dilly-isious,

Scary.

So, occasionally I, like all the people filling congregations, try to gain a comfort level by seeking the company of likeminded others. And that's why, the minute I came across it, I adored The Option Institute, where, they understood, with me, the symbiosis between feelings and beliefs. Oh joyous day! It felt like coming home, to the wisdom of my elders.

Because, though I already knew the truth,

They not only knew it better than I, they also knew what to do with it.

However, my ability to understand these concepts, came, a year before finding out, that there were others like me in the universe.

At that time, my thoughts stood alone, and I knew no one, who could validate my beliefs, by believing them too. And at the time I thought, I needed outside agreement, which left me uncertain, of how to proceed.

So, since a brain never stops working, mine questioned the concept, wondering if it was true. Were my feelings always so completely manufactured by my ideas? Could I act happy and then become it, if I remembered to insert the belief that I was? Like, believing there was nothing wrong with Talk Shows and then suddenly not minding them?

Or was I just performing mental gymnastics in order to justify my vengeful, get even with Dana and hide my own embarrassment path? And,

To keep me from noticing,

How suicide cruel,

This show

And that show,

And I,

Really were.

And that's when I realized that, having my desire for revenge drop me into the middle of the game, had made me the perpetrator of other people's pain.

Done, because I had wanted to see myself as the Talk Show police, person, savior.

And had instead, discovered that; the minute I created police, I created crime.

My crime, of fraud, highlighted the irony, as I realized that I'd become what Shirley had accused my children of being: a girl fibbing to get on TV.

Upon arriving home from the Gordon Elliot Show, unchanged and intact, I pushed play on the answering machine and heard a male producer completely unaware of the day's events and of who we really were—inviting us to be on the Gordon Elliot show. The double-duty distraction to my otherwise difficult life was devilishly tempting.

Especially since, I was to be a man on this one, and being that different from myself always tempts the actress part of who I am, promising to teach me things that I could never have otherwise known.

Besides, Lenny was the only character for whom I had a proper disguise.

And of course there was that other element, the one that coaxed me to consider, continuing on this quest.

The Elliot show staff had sent us home promising to say nothing to the other daytime talk producers. It seemed as if they wanted us to continue our spying, to get away with it and to give all the other show hosts a very bad report so that they could pull out their glowing taped version of what I thought of them, proving that only they were genuinely caring and diligent enough to catch us in the act. I loved the possible irony of catching them instead, or even, of proving them right, since either bit of knowledge would be carried by me, through a story, for my book.

So still, even after the journey, we were the same, people, wanting to use each other to benefit ourselves, while each of us remained emotional burrs, piggyback riding to success on the efforts of the other.

And even though I noticed the process over and over again, it was as if I was, like the guy in the movie "Memento," suffering from short term memory loss: unable to see beyond the brainwashing, only minutes, after seeing beyond it,

As I wove in and out of myself, re-becoming, over and over again, one of them:

The truth-telling liars.

I propped my eyes open to keep them from closing and saw the never-ending circle of revenge. I looked, inside families and neighborhoods, feudal grounds and warring lands, individuals, religions, nations and friends, and saw, the "getting back at" truth of no beginning to the crime.

Because,

The he who starts it,

Is me,

Every time,

I forget to say, "No,"

To having that in my life.

So, that's what I did. I said, "No."

I looked through my memory into the pupils of the producer that had been responsible for our first invitation to the Gordon Elliot show. I saw the fear, pain, and feeling of betrayal in her eyes. I knew that she couldn't see outside her portion of the game, couldn't see any possible justification for what we'd done, couldn't see anything, other than the honest fear of losing her job. It sat in direct contrast with my memory of Dana Danvil's pretended fear over the same issue, fear that she had used to manipulate my children, fear, that I now considered, could have possibly been real, especially, if she believed it, was.

My thoughts turned to her, thinking, of the possible effects of my actions that she was about to suffer. It was too late to back out of exposing her; the "Spin"" article would be in print soon. Besides, in truth, where this journey was concerned, I was taking care of me, not Dana. I needed to call a halt to what she had begun because I wanted to stop swimming, in this milder version of the same momentum driven fixation that had consumed me when my brother was killed.

As it turned out, in both cases, it wasn't a sadistic form of vengeance that I was after: it was air, fresh, clean, unpolluted air.

I hadn't needed to watch his killer die or see him suffer pain on my brother's behalf. I simply needed him to stop, breathing, as my brother had done, so that I could start, to breath in Henry's place. Just as I had needed Dana to stop, having a position from which she could entrap her friends, children.

And since she wasn't being fired I had to do something to nudge it along the way, because I felt I needed to believe her prevented, though I didn't need to see it done.

So I used the press to affect my goal: Funny how willing I am to engage the media to fight my battles while at the same time loathing their manner of war. I don't approve of TV, newspapers and such, so I attack and ban them from my house, often. And yet, like the police, when I need them, I want them there. I'm a hypocrite!

Perhaps that is unavoidable.

I cancelled the other talk shows, and stepped out of the arena. Allowing the fated article to make, or not make, me even, was good enough, for me. Because,

In this righteous process of revenge,

I had merely become a person,

Hurting other persons,

For the right to speak,

Crap,

Out loud.

So once again I stopped writing and walked away from a project that could have made me rich because, I didn't like what the project was turning me into. Despite the fact that I had seen and heard enough for a four hundred-page novel, I closed the book never having written it, both sighing with "Spin" magazine relief for stopping Dana and shaking with "Spin" magazine shame, for doing the same.

I didn't want that to be me, someone cruel, in order to expose cruelties. Even though I was beginning to understand that no one can be perpetrated upon, not even my brother, my children or me. "No one can be perpetrated upon." I pondered the thought. "That would mean that even if I want to perpetrate upon Dana she has to agree." What a paradigm shifting thought that always was, "So I guess that means that I am doing their dance as well when I think I am doing mine, which puts a whole new spin on the concept of punishment, except in the arena of parent wherein I had already always seen the dance as a contact improv jam."

In a different mind, a concept like that could be dangerous,

As long as everyone around him, agrees.

And with all that license to behave in any way I wanted, I found I didn't want, to be the person acting out the role of cruel, that's just not the part I wanted to play. I wanted to be the good guy. But the good guy 'I', I realized, could only be good if there was a definition for bad, which could only be created if some generous soul was willing to play the part opposite me, in order for us both to learn, something we wouldn't have otherwise known.

I began to feel grateful to everyone I didn't want to be.

❖ TWELVE ❖

The more I thought about it, the more it seemed that cruelties, like truth, were only cruel if somebody like my editor, producer, publisher, me or the people involved packaged them that way.

Even global cruelties—like the right or wrong, good or bad, winning or losing of wars and televised tragedies—appeared so related to the perspective that I as a writer presented, a person to have, that,

It occurred to me that, perhaps there is no actual truth or fiction to be derived from the scripts we all write, for ourselves and others, no absolute facts to be gleaned,

Or even distorted. Then I considered the possibility that what is, is simply a decision decided by the focus I give to the characters I portray.

"Probably so," I thought, "if in order to turn cruelties tender we need only wrap them in smiles and gentle tones,

To call them kindness,

Reminiscent of talk show hosts,

For whom,

Manipulating public opinion, is a self-preserving art form,

Called "Spin Doctoring,"

That movie stars and politicians often use."

I watched Monica's persecution as she gave witness to her possibly spin doctored version of the truth and thought of what was being media labeled,

"CLINTON'S LIE,"

And wondered if it was.

A lie.

Perhaps he did actually believe that not inserting his penis into someone's vagina equaled not having sexual relations,

Inappropriate or otherwise.

Perhaps he did.

How many husbands did I know who felt that same way?

Who played and played and played at touching and kissing and the skin food of caressing,

Who paid and paid and paid for hand jobs and mouth jobs and let's do ourselves jobs,

All the while retaining a belief in their own fidelity?

How many spoken for men meant it when they swore adamantly that they had never cheated on their wives,

So long as their penises only entered rectums and hands and the mouths of their friends,

But never, never, never, any non-mate vaginas...of human origins?

Because,

Of course, there is a guilt-free, no-marriage-vows-broken ride, with beasts,

And/ or rodents,

Enjoyed by the masses.

Or toys and apparatuses,

With imitation asses,

Bearing STD-free holes,

For their love lusting splashes, safe,

Because they are inanimate and cannot wave blue flags,

Of D.N.A. smeared on dress patches.

Besides they can be run through the dishwasher and sterilized for future harasses.

How many husbands, other than mine,

Have I known?

A lot? Yes.

Hundreds in fact.

But not only husbands, wives,

Have crossed my personal path,

From as far back,

And into as many lives,

As I can remember.

Husbands and wives confiding in me their,

Monogamous non-cheating,

Sex without their mates,

Beliefs,

That they never seem able,

To confide in their partners,

With quite as much clarity,

As they do with me.

I know. Because I ask,

The Penis-in-Vagina believers,

Who admit that, in truth, they haven't explained these convictions,

As clearly to their mates or social peers,

As they explained them to me:

The, all-accepting, bisexual, hetero-queer.

So, I guess, I know a whole gaggle of men, and a giggle of women,

Who sleep with a clear conscience, undisturbed by the fact that they've been not-sleep-ing,

With non-mate genitalia.

They are undisturbed because,

They've been behaving like those hookers that,

Despite their open legs and undressed labia,

Think they maintain a lack of intimacy,

By refusing to kiss.

Personally, I kiss.

Because I don't want to be one of them: the purposeful hypocrites.

But then, another person's intentional hypocrisy is an assumption on my part.

How do I know if that's what they mean to be? Or are?

Are they hypocrites if they mean what they say?

And if they mean what they say,

Then who am I to call them any kind of "liar?"

Even if their name is Clinton?

I can conjecture but never know,

The complete truth about, even, myself,

Never mind someone else,

Of whom I am a part, though separate by design.

I cannot know and even if I could,

Why would I want to spoil the mystery,

And loose the lesson,

Of "never assume?"

Regardless of what my opinions might be,

About people, like Bill Clinton—America's song and dance President of the 1990s—

They are only my opinions, which, very often, bear no resemblance to the truth.

But it's my letter, my book, I get to say what I want, so I'll share my opinions a.k.a. my truth,

Anyway. My truth, like that I think Clinton should have been named Bob instead of

Bill.

After-all, regardless of the turbulent waters he reigned down upon himself,

Regardless of the swelling flood, the depths, the undertow,

He didn't drown; he Bobbed,

Like an apple,

A rooty tooty piece of fruity,

Rising to the surface, every self-induced scandalous time. What a trick!

He was for Monica.

Still, that didn't really tell us anything about the other aspects of his character: resiliency is not a true indicator for intention.

Resiliency is merely an indicator, for resiliency and Clinton's resiliency, may or may not have been totally his doing. It seemed impossible to know what to give him credit for: how he meant for it to go, what he meant to do, or say, or be, or even what he really was.

It seemed impossible for me to know his level of honesty,

Because I could not know his truth,

Confused as I usually was by his and the media's presentation of it.

And since I could not, know what really happened or how he really felt about anything, having an opinion began to feel somewhat ridiculous. So I tried not to have one.

Jeff, have you ever tried not to have an opinion? About something everyone is talking about? It's a very hard thing to do. At least it was for me, especially since, at the time, I could often hear thoughts feeding me the beliefs from which opinions sprang.

I could hear thoughts, other than my own. The more people I held in my arms the more thoughts I could hear. Until eventually I could hear thoughts, that came from those outside the circle of my long term or hourly affection. I could hear thoughts that came from some, though not from all, the people I passed. I could hear thoughts springing from everywhere and inside the din inside their minds a repeated refrain began to skip and skip and skip and skip. They were consumed with Clinton's affair. I could hear, beliefs, beliefs, beliefs that were never Clinton's because, he was never close enough to me, for me to hear his mind sing out its truth. After all I'm a Canadian. Which apparently meant that our relationship was somewhat thin.

A fact I had just recently become embarrassed to learn.

Because, OH MY GOD, JEFF!! TWO AIRPLANES FLEW INTO THE WORLD TRADE CENTER!! OH MY GOD!!! WHERE WERE YOU WHEN IT HAPPENED? WERE YOU THERE? PLEASE!..NO...Please...no....please...no...please......no.

And with the memory of the towers I found myself whispering in the far reaches of my wishes. "*Do not be a part of history. Do not be a hero. Do not be a ghost beyond the reverie in my mind. Do not be lost "Somewhere In Time;" never to read the words that I hope will bring you back to me. Please, take care of you, who are, my other Canadian/American me.*"

Jeff do you remember that time you and I went to see an Immigration lawyer in the hopes of moving to America? That was back in the days when I believed Canada and the States were symbiotic siblings, brothers, friends. That was before this recently part of my, just recently becoming embarrassed to be a Canadian: an emotion which only happened after the high tower horror changed us into a whole other time.

It was November 2001 when, two years after writing this love-letter book of thoughts, I was taking it through the final edit in preparation for publication and saw something that brought the hue of shame to my cheeks, flicker from the TV screen.

America had engaged in a war against terrorism and a few of my overloud Canadian countrymen were gathering in anti-American rallies,

Protesting this war, of retaliating; for towers that crumble and fall,

On their residents.

I considered dropping my accent.

I was ashamed,

To be related to the protest in any way at all.

Because I did not,

Protest,

Closure,

Or prevention, or even, occasionally, revenge.

I shuddered, certain I could never publicly object to,

Erasing the danger that threatened my neighbor's life,

Never protest the possibility of regaining a victimized family's freedom,

To breathe, into the days ahead. Never, confuse the cause with the effect. Never,

Feel comfortable with my own perceived guilt by association through nationality.

My mind flipped and flopped about, trying to squirm out of its, barely there, rather obtusely angled relationship to my fellow countrymen's minor indiscretion that stood in direct contrast with the rest of the non-Middle Eastern world's steadfast support. My heart, bled empathy as it turned its attention to a suddenly there, up-close realization. "If I feel like this about such a silly thing as a protest imagine how all the Muslim American innocents, related merely through religion or nationality, must feel about their undesirable terrorist-leader cousin, Osama Bin Laden?" I was ashamed of my pettiness for being ashamed of something so small and became aware of my Canadianness even more, because we Canadians are often disturbed by the little things in order not to have to have an opinion on the big ones. It made me feel small,

Until, December,

When, I went home for a visit, and discovered that it hadn't been an anti-American rally at all. In fact, it was nothing more than the annual labor rally that was, crashed by a few sign carrying anti-war protestors looking for fame. They made a scene because they wanted media coverage.

They got it.

Because the media needed something, anything, to cover as long as it related to the war, for 24 hours a day

"So who is it," I wondered. "That manipulates the media propaganda machine, and is responsible for all that confused emoting we are led into; the professionals or the populace?" And not knowing who is to blame reminded me that if the source for all my learning came from the media, I couldn't know anything for sure. And then it occurred to me that I was the one responsible, for how and what I chose to perceive and for what I chose to believe as a result of what I believed.

I closed my eyes and saw again and again the September 11, 2001 image of the second plane flying, directly, with no hesitation or swerving attempt to miss, into the middle of a tower full of people, who were jumping to their deaths, in order to avoid burning, in the fire of hell's fuel.

How do you get closure on that? ...Maybe you can't.

Maybe images like that are why the cultures and tribes, within some countries, don't,

Ever move on,

To peace.

Because they, have, so many images, that we are just beginning to see.

Maybe that's why their wars go on for centuries.

Maybe that's why, we must...not...

Be,

Them.

Four weeks after the planes took the towers down, I stood at their base, and saw the smoke and the ashes of ground zero,

And felt what I had up till then, only known:

The massive scale of the thing.

And so, life changed, and became, for me at least,

Filled with wonderment, horror, empathy and admiration for,

Without exception,

This race of humans, of which I am a part.

And I—who never watches the news—watched, as new events evolved and unfolded.

I was excited: believing that, what was happening, in other countries – in defense of America and of themselves—could in the end, safeguard the world.

I watched, as the leaders of various nations came together, moving us forward into the future—for which Osama Bin Laden had set the scene—becoming one, group of citizens, united against a common enemy, from within; policing ourselves, and each other, in an attempt to achieve our common objective: safety. The plan: to extract or enlighten, the terrorist devils inside, each of our borders, that had assimilated into us, like the dark side of the soul attempting to obliterate the light, by pretending to be it, reminding me of my talk show adventures and diminishing them into nothing important.

But even the darkness of my soul was under my influence, I knew, because, I had lived inside it for awhile. Until, with painstaking effort, and much self-education, I had illuminated it into a rich brightness composed of depth and decision that left behind only the memory of its suffocating presence and the dormant existence of its spectacule seed.

So, you see, I knew: "It is possible to adjust the dial on the darkness of a soul." I knew, because I'd done it. "Thus" I thought, "if one soul can be illuminated from black to gray to white, why not have that one, be **The One**, the one we call the collective, the all, the each of us? That way," I hypothesized, "as the collective grows love, the quicksand effect of this black hatred against the United States, will reverse its sucking action and throw out, rather than swallow down, the life shaping idealism of man."

It was my opinion that the world need only to be shown a new truth, to help its darkness see, that it was not the light it thought it was.

Which would of course allow it to become, brilliant.

And with that in my eyes I watched us becoming, one, delightfully different, same.

And while my optimism tried to perceive the tragedy of 911 as a lesson for our connected souls, my realism watched, repeatedly, the televised replay of events that began this police action called a war, horrified, every time. I froze, hypnotized by the airplane's steady descent into the tower, as my whole being suspended its breath. And each time I watched, I found myself believing that this time could be different.

Taut with suspense, I silently begged the plane to pull up, to turn, to hesitate, to STOP, at least once.

It never did,

Stop,

Though it stopped,

Being shown,

On television,

Which for some,

Is the same.

I paid attention, looking to see,

What I was getting out of this reality,

And why I'd manifested such a horrific tragedy.

I found that in paying attention I became passionate and carried my children with me, into a concern for the world around us. We talked and conjectured and huddled as a group. "How, in a world so connected by the Internet, satellites, telephones and international travel, could these suicide killers with the ability to traverse the earth and expand their outlooks, have been cocooned sufficiently enough, to remain separate enough to nurture the hate fostered abroad by a man who asked them to die for the sake of killing?" And these questions about others raised questions about ourselves, giving us new insights into our own family's minds.

We turned our attention to the rest of the equation, "How could these angry men then grow that hate to such mammoth proportions that though they had infiltrated a society filled with people extending the loving hand of help, they stayed focused on their goal and remained bent on burning that handshake into oblivion: killing, for the sake of dying?"

And, as I fielded the questions my children asked, I was shook by the memory of my talk show quest. I remembered the way I had continued down that path of teaching (Dana) a lesson—doing whatever came next, regardless of the fact, that I hadn't yet learned the lesson I was trying to teach—and realized, that even as I'd walked it I'd known I was lost, had known, that the direction I was traveling no longer made sense, if indeed it ever had. It was then that I noticed how absurd my mission had been, in spite of how important it had long ago seemed.

I shuddered, remembering also, my brother Henry, for whom I had sought some kind of revenge, fantasizing incessantly about how I would murder his murderer,

In order to stop mind-staring at the peripheral image of my brother's bloodied face.

I needed to plant the image of someone else's in my memory.

I was humbled,

Into a semblance of understanding,

That, no one without it,

Can comprehend,

Hate.

And understanding that I understood that I was grateful to myself for choosing,

To no longer understand that.

Because sometimes it does not benefit me to see, through someone else's eyes,

That used to be mine. And that's why I didn't do it more often.

Normally, I seeked to understand through my own presently realized emotional experience.

And my experience told me that if what I believed was true was, if I, along with everyone else in the world, was truly responsible for creating our own existence, then I, along with everyone that lived through or died because of, these events, created them. We built it, this time filled with tears and the clarity of a job to do, in some hidden agreement for what was to come.

It occurred to me that such a concept should be a hard pill to swallow, but it wasn't. It slid down easily and rang true in my heart, where the understandings lie. I thought about the fact that I had already—pre-tragedy—been talking with excitement to anyone who would listen, sharing my opinions on the unifying force the Internet could have in redesigning our next generation into borderless children. I was certain that this free access to universal multicultural communication would eventually shed our thus-far-very-human fear of the unknown, by erasing that factor, of stranger, believing that, with the Internet, eventually everyone would be extending an electronic hand and shaking their introductions and sharing their experiences. And maybe I was right, except, I'd left something out.

The part I hadn't foretold was the catalyst part.

I had expected this development to be a slow-growing fuselage, not a spontaneous overhaul by the engineering firm: "Impetus In The Form of Murder." But if I'd really thought about it, common sense mingled with a higher level of world events awareness, would have helped me see it coming. If I'd really thought about it I would have recognized that you can not unify countries via the computer if some of them haven't yet reached the point of free access to radio. If I'd really thought about it I'd have noticed that even my house had needed the catalyst for it was one of those hands on, non-technological, barely a vacuum cleaner let alone a web connection, hermit, country unto itself homes, with no way to hear, no way to become a part of everyone else, in the absence of a very loud noise. If I'd really thought about it I'd have known that the pendulum had swung. Unaware Good had become Unaware Bad and it was time to change the rules, and learn to participate.

But I hadn't really thought about it, not completely, not beyond the part I found intriguing. I needed an interrupt: something to distract me from my mode of proceeding and put me back in the fray, to mix it up, and find the commonality even as I protected myself from the soldier, whose boots I was marching in. So there was nothing slow about it, this alarm bell awakening. Suddenly it was here: a cause, creating one global enemy and unifying the rest.

I considered my wish for no enemy at all, and contemplated the concept that, "It is impossible to lose the existence of foes, completely, without losing also, the definition of friend."

What a bummer to realize,

Until I thought again.

And realized,

That the difference is in the degrees.

"*Why deaths? Why not deaths, aborted?*" "**BECAUSE IT WOULDN'T HAVE HAD THE SAME EFFECT!**" the answer screamed inside my head. "*I know, I know, I know, I know.*" I whispered my acquiescence. "But," I wondered, "Was such an effect so needed?"

"If I created my existence, why did I decide I needed so badly to be blasted into a state of wakefulness? Or for that matter why decide the pendulum swings at all? What's so bad about slumber? Why not make it OK to bury my head in the sand and, having no involvement with my community, remain unaware of the affairs of prime ministers and presidents? After all I tried involvement while raising my kids, I'd done the teacher parent politics, the neighbor-neighbor politics, the government, the workforce, the husbands, and the streets. I'd done it all, on my knees, spouting a mouthful, of putrid, white, bread, shit, kissing ass and never loving it. So I quit and,

Refusing to wear figurative feces on my nose any longer ended up risking to wear it literally for the groceries and the rent: by far a more honest expression of my talents and myself.

Because, I'd rather make love,

Than war,

With another teacher,

As she summarizes what she thinks I've done wrong,

In the raising of my children.

It was a thought that reminded me of the time I was supposed to be doing a dress rehearsal for the teachers in my son's Catholic elementary (or as they say here in the good old U.S.of A., grade) school. The teachers had agreed to stay late one night and be my practice audience, giving my troupe some much needed exposure to the possible laughs within our prison tour play. Five minutes before driving the two blocks to the school to set up the props for the performance, I got a call from Children's Aid saying that the school had reported me for some bullshit crime that I can no longer remember. I was sick of it. This school had been harassing me ever since I reported my son's teaching assistant for sexual abuse. As if that situation hadn't been hard enough all by itself, the principal made it harder by trying to point the finger of suspicion in my direction as though I had made it all up and coerced my son into the accusations. I supposed he was trying to destroy my credibility, in order to make it easier for him to protect, one of his own. Sound familiar? I think I might have said this before, about, Deja's mom, who may have taught him the technique? Or maybe he was a coarse graduate in: How to Help Your Friends Escape Detection for Sexual Molestation 101.

Perhaps! I mean there must be such a course since so many molesters use that same: gain a position of power in the community (be a prominent doctor, lawyer, teacher, massage therapist or priest) in order to escape suspicion strategy. At any rate, regardless of the principal's mentoring influence, the fact was that he had been treating my family with a heaping helping of crap. And, as was often the case, where the mixing together of teacher ego, school politics and me protecting my children was concerned, my son's needs got lost in the process. I was fuming!

Too much to pretend I was not.

So, unavoidably, on that dress rehearsal day, I lost my professionalism (Actually I hadn't really ever had a good grip on it any way.) and in the middle of our act I began yelling at this poor group of teachers ninety percent of whom, had no idea, of what I was talking about.

According to my memory (and the prison tour footage that those nasty college students stole) I yelled, all my frustration anger and pain in the faces of those confused and frightened educators. I swore that they had no right; that I was the one who had adopted these children; that I was the one who had taken them on; that I was the one that was committed to their mental health; that I was the one that ya da ya da ya da ya da ya! Every body squirmed, coughed into their hands and when I wasn't looking (while the vice principal took the microphone from me) left.

I can only hope that they thought it was part of the show.

Regardless, the point is, working within the system and trying to be a participant had been an impedance to mine and my children's development because, fighting pushed the pause button and stopped us from growing, and since the system didn't fit our group, our group fought to force it's round self, into that square school, kid by kid by kid. Fighting seemed inevitable. And since we were on pause, too busy grappling for position to be able to move forward, it wasn't until we dropped out, (into home schooling) that we dropped in, to ourselves, and advanced in our learning.

And that's how being involved had awakened me into the need to not be involved: in an opposite awakening to my social consciousness awakening of Sept. 11, 2002.

I suppose that all realities left to idle in one place will eventually change sides as the pendulum swings by, swishing them from bad to good or good to bad. I guess that such oscillating is necessary to create the appearance of forward motion. And I guess that since the pendulum dips into each reality on its way by some of what was there sticks and becomes mingled into some of what will be, effecting a change ever so slightly with each pass of the wand. And I guess all of that adds up to mean that nothing remains what it is and that the appearance of forward motion is in fact a kind of snakelike progression called change, which I embrace most of the time because motion is, as near as I can figure it, the definition of being alive, and a snakelike progression is better than the tedium of treading water, circling, hovering or jumping up and down; in a polishing the stone kind of evolutionary life. And so things change, regardless of if they seem dead still, which is impossible even for the teeming-with-parasites dead.

Thus the towers illuminated what the pendulum had flipped, changing my turtle-type solution of pulling us into a shell, from what was right to what was wrong.

It was time to go looking for a different house in the forest: That different forest made of man.

Urban life! I wondered if we were ready for it. And that question raised the need for my feelings about that reality to be revamped, or maybe just balled up and thrown away. "So," I thought, "I'll believe in watching the news and playing in the forum. We'll get satellite TV and subscribe to the Internet. I'll expose my hiding spot, raise up my voice and take part in the world." And suddenly, from no place I recognized as my memory mind, I got a message that connected this decision to something far greater than anything I could have foreseen, though I suppose in effect, I was foreseeing. Returning to the world, I was told, would bring me the opposite of what I had expected. Instead of sacrificing my son to the activities of city life, instead of losing touch with his development and leaving him to flounder in the neglect of my busy-ness, my busy-ness would enhance his learning and free us into independence.

The message was clear: Dar's tongue would not gain the agility to enunciate clearly, till mine did too. And I got; that he needed me to lead him as though expecting him to follow and without watching for him to change because he needed me to treat him as though there was no question of whether or not we could, do this thing, called walking the path.

He needed me to be brave enough to convince him that, there was nothing in succeeding, or even in being visible to fear. Which would help him to perceive that there was no need be brave in the first place, which would be good, because he believed himself not. And for the ga-zillionth time in my life one of my children's needs forced me to know again, something that I now needed to teach:

There's no need to be brave cause there's nothing to fear.

A tear rolled down my cheek and moistened my lips because suddenly I understood, "I must stop using helping Dar as an excuse to stay put and hide out from society." and my bottom lip began to quiver, as the revelation dawned in the form of an image that was gifted me. "*Oh, my son!*"

I knew what my child had given up, in order to gain, such a bond with me.

And I sobbed with gratitude and admiration as I recognized Dar for who he really was: my angel-incarnate, here to coax me to stretch my wings, and fly.

And I wondered if Osama had any intuitive idea of what a wonderful thing he was doing for me, when he inadvertently positioned me to see things, differently. And then I wondered, if he had any idea, if he understood at all, that he had probably given similar gifts to millions of people, and wondered how he'd feel about that: my grateful joy? And as I wondered after Osama a revelation began to quiver and quake and call for my attention but it was a revelation I wasn't quite ready to notice, out loud.

So I changed the subject back to its beginning and thought, "I guess the towers were a kind of spiritual wake-up call." and wondered, "But if I needed to wake up, why do it at the expense of lives? Why not just wake up? Why didn't we all just choose to wake up, slowly?" But I already knew the answers—I was just being shit scared redundant—to avoid hearing myself, reveal, anything, ahead of my acquiescence.

So I stayed distracted from the nagging revelation by wondering what some of the other people's stories of benefit as a result of the Trade Center planings were. I knew there had to be many and wished the news would show us some of them, a little joy to lighten our hearts with and thumb our noses at the pain, the same pain that, even as I felt it I knew, didn't need to hurt.

And listening to my thoughts, my ideas and my summations I wondered over my sanity. "Is it possible to believe the way I believe and not be nuts?"

I decided it was, because that was more comfortable, and a lot less work, than deciding it wasn't.

Besides my way of believing, was logical, according to me,

Even if I did believe that I was God, and the Devil and everyone on earth.

Even if I did believe that I deserved the credit and the blame,

As everyone else.

Even if I did believe.

And as I wondered over my convictions, my beliefs and my chosen deity, I watched the news and believed,

In most of the images I saw,

Even though the previously reported Canadian Anti-American protest that wasn't, should have taught me to be more discerning.

I believed, because, seeing is—-

Able to cause a conditioned response.

And I believed because that Canadian misrepresentation that taught me not to believe, happened, before I revamped my beliefs after the pendulum swung.

So I watched, searching for answers everywhere, using multidimensional vision I looked, with an eye on the future and an eye on the past, and evaluated, and pondered, and created my world out of the pieces I could see, all the while remaining aware of my present, wherein news about Canada was coincidentally (?) once again causing me embarrassment,

I reconsidered trying to hide, my accent but I didn't really have one anymore.

Admittedly, on this occasion the blush of my cheeks could not be blamed on the American newsman's predilection for sensationalistic reporting.

This occasion was Canadian-grown because this time I was standing on Canadian soil reading the story in a homegrown paper from a homegrown press. Apparently Chretian, the homegrown Prime Minister of my homegrown-land, after promising to deploy one thousand ill-equipped (the ill-equipped part wasn't a promise so much as a reality) soldiers into Afghanistan, reneged, because a British (not even a Canadian) landing at Kabul airport met with resistance. This bothered the Prime Minister who apparently preferred to have the enemy roll out the red carpet in an open armed welcome whenever he sent soldiers in support of the war effort against them.

According to the press, Prime Minister Chretian tried to excuse his boomeranged promise that let down the States by saying, " We don't want to have a big fight over there."

And I wondered what he did want: a game of Red Rover perhaps?

And wondered if he had any idea that his neighbors were in trouble?

I considered the possibility that Chretian—aware of the fact that wars are expensive— was trying to time it so that Canadians could get the glory of being bravely supportive, while keeping the cost down and the voters happy by ensuring that they didn't show up until they were not in danger and there was nothing to be brave about. Playing both sides of the fence and not accomplishing anything, I think they call it.

And with the concept of bravery popping up again I realized that my recent re-revelation (there's no need to be brave because there's nothing to fear) would sound trite in the ears of a soldier being told to kill or die or take an arm or lose a leg. And I also realized that these soldiers, facing just such an eventuality, might adore Chretian for his wishy-washy going-to-war-later attitude.

As well they should.

But I did not,

Want to believe that the countrymen of my homeland felt less empathy, less little brother gratitude, towards the States, than other nations did who were an ocean away and far less dependant. I wanted to believe that my country felt as I did. So grateful in fact that they would fight, and risk stopping the beating of their own heart, to protect our way of life on this continent. So I asked my Canadian friends what they thought. They echoed my sentiments and worried over a leader who didn't lead, any of us. We were afraid of being painted yellow: coward by association, in the eyes of the

Americans and mostly of ourselves. Of course none of us were soldiers or the family of soldiers so it was easy to be brave.

It was easy to have an arms length commitment to this action we knew nothing about, fun in fact. And then I thought of that re-revelation about feelings and, noticing my emotional commitment to the opinions I was arguing for I realized I had got caught in the game again. I had been passionately evaluating the actions and motives of leaders with less than a full compliment of information, experience or observation.

Was it the lack of information or the game itself that caused my fear? I thought of Osama's suicide soldiers and decided no, it was the rules of the game that made the game and our commitment to those rules and our belief in how carrying them out should feel that made the fear, or whatever emotion we chose to have.

I blinked away the above-the-crowd perception that allowed me to see us sitting at the game board and returned to playing amongst my friends.

Immediately I joined them in finding these political events unnerving because, we realized how much a leader creates the world opinion of the people he leads and for many reasons that we created at the time the opinions of others mattered right then.

And though Chretian, who I'm sure must have learned something from all of this, didn't lead me, or even you, Jeff, for we lived in America, I didn't want to be painted coward by the association of country kinship.

And then I reassured myself by imagining that, in many ways, Canada was seen as a neutral country somewhat like Switzerland is famous for being. So probably nobody expected anything of us in the first place. And somehow the reputation of being unimportant bothered me less than being seen as disappointing had. So I saw it that way. I took comfort in the Canada Switzerland sameness till I noticed the parts that weren't the same; like Switzerland's geography, which lends itself to a position of neutrality. The Swiss may not owe a debt of gratitude to those mountainous Alps but that is only because mountains are inanimate and afford their protection in spite of themselves. I'm sure the Swiss appreciate them anyway.

Now Canada's geography is a little bit different, her mountains run down one side and are in no way related to border protection from especially the south. The typical Canadian's feelings of living in a safety zone is vastly different from Switzerland's because Canada is protected not by enormous mounds of rock but rather by being located next to enormous mounds of military power called ally, a.k.a. The United States of America.

For that, a country's people just might owe a debt of gratitude,

To be expressed when their protector is in need.

But that's just me, and my opinions. I could be wrong

Even when I'm right.

Then, in need of a way to end the ruminations about Canada and Chretian, I remembered the glory stories of Canada's role in the Second World War, during which time Canada led North America in the march against Hitler. I put down the Toronto Star and stopped reading, refusing to observe any longer, this Prime Minister as he misrepresented my homeland, into appearing as nothing more than an inert pile of ineffective pebbles. And thinking of how leaders create the world opinion of their constituents I was reminded that constituents can create the world opinion of their leader. Which reminded me of how nauseous I felt watching the people of the news paint Clinton as playing with 'privates' rather than politics.

And remembering why I didn't like to watch the news,
I closed my eyes
To the memories of oft-forgotten current events.

❖ THIRTEEN ❖

And the act of sticking my head in the sand made me feel, you, and remember another time, at the donut Shop, when I defended my position of refusing to watch the news, not wanting to be aware of the world, outside my world. And you, accepted my position, while nudging me gently, to at least read the headlines, knowing it would help me keep my stand up comedy more current and also to lead my children into a more conscientious citizenship of the earth.

It was a good idea, that I followed,

For a while,

Keeping you in my memories.

And that remembering it now,

Encourages me to take my head out of the sand again.

So, Jeff, you were always my leader.

Eh?

Do you still use that term?

Eh? As in the Canadian euphemism for "don't you agree? Huh! Huh! Don't

you agree??"

Eh, which sounds like "A" as in "A," B, C,

"A" as in Ashamed, of a Prime Minister,

Whom I'm afraid will reflect poorly on me:

The Canadian, happily living in an American home.

"A" for Ashamed,

And, "P" for Proud,

Er, than I am ashamed. Proud,

Of my fellow humans,

And every story ever told,

And the heroism displayed.

"P" for Proud and "V" for Victory,

Over ourselves,

And this war,

That underscores peace.

SHOUT IT!

"P" and "V"

"P" and "V"

"P" and "V"

Hey! Look at that!

"P" and "V" can stand for something other than,

"The Penis-in-the-vagina.." Who knew??

And I was reminded that life's little definitions all depend upon one's point of reference.

And all those penis and vagina abbreviates, for some reason led me to remembering the words to Rizzo's song, from the musical "Grease":

"There are worse things I could do, than go with a boy or two."

And as I remembered the words it occurred to me that yes, there "are worse things;" things like refusing to fight for the country I am positioned next to, even while expecting that that country would fight for me, should I ever need it to. Especially if I also simultaneously had a sense of knowing that it may have been that very same 'Big Brother is waiting in the wings.' expectation by other countries that has thus far kept me safe, by keeping all those others at bay and away from my borders.

There are worse things I could do.

Like bite the hand that feeds me by justifying my running away.

Yes. **There are worse things I could do, than go with a boy or,**

Three hundred:

I could cluck my tongue with pity while I watch the results of someone else creating widows and orphans out of suicidal maniacs and then go back to what I was originally doing as though nothing had really changed. Worse things, yes, I could be the one who made the widows and orphans plan.

Worse things I could do,

Than have sex.

I could, become a celibate religious leader and then call myself an expert on the morality of all the others I have never even touched.

Or I could be me, and I could touch.

And with that in mind my life gained a new guilt free perspective,

As my thoughts returned to the subject of monogamy,

And the ridiculous lies and un-keep-able vows that the expectation of it forces people into.

And perhaps, since these vows, except when based merely on intention, are impossible to make with conviction, unless the person making the vow is gifted with super duper, long-range, observatory-telescope-style, precognitive foresight,

Perhaps that is why, so many of the people in my experience rewrite the meaning of monogamy.

Thus they can make the vows with sincerity and, no intention of holding fast, beyond the Penis-in-the-Vagina lovemaking limitation that even my first husband believed in.

I considered the possibility that perhaps these vowed-to-love-forever monogamous mates that play the field are not merely presidential jerks after all, but rather brilliant moralists with their fingers on the pulse of fidelity?

Perhaps they have discovered the only way to remain fidelt,

For twenty-five to thirty years of married life.

Perhaps Clinton was one of them and has been unfairly maligned.

Perhaps he was the penis-elect destined to sound the banner and ring out the message of literal enlightenment to his fledgling children the American people.

Perhaps, Clinton, along with all the rest of the persons,

In the "Penis-in-the-vagina" congregation,

Was merely a victim of social moral abuse.

Or perhaps these mental tongue-twisters are all backwards from the truth and Clinton was the perpetrator of spin-doctored sex.

Or, (if you can take it) even another perhaps, perhaps, he just wanted to exercise his civil right to practice his own particular sexual religion without fear of persecution or prejudice.

But it seemed more likely to me that he was just a person,

With a penis in his pants,

Standing next to another person,

Offering to help him take it out?

Which, not wanting to hurt the feelings of any of his constituents, he let her do.

It's all about good manners,

And voter recognition.

So, occasionally,

Just to save her the trouble,

Perhaps he takes it out himself.

In a cocksure attempt to impress by displaying himself proudly,

In order to meet the criteria of,

Introduction,

As defined by his understanding of what is,

Genteel.

Perhaps!

So what did you think about all this pretended presidential outrage, Jeff?

Did it remind you of the rich indignation so many drivers suffer from as they yell at the driver in front of them for doing exactly what they themselves did to someone else only moments before?

A behavior I saw you display only once upon a long time ago.

Were you involved,

In the hullabaloo,

Of driving the satellite trucks from state to state, yelling at other drivers, racing against the competition in an attempt to capture the minute-to-minute update on the popular opinion for the proper use of the Presidential penis?

Were you? I wonder.

And as I wondered about you wandering after Clinton, I began to wonder about you wandering after satellite links to footage of Osama and Bush and New York mayor Giuliani. And once again, the current events that surrounded me, brought me up short in the process of editing this book because it was hard to focus on my love for you when death was in the air, though there is probably no better time to do it for most people.

For me, however, focusing on loving you brought up you, which brought up your work, which brought up the news, which brought up those current events, which brought up the dead. And left me trying harder than ever before not to think about you. So I focused on the tragic dead in order to not. Because conversely, focusing on the unfolding story of America's choices for retaliation radiated love, because I wondered while I watched President Bush who has taken over for President Clinton:

"Did you set up the truck that shot that footage? Or that footage? Or that?

Were you there? Or there? Or there?"

Being mindful of the news put you back in my life, and reminded me of the other reason I stopped watching and looking for your fingerprints,

On the events that make you current:

Because there's someone new in my life and I'm supposed to move on.

So as I tried to climb my mind away from thoughts of you and of our sex, I turned my head to presidents and ended up laughing instead, at popping up images of Monica's blue dress, bearing dried-up DNA flakes of Clinton's little mess.

And, over-laughing to push you from my mind carried me to the outrageous. Perhaps Monica was more than met the eye. Perhaps she was, in fact a long-range thinker envisioning her future. Who knows? She just might have done it all—enshrined Bill's DNA and refused to wash her dress—for more than the purpose of proving herself in court. It may have been a simple: virginal-pregnancy-make-it-to-heaven plan. Maybe she intended to live until science advanced enough to re-hydrate those stains and impregnate her—cigars don't count—presidential virginity with the sire of a leader. WOW! There's a thought!....... That could only come from me,

Or some fanatical religious leader with a self advertised pipeline to God (Allah, Jehovah etc.) who sells his conditional, make-it-to-heaven plans sounding, to anyone that doesn't agree, equally as ridiculous as my Monica jest, jest did.

Good comedic subplot in a Comedy Science Fiction movie though. Perfect for the South Park gang: assuming they'll do it, of course. The plot could be centered around the suicide planers as they try to make it to the highest place in heaven in order to be surrounded by seventy (or a thousand or whatever number; dependant upon what teacher they may have listened to and/or the number of people they took with them into death) Houris, which are beautiful virgins provided in Paradise to all faithful Mohammedans. Bin Laden could usurp Hussein and play the devils new bun honey: Cute little subplot playing off the last South Park film and pitting a jealous Saddam against an upstart Osama.

Monica, who was after nothing more than recognition and a high station on earth, could die giving birth, and end up as a result of her virginal presidential pregnancy earning a high station in heaven.

Poor Monica: important in all the wrong places.

Monica could be disappointed initially, until she finds herself surrounded by thousands of male and female sluts completely un-hung-up about sex and willing to do her bidding.

The movie ends, as those poor suicide airplane terrorists—whose blown-off arms never materialized due to the rationing of magic in the very lowest regions of heaven which is as far as they got—look upward in misery, surrounded as they are, by the enticement of those exciting, virginity-protecting Houris. Finally they understand what the Christians meant when they said that suicide leads to hell: stuck, for all eternity horny and handless with no way to release their frustration. Meanwhile back at the Ranch of Fire and Brimstone, Saddam and Osama, are so fuming mad at each other that the two combust into a heap of white hot charcoal leaving Satan with nothing but charred flesh cheeks to chew on ...THE END.

Sorry, Jeff. You can just skip over that part.

Sometimes imagination is the only way I have of distilling and reducing my thoughts,

By spewing the mental diarrhea piling up in my head, into something that makes me laugh.

Occasionally, my imagination even splashes upon the truth: Those Houris just may actually be teasing, at this very moment, every terrorist who ever killed in the name of Allah. Perhaps those airplane murderers did wake up in heaven, surrounded by almost every man's dream: the experienced virgin, only to discover that the word "experienced" applied to her experience at remaining the untouchable Houris, brazenly belly dancing just out of reach, her chastity belt of heavenly chasteness.

What a (blue balls) dream come true, that religious rhetoric has implied.

No wonder young men jumped to sacrifice themselves for the cause of naming this unholy war holy. They forgot to read between the lines.

But for all the jokes (if that's what they are), especially the ones about Monica's splotchy dress,

The humor pales and becomes unfunny when compared,

With the color of splotchy reddish brown staining the hills and deserts of Afghanistan,

Even before the Americans landed to fight. Those poor dark skinned people had been abused, victimized, murdered. They had been prematurely dying violent deaths, cradled by the sadism of others, for over twenty years.

Yet, for us the color of their suffering pales in comparison to the ashy gray,

On the mound of Ground Zero rubble,

In the heart of New York,

Where two towers, full of people from all around the world used to stand.

And so we cry because we in the world are at war,

Against our own evil propensity to grow up confused,

By the beliefs we adopt from the religions of our elders.

Religious beliefs: that cause irreparable damage, as we suffer and kill, ourselves,

In the name of being saved, from something made up.

I hope we win. For,

At the moment I could use a little saving. For,

In the past two years,

Ever since writing this book that will be published soon, so long as I meet my deadline of editing it down to size instead of growing it bigger as I am doing, I have lost sight of the good, that this letter gave me.

I've become re-confused.

And forgotten the secret this journey revealed,

The secret that, answered all my questions,

About climbing into love, like you climb into bed, to cuddle, to rest, in the arms in your head.

So I read, edit and look about me, searching my world for clues, to what is true,

Just as I did two years ago when this chapter was given birth, brand-new.

Re-reading my thoughts,

On Clinton,

Has highlighted for me how much has changed and yet, the changes are too few.

For now looks remarkably like then,

So much has stayed the same,

Including my heart.

I looked about me asking "*Why? Why? What does the world have to teach me?*"

And heard the answer as I saw us all circling in the sameness between then and now, sameness which are made most obvious in the news.

True, Bush didn't seem the type that was likely to be caught in the sex scandals Clinton did. But the president doesn't always have to be involved for a political scandal to appear the same as the one that came before, since the look of such a thing is generally created by the way the press colors the pictures. Truth is, as long as sex can be considered scandalous, if you look hard enough, there will always be some Swaggerty styled religious figure or some heretofore unnoticed politician like, say, Gary Condit, filling the bill and grabbing the headlines.

And as long as sex is considered scandalous it will remain deliciously tempting to those who have the most to lose because the greater the pressure the greater the demand for its release. Thus people, like the ones in politics, the ones for whom a scandal could jeopardize a hard-won, much-loved career, people like that, might find themselves 'driven' to cheat. Then, unfaithful but remorseful, they drop to their knees to pray (ing mantis) that it had never happened or at least that there were no observers when it did. They might then look straight at the lover they had just minutes before so ten-

derly humped and realize that, of course even if nobody else saw, there was this......
one....... witness.

Under those circumstances what leader who believes he has something to offer the world, who believes that being free to perform his other duties means there is more at stake than one piddly little life, what leader wouldn't then bite and effectively sever that lover's head, sacrificing one, in the throes of their political passion, for the good of all?

Many. I hope.

I and probably others think things like that because we have seen a goodly number of scenarios such as these on TV and in the movies and at least I, a media educated child, have been programmed to suspect a sordid truth. So I continue to obsessively cluck my tongue as I watch others who watch the news for bits and pieces about those we decide may have committed the possibly uncommitted sex and or murder we pressured them into (though they are still to blame) in the first place.

In spite of us,

The pre-catastrophe crass media led American public's,

Pre-occupations were the same this time as the last time bombs from here whistled their way to the other side of the world in search of Bin Laden. On both occasions it took war to push sex out of the headlines.

I suspect that the timing on the first occasion was a relief for Clinton whose penis had long been sizzling in the limelight of be kissed and tell, in the hands of Monica's, no thank you Mr. Clinton—predecessor, Paula Jones. I suspect that the president felt he needed a distraction, a big one, especially when the discovery of Monica completed the picture of "lecherous man only sometimes rebuked," and that radiantly warm member of his, began to really fry.

Monica added to the fuel, infused it with life, and fed the blazing media, energy, like oxygen to a flame.

It was the year of the embassy bombings in Africa killing 224 and injuring 5000. It was the year Clinton froze Bin Laden's American assets and, backed by several European countries like Britain and Germany, bombed Sudan for hiding their weapons of mass destruction.

It was one of those years when the focus shifted from the missile on the President's groin to the missiles leaving the country's armory.

In all cases, there was lots of show, lots of noise, and very little substance,

As wars,

And torrid affairs,

Go.

Throughout Clinton's tenure the terror (1993 World Trade Center bombing, 1995 Saudi Arabia, 1996 Khober Towers, 1998 US embassies, 2000 USS Cole) and the terrorists grew in power. As residents of America we cried out our need that the President be a man and make strong decisions, for the sake of our futures: futures that, some of us, no longer live in,

And haven't,

Ever since the past of September 11th 2001.

Also during his tenure we talked, debated and conjectured our need for the protection of,

The kind of man that will,

Fight,

And fuck,

And slay all the dragons.

Except no one wanted Clinton to screw,

In our faces, any non-Hillarys,

That caused such disgraces.

So I guess in our wishes we were the hypocrites who,

Caused rippling reactions that simmered and stewed, because we wanted it both ways.

Now lay on top of that this weird idea of mine: I think our society finds it more long term fascinating to watch and imagine our public figures extra-curricularly copulating than to observe news about people as they unexpectedly expire. It seems to me that the moment of becoming a dead neighbor-leader, Afghanistan, while fleetingly engrossing, has limited continuous appeal, because we can only observe, obliquely, the act, once, (excluding replays) in each person's lifetime. Similarly, we can only, ourselves, perform the act a single time per existence while, conversely, sex is a multi opportunity activity.

(So Jeff, perhaps that is why I can't forget you, because with you the blur, wasn't.

I remember with snapshot clarity, the feel of your fingers as they indelibly traced love,

Upon my body.)

Point is sex is more wonderful to think about than "croaked," which is less appealing, less familiar, less of a friend and seemingly, beyond our control. So, though in some ways that very lack of familiarity should help to create a feeling of mystery and make death more interesting than coitus is, to the masses, and it probably does, I just don't think it sustains everyone's curiosity for as long as things like secretive affairs or fetishes do. At least it doesn't sustain mine. I think it's harder to empathize with the unfamiliar, activities, of heart attack, suicide or murder, at least until they become familiar through some sort of familial experience. And even then it is my wish to forget,

To move on,

To love...making.

And, mass dying, until it happened at home, seemed to me to remain even more unfamiliar, more un-understandable because it was beyond my scope and too hard to hold in my mind.

Thus, I doubted if terrorists striking terror upon the un-famous nondescript, an ocean away, sold as many papers or drew as many viewers for as sustained a period of time, as the stories of sex and romance in the presidential pants did.

And maybe that's not something to feel bad about. I considered the concept.

At first glance it seemed trite to be so focused as a country on the happenings in someone else's bedroom (or office or elevator or trampoline or cornfield or closet or bathroom or chicken coop or jalopy or walk in freezer). But then, I found myself wondering if, in the countries where: death from famine and/or government sadism and/or terrorist action and/or internal war, is so prevalent as to be considered commonplace, in these countries wherein, everyone can relate to mourning for the murdered because everyone is related to more than one someone who died prematurely; in those cultures is it sex rather than death that becomes the kind of news that splashes the front page but is unable to sustain public interest? In countries such as those, is it the raging rhetoric of religion and politics that shines brighter and becomes more riveting, more ratings rewarding, than making love and flailing in an inappropriate bed?

Is it merely the promise of drawing another breath—from whatever fearsome faction feigns the pledge—that holds the attention of a threatened people? If so, if constant war and starvation is the recipe for fear-based political social concern, maybe being a sexually fixated society becomes a reflection, not of our decadence but of our freedom from fear. Perhaps we simply have the mental space, for voyeuristic leisure because of our greater piece of peace and should be proud of our exercised right to be politically trite en masse.

Though I merely conjecture and do not know...Frequently.

I wonder? Did that more abundant peace and/or that more abundant talk about piece, help lay the foundation for attack? If one examines the dates of destruction and then lays it against the dates of media prying, would a curious pattern evolve? Could it be that every time the country turned up the heat by attacking Clinton's sexual integrity, the terrorists also turned up the heat, with bombs, effectively attacking Clinton's ability to protect his long-distance constituents. Was our lack of focus on security at home and abroad a signal to terrorists groups, giving them the green light to do whatever they chose?

While our backs were turned in the direction of scandal? Is that how it went? Ping-ponging back and forth throughout Clinton's term of office, beginning in the year of his inauguration, and ours, and the not-very-sexy Whitewater flood scandal?

If we strip away the details and deflections does the story look like this: Paula points at Clinton, a terrorist bombs the not-yet-demolished trade center, everyone points at Monica, who misty-eyed moons over the President, terrorists bomb Americans in Saudi, Kenneth Starr goes for impeachment challenging the honesty of Clinton and his Penis-in-the-Vagina justification, the U.S. embassies in Africa are bombed?

Is that how it went or the other way round, or is there even any pattern at all?

Was sex being talked about in so many quarters that everyone was using it as a meter for action, even Clinton? Was he scared? Or was he relieved to have an excuse to go to war as long as it didn't last very long, while still,

Affording him a small reprieve and enabling him to tuck his scud away, out of our sight and out of our minds.

I remember hearing about the pharmaceutical missile-drop and being amused. I reacted with the absolute irreverence that distance from repercussion and a lack of knowledge permit.

And I ran off at the mouth, insisting that maybe President Clinton planned this pseudo war himself. *"You know. Just to play hero instead of scoundrel for a change."* The thought amused me and I toyed with the idea of writing a movie along this theme. I tickled myself with tentative titles like, "How The Boss' Bits Got Cooled By The Fire" or "BAH! BAH! BAH! BOOM!" Six month's later I was to learn of a movie scripted along this theme with a subtler more artistically brilliant title, "Wag The Dog." Critics loved this movie,

Which gifted me and many others with eye open amusement, proving to me that I was not the only one who found Clinton inspirational.

However, Clinton's inspirational, fisted retort fizzled out after a missile or two, leaving me wondering which role he enjoyed more: beast or bastard? At loose ends and with no more projectiles to focus on, the people and the press turned again to Clinton's affairs to keep us entertained. He succeeded, in making that same old "Scud thing" new again, as he played the starring role in Kenneth's play and brought up the question of "Where's the truth in what you say?"

And as I thought about Clinton, bebop-bobbing on the turbulent waters of public opinion it occurred to me that his entire run as President resembled a Warner Brothers cartoon with Bill skedaddling around like the roadrunner while we played the coyote trying to catch him. Meep! Meep!

He found it easy,

It seemed,

To amuse me,

Though I'm sure,

I was beneath his intent.

Regardless, I was amused,

Especially, as I said, when he long-distance-retaliated for injury and murder and diabolical weaponry lies by bombing that pharmaceutical plant in a recently sort-of admitted to (possibly spin-doctored confession because of Osama's bragging involvement with the trade tower tragedy and Clinton's need to not be to blame for Osama's being alive) bungled assassination attempt (done en mass so as not to be labeled an assassination attempt because Clinton had declared assassinations illegal) late at night, after Bin Laden had gone home,

Leaving, many,

More than me,

Amused,

And at least slightly,

Suspicious,

That bebop-bobbing Bill might have just been trying to razzle-dazzle-bomb his way back into missionary position: on top, and humping the hell out of the press without really doing anything of consequence.

Funny thought, then,

But not anymore,

Because this time the war is not pseudo and thousands of people weren't just injured, they were vaporized:

The day dead became more than a far away world on the six o'clock news.

The day when, once again, the Taliban and consequently the Al Quaeda were illuminated on center stage, by the reflected light of mass destruction, they eventually proudly wore, as they once again ripped our sordid obsessing eyes from the picture of a politician's (though thankfully not a president's) suspected surreal sex life.

The coincidental sameness was intense. So perhaps the public's pubic preoccupation was what signaled our lack of focus on home security readiness, after all. Perhaps there was no joke, in suggesting, that our getting greater piece threatened our greater peace. Perhaps it did, a little, or perhaps, a lot.

If a lowly married congressman and his missing intern lover were the most shocking thing we had to talk about, as the preoccupied press propagandized the public, with mental pictures of Gary Condit's possible crime, then perhaps we were in a comatose nightmare ridden sleep, and needed to be scared awake?

And so we were blasted into consciousness;

By the shadow of the towers as they tumbled into the vortex of terror,

Bringing us with them into the solidarity of sorrow,

And symbolizing,

Every possible,

Not possible.

And the towers that weren't, consumed me, became they were all I could think of, related to everything, even as I read my thoughts from two years ago, about Clinton, who was already gone.

Two, once strong, towers, had stood together, husband and wife, like breadwinners and caretakers of a great city, watching over their wards, keeping them safe.

Two annihilated parents, dying, all over their family, crushing their children in the process of crumbling under hate's heavy weight.

Obsessive, focused on symbols, devastating hatred.

How could any marriage survive that?

None of mine ever did.

But then, none of mine ever tried. Perhaps it is true what they say about suffering making us stronger, growing character, and cementing relationships. Perhaps, Bill and Hillary have a richer marriage for all that interference and attention:

Assuming, of course, that finger pointing and infidelity are the kind of things that stir up the strengthening agent of suffering for families like the Clintons.

Who really knows? Maybe it didn't sting at all. Maybe they loved it! And maybe it's love, not sorrow that makes us stronger in every respect.

So maybe a political marriage thrives on difficult for different reasons than some may assume. Maybe it thrives not because it is reinforced by the difficulty, but because it is already reinforced and can therefore thrive.

Or perhaps a political marriage simply stays intact,

Because we tell them to, at least on the outside,

The part meant for us, to think we see through,

As we rail against hypocrisy and beg for the truth.

Hence the world's continued adoration for Lady Di's honest daring to be different,

Rebellion,

Of divorce.

We seemed to admire her for breaking the bonds of marital vows that, I believe, it is shortsighted to be vowing in the first place (Though admittedly that never seemed to stop me).

What do you, who loved Dianna, think, Jeff?

Is it possible to make any promise especially such a long-range one without full knowledge of what is yet to come? Here's an idea: what if people changed their vows to reflect the contract of agreements made between them? And what if those agreements became the legally binding definition—in their particular case—of what was or wasn't enough of a breech to warrant divorce?

Don't you think that cheating and the lines for what is or isn't extramarital sex should be defined by the beliefs of the people in the relationship, instead of the neighbors, judges and clergymen with whom they will not be sharing their bed?

Does it seem to you that the citizens of the world are staring at each other, in order to not see, themselves? And if it does,

What do you think Jeff?

Should they stop? I think, I think they should.

Except; while I think it, as I hesitate to publish this intimate book about my spiritual, sexual, love evolution; I realize that this journey required obsession in order to be experienced, in order to be written, and yet, here I am tsk-tsking my tongue at the obsessed obsessions of both the populace and the press.

And it occurs to me that,

I should laugh at myself, again.

I so frequently complain about and so passionately avoid being influenced by the media, and yet, it is from the media arts that I have received most of my inspirational teachings. So, as I rail against the media, though I try to hang onto the baby whenever I throw out the bath water, on occasion I toss an infant or two and miss rearing to ripeness some of my most promising prodigy, called perceptions, because I'm looking with my eyes closed.

Silly me, silly me, silly me, silly me, even more than, and along with it all, it is the media and its arts and the elements therein that I most often comprehend, as my creation. Thus, if I wish to attribute its genius to my credit, then so, must I also attribute its stupidity (unless I am right and I really am God, who always only gets the credit, and passes the devil the blame).

But, in that moment, when I could if I would, see the me, in the ridiculous, I—not liking to be laughed at—refused to be both God and the Devil, refused to take the responsibility for wrong, until the next moment when I did, take it, and joined in the joy of self-amusement as I made myself whole temporarily.

And it was then, while I was whole, that I re-remembered: we are all one, with no true separation between science, spirituality, religion, Bin Laden, Bush, Clinton or Condit, though each from each, is a world apart in ways upon ways.

And I wondered: should I stop seeing the problems of love and relationships as too petty for newspapers and TV and such? If we are all one, then are we not all worth the price of admission? Are we not all interesting? Is any cause more, worthy, than another? Perhaps I have misunderstood, and the status of Condit's missing intern is not less important than the tragedy of the towers, in spite of the numbers, multiplied. Perhaps sacrificing one to save many is the same as sacrificing all? Perhaps, perhaps, perhaps we fixated on our sordid suspicions over his alleged affair, not because we were a world at peace, but because the problems of love and the value of each individual, was the only important reality we had enough power to actually work on: the only reality within which, we could make an immediate difference, from home,

Each of us, around the world, creating, within a different culture, working, within different rules, to love by.

So, what, and who is right? How do we love, truly, deeply, faithfully, forever, in a manner that all would deem correct? How?

Maybe the definitions created by the merging together of the individual beliefs of the persons doing the merging,

And then agreed upon,

Are the true vows of being faithful.

Eh? **Don't ya think**??

Or has being married changed you?

Jeff?

Has it?

Are you changed?

And even if you are changed, how can, making rules you're both happy with be wrong? Isn't that how all contracts are supposed to be created,

With full knowledge and consent,

Agreement and trust?

Isn't that the only way to be in concert with another? The only way to know when a lie or breach or misrepresentation has been perpetrated,

Between the two of you?

And if it is not the two of you who can see the rift,

In the delivery of the promised responsibility,

Then who?

Gordon Elliot?

Carnie Wilson?

Barbara Walters?

That Bill guy from Politically Incorrect?

(I don't mean to Maher your opinion of me with my political incorrectness of not knowing Bill's last name. But, oh well, I never was very good at behaving according to anything other than my own ever-changing rules.)

You know, all this multi-perceptual understanding makes it hard to have an opinion.

Who has the answers to how we should behave anyway?

The parties involved or the uninvited voyeurs?

What do you think, Jeff? Are people who think they have a right to their own marital definitions, their own commitment agreements and beliefs, are they merely dreaming?

Are they deluded?

And what about you and your wife, did the two of you even remember to agree?

Or is cheating something different to each of you? And if so, which one of you is wrong? Both of you? Neither of you? Could you both be right?

Could you?

Do ya think?

That the rules belong solely to the person who makes them? Does their guilt compassion and duty have no real bearing on the person they stand beside? Are we all—like the terrorists on the plane sitting next to the victims whose families they are about to maim—believing only in our own justifications?

Tell me, Jeff, in your married moral code of ethics, are you,

And I,

And Ted,

The rule benders because we do insertion?

Or are the Clinton style outercourse innocence propagandists, the lascivious loophole lookers?

Who knows who is the absolutely, right, literally accurate,

"By the book" fucker?

The book?

I'm afraid,

Not even The Book, has the answer.

For like society, my $100, 2,230-page Webster's unabridged dictionary is having trouble deciding the meaning of sexual intercourse.

In fact their definition isn't,

Anything more than a loop of words,

Fully designed for loophole lookers.

This "Bible of definitions" defines sex as sexual intercourse, which it defines as coitus, which it defines as sexual intercourse, which it defines as coitus, which it defines as sexual intercourse,

And on and on and on ad infinitum.

No wonder I sometimes feel confused by all my casual coitusing I've been looping around at such dizzying speeds that I've thrown off my equilibrium.

Perhaps I've lost my balance and that's why I keep bumping into,

Butts and lips,

And legs and hips,

Elbows and knees,

And toes and Febreeze,

Vibrators and creams,

Whimpers and screams.

And perhaps all my fetishes are nothing but dreams,

Caused by the hallucinations, that were caused by the circling,

Around in search of an accurate definition to believe in.

And having found none,

Decided that, unless the act of what is or isn't sex,

And of what is or isn't inappropriate is allowed to be defined by the people involved,

Maybe we should all just keep our sexual organs on our own side of the bed,

Especially if we are married,

To each other.

Wow! Sometimes my mind is a scary place!

That you never made me feel I needed to apologize for,

Because you never once acted like the rest of the world and told me calm down because I think too much.

I guess that's where it came from: "Our Silence,"

From your acceptance, from your never pressuring me to not think. From you.

I gave it to me.

And so because you let me think, I didn't need to, and my mind grew, sometimes still,

In the quiet.

Thank you! I wish you were here to help me calm myself now, for I, on occasion, still think,

Myself, into fear.

But maybe that's a good thing, from time to time. Maybe if people like myself had been busy with scared instead of amused, maybe if we hadn't been so suspicious, so lacking in support during Clinton's tenure, maybe he would have behaved differently and then maybe the war would have been averted? Maybe if we'd been supportive he'd have been brave, because basking in our support it would have required no courage to be brave, for in our loyalty there would have been nothing to fear, until he did, fear, taking a strong enough action to stop the terrorist trend, did fear, us, and our displeasure. Maybe that is how it went. And maybe, once the fear stopped him from taking conclusive action and preventing the future, the future became the thing to fear,

Because he had.

And although President Bush has been more decisive as a leader—formulating and following through with his plan to retaliate against the homeland devastation—admittedly—since an averted war cannot be proven—Bush, with his war to win, appears to be in a better position than Clinton—who only had a war to prevent—was. Thus,

Clinton must have feared much more than I can imagine, must have feared much, like trying, and succeeding, and no one—not even him—knowing, if he had,

Stopped...Any kind of something.

Rightly so, since a non-event, is just that; non.

❖ FOURTEEN ❖

And so because an event to stop an event appears like aggression and causes dissension while "unknown action causing an event avoided" is even harder to use as leverage for garnering votes, something a leader is morally bound to try and do if he believes himself right for the job, Clinton would have been in a kind of no-war, no-win situation: A reality which became a good-war, (their fault, not ours) good-win situation for Bush.

However, when I stripped away the politics and turned my head to look away from the leaders and see instead their people: no war might have been better for the dead victims in the planes, the Trade Towers and the Pentagon, who weren't just crash test dummies hit by weapons of mass destruction late at night after everyone had gone home. A thought,

Which led me to think of Clinton again, and I wondered something in a different light than I have otherwise heard myself think it. Maybe it wasn't that Clinton couldn't keep focused enough to keep his repeated promise to hunt down and punish the perpetrators of the various acts of terror during his time in office. Maybe we the people didn't let him.

Maybe it was we, who couldn't stay focused on such dreary priorities as death and decimation, maybe it was us—the masses—who interfered and didn't let him do his job. Maybe it was, the residents of America, not the media, nor Clinton's need for self-protection that kept him busy defending his manhood, marriage and integrity,

Instead of using it.

Perhaps we pushed him, caused him to stumble, then reveled in his graceless fall,

Until he buoyed up again.

I, head-down-hear myself wonder, what I've been wondering for some time, without noticing. Was it us? Even if the magic I believe in is wrong and there's no such thing as creating your own reality, was it still, at least partly our fault. Were we complotting conspirators? Us: the public at large in North America for whom the dead bodies that were an ocean away, weren't as fascinating, as the close up imagining of live bodies doing the squirm-and-sway.

Was it us,

Who failed to protect our way of life?

Is it our responsibility, shared,

By my fellow Canadians,

Also, culpable, albeit conversely, for their embarrassment without action against a Prime Minister that reneged a promise to allies and represented his constituents as cowardly unreliables? Canada's Prime Minister, Chretian, whose cowering in plain view gifted me with a new vantage point, and the realization that I must learn to be what I wished he were: proactive and leading head on. I must use my voice, if I wished my children to,

Learn, to speak,

Out, with their hearts.

Was it all of us who at various times in this complex process failed to protect our way of life?

While fooling ourselves that we were protecting our way of life?

Was it us that pressed the then President into unveiling himself on the highly rated (by our mesmerization) Kenneth Starr Talk Show of the American court?

Did we teach Bin Laden—by displaying our determined decadence – the weakness in our system? Did we teach him, the way we teach our children, to become educated delinquents, maneuvering their way around the courts, manipulating the repercussions and the rules?

Schooled by the system,

Instead of screwed by it?

Did we? Forget to screw Bin Laden?

Out of any opportunity to be his contagious cantankerous self, teaching hate filled opinions, attitudes and beliefs that reinforce, and feed, and spread, his nihilistic disease?

Is it possible to war against the nihilistic without evolving into them, without also coming to hold that the other group's existing social and political institutions must be destroyed in order to clear the way for a new state of society? Is it ever possible to fight without joining in?

If my experience contains the answers, I would guess, it is not.

And pondering my experience passes my mind over the talk shows and the lessons they taught me: about pretending to be one, to catch one, leading to catching only myself; for I'd become what I'd pretended to be which was what I was out to catch: a phenomenon that occurs no matter who's deceiving who to catch who at being who. And I ruminate over learning to let it go, to accept the loss, perchance to win. And I think about the world I live in as it takes shape outside of me and jumbles together in a mixture of events:

As I think about the phenomenon of becoming what I pretend and then hating myself for becoming what I hate; like some of the terrorist planers whose rigid morality ruled that full body clothing – including total face coverings—must be worn by all women, it seemed to me that I was like those terrorists who evolved into us. They, the airplane terrorists, were like a society of peepers into other peoples sex ; as they languished, over and over again, looking into naked woman after naked woman in the intimate environment of the American strip bar before flying to the deaths of man upon man upon man upon man. I'd become like them- peeping into other peoples motivations and finding them dirty, setting myself up as henchwoman once I had fulfilled my duties as judge, jury and undercover police- except I had changed my mind when it came time to "wield the axe", "write the book", "fly the plane," because I'd gotten caught in the act of pretending to be and given myself the opportunity to look again.

But even more than being like the terrorists I reminded myself of those college student documentarians that dissolved into my family, that hung and played and pretended ally by pretending friend, that encouraged questionable activities like the black market selling of cigarettes so that they could catch me selling, so that they could gain from their exploitation, of me and mine as we obliged their request, though it would be them—our partners in crime—that we sold them to. As I thought about my used to be in college "friends" they reminded me a lot of every John who ever disdainfully called a prostitute a whore, who ever, while soliciting the purchase, avowed his own superiority over the behavior of solicitation. And they reminded me of me, declaring that the talk shows I was faking to get on, were deplorably fake, while believing I wasn't.

And finally I felt like Dana, in more ways than apply to this book length letter of love.

"How often have I tried to create something for me at the expense of someone that I thought I might save?" I wondered. But then, as I remembered Dana punching out my children's self-esteem in the name of opportunity, I decided not to search myself for the answer. And all of it all, jumbled together, becoming the same as I was, as they were, as they pretended to be, me, whom they despised. And vice versa. All of us becoming the thing we loathed and then loathing ourselves, while blaming the other, for calling us into it.

And so we struck at the loathsome and in doing so we struck at ourselves, in the form of others.

I, and I'm sure they, wanted to be the good guy. But there wasn't one, there were many, in fact all—depending on where you stood—were, the "good guy." I suppose that's true of everyone who spies: Each belongs on the side of right to about half the people involved.

So we spied on, and plotted against each other in the name of getting even, even though there is no such thing, even when we think there is because it feels as if we did just get even. Like when sweet Henry's killer died and I felt even, even though Floyd's death had nothing (except in my fantasies) to do with me. Or like feeling revenged because the "Spin" article was published, telling my truth about Dana and all the people in her vocation, feeling closure as though I'd evened the score, even though, the article possibly, never affected Dana or anybody else in the least. Feelings all generated by the emotional mathematics concluded in my head feel real, for in fact they are always only that for everyone.

Always, my feelings are uniquely real, like feeling freed by my decision to vacate the politics of the educational system by home schooling my kids; an act that would, for some people, be the opposite of freeing. My feelings of freedom though, were so strong they bubbled out of me, creating, growing, gifting, their power, to my children who began to learn. I was convinced, that it was the system that had imprisoned us, rather than my beliefs, about what the system should be and how I should feel if it wasn't. I was wrong, even though I was right.

So closure and the freedom to move on, is a decision I have made and can make, at any time, for any made up reason. Still, I selected keeping the dead past alive inside myself whenever it seemed proper to do so, because of my beliefs. Thus, it was my beliefs, not Clinton or Bush or the Talibans that I ought to have defended myself against in order to create free, so that I might benefit in the fallout of the 9/11 events, by choosing to gently go to war with my own upside down pyramid of ideas. And I wondered if Kenneth Starr who salivated so salaciously over the details of Clinton's amorous encounters might not some day read these words and reconsider obsessing over sex in order to fight obsessing over sex as I learned again and again to stop pre-deciding the outcome, and to watch or not watch the proceedings, in the world around me, for new reasons, rather than simply to reaffirm, that I should not watch. I closed and rubbed my weary eyes.

The darkness behind my lids was blast brightened as it flashed on that image of the second plane injecting itself into the not-yet-an-inferno tower.

It occurred to me that erasing the cruel presumption of pre-decision against, might be some good advice for Mr. Bin Laden as well.

If only laden Laden had been paying a less prejudiced kind of attention to our open book society. Maybe he'd of liked us. Certainly he'd have at least learned, how to put a smile on the face of his opinions of our,

Underdressed Silhouettes of America.

Just as his terrorist planers did. Perhaps all he really needed, was a closer look, in order to feel, better, kinder, happier, unburdened, relieved, by,

The vision of an experienced non-virgin, kickass, lotsa lovin naked American girl (or boy if he preferred).

Because sex in America, as in most of the free world, will lighten your laden load every time, as long as you're not our,

President,

Or a puritanical, radical, planer, with guilt and duty and rhetoric in your eyes, blocking your vision, from the beauty of what you see, and forcing you to hate the people that showed it to you.

Every aspect of America The Beautiful is,

Only to those who let it be.

Right, Jeff? Hey, can you imagine how equally cranky Americans would be if our women hid their faces and weren't allowed to screw?

Because after all, screwing,

Is what I was originally talking about,

And something I personally define as,

Placing the penis in the vagina. Because, that is, the understood definition.

And if copulation,

Which Webster defines as sexual intercourse,

Is the only thing Hillary has deemed inappropriate for Bill to perform with someone else, then maybe,

Except for the fabrications that were made in order to hide such a socially rebellious approach to marriage,

There were no lies that we didn't ask for, told,

Under oath,

By the Clint-ewinskies,

In regards to sex.

Maybe all that happened was we came face-to-face with the moral dilemma of wondering whether or not a good president even has to be moral sexually, according to us, and our varying definitions of what that might be. The thing about moral dilemmas in regards to seeking agreement amongst the views of many is: they can't help but be dilemmas, since a dilemma means to be unsure of which way is right and though each individual may be unconfused as to their own answer, only a citizenship of one has any chance at finding no opposition rocking the boat of its hard held ideals.

Anyway all the conjecture was fun, for us. That's why controversy sells.

And thinking about moral dilemmas reminded me of the ironies buried deep in the lessons of one of mine: the Cigarette Selling (to do or not to do that is the) Question. It was in the early 90's, back when the Canadian government raised the price of cigarettes to—in some places—as much as $7 a pack. I had the necessary connections to go into business selling black market cigarettes at wholesale prices. Many of my friends wanted cheaper smokes than were available in the retail outlets and saw no "bad" about it if I was willing to help them out. I was a reformed smoker and hated to contribute in any way to the continued health of the cancer causing industry that had killed my father and that the government seemed to be trying to squeeze out. "*It seems wrong!*" I worried to a fellow colleague who pooh-poohed my objections, greatly amused over my misplaced morality.

"People are gonna smoke anyway. At least if you help them now they'll be able to afford the cancer treatments later." She laughed.

"*What are you talking about? We have socialized medicine.*" I retorted.

"True." She paused, "Well, anyway make sure you get DeMaurier Kings."

She certainly hadn't convinced me that it was an acceptable thing to do.

However, even though **she** hadn't convinced me it was acceptable, **life did**, when, while visiting you, Tsara wrecked my brand-new blue station wagon and left me another $10,000 in debt without a car. At that point, with the temptation to sell grown bigger, I found a way to justify the act. I got the idea that using illegal dollars (bad) to help fund the prison tour (good) could turn my answer inside out. I had found a way to make amoral moral by using it as an artistic tool within the docu-drama to illustrate the theme of turning something bad into something good. I was truly proud of myself for being a good enough bullshit artist to pull the wool over my own eyes.

However, at the time when I began the project; feeling perfectly justified to sell the cigarettes and sacrifice a few lungs for the greater good of educating a society into breaking its own patterns of assumption and teaching them to think again; I began getting more media attention than ever before. Consequently a few of the people smoking my black-market brand decided they wanted a little attention too. They began pointing at my immorality as if they themselves would never have done such a thing (which is true since they didn't have the connections). Then the law changed as a result of the pressure people like me put on the government by lightening the weight of their alcohol and tobacco-tax coffers. I'd helped to change things by spreading the wealth.

I began to feel like a modern day Robin Hood alleviating the immediate problems of the lower classes as my inner circle of friends touted my subversion as heroic. They extolled my virtues for changing the face of things while I awoke from my justifications to realize that my short term experiment was about to have long term results: Canadian children by the scores would be able to smoke cheaper now, possibly for good.

And it occurred to me that the concepts of right and wrong were much more abstract than the concepts of legal and illegal. Because, even though the law had changed to a position of sameness with me and my activities by dropping the taxes and returning the price of tobacco to a more affordable level, that didn't make me right, I realized, as the effects of my actions rippled into the future. So, it seemed, my thoughts had circled all the way back to the question of whose morals should define morality. Comparing the two (what is or isn't ethical and what is or isn't against the law) is like comparing any of The Arts with Mathematics: math can be clearly defined and easily proved (and even that can be argued), while art is up to interpretation and cannot.

"So, perhaps" I thought, "cheating and whether or not you have, is dependent upon the arena within which it takes place: relationship or courtroom."

And maybe, even if Bill did play at sex with other women,

It was Hillary, the one who didn't get to have sex, who cheated,

By changing the rules,

By getting upset,

By not emotionally sticking to their agreed upon definition of inappropriate sex, for Bill? Like my cigarette-buying friends who couldn't stay decided about what was or wasn't right, for me to do.

And maybe, like me, Clinton woke up one day after he'd gotten away with it all, and realized that his protestations were a crock. He just shouldn't have done it.

Or maybe, I'm just making all this up!

Because, eventually, at some point, the fantasy I call truth ceases to matter,

Even to me.

And what I think becomes irrelevant,

For the true truth is,

Even if I don't agree with President Clinton's, "Her vagina never inhaled my penis" justification, if I believe that he might believe it, then the case is caught on yet another catch-22. And the crux of the issue becomes, what it always was, the audacity of any audience to assume, that it's beliefs about someone else's beliefs, should carry with it the power of accountability.

Perhaps it was that kind of audacity that carried Bin Laden over the edge of our horizon as he set out to punish us for what he perceived as our immoral crimes. He spoke to the world, in voice and in deed, possibly because like the priest or parent or talk show host sermonizing, he thought he had something important enough to say.

In fact, I suppose all of us think we have something important to say.

But that doesn't mean we have the right to force others to listen or even that we can, make them hear, the meaning we intend.

Still, making judgments is part of the fun of being human and at times I have become enamored of it even as it built the walls that curtailed my freedom and blocked out the horizon. In issues like presidential infidelity, occasionally it even seems necessary, almost as if it is our duty to judge, since that is what we do in order to vote.

So of course, since Bill was the President it was easy to get caught up in the idea that this societal audacity was acceptable because of the agreed-upon responsibility of person's holding a public office. However, the President is still only a person and since we can elect neither a singularly focused Cyclops nor a driven by singularity of purpose Cyborg, into office, maybe we should stop crying outrage at presidential humanities.

Maybe.

Who is right? And who is wrong? And who decides, the degree to which a punishment should be levied, for a crime perpetuated upon the beliefs, of the uninvolved? What is the difference, between the corrector, and the corrected? What is the difference when they all look the same?

All the men,

The women,

The Lewinskys,

The Clintons,

The Val and Ted McRenolds,

The purchased ones,

The rentals,

The sane ones,

And the mentals,

All resemble,

Me,

And Bin Laden,

To a T.

We all look the same when caught in the cloning of media makeover madness.

We all look the same unless the reporters,

Whose job definition and bosses demand that they have something new to say,

Want us to not.

So the media decides how they want us to appear,

In accordance with what the media decides we want to see.

And everyone decides what ought or ought not to be,

About everyone else, in society,

Right or wrong,

Assuming there is such a thing.

Reporters and readers comfort themselves and assuage their fears of reciprocity with the belief,

"That the public has the right to know:" A dogmatic statement that gives free reign to the news, when it's bogus, as well as when it's not,

To tell all, to all, all, ways, with flair.

The news mill, like the gossip mill, is forever rewriting itself, evolving, becoming, something, other than the apparently tangible story, from which the seedling grew. And sometimes that's OK. Sometimes. Like when my friends and I decided to play a practical joke on Howie Mandell, as payback for all the jokes he'd been pulling on his opening act Howard Busgang.

According to Howard, each night while he was on stage warming up the audience for Howie, Howie would, unbeknownst to the crowd, do something outrageous in an attempt to break Howard's concentration. Howie had been driving Howard batty with pranks; one time even going so far as to sit in the front row during Howard's act and shoot him repeatedly with a water pistol. It was time to turn the trick about. But, nobody knew what to do or how to phase the unruffleable Howie Mandell? "Nothing throws him," Howard insisted...After some discussion it was decided that something might.

I took off my top, removed my bra, put one foot on the stage and over my shoulder whispered, "*This should do it.*" I waved regally to the audience as I sauntered, moving at the pace of a royal woman walking, across the stage, just behind Howie Mandell. Howie may not have been thrown but he was, at least for a beat or two, definitely confused by the overt audience response, to something he knew not what. At approximately two thirds of the way through my bouncing, bare-breasted journey, he turned to face me, nose to nipple...and stammered. I think he would have recouped then and come up with something funny to say but before he could respond, Howard (whose warm-up act is reminiscent of Woody Allan's whiney, can't-get-a-chick-to-love-me routine) screamed, "WAIT!" and came running after me with his pants half down. The audience fell over laughing.

We'd done it! Howie was flustered.

The next day I was driving my kids to school when I turned on the radio and, while flipping channels, heard three sound bites reporting that some hotsy-totsy had run across the stage naked at the Howie Mandell concert. (Hey, I wasn't running!) I even listened to an interviewer asking Howie all about the Naked Lady Of Mystery. Howie appeared to know nothing about my identity and made no attempt to correct the misinformation in regards to my total rather than partial lack of attire.

Better for me, better for him. In this case since nobody was hurt by the fallacies in the story the inaccuracies were fun. Meanwhile, I pulled over and parked the car so that my guffaws would not jiggle the steering wheel and laugh me off the road. My children waited, accustomed, to their crazy mom.

Yes, in this case the inaccuracies were fun but sometimes they're not, sometimes it does hurt, reputations, and lives. Sometimes, being misrepresented or even simply represented in an unflattering way, presents people with an opportunity from which they may choose to commit rash acts. And the memory of such dramatic consequences brings to mind my often held beliefs that accountability and the onus for the presentation of ideas that grow rather than diminish or even purely reflect the minds of the populace, rests with the media. And I realize that if I am to return to the public forum, then that burden will also fall on me. Again I am afraid, to publish.

Though if I do, publish, I suppose I could protect my heart by returning to my previous head-in-the-sand newspaper habits and refuse to know what people have to say about what I have to say. For I take the news personally, even when it's not about me, imagine how I'll feel when it is, again.

Yes. Imagine how I could feel. Proud? There's a thought! I mean I guess, yaa.

Maybe proud? Hmmmm. Actually,

Maybe,

I'll keep my eyes,

Open.

It is a conundrum, a quandary, an unsolvable riddle and a bloody scary thought. I wanted to be alarmingly honest, to tell it all, even the bad parts and especially the fantasies because I thought it might help some other else, teetering on the edge of self loathing. I thought I might help them to walk the path of a healthier, more loving mind by teaching from my experience, not to bury feelings of rejection and loss but to instead recreate them into something new like opportunity and gain.

But it occurred to me that my revealings might instead be used for the total opposite purpose of titillation, and I might end up having a hand in creating just what I was trying to expunge by taking such a risk.

I worried, mostly, that my story might increase, rather than decrease, the number of pedophiles in our society.

Even though I believed, that a healthier me builds a healthier world,

It dawned, that I couldn't take the opportunity to help prevent the evolution of any victim enroute to becoming a pedophile, without also being willing to risk aiding, in the creation of another.

I supposed that this sort of dilemma was a constant state of being for the ever-evolving folks in the media; from whom we desire mature decision-making skills even while demanding that at least the visible participants be largely made up from the icons of youth. I felt a little like Clinton must have felt when pussy footing with Bin Laden, tempted not to do anything, because I knew that only the negative repercussions to my tellings were likely to be advertised by the media mill. While the people I may have helped, were likely (and wisely so) to remain hidden.

But then I thought about the time when, while waiting for school to let out, and with Rye in tow, I threw a chocolate bar wrapper out my car window. A female stranger came over, picked up the wrapper, crumpled it into a ball and, while shaking it in my face, lectured me on littering our world and reminded me that I needed to set a better example for my children. My cheeks burned red with embarrassment as I huffed and puffed and tried to make excuses for my faux pas. But I couldn't, because she was right! She had drawn my attention to a flaw that, I hadn't ever noticed in my character before. And I changed my trashy trash habits right there and then.

Though, by my reaction, she will never know that, she made a difference in my behavior. Now, though I do think unasked for advice when batted about on a continuous basis can be very abusive, still I have often benefited—mostly without good grace—from exactly that. So since that story is merely one example out of my life's many, I am reminded every time a similar event happens that standing up for ones ideas can have a positive affect. And then I try, to remember not to be afraid to avail myself of the opportunity to teach someone else (though hopefully I won't do it with so much crow bar and heavy wrench attitude in my approach) the things I have taught myself. More importantly though, than learning to teach without fear of the possible reactions of others, incidents of this nature have taught me to do so, void of the need to know, that I have, gotten the message across.

Being a part of the media has been like that for me: you put it out there and hope it helps, believing it will, knowing there's a good chance it won't, be understood beneficially. Sometimes it can feel like a no-win situation, especially if I look at it that way. But then, according to what I have thought in the past, so can being the audience, appear imprisoning, into fear. I, we, want accuracy and information, entertainment and silence. And we want it all NOW! Sometimes, like when the news media reported everything America planned to do to the Talibans even before it was done, I just wished the journalists would make it up, like parents do, telling us only what we ought to hear. Especially in situations like war of any kind, because chances are we are not the only ones listening. I wished it, until I considered the fact that I wouldn't be the one deciding what "what we should hear should be" and then I flipped opinions and changed to wanting it completely uncensored.

Thus I oscillated: wanting them to tell me, and wanting them to not.

However, in our system, and with our constitution, it's a no decision choice: the news cannot rightfully be stopped. So, we simultaneously inform the populace and give information to our enemies who, most appreciate, how generous democracy is with its military secrets.

A fact which, coincidentally, probably grants my no-longer-desired media censorship wish by pushing our sworn-to-uphold-the-Constitution government into protecting us by misrepresenting or possibly even lying, making it up, like any good parent would do(?), protecting us,

So that we can, in the future, still be alive to be aghast at their deceitful behavior,

Because, we believe that the public has a right to know whatever anyone can think of to tell them.

And those were the thoughts I was thinking as I watched Monica's persecution,

Mixed with the thoughts I was thinking as I read about the thoughts I was thinking as I watched Monica's persecution,

By every news celebrity and station that could find a way,

Meaningful or not, to cash in on the story.

And as I said, it was while I was watching that I realized; the apparent coincidence,

Of Monica's interview being broadcast at the same moment that I decided to search the television for advice,

Meant, something about me. And I knew I was once more,

Using the media to talk to myself.

And understood,

That very loud message,

Yet again: **Obviously, I believed in persecution.**

The evidence of my world had been gathered and I used it to point out as well as to fortify a belief that, any person or thing standing above the crowd as a symbol, risked standing within reach of the angry fists of discontent, some armed, some dangerous. I longed to follow the chosen path of King, Kennedy, Lennon, Ghandi and even Christ (or maybe Mary Magdalene). But I was afraid to be so visible, unsure of my ability to stand, unflinching, as I died, crumbling, like the towers, that were melted by our planes. And knew, that if I was afraid to, I probably would, suffer.

I closed my eyes on the visions of,

Planes and towers and people we no longer see,

And then I remembered that it didn't have to be,

This persecution way, unless I wanted it to.

Because there are no "have to's."

A fact with which, I felt certain, Neale Donald Walsch, author of the "Conversations With God" trilogy, and all the people who have been similarly affected by his work,

And you,

Who has heard me,

Tell of my experiences before,

Would agree.

And as I recognized my own complicity I found myself crossing the border between Canada and the States wishing we were just one big country. And something special happened, in answer to my wish. I raised my eyes to look at the girders above me and opened my soul to the sight of a banner, stretched across the bridge, flying between Detroit Michigan and Windsor Ontario.

There it was swaying in the wind beckoning my heart. Between my two worlds, were hands of peace joining them together and grandly displaying their intention to stay that way. I peered through the blur of the tears in my eyes at the Canadian flag and the American flag which lay on either end of the banner separated only by the words—"UNITED WE STAND"—and melded into one. I choked back and then gave in, to my tears,

And that was when I realized, my own audacity. I didn't know anything, about my country's politics and I had no business being ashamed.

It was a thought that could have helped me to re-choose ashamed,

But I was too busy experiencing awe.

And then I wondered, if there are no have tos, and we create our own realities, why had I chosen to create so many catastrophic events, with which to blow up life,

Just to be able to put it back together again?

And I wondered,

Can we not just live in a world filled with fluctuating positives? Can we not just ride the subtly shifting waves of joy for the sake of euphoria?

Without fearing ourselves petty?

Must we suffer in order to validate our existence?

And as I considered all the recent suffering, I feared my answer was, yes, though not necessarily so often nor in such heaping helpings of opportunities to hurt.

Still, the degree of how piercing the pain is depends on me—depends on how I validate my existence via my ideas about how I should feel – rather than the event I find myself aching because of. And so, knowing that, and feeling responsible to it, instead of crying I stood tall. I swelled my heart with pride, compassion and awe, for the heroes: the firefighters, police, citizens and military: all risking the sacrificing of one life, (their own), to save another, stranger's.

I felt changed, back, into someone I used to be,

As the pendulum swung across my mental screen Etch-a-Sketch erasing my past beliefs about my past reactions to those parts of my past, filled with:

> The married minister who invited the little girl me, to open her mouth, so he could caress her teeth,

> The other minister who, after his wife sent him to comfort me in my home because my husband had deserted me used his position as confidante with God to manipulate me into pleasuring him with my nineteen year old hand,

> The police officer who took sixteen-year-old me out on a date and then flashed his badge whenever he was caught: speeding, feeding alcohol to a minor, handcuffing me to his cruiser and—deciding that I belonged to him—becoming my stalker, till he was reassigned out of province,

> The traffic cop who pulled me over (because of my Canadian plates, I suspect) and falsely charged me with driving my overloaded, could-barely-make-it-past-fifty-

miles-per-hour, on her last legs van filled with children; at 99 in a fifty. He refused to let me see the radar and instead took us, immediately, in spite of the fact that it was 2AM, to see the judge who threatened to incarcerate me and put my kids in detention centers unless I shelled out $250 right then and there. I did, which left me broke and entrapped me into financial creativity in order to make it home,

The doctor who explained the operation he would be performing on my stomach while talking about my heart as he squeezed and fondled my breasts and reacted shocked by my objections, as though this were normal procedure. So, I reacted embarrassed for objecting,

The gynecologist who, without my permission, invited fifty students into the room to watch, me scream, while all the interns took a turn, pushing the part that hurt, inside my vagina,

The teacher who molested my son,

The coach who molested me,

The Dads who molested a lot of us.

And all the other things that picked and picked and picked away, at my naivete, eroding my attitudes, towards every uniformed or authority figured, they.

But they picked no more.

I felt changed back from the person whose authority figure attitudes had transformed into ones of distrust, who had lost sight of the difficult parts inherent in all authoritative jobs and the strength of character it takes to do them. I felt changed back, away from, the someone who was careful of what she said, for fear of garnering attention from the people whose intention it was, I believed I was supposed to believe, to serve me. But I hadn't believed it because the evidence I attended to, the evidence against such a thought, mounted a wall of carefulness around me. It was from behind that wall that I began to speak selectively, telling only what I thought I needed to tell, in order to remain safe, and protect my family from any negative repercussions, my normally verbose personality might cause, in any given situation. I turned my back on the world. I hid myself from close contact, concerned that who we were might be misunderstood and thus found hateful. And as I shirked trouble I shirked the systems that had been put in place to help me.

I came to realize, as the pendulum swung, that those play safe attitudes that had cocooned and helped me, had changed, from good to bad. What used to heal had begun to hurt. I had in the first place begun my relationships with an open and trusting face. And then I lived, to discover that wrong. And the hiding that my life experience had in the second place allowed me to teach myself to do became the thing that the third place allowed me to teach myself was most likely to get me in trouble, and did. Like the time I hid my car (not an easy task) from the customs officials at immigration because the safety had run out before I could get back into the country and renew it. I knew it wasn't really such a big deal I just didn't want to have to cope with any customs interrogations. So of course I did, have to cope with them, not because they cared but because I'd been afraid that they would, which made them think they should. So, I ended up briefly incarcerated while they interrogated me (exactly what I had been trying to avoid) and thought to myself, "I knew they'd do this, no wonder I tried to hide the car!"

Unfortunately for Tsara who did not have her green card yet, she was with me. And trusting in me—her authority figure mom—she had gone along with my plan to avoid all the hassles she ended up getting. Tsara and her crying children were not only incarcerated, yelled at and left without water, they were temporarily kept out of the country I had come to love. And that's when I noticed: my way of protecting my children had a way of not. Perhaps I was the authority figure to be wary of. It came to me that it might be better to just decide what's right for me and mine, at every given moment, by examining the elements involved without any pre-decision about what might happen. Maybe then I would stop marrying myself to beliefs that set up my pattern of actions: actions that self perpetuated and caused the need, for that pattern of actions.

Maybe then I could jump ship and get out of the loop.

I began to change the order of things in my mind, back to chronological, in order to remember all the good parts I'd left out, of my memory banks.

I began remembering the whole thing, the other parts of the story; parts like that the Children's Aid people, who had so harassed us, were also the ones that gave me my children in the first place. And that, though both my father and my brother were dead they'd once been alive and warm in my arms. True, when I walked into poverty and began driving beat up cars I attracted the resentment and eyesore-annoyance of some neighbors who petitioned to be rid of me and my motley crew, but I also attracted the attention of many others who held us aloft, kept us from starving and tethered the rope we climbed ourselves up on. And then I remembered that most of this aid came from religious groups who didn't seem to mind that I was not. I marveled at how much room is left in the heart and mind of a person who is firm in their beliefs: how much room, for doing good,

Or doing bad,

Saving lives or taking them.

Like Mother Teresa, like Bin Laden,

All taking orders from God, A.K.A. many things,

Because religion is the business of beliefs and beliefs design people out of feelings and feelings cause them to act. I knew: my prejudice against Christianity often kept me from seeing the good even as I held my hand out for food from the ones I was judging. I decided to try not to assume, at all, about anything.

Changing the focus of the light on my memories, changed everything. It changed the light I saw the system in, changed the light I saw the me, of my past, in, and changed to light, all the darkness in my eyes. So, as I looked about me, at my past and at my present, my feelings changed from this to that and I saw things differently again, almost erasing the word bad from my perception, understanding that I could choose, correctly without it.

One of the things I focused on was the time I had tried to fund the prison tour by selling black market cigarettes. Suddenly I could no longer justify why I had ever decided to do that. Also as suddenly, I stopped feeling bad that I had: no longer needing to judge it as anything more than, something I did once upon a time. Still, even without judging it, I knew it was something I would not do now, because, at this point in my life I knew that I created my own reality. Thus, I must be able to create better ways to affect the same result, better ways to feel. And, leaving desperation out of the equation, I became a searchlight seeking, the beauty, to illuminate. I found it, in all the people who helped, others, called me.

I felt closer to the source, unburdened, young, as my respect for politicians, teachers, police, clergymen and doctors, returned. (I didn't mention firemen because I'd never known a fireman to do me harm. Thus, they never were outside the focus of, my admiration.) And, as filling myself with respect returned me to my childhood opinions, my actions changed:

I stopped ducking the traffic police and customs officials. I put on my seatbelt and prepared to declare the smallest of items; anything at all, that I may have purchased abroad. I became grateful for security and immigration and soldiers and police. I found myself happy to be given rules, laws and orders, searched or interrogated, all for the cause of keeping me, us, safe. Suddenly, for the first time in years, I appreciated the system and why it was there: Finally, I had come to believe that it was my friend. I emerged like a butterfly, proud of the wings that proved I was new and reminded me to fly.

I felt warm in that brand-new old something I used to be when I was young.

It was a feeling of completeness re-becoming the person I had started out as in life but with the added element of experience. Good to be the one for whom a uniform meant comfort and safety instead of annoyance and the threat of an irritating inconvenience. Joyous not to see getting caught as a type of persecution that, because I had drawn it to myself by breaking the rules, was my fault in the first place.

Thank you, Osama, for I like this new me, comfortable in her own skin and proud to be a part of the flow. Thank you, Osama, because I like this new world full other stories just like mine wherein many have responded to this crisis in a similar way. "Thank you, Osama, because I am now someone for whom bending the rules has turned from being the only way to be, to being the way to avoid." And as I walked the streets plump with all the other others who were filled with gratitude for our defenders I felt strong in my belief that my beliefs helped to make our defenders strong enough, to not have to defend us and that let Clinton off the "it's all his fault wishy-washy hook."

Thank you, Osama, for being willing to be the devil so that we might earn our wings.

It seemed that it was easier for people with a common enemy to feel common to each other. So, as even many of this world's leaders joined hands, it strengthened our unity and let us separate apart from the "evil" we chose to eradicate, the "evil" that Osama had chosen to be.

He stood in the middle of our circle of hands, with all of our focus upon him, and took the role of different from, us. In the face of this difference, the animosities that joined the rest of the people of the world, withered. And I wondered why we couldn't have simply behaved like this all along,

Even though I knew the answer.

I listened, opening my ears to the whispers in the world, within my world, and heard:

"There are no heroes without danger, no ghosts without death, no smiles without facial muscles, nothing stands alone and all support systems lead down the path toward the opposite of where they began. And so we end up at the beginning, every time, a little richer. Life is never stagnant, even when it moves too slowly to feel."

"Yet," I wondered, "Why?"

"Why do we always attach things to their opposites? Why can't we find another way other than suffering in pain just to feel joy?"

I knew that a broad understanding of these things was what painted the backdrop, for the why, of this turbulent tower time, in my own personal existence.

I understood the generalities.

But I wanted an answer to the specifics.

So I stopped writing and allowed the answers to come.

I closed my eyes,

And saw:

That indelible image of two towers. With one already in flames, and the other about to be, the second plane approaches, with the absolute deliberateness of suicidal bliss. It buries itself into the second tower. And I got it. I got that for me, the message is about hate of self, and lovers and being happy.

And I understood, as I have understood about other things before, all the somethings good that will continue to flow from this horrible something bad.

And wondered, if the reason those ghostly images of people jumping from the tower were haunting me now—just as your image haunted me then, back there in the cabin, watching Monica Lewinsky talk—was because I was wrong in my assumption about myself. Wrong, that I could do it: be brave enough to jump, in, to tell these truths about my most intimate thoughts. Wrong! That I could tell it, even to you.

For though I'd been buried in anonymity, hidden from public scrutiny, safe, free to see life in any way I chose, I hadn't remembered to hear the continued harmonics of life for one, let alone two, of the last few years. How was I going to do it now? And then I realized that I was going to do it because I was going to relearn what I had forgot, and that, that's why I was here, editing this book, in the same way that, that's why I had been there, in the cabin, looking at the TV and writing it.

Apparently, after I learned the lessons of this book the first time, I forgot,

That one has to remember,

To know,

Everything they've learned,

Every single day.

And I saw that the problems and the deeds left undone were once again mine. For in forgetting everything that writing this book had taught me I had made the journey and then lived, as though I'd not learned to swim in any direction other than still, as I hastily treaded water to appear busy.

And suddenly a great excitement swept through me. I realized that, all solutions to all things throughout our world are created from our beliefs. And I realized that I wrote this book for everyone, including me,

To read, to edit,

To sleep, to breathe,

So that I could once again learn,

What the writing of it taught me.

So that I might find myself,

From a new perspective,

Again.

I could hardly wait to turn the page.

To drop my editors pen and go back to the moment,

To relive,

To re-experience,

With virgin eyes,

That answer,
That enriched the soil from which I and the world I lived in could become,
Anything,
So that this time I might finally learn, into antiquity, the impossibility,
Of humanity's dischord, laid against the other impossibility,
Of unrequited love.
And so I read.

❖ FIFTEEN ❖

"Conversations With God," book one, was SMack's gift to me so that, I could find my way to letting go of you, though at the time he had no knowledge of your existence. He merely knew: I'd be helped by the book.

Just as he had been helped,

Into,

Letting go of Lisa,

Though he had no knowledge that being immersed in its pages was how he had gotten free of his obsession.

That book laid the concrete on the road I would travel,

To you,

And him,

And me,

And this love letter book that that book released,

Out of its prison,

Called my heart.

The philosophies Walsch shared supplied me with two great learnings; one of those learnings was the catalyst for Colorado and the other, well the other was the answer to a question I'd long been asking the universe about the reason behind a pattern, of mine.

And the answer came,

One day while I was alone in Deja's apartment. It was about the third or fourth of January, 1999 when I finished reading what I've come to refer as "The God Book." It had been an inspirationally intimate journey and as I neared the end I found myself crying and laughing aloud from the sheer emotion of being uplifted into the unencumbered freedom of spiritual ecstasy.

I closed the book and sat,

Still,

Feeling,

The joy,

As it morphed into something else.

I got up, paced, and pondered. Somewhere in the stillness I had heard an unacceptable, to me, concept presented by the book. I was confused, bothered.

How could words with so much truth still carry warnings of inescapable persecution for anyone who chose to be a master of spirituality?

My mind balked at the possibility of such an absolute law.

I opened myself and asked for a response.

Within minutes the answer came and I understood. I decided to talk to my Oversoul: the energy essence that, I believe, some people mistake for God.

My Oversoul, I knew, must still believe in the persecution of messiahs,

Or my world would not behave as it did.

I considered the sound of such a concept.

But first I laid my knowing against my believing,

To see if they matched.

I paced circles on the living room rug, contemplating my theories and trying out my logic to see if they fit. I searched for my beliefs so that I could discover the effect they were having on my emotions, and hence my reality, so that I could decide whether or not I thought they—my beliefs—served me.

So that I could decide,

Whether or not I wanted to keep them.

This was a method taught by The Option Institute for coming to understand how we motivate ourselves and what causes our emotional responses.

I used the method both with my spiritual and my earthly beliefs.

Though lately, for me,

The chasm between the two worlds,

Within and without,

Was quickly closing and becoming one.

I internally followed the thought paths as one idea led to another, finally uncovering the hidden obstacle upon which I was constantly stubbing my spiritual toe.

And at the moment that I discovered the previously hidden obstacle, and thought of the analogy "Stubbing my spiritual toe" my physical toe began to scream and burn with pain as if to underline the authenticity of my internal discovery. Without cause or accident the bone splintered on the big toe of my right foot and when the sharp pain and burning faded a chronic numbness that refused to heal was left behind.

Until just now, when I decided to tell you about it and wrote that sentence:

The numbness faded and the sensation of normal feeling returned.

Amazing! But, not really a miracle healing, just me using the physical world to talk to myself again.

And talking to myself is exactly what I was doing at Deja's as I continued to search my psyche for an understanding of my place in the universe.

"OK," I thought, "Let's go through this."

"Every time I get an idea about some movie or book or television show or song or poem I want to write, if I don't do it myself within six months it'll be done by somebody else."

This in fact had been happening with so much regularity that every time

I opened my mouth Tsara would say, "You better hurry up and do it. You only have six months to beat the competition." Remembering her teasing tones, I chuckled to myself,

And continued to pace and think and talk out loud.

"What causes that miraculous creation of my ideas by others? All right, the hundredth monkey and collective unconscious and all that is a relatively good explanation for this...?" I snapped my fingers and searched for a word. *"Phenomenon, I guess? But——"*

I became more and more animated, *"But the whole thing feels more, me directed than that!"*

I was waving my arms and vocally emphasizing certain words, immersed in the drama of seeking the answers. I was enjoying, enjoying the drama, which as you know, is true to form for me: a fact, which even my grandchildren, who call me Dramma, have realized.

"Truth is it feels like I'm creating the work, writing it, performing in it, whether by my hand or not." I insisted to myself.

My daughters and I often joke that I should actually do the physical work on one of these inspirational money making projects I conjure up.

They insist that, if I'd only finish a project and make some money, they could teach me how to shop and then we could all be benefited and thrilled into learning by the "bucks" bombardment of success. We laughed and chided each other as they vowed to help me spend, those little numbers on a piece of paper, called cash, or check, or I.O.U.

"So," I thought, "Everyone in my life knows that if I think it up it'll probably happen." Because it usually did. (In fact it still does. Like when I laughingly designed the necessary propaganda response The United States would have to perpetrate on the Afghanistan people in order to re-educate and recreate their opinions about America, a month before they began to do just that. I wonder, is that foresight, intelligence or some kind of psychic intuition?) *"What does knowing plot ideas and scripts for movies, T.V. shows and books in advance of their creation mean about me?*

That I understand audience trends? That I'm plugged into the artistic ether? What?"

I thought I knew.

"So," I continued to investigate the possibilities, *"If it is true that I am creating the finished product, albeit through someone else, simply by having the idea. Then, since I often don't realize I have ideas till I start talking about them as though I already had them, it follows that I have more idea's than I realize I have. HMMMMM"* I mused.

"I may actually already have all the ideas there are to have."

"That's a thought! OK, let's go with that. Accepting those weird coincidences of others creating what I conceive of as my own idea constructions creating others who create what I conceive and accepting the possibility that I even could know everything, maybe Science is wrong. Maybe we do use all of our brains."

"And maybe psychic reality has nothing to do with science."

"Maybe the real question is not how can we use it all but how do we come to understand that we already do?

How do we remember,

What we have decided to forget?

How do we access,

The Top Secret access codes,

To the secured areas within,

Our own minds, within,

Which the magic lies?"

And hearing myself ask the question I heard the answer, which lay in the asking.

It was easy:

I had simply to change my mind, and decide to remember,

What I had previously decided to forget.

And in knowing the answer,

I also knew that deciding to remember would change the game,

And the reality,

And make magic,

Wonderfully,

Commonplace.

But I wasn't yet ready to stop solving my problems in linear time so I stepped away from deciding to remember and returned to my fun of ruminating on idea constructions. *"If my observations are correct and accepting that thought is moving energy and energy as related to mass is already moving at, at least, the speed of light squared, making mass something like energy stilled,"*

"Then creating physical reality out of one's own idea specifications is scientifically logical."

"Now to prove that hypothesis, just add the constantly repeated occurrence of my ideas for stories and movies and self-help and skill development books and for computer software and business inventions and designs becoming materialized into this reality with no help from me."

"Then,"

"I suppose I could further hypothesize that if my mind is the projector and the film for the movies in my world,"

"Or more precisely the movie of my world, "

"That could mean that I am the author of everything there is,"

"Whether it has my name on it or not."

And suddenly I had two memories at once:

I was a young child in Sunday school listening to the Bible story wherein God and the devil were messing with some guy, tempting him to make a choice between infinite riches or infinite wisdom. I was only a child but all I could think was, "It's just like that stupid the Genie story! Wish for the magic! Where's the confusion? In this story the magic is the brains." I never understood,

As a child,

Or even now,

As a rememberer,

How the choice of whether or not to know, how, could be a dilemma.

I never understood, despite the fact that I had, only moments before, had the same dilemma and decided not to know.

Because knowing would change the game I wasn't done playing.

The second memory was more of a revisiting,

To a vision I often gave myself as I fell asleep.

I would imagine a cone-shaped library containing all the existing knowledge for worlds upon worlds upon worlds upon worlds.

The walls were coated not with books but with molecular energy cells of information that were,

Easily infused,

Into me,

And I looked like a whizzing comet,

Zipping about with its glittering tail.

Swirling and swirling and swirling around

As I gathered up each morsel,

Round and round like a stick in a cotton candy machine,

Attracting every shimmering grain,

Building and building,

Till every minute particle of simple carbohydrate,

Thought,

Energy,

Was got,

And swallowed,

Absorbed,

Recreating me,

Till I was,

All the knowledge there is.

And this was the point at which I would, full of dreams, beliefs and ideas fall asleep knowing,

Everything.

Like at Deja's, when I re-experience-remembered,

Every thing,

About the everything.

Including the words on the pages in "Conversations With God,"

Which I hadn't yet read, although I had.

The memory was like a conversation of its own, a reawakening, dumping upon me the re-realization that I'd always known the contents of that book even before it was written. And still, because knowing the ideas, for me, means questioning the meanings, some of the passages within the book, "Conversations With God" nagged.

"OK, So let's keep going with this."

"Accepting that I create my own reality and that everything is just a thought solidified, although I already know everything, I can't stay aware of everything at all times because then there would be no way to experience the stories within. Is that true? HMMM? Why couldn't I experience them? HMMM? Well, because, there could be no story lines to experience without a point of view to focus on. And there can be no point of view without a narrowly focused awareness. So I have to let go of some of what I know. HMMM! OK, so that's why life seems the way it does, so linear and individual, even though I may be nothing more than thought, projecting all that is.

HMMM! I guess, if I created everything, tangible and intangible, then, whether I know it or not, I created that book.

OK, OK this is starting to make sense. So if I wrote the books then it follows that, just like when I watch TV, when I read I am talking to myself. So, if I don't agree with what I've said through someone else then perhaps that is the point. Perhaps I am teaching myself by revealing my areas of misdirected thought. Because if I only want to read what I already agree with why not just stand in front of the mirror,

For the rest of my life?"

"OK. That sounds good. Well, not the mirror part" I chuckled, *"That sounds like a boring invitation to make up all the beautiful and ugly parts of existence out of my own appearance. Just a little too self absorbed even for me."*

"So, let's look at the beliefs in this book, the ones that bug me, and find my misdirection."

"Unlike the God book I do not personally believe that anyone is ever "stuck" with persecution, they have to choose it. A truth like that should be even more evident in the life of a master, which is what the book said Jesus was. According to Conversations With God. Jesus was both a master and stuck, unable to tamper with the fated coupling of persecution and saintliness. That's just got to be wrong!"

"So, if I don't believe it why did I cause it to be written? Is the error in my thinking or in the writing,"

"Which is also mine,"

"Albeit through someone else's pen?"

Then I wondered, "If the book is me talking to myself then maybe so is my life. I looked at my own history and the patterns that I'd followed, the fear of persecution and societal prejudice and all the resulting real life dramas I'd endured,

And I saw it,

The lie about myself,

Revealed.

"There it is!! I am constantly saying people persecute me because of mine and my family's difference!! And of course since I say they do, they do. WOW! Aren't I wonderful to adopt those kids and suffer so on their behalf??? Man, sometimes looking at yourself

*can be embarrassing. No wonder I don't want to stand in front of the mirror. Well, look at that, apparently it **was** my reflection I was looking for!"* And I laughed and laughed and laughed.

"OK, Maybe I do believe in persecution, but I don't want to."

"And I KNOW I don't have to." I insisted.

I threw my arms up in excitement.

"I got it!" I snapped my fingers. *"I **am** talking to myself. I'm saying "You still believe in that. And so, you shall have it, even in this book.""*

I was exhilarated into exhaustion with the joy of this wonderful revelation.

Now normally the revelation itself would have been enough,

But this time when I plopped myself back on the couch, to revel in my spiritual after glow, something still bothered me.

"WHAT?" I asked myself with my hands in the air, *"WHAT?"*

And waited.

And remembered,

Something,

I remembered,

Often.

I remembered:

The time when I was seven or eight,

And still a visionary,

Because I was still close enough to my birth,

To have not yet decided,

To forget,

All,

Of me.

I was standing in the school yard, waiting for recess to end, talking with a friend, about God, Jesus, the Bible and how,

"If God is really the guy in the Bible then it's probably better to go to hell. I mean God kills babies and burns cities and turns people to stone. And he's such a bully he can't even forgive sins without killing his own kid. The Bible is stupid."

My friend's responses made me realize that I might not be making any more sense to her than the Bible was making to me, that not everybody hears, sees, or comprehends reality in the same way.

And in less than a fraction of a second I thought about,

The understandings, created by,

The chain of events, we think we see.

I thought about gossip,

And "General Hospital,"

And Perry Mason court rooms.

I thought about teachers who thought you were smart,

And frustrated parents who needed you to be.

I thought of how the world looks to short people,

And imagined how it looks to tall ones.

I thought of understanding less,

And understanding more,

And of what that did to all your understandings.

I thought of kids and cats and trees and bugs and the splintering into infinity of their various perceived realities and knew that none of these thoughts scratched the surface of the truth.

Then I thought of make believes and believe it mades,

And the boring redundancy in the lives of Dick and Jane and Spot and wondered if my classmates were reading the same book I was,

When WHOOSH!!

The walls of singular focus,

The walls that make our world seem real,

Turned translucent,

And melted away.

I have tried repeatedly to express the awareness I gleaned in that moment, to articulate the feelings and paint the picture of the vision, that stayed with me, in and out of focus, with varying degrees of intensity, nurturing me and answering my questions, for the next three days.

And each time I try to teach it,

I go back to that place,

And almost understand it,

All over again.

If you've ever pondered all reality while looking into the picture, of a painter painting a picture, of a painter painting a picture,

Or stood between two mirrors facing each other at an angle, and studied the slight differences caused by the barely perceptible change in position in each subsequent reflection of yourself,

Due to the barely perceptible change in your perceptual stance from the object of study as it recedes into the, no distance, distance,

Getting smaller and smaller and smaller and smaller,

Than we can see,

Though mirroring itself still,

Then you've got a base on which to stand while we imagine together the place I've been.

For that's what the world did, everywhere I turned, with each mirrored reality, having mirrors of it's own, from every conceivable angle and then on, into dimensions of angles we don't even have...though I saw them still.

And that was only the beginning.

As in each fraction of a fraction of a fraction of a second so close together that no time elapsed, every thought or thought of a thought gave birth to whole new worlds of images reflected.

And after a few dizzying seconds of my classmates filling up the spaces and crossing into and out of each other I managed to think on two levels and simultaneously carry on the conversation while retaining my immersion in this multi dimensional spirit play.

And in the inkling that I thought I had to carry the conversation in order to not frighten my friend,

I knew that I did not.

That she heard what she chose to hear, and that the sounds splintered in the same way that the images did,

As did smell and touch and taste,

All banging into birth in creation of their own realities.

A zillion, zillion choices to hear what she chose to hear,

And see what she chose to see.

And I saw,

Her decision.

She would experience what she chose to experience,

And I only had to worry about what she thought of me,

If I did,

Worry.

My world could cease, wait, freeze, call me crazy, kill me, care for me, whatever I wanted, while I chose to have or not have, this multidimensional experience.

I chose to have.

I walked in what my child's mind could only liken to the greatest grandest house of mirrors at the fair. I asked questions of the ethereal silence trying to learn from what I saw. I didn't talk or converse, I merely let the questions fly through my mind unformed into words. I thought of religion and science, human nature and never any math,

Because there are some things you just don't want to know.

I played with the clarity of the visuals, sometimes letting the physical world dim to nothing other times bringing it into focus,

Occasionally I froze the frames, often times I let the movie run.

Till after a millennium or two,

Of seconds,

Learning the nature of reality seemed,

Trivial,

And playing in the playground seemed a lot more important.

So I allowed three days to have passed, switched from the end of morning recess on a cold and cloudy day to the beginning of afternoon recess with a warm bright sun,

And feeling the need to put to words the last of my questions, I thought-spoke, "*But if it's up to me, why does my Mom hit me?*"

And so she did.

She hit me,

Not because I missed the point,

But because I hadn't.

I understood it to be my choice,

And knew the reason,

Had to do with my dad.

And also knew that even the reason,

Was a choice that could be changed.

And then I knew something more,

And forgot just what that was.

And in choosing not to remember,

Chose the path,

Of violence,

And allowed the molecules of,

Moving masses of thinking energy,

To un-form and fly away.

I was energized and awake, in the after glow of revelation.

I ran to my friends, to skip, to jump, to talk, to teach,

A lot of kids that thought I was nuts,

And a mother that just felt angry,

With my difference.

Eventually I grew quiet, knowing it didn't have to be this way, no longer sure why not, waiting until my language skills could match and hence impart my philosophical viewpoints,

Hoping I would remember what they were.

And as I was in Deja's apartment remembering this, I thought of Deja who carried none of my blood yet with whom I felt so connected, and marveled again at our absolute sameness.

I wondered if our similar child hoods had designed us into,

One person of different ages.

I questioned why being molested as a small child had been my,

Choice,

To share,

With her.

And knew that I had created her,

To love myself enough,

To try and save a soul like me,

From the anguish of any more,

Sameness shared.

Deja had given me the chance to give her what I had wanted to give myself:

A family to return love to.

And maybe that sameness is why Deja and I too often protected each other too much.

And thinking of Deja reminded me of Dakota's birth,

With awe.

Which took me to the thought of a child in a womb,

Coming from a child,

Who came from the womb of a woman ...who came from the womb of a woman...who came from the womb of a woman...who came from the womb of a woman in the ancestral chain of life...,

Till I understood the answer to the problem I had been pondering.

And that's why I stood up to talk to my soul,

Whom I knew was in the room with me.

I knew it because:

As I have grown and developed and tried to explain,

My version of truth in accordance with the revelation revealed, to the seven-year-old me,

I have studied dreaming,

And created new analogies to help impart my sense of things.

My most recent favorite analogy on the question of life after death,

Especially when teaching my children, whom I assume are just little versions of different parts of me attempting to understand,

Has been to dissect the experience of dreaming.

And the analogy picked apart looks like souls inside of souls as the awake person sleeps when the sleeper awakes.

For example, as the dreamer I create realities wherein the rules change at will. I am sometimes a watcher, sometimes a participant sometimes a man, sometimes a woman, sometimes each, all.

Sometimes I am,

Every,

Character,

Animal,

Thing's,

Consciousness.

And the sometimes,

And the combinations,

And the possibilities,

Are without end.

And as I dream at times I am aware of being the dreamer, at times I am not,

Now as I said when I used to explain this I was generally talking about death, and was using the analogy to symbolize that dying,

Is like waking up,

Back in your room.

Normally I go on to explain that the person in our dream is like the little wooden doll inside the bigger wooden doll,

And that perhaps we are all just a lot of dolls inside of dolls.

However, while sitting on the couch the memory of those teachings startled me into realizing that,

If I taught it this way,

It was.

And if I was the creator of my own parts,

Then the doll that was bigger than me, that was the sleeper to my world, would be using the free will I had given it through my belief in such an entity.

And in using that free will it would have formulated its own ideas about reality,

Possibly even based on its observations of my life.

My sleeper might be being taught by me the person in its dream,

Just as I am often taught by the person in mine.

And since my concerns and fears often form the background for the world inside my dreams,

Then my sleeper might possibly be having the same effect on me.

And my sleeper I assumed,

Was A.K.A. my soul.

So it followed that, my soul and I had to get in line, and cooperatively collaborate on our beliefs if, I wanted these experiences of self-proclaimed martyrdom, and persecuted cruelty to stop.

And as I understood that I needed to talk to my soul,

I felt its presence,

Never seen.

And told it,

That we didn't need to believe in persecution,

Anymore.

That helping didn't have to be chained,

To the sentence of hate,

And that since everyone could be a messiah,

No one had to be left out,

To feel resentful enough to cause us harm.

And then I explained that,

If we see the world beautiful,

It will be.

A lesson learned and quickly forgotten.

Lost in the living of the past two years,

Culminating in that catalyst of chaos,

Reminding me of my responsibility as the towers tumbled down,

Bringing me back to these writings to edit, and to relearn, how to blend the colors in my painted reality with no harsh lines or separations between the images.

And as I came to see, to understand how: all around me the world softened into supportiveness, reached out, held hands and unified,

Into One,

One at a time.

And just as back then, back there in Deja's apartment, when I experienced that conversation with my soul and I felt the world change, so do I re-experience the lightness of flying from within, every time I read about it.

The next time I looked in the book "Conversations With God,"

The words were slightly different,

For a while,

Until I rewrote my awareness, changed the lessons,

And forgot to notice that they were.

And since, back then, the Colorado quarrelling between SMack and his pillows and I happened just shortly after this mind broadening Oversoul experience, so shortly that, my brain was still running circles on the teachings of patterns,

It was easy to be the wise man on the Mountain, in the hotel room bed.

Because I understood. I understood, that one only needs to stir it all together in order to see the absolute nothing of the everything they're in. And so I saw the circling stuckness of all the self invented crappy zeroes,

And one by one,

I broke the loops.

It was like the game of first blowing and then popping the bubbles,

That evade and swirl about in the wind,

Seeking survival till the last possible second.

I attacked each created thought balloon with merciless vengeance,

There, in the mountains, laying on one bed listening to SMack sulking loudly on the other,

I searched my thoughts for the reasons behind all my choices in an attempt to stop this constant life long waffling of being blown about,

Caught in the warm wind tunnel of the changing moods of men.

I thought about all the things I already knew and all the places I'd learned them in.

I thought of my last similar revelation experience, a year and a half ago when-

I had been extended in every direction, trying to pay bills, fighting with ever-angry Chance, never finding time to teach Dar anything because I was too busy teaching his teachers who never seemed to learn. And because I was too busy making a living putting smiles on the faces of other people's "Happy Birthday Children"—

And remembered how I had gotten fed up with giving everyone but my family the best of me.

That was when I discovered, "Happiness Is A Choice" by Barry Neil Kaufman.

And that's when, as I read that book about choices,

And discovered that part of me was afraid to be,

Happy,

Afraid,

That if I were,

Happy,

There'd be nothing to work for. Afraid,

That I would give up on the system,

Quit playing with the teachers,

And play with my kids instead,

By taking them out of school, and influencing them,

All day long.

Afraid!

That if,

I were,

Happy,

I would just,

Smile,

Play,

Love,

Myself and,

My kids,

Freely,

Without strings,

Until all of us,

Liked who we were,

And learned,

At break neck speed,

That we didn't need,

To struggle anymore.

And I was also afraid,

That if I stopped fighting the urge,

And got happy,

And home schooled my children,

I'd never get any of my career focused work (The work that I was already not getting done) done.

I was afraid,

That if I was already happy I'd lose my strife-born drive and never become a movie star,

Which is what I thought I wanted,

Because I believed that,

Being a movie star would solve all my problems,

And make me happy.

The joke of it all began to bubble in my chest, which erupted with giggles.

"HA!" I thought reiterated, "I've been afraid to be happy because I wanted to become a movie star to get happy. And I believed if I was already happy I'd never make that choice and become happy.

I'd never want to set myself up for all the criticism and misery of being an actress,

If I was already happy.

I needed the extreme misery of living to help sustain me on the actor's miserable path that I believed I had to follow in order to not be miserable anymore.

Where would my perseverance come from,

If I was already happy?

How could I succeed,

And solve my problem of being unhappy,

If I was happy?

And how could I ever end this cycle of poverty I'd grown so fond of punishing myself with? If I was happy I wouldn't hate being poor and if I didn't hate it,

I wouldn't suffer enough to be motivated enough,

To make me want to get rich?

Which was the only way I knew of to ease the suffering, of self induced poverty,

So I could become Happy?!?!?!?!?

And I laughed, and laughed, and laughed at the sound of myself.

And laughing changed things,

Every time,

By disintegrating the thought rays that reduced my world,

Into a fast-food-style SMackburger and fries and re-acquainted me with the buffet style smorgasbord of pleasure that I called my life,

Laughing made me realize that even if being happy,

Meant I might become somebody with different dreams and beliefs,

Than the ones I had now,

So that I could be happy,

If I was already happy,

Then, I guess I didn't give a damn!

I put the book, Happiness Is A Choice, in a safe place and immediately set about changing my life by re-arranging my commitments,

So that I could stay home with my children all day long,

And play,

And live,

Happy.

I decided not to work, to live in an RV and, using the entire North American continent as my home, teach map reading and geography while I travel schooled my children.

And things started to happen.

The minute I decided to do the impossible,

By calling money from the sky, it fell on me.

It dropped on I,

The previous happiness chicken, little,

By little by little,

Miracle after miracle,

Making fantasies into realities.

And that's when the persecution stopped and people appeared, out of the most improbable of places, offering to give me money pay my bills and solve my problems,

While my choosing happy allowed playing with my children,

To make me happy and turned me into someone else.

With different goals,

Oh! Glorious day!

The magic of that RV happiness lasted for one full year,

Until I forgot how,

To just choose,

And remembered instead,

The socially understood romantic misery,

Of dissatisfaction.

And fell backward into the struggles.

As I lay in bed listening to Ted grunt and groan and SMack and throw his weight upon the bed,

I knew that somewhere I must have changed something.

Somewhere.. somehow...I'd fallen out of the winner's circle.

And landed here, on the top of the mountain.

I tried to remember when, so that I could remember why,

I curled up into the fetal position thinking of circles and Ohs and zeroes and woes as I attempted to disappear myself, into the bed in Colorado,

Where I was busily going about the business,

Of bursting bubbles.

I analyzed, contemplated and looked for answers.

Where had I put the magic?

And why had I stopped believing in the ???? What?

When I FOUND IT!!!

There it was.

The not-enough-ness that the "Conversations With God" book had warned me about.

I had been self-creating problems not because of what I had stopped believing in but because of what I had started,

To perceive: A world of Not-Enough-Ness.

I had bought into the concept that there was not enough money, not enough time, not enough love, not enough clothes, not enough jewelry, not enough health, not enough kids, not enough homes,

And not enough, not enough, not enough,

Owns,

Everything it knows.

That's what I'd forgotten,

That you get what you believe.

So I created a new mantra to recreate with,

Every time Not-Enough showed its starkly featured face;

"*There's always enough, in fact there's a surplus.*"

I used the mantra, as I asked myself,

"*What do I want?*" and, "*Who am I?*" and,

"*OK maybe that's who I am but is it who I want to be?*"

And the minute I knew the answers new questions came.

"*Well, then who?*"

And I used the mantra every time,

Not-Enough jumped into the argument and tried to justify my patterns of financial fear.

And suddenly I didn't feel tied to my money-making married boyfriend anymore.

And despite SMack's angry energy zipping about the room a saintly calm overtook me,

While I made apparent logic-defying choices.

Void of financial resources,

Or solutions,

And for the second time in two years,

I chose happiness,

Chose liking myself and the family that I'd built,

Instead of practicality.

And went home to play with my children,

To change my life,

Back,

Into,

Something worth having. Again.

And that's when I noticed that changing, my life,

Had also become,

A pattern of mine.

But in trying to rid myself of patterns I came to understand that a world without patterns would be a world without sameness,

And a world without sameness would have no sense of familiarity,

Or difference.

And with no different from the same,

Illuminating the,

No path to follow,

There'd be nowhere to go.

So I settled into the idea that some patterns make the story,

Better.

Like on the way home,

While at the airport,

When I bought a lottery ticket,

Because that was what I did at the end of every relationship,

Since you.

Sometimes it felt like a desperate futile attempt to turn losing into winning and other times it marked the beginning of freedom and of walking away.

At the airport it felt like both.

I did buy the ticket but unfortunately I still couldn't remember what the winning numbers, I dreamt that morning when you took the kids to the zoo, were.

And not remembering made me feel fated,

To lose,

At my attempt to win.

But,

I bought a ticket anyway,

Because,

They only cost a buck.

"*And besides*" I thought, "*Maybe I'm wrong about all this spiritual stuff and finding money really is about luck.*"

I was using my inner tongue to deny my faith and hedge my bets and not feel crazy.

Like going to church, just in case,

What other people proclaimed as truth,

Was.

Such namby-pamby believing gives authorship to too many plot devices and always makes a big messy hodgepodge out of the life I design in my creation of the universe.

Yes! Namby-pamby believing makes a mess!

And I know that messy means losing because mess fills up the spaces and makes the world smaller,

Than the freedom of a win.

While winning against no one,

Exhilarates life into a clear and simple and infinitely there,

Single note of music.

I have all the answers,

I know that,

Some of the time.

But at that moment I was in the mood for the cacophony of noise,

So I denied what I knew and tried to believe otherwise.

I bought a ticket, knowing that the odds were against me,

And thus,

They were.

And actually, now that I think about it: that is the spirit with which I buy most of my lottery dreams.

Maybe I should change that,

Since winning millions of dollars has turned into a quest of mine; a goal towards which,

I buy five dollars worth of tickets twice every week.

Perhaps even the lottery is a pattern meant to keep you near me.

But I don't care if you are the reason I've decided to win the lottery.

Because the process of trying to figure out how to win the BIG ONE is a fun way to learn.

For example,

Every once in a while I am solid in my conviction that winning has nothing to do with the odds of winning,

But everything to do with believing in them.

So I try not to.

And if I succeed in maintaining my clarity then that's when I see clearly enough to purposely manifest and manipulate,

The result.

That's when,

I win,

Small amounts.

Just like my ex-husband, Jim, did,

Until he hit it big.

In fact the more I pay attention to life the more I realize that mathematical odds, like logic, are constantly defied and are therefore not logical.

And that's what I was thinking about,

Alone in the airport having spent my last dime on the Texas lottery and needing to get home.

And that's when,

Against all odds, my Visa materialized extra credit and I rented a car to get me there.

I began the two-hour drive to surprise my children, contemplating all the gambling influences of my thus far life:

I thought of the time when my father had spent too much money, been too extravagant, gone so far as to fly guests (Well, one anyway, he paid for my ticket.) from all over the country to his part of the world,

In order to give my mother, his longtime bride, a surprise party on her fiftieth birthday.

It was a party that she seemed to hate.

Once the festivities were over and I was leaving to catch a plane for home I noticed that my father seemed sad.

The sadness didn't feel related to my exit but rather to his wife's dissatisfaction and his own depleted funds. I saw the scratch and win tickets laying next to his hand on the kitchen table. I wished for him a winning scratch.

Then, 1300 miles later, as I walked through the door to my house the phone began to ring.

It was my bright and cheery dad,

Who had removed the gray film,

And won,

Happiness,

In the form of,

A brand-new,

Car.

This was especially exciting because to the best of my knowledge, my dad, who was a whole lot nicer than my husband, had never been the constant winner my husband was.

My husband won,

Little bits,

Often,

From everywhere.

He loved gambling. He enjoyed the thrill and believed in his own ability to pull "luck" from the air, building, building, ever building...Till he hit what was for us "The big one:"

One hundred thousand dollars from the 649 Ontario lotto.

He won money,

That he shared,

With the kids and I,

Only one thousand three hundred,

And not a penny more.

Because he was never one to see us as in need of comfort. Besides, he'd left me,

After I kicked him out,

For molesting my daughter, Tsara.

Be careful what you wish for,

Because wishes come true,

In some form or other.

Like wishing for opportunities to prove how much I love my children,

Which included wishing for opportunities to suffer for them because I wanted to pre-pay the dues that life would exert.

Wish upon wish of my wishes came true,

And I gained a new respect for wishes.

Be careful what you wish for,

You never know what shape being a hero will take,

Or how much ownership to the danger of the damsel in distress,

Belongs to you.

Like Tsara, the child I tied on the tracks in order to save:

Jim was not her father. I never would have had to protect her from him if I hadn't brought him into her life in the first place.

Of course, if I hadn't brought him into her life in the first place, I never would have had the opportunity to prove what a great mother I was,

By protecting her.

On occasion I wish that I still believed in fate,

That way I could remain blameless and not see how lacking in coincidence,

Coincidences are.

But then I remember that taking no blame for what happens also means taking no credit.

And that taking no credit means never learning from the result,

Of what I would then believe I had no control over in the first place.

Because, whenever I've bought into the belief in fate or karma or God's revenge it has ruled my world with coincidental misfortune,

That left me carouseling on the repetition of life.

And so I stopped wishing,

In my innocence,

And looked at my complicity,

In order to get off the ride.

And thus, the old believing was why I couldn't see the abuse between Jim and I, until it landed on someone other than me?

Because as I now see,

Until then the plan had been,

That I not see,

My own hand in the design.

And so, forgetting to remember that whomever I picked for me I picked for my children,

I brought the predator into the house to keep me safe,

From other predators.

I even went so far as to think that living in the lion's lair with a grizzly bear was good for us,

That it would sharpen our instincts,

That the fear would create a constant condition of being on guard,

And prepare my babies for the dangers of life.

Strange that it never occurred to me that,

When the danger ceased to hold us and we tried to get away,

Our protector might turn on us,

And eat one of my cubs.

He had been my champion,

My God,

My thinker for me.

Because he told me that he could do things that defied the odds?

And then did.

He was like a magic man,

Full of the sexiest,

Impervious force,

Of will.

And when he told me things,

Like that he was going to win the lottery,

And then won the lottery,

I stood in awe of his power, and bent to his desire.

He seemed omnipotent,

Especially since I still didn't know that he was so,

Simply because I had written it that way by believing he was,

And not knowing it was so,

Had simply believed,

He was.

It made me afraid.

Mostly because,

Though this may be hard to understand,

I didn't want to win large amounts of money.

I was terrified that we'd get sinfully rich without sufficient suffering first. I wanted us to be piously grounded in humility lest we become television's stereotype for the wealthy, the worst of all things: a family full of selfish, snotty, horrors.

Embarrassed that we might be seen as the kind of people who wanted life to come easy.

Sad to be cheated of the possibility of paving the road to success alongside my husband.

Every time Jim bought a ticket I would feel the threat of impending doom,

Until he checked it.

And the loss,

Or small win,

Brought relief.

But the relief was fleeting,

As he bought,

Another one,

And checked it,

And another one,

And checked it,

And another one,

And checked it.

And ...so it went.

Until, I bored of inventing ways to survive poverty,

And changed my opinion on the attributes of wealth.

That's when,

The mental anguish I self induced with every purchased ticket,

And the wished for suffering of poverty itself,

Lost its attraction.

Though, it continued still,

As I moved into the next phase of wishing,

For wishing for money.

While my husband,

Who was ahead of me a phase or two,

Actually won.

The day that he left me.

And finally,

I knew it to be because of my believing more than because of his.

For every nuance of every phase from every angle,

Was just another lesson for Lynette.

And the deja vu dizzied me with advance recognition,

That I didn't yet recognize.

Jim bought a ticket on the day that he left me.

And followed the pattern I would later create.

However, unlike him,

When I follow the pattern,

The winning continues to evade,

Because I am still stuck in the wishing to win,

Of the lottery-buying phase.

Still stuck, despite the evidence that should give me the tools to free myself,

Into riches.

Still stuck,

Even though my husband's temporary financial affluence has already made it obvious to me that I had a part to play,

In Jim's acquisition of the long-sought-after pay day.

Because he hadn't been able to win until after he left me,

For I had wanted him to not.

And the day I recognized that, was the day when,

The guts of my journey towards spiritual enlightenment began.

And that's why,

For me,

Learning to win means I am rewriting effectively those previously held Christian beliefs that affluence or opulence or health and prosperity mean,

That I am not the good little martyr I ought to be.

Martyrs suffer,

By losing now,

So they can win later,

Acting as though,

Constant winning,

Does not exist.

And though I see no error in my concept of martyrdom,

I note a grave one in my belief that I ought to want to be one.

Because what I had meant to want to be, was a savior,

Not a sufferer,

Needing to be saved.

But then even being a savior is only possible if there are creatures who suffer.

Creatures like my disabled children who had to be disabled in order for me to help them to be not,

Who they were when they arrived. Thus, choosing to be a savior originates the need for suffering.

And as I read, in order to edit power words like "Savior" and "hero" I found myself reflecting on the recent deaths of the firefighters, postal workers, police persons, citizens, and military,

Never saved while saving, heroes.

I wondered if pushing away from myself over the past few years this decision to be a hero, gave the job to all these someone elses,

In an arena that never had to be.

Maybe even these lessons could be seen as lessons for Lynette,

Given to myself so that I might see,

The face of heroism and be moved into making a new choice. A choice wherein,

Nobody suffers.

A choice that in itself could fulfill my wished for destiny of saving the children,

That never had to hurt,

Quietly without fuss, by removing the existence of danger.

By removing it so completely that no one would know anything about anyone being saved, giving birth to a strange kind of true heroism void of kudos and Hallelujahs,

And any need to hero.

And, I suppose, that would make the life choice of being a hero, somewhat, uninspiring.

And I thought again of Clinton, uninspired to prevent ...and realized that in this new world he would have needed none, no inspiration, for there'd have been nothing to fear.

Perhaps such a world incarnate would sacrifice not only the hero's role, but also the joy of inspiration that brought him to,

Want,

To remove the pain and suffering,

Of others,

In the first place.

Perhaps we lose,

Even more than that.

Perhaps we lose also the joy of healing and the quest to understand.

And as I made note of how filled our lives are with these co-dependencies, I wondered what we would end up with, how we would live in such an empty utopia. And having no frame of reference for imagining such a world, I found myself once again revisiting the fear of total happiness.

Though happiness was the thing,

I and every version of me,

Desired most.

After a few deep breaths the fear dissipated and I contemplated the world unity President Bush was managing to (at least momentarily) gather around our victims. I found myself thinking him a heroic leader, re-arranging the world into something we'd never seen before and, realized that sometimes the unknown is friendly and should be embraced. Like this, The New World, made new all over again, as through the pain, we mixed happiness with pride and erased the discomfort. This new, awesome, previously unimagined, world, felt better to me than the one that came before, in spite of the fact that, I didn't have any frame of reference for it's creation, in my eyes.

Or perhaps I did have a frame of reference, in those enjoyed by me futuristic movies which displayed a time where-in world leaders would govern whole planets,

All around the universe.

But movies are just a game of pretend,

And so, I believed, is this new, world unity,

An illusion,

That merely exists,

Because it doesn't.

We only came together strong, arm in arm, as one, because we had an enemy to defeat and,

An enemy from within the world united,

Cuts us in two.

Which seemed preferable to the millions of pieces we were in before,

When we closed one eye to not be bothered to see the world as all divided up,

While the terrorists attacked insidiously from within, like bowel parasites in our feces.

So the parasitic enemy, with its fermenting beliefs twisting up their hearts and pumping out their poison, gassed up our bellies, bursting through the intestinal wall and breaking down our guts: they sprayed our own feces upon us. We were left to fester in a public pool of putrid persecution: infected pus within which only the parasite-turned-sewer rat could languish. It was this hatred, this fermenting rot growing like a cancer in our bellies that, not wanting to wear the tortured faces of our enemies,

I think we feared contracting. Though, since we'd already swallowed the cyanide of revenge I feared we already had,

Become the same,

Contorted,

By the more poisonous than Anthrax,

Symbiosis,

With Suffering.

We'd become the same yet different,

Like the mirror and the image it reflected.

We did appear at first sight to be using hatred against a common enemy to make ourselves strong,

Killing,

In the name of retaliation.

Just as the terrorists, mistakenly we believed, believed,

Their killing to be retaliating against us,

For political issues of co-dependant abuse.

We however, I chose to believe, made ourselves strong enough to go to war, not out of hatred but out of love: the love of peace.

Still, as always seemed to be the case with issues of domestic violence—which (if you think of the earth as home for our race of beings called humans) this was—the lines of "different from each other" became starkly fuzzy once dissension was introduced. It seemed impossible for those involved to agree on who was to blame for throwing the first punch, the antagonizor or the retaliator, or even, indeed, which of each was which. And as the argument ensued passionately, as if the order of events mattered and carried some relevance in this world where all time exists at once, those starkly fuzzy lines faded into invisibility and we became the same.

Because for us the order did matter, since linear time is the illusion we live within. It did matter, a great deal, especially when we tried to learn from our past, tried to glean knowledge out of the order of historical events. It did matter. It did. Didn't it?

Perhaps! But mostly I think the thing that really mattered to me was that,

I no longer wished to play with a losing hand.

And in my created existence,

Americans win,

With love. They are strong fighters, with a conviction born not out of anger and hatred,

But out of love and responsibility.

To me, Americans marched down a path grown not from religious fervor soaked in a dependency creating fanaticism of being consumed by the devil they desired to destroy, but the rock-hard determination created by an addiction to freedom and a desire to protect,

Everything,

That made them proud.

And as I watched, "The World According To CNN,"

I saw countries uniting,

And was proud and ready to fight,

By believing it so...Possible.

And I wondered again if I would ever create into my life a time wherein we all are heroes,

From within,

The womb,

Unborn,

In the absence of,

Danger: the birthing room of courage.

And wondered if that would be good.

And noticed another something about myself. It seemed I was always creating a world to live in that is ruled by the power struggles of primitive religious beliefs, which enslave their oxymoron followers, seeking the path to freedom of choice, in the consequential halls of heaven. I wondered why?

Did my fascination magnify its power by polishing it up and looking at it from every angle? What was so mesmerizing for me in these competitive, mythological, religious doctrines from every culture and country on the globe that proclaimed themselves the authority, standing righteously against all dissenters who did not fall to the ground and worship their ideals? And why was I so righteous in my distaste for all their righteousness? I prayed for the death of rule bound religions that made enemies of those who did not kiss the ring of their rhetoric. And prayed against all the religions that made martyrs out of misery. And prayed to find a world without prayer.

And catching myself praying.

I prayed,

For a less religious way to communicate,

Outward.

Then, having answered my own prayer,

I switched to contemplating,

The heroes,

In the planes, and the towers that tumbled and fell.

While, all the kings' horses and all the kings' men couldn't put life in their eyes again:

Those ghosts of our, martyred, never forgotten, stranger, friends.

Which is what Osama Bin Laden will be,

Martyred,

If we manage to kill him.

And though I didn't like the power that death could give his already spoken words,

I guessed that a dead martyr was better than an alive Osama,

Throwing bombs,

Made out of people.

Still, I would have preferred to lock him up in a cabin with Harvey Keitel wearing a dress and playing the part of the cult re-programmer.

Perhaps, once Osama is converted he could preach a new message of love and non-judgmental acceptance, to all his followers,

Before we 'do him'.

Because he couldn't just be allowed to assimilate, in case he was fooling us, by pretending to be converted by following the advice in his own, "How To Assimilate In America" manual.

And since, there was always the chance that he was pretending to assimilate,

In order to annihilate,

Like I said,

It occurred to me that we would just have to 'do him'.

Thank goodness they lifted the ban on assassinations otherwise our buddy, the doer, would run the risk of ending up in jail beside Osama's buddies, the even more doers. Whew! What a relief! To not have to actually do any of this.

Still we couldn't save Osama,

Because saving him would mean,

Denying him his right to be a martyr,

Which would be his damnation. And who wanted that responsibility?

Which brought me to a question about the concept of salvation, *"How can you save people from suffering if suffering is their salvation?"*

"Wouldn't then saving cause them to suffer the not suffering,

And bar them from sainthood or even a ramshackle cardboard box house in heaven?"

And, Jesus Christ!! I found the hole, in the hands of my beliefs.

The same hole that had sucked me into a whirlpool pattern of circling poverty.

Because I'd mistakenly believed that the word martyr was synonymous with savior.

And once I saw the difference,

It became easy to remove layer upon layer of,

"Not-Enough-Ness makes you a better person" beliefs.

Till slowly the magic happened,

And I invented luck.

Like when:

A friend asked if I wanted to learn to play poker. I felt a zip of tingling awake-ness and knew I would win the two hundred dollars I needed for rent. First I knew it. Then I did it,

That time, and this time: when, I walked into a bowling alley and the only lane open was under the control of some regular leaguers. They invited me to join them. I didn't know it but they had automatically entered my name into the surprise prize box. For no normally apparent reason, the minute I heard the voice announcing the contest on the loudspeaker, I knew they were going to call my name.

First I knew it. Then they did it.

The main prize had a condition. If I didn't want to be stuck with the bowling-pin-key-chain consolation prize I had to bowl a strike. My arm tingled and my attention focus-pinpointed to the end of the alley. I never questioned the outcome. I knew that, as long as I continued to choose it, I would hit both, the strike and the pot of a thousand dollars.

First I knew it. Then I did it.

It was a strange sort of confidence for someone who couldn't bowl,

On any other day.

I won,

And won,

And won again.

Teaching me to believe, in my ability to create,

Money,

Out of need.

Like in Aruba,

When I walked into the casino, sat near the black jack table and waited for the tingle that didn't come.

Instead I felt a compulsion to step away and walked, as in an underwater dream, never having played slots before, up to one of the many machines.

After five pulls of the handle, I won, the fifteen hundred dollars, that I was behind in for the month.

Over and over, little things coming my way, and each time that they did,

First I knew that they would and then they would, come my way.

And so the lottery had become for me a challenge, a meter stick with which to measure spiritual evolution.

Because winning required a complete decision wherein: losing never entered my mind,

And desire rather than need created the outcome.

Of course I knew that once I mastered this it would mean I had no real need for money,

Because, I never feel the need for what I already have,

Though I use it often.

However it still seemed like a nice idea since I was trying to get to an emotional place where not needing money because I already had it would be a good thing. Besides, I believed, if I could manifest winning the lottery,

I could manifest anything,

Even a world where money doesn't exist.

Though I knew I might not choose to,

Since I would finally have a lot of it,

And might want the fun of spending some.

And though I knew that I could,

Create a world without money problems if I wanted to,

What I didn't know was how.

So, as I drove the car home while ruminating on rubles,

And wondered if the clarity of my decision in Colorado,

Meant that I'd managed to break out of the circle far enough to find the loop hole,

In this create-your-own-reality,

Money game of the mind,

I realized that,

In wondering,

I made it not so.

"*It's OK.*" I consoled myself for my inability to know everything.

And reassured myself with the memory of Deja's words,

"Am I ever glad you didn't ski because I was driving home counting on your statement that money is coming to me because I don't have any and the lease is up and "you know who" isn't calling and I thought, oh no she's in Colorado and she didn't think that trip would work out and that means that her psychic antennae is out of whack and I'm about to end up living on the streets, even though I know I would never really end up on the streets as long as you're around mom but you know what I mean. Then when I got your message about not skiing, I thought, HALLELUJAH! I guess I am gonna pay my rent after all."

First I knew it then she did it.

I was reassured that,

Though I may not know everything,

I definitely knew something,

Not really caring what.

And though the money didn't roll in,

It did drip, drip, drip my way, keeping us afloat,

In spite of the fact that I stayed with my decision not to work.

And all these magic money memories circled me back to Valentine's weekend and the events that sent me catapulting to my computer,

To be with you,

In spite of the fact that, I was meant to let you go.

SMack only had to read "Conversations with God, Book I" to let go of Lisa and I'd already read books I, II and III only to discover I was still holding on.

I guess "God" was on your side,

Valentine's night.

Ted and I were in a Louisiana casino two hours from Houston.

We'd come there because I wanted to,

Respect the fact that I'd tingled,

Just a little,

When we thought of it.

I was hoping for, maybe, enough to pay the mortgage.

The problem was that Ted, who already had lots of money, had come to the casino to have fun and be with me. While I was there for the sole purpose of making money.

And making money meant that tonight's fun was going to entail focused work.

Because it didn't feel like the cash was going to arrive in great big buckets of over-flowing bills.

Unless I believed otherwise,

Which, having already thought of it, I didn't.

So there I was, trying to stay focused enough to continue to choose to win, while Ted rocked behind me from one foot to the other.

I could feel his feelings of rejection. He was preferring to have my attention and throw the money away.

I couldn't,

Afford to have a lark,

And chalk it up to entertainment.

I had won at first, but Ted's "wishing I'd hurry up" energy was splitting my focus and bugging the shit out of me.

So I asked him to please leave me alone and go play something, somewhere else.

I knew his feelings were hurt, had felt them ache, but I'd started to lose and needed to make the money back,

Getting rid of him was a must.

Freed by his absence,

I started moving about the room, turning away from blackjack, trying to feel the machines. I was making the money back but I was working for it.

SMack came up from behind, touched my shoulder gently and, trying to pretend he wasn't upset, told me he'd be waiting in the car. I smiled and said I'd see him in a little while. Then he left the building and I dismissed his actions as a manipulative tool to make me feel guilty.

As soon as he was gone I started to win,

And then I stopped,

Playing,

And sat,

Amazed,

At what,

Had just happened.

I'd forgotten my mantra,

My voice of love, reason and choosing to care.

I'd regressed into believing in the Not-Enough-Ness.

And sacrificed a friend,

Who was trying very hard to be,

All that he thought I was.

I'd lost an opportunity for a shared adventure,

And chosen singularity instead of togetherness.

I'd stumbled across one of my patterns,

Being alone,

By being separate,

Even when together,

To not be hurt,

By losing,

Again.

And so I was convincing myself,

By acting as though there were not enough love,

To last,

All,

My lifetimes;

Like a love martyr,

Afraid to use up the together,

Lest "alone" be the fabric of eternity.

I thought of you, and us, and wanted, that again.

Yet still,

It wasn't an easy choice,

This question of,

The money or the man?

Until I saw—

Though I knew it was a mirage—

Two sparkling silver roads forking away from themselves.

One led to the mortgage,

The other to a friend.

And even though I was used to scoffing at the need for friendship,

Claiming friends to be highly over rated,

As I looked at the roads glistening in the beckoning riches of my mind,

I was suddenly unsure,

Where the pot of gold lay.

And then, though all my mother,

Food-on-the-table household supporter training,

And all my tingling body wanted to stay alone to win,

I left,

To do just that.

And as I walked down the hall toward the exit I ran into SMack walking down the hall,

Toward me.

We had chosen each other.

My path had been,

The roadways in my mind,

And so had his

Been the roadway,

Inside his:

While sitting in the car he had read some excerpts from, "Conversations with God,"

And, remembering my advice on happiness,

He followed his thoughts to clear his head.

He had copied me, done what I do and tried to understand his feelings by traveling through his beliefs.

He had searched his ideas and stopped to examine each connected doctrine. Then, without hesitation, he had discarded the internally adhered-to concepts that he didn't want while keeping the ones he did.

SMack said that he had riffled through his mind,

Looking for love

And how he wanted to define it, till finally,

He reached his desired destination,

Me.

And came back.

No attitude,

No strings,

No intention to manipulate my choice.

He'd just come back,

To be next to me,

As I played alone,

If that's what I wanted.

And I did,

Want, him.

Though had I been listening,

Void of my own love choosing beliefs,

I might have heard,

The difference,

Between what he'd learned,

And what I'd taught.
I'd taught: searching the mind to find the surprises,
In order to rewrite the story,
Inside and out.
He'd learned:
Rewrite the story,
Then read only those pages,
Containing the desired picture,
For the outside,
He wanted to draw in.
The two were very long term different.

❖ SIXTEEN ❖

I talked and talked and talked all the way back to his place,

Having chosen the two of us together instead of side-by-side apart.

I was possessed by the excitement of anticipation, knowing that such a change in my choosing was bound to be accompanied by some as yet un-experienced brand-new thing exploding out of me.

And since there was nothing to write on I rapidfire-talked us into awareness.

I explained and explained and explained some more,

Seeking to understand,

What it was that I was pretending to know,

And telling him about the moment when,

Upon seeing him walking towards me in the hall,

I felt my feelings paradigm shift,

Into new beliefs, perspectives and possibilities,

Making me sure that something big was only moments away.

I was right,

It was.

Valentine's Day!

The day of "the happening."

The day SMack set the scene using movies to stimulate my senses,

In the same way that Ian had used the book: "Bridges Over Madison County" to romanticize and ensnare. But, Ian's motives seemed to be about conquest and the sexual greed,

Of a con mans unconscionable need to string girls along and implant the seed,

Of; "though I can not have you I will love you for ever" misery.

Ian was a grandiose farmer spreading many seeds, ensuring a good crop of,

Hearts grown out of me, the many possibly romantics.

Ian hedged his bets kissing with his eyes open so that he could scout without pause for additional rich soil within which to lay his crop.

Ian's sensual way was the way of an up-close distancer, more afraid than even I of proximity. He wanted to be wanted without wanting back. So that he could feel free to want to be wanted all over again without ever being to blame for the breaking of a heart.

He was a cupid,

That could shoot a gun, or pluck a bow,

But never wield a knife,

For fear of becoming involved.

Because his work was the work of someone who needs guarantees,

Before taking a risk and, coming in close enough,

To be touched,

By the arrow he shoots.

Different,

Same,

From the romantics that, when falling in love, land on the safety nets that they imagine their lovers have knit. Like SMack,

Having an old wife,

While searching for a new one.

His was the work of someone,

Who wanted to be able to hide behind the bush,

Of intention,

While he shot, just,

In case he missed,

Or lost his taste,

For devouring the kill.

His was the work of someone who wanted the possibility of escape,

So that he could run away and pretend,

He never shot anything,

Let alone the fantasy,

Of concocted love,

Inside my head.

But then as I write these words I realize, this description more aptly suits Ian, the paper sniper, than SMack, the movie shooter,

Because, SMack did come in close,

Enough to follow Ian's lead by passing me books to read.

Books were his way of sharing, for the purpose of showing and building, sameness.

While the movies were merely,

His honest,

Propaganda,

Like bow and arrows of love,

Sermonizing the belief in happily ever after,

Meant to divert my attention,

Onto the fact that we were an us;

Something that Ian and I never became.

And though he also used books SMack was different from Ian,

Because he wanted to hold the prize in his hands,

And be part of the biography.

Where as Ian simply wanted to be the lead character in a fictional work,

Of made-up memories,

That made it harder for women to choose not to pine for him,

For,

Forever.

It was his game, that we all played well, for such was the way,

He juiced his masculine pride,

While we fed our femininity.

I believed Ian fancied the notion,

That there were woman strewn everywhere,

Aching into their dying breath,

For the orgasmic beauty,

Of his already spoken-for,

Caress.

He seemed to me to want the story to be the ending,

That wouldn't end.

While SMack seemed to me to want the ending,

To never come,

And chase the story away.

So SMack,

Came in close,

To cut us both,

But used a gun instead of a knife,

Because,

Like me,

He was an efficiency freak,

And the big bang created by the visual assistance of a movie is a quicker journey toward everlasting love,

Than the insipid use of words alone could ever be.

That was one of the lessons that SMack had been learning,

Since the day after we began, this version of the "Love Connection" game.

SMack was also using movies on himself,

Helping himself to formulate the picture,

To write the story,

Of him,

In us,

My family,

My fragments,

Me.

So SMack talked to himself the same way I talked to me.

At first he thought it was an eerie coincidence that the second he learned about autism it existed everywhere in his world.

That supporting ideas and stories about the disorder came barreling down on him,

Talking to him from places within which he was willing to go.

Like guy movies,

With Bruce Willis,

In "Mercury Rising."

As SMack's understanding grew more sophisticated, so did the information that came his way. And he watched himself,

Learn,

Immersed in the metamorphosis of the SMack in us.

Then, an ever-willing student,

He took control of the method.

And got movies for me,

To watch,

And metamorphosize because of,

Because he didn't want to be the only new creature in the room.

He got movies to make me see,

His dreams,

Of soul mates and connections,

And like with the book from Ian,

It had worked,

Though not nearly as well.

Because, though the method was strong, I was a much tougher cynic now, where romance was concerned.

Because, after all I did it for a living.

And I knew how easy it was to fall in love for an hour,

At a time.

And knew that like happiness,

Love is a choice,

To have or have not.

Besides, for me,

Books are the better weapon as they inflict a deeper wound,

Because, for me,

They are more intimate, more convincing, more personal,

Far less hokey than film.

For me, it is more me,

To experience love through my imagination,

With myself as the main character.

It is more enticing to imagine myself,

Than to have the imagining done for me,

Represented by the starring of far more beautiful, women,

Than I.

Women like Meg Ryan,

In "You Got Mail;"

The first film SMack ever took me to.

The plot was about two people creating a romantic relationship from nothing,

More than anonymous letters over the Internet.

The movie matched the reality of our lives,

As we sent e-mails back and forth,

In place of contact, though we knew each other first.

In the movie, Meg and Tom (Hanks) sent e-mails that were more honest and forth-
coming than their authors,

Were used to being,

In that reality,

In their world of pretend.

And the messages matched the real,

In the real-life people,

Watching the film,

About people being real.

And so,

Though I rolled my eyes at the "cheesiness of it all,"

Our e-mails,

Our ties between sightings,

Were enhanced,

And took on more substance,

And became,

Us,

In spite of my resistance.

And thus the movies rolled in.

Purposeful influences from him to me,

As he tried to author a romantic us.

Movies like Richard Gere and Julia Roberts in "Pretty Woman;"

The story about the prostitute that stole the heart of a millionaire.

How appropriate!

This time though the message wasn't from him,

It was for him,

From me.

When I bought the gift I just thought I was being cute; a video gift from SMack's favorite whore about a whore portrayed by SMack's favorite actress. Ahhh sweet!

However, as we watched the movie I came to realize that I and Ted were the same, that like him I was using the VCR to attempt to implant a desire or blueprint to live by.

Ironically as Ted became enamored by the onscreen design I found myself repelled,

By his dreamer's delight,

In the movie's lack of depth,

And found the pattern I had prescribed,

Tacky.

I watched Ted fall deeper in love,

With me,

As he watched Julia,

Portray the experienced virgin,

With a magnetic childlike innocence.

Julia, the ever-beautiful, ever-cute, never aging, unencumbered by disabled children, debts or emotional baggage,

Rosy red flower.

I shuddered, understanding some of the problems we were about to have,

Knowing that Ted would soon try to rearrange my position from mistress to wife.

And I thought about the wife.

The Pretty Woman,

Present had been for Xmas from me,

And for some other occasion from her.

Our gifts matched,

For different reasons.
She had bought her copy for him,
Simply because,
Ted loved Julia Roberts.
He loved Julia Roberts,
Because she reminded him of Lisa,
Of whom I reminded him,
Though I looked more like Val.
So when Val gave him the video,
She reminded him of me,
Kind of made a present out of my existence,
Just as my present reminded him of hers.
So, though she didn't know it,
Val and I shared Ted,
With an unexpected sameness,
As though we were,
His flames of reflected self,
Burning at either end of the candle,
In an attempt to keep the middle warm.
We glowed and undulated heat,
Seeing the world from a different place,
Search lighting the future,
Seeking some love control over the role we would take,
In our own lives,
With,
Or without,
Him.
And so, as always happened when I gave messages to others,
I gave them to,
Me.
I thought of our similarities and my ghostly role in the haunting of this woman's life,
And knew that,
Hurting Val,
Who was also me,
Meant hurting me,
The audience to her pain.
And Val became real to me,

From the real in the real life actors,

Playing real people,

On film,

In a world of pretend.

Like this weekend's video romance,

With Kevin Costner and Robin Wright Penn in;

"Message In A Bottle"

Wherein the unshakable ghost was the wife:

Movie warnings for the future.

And the world I shared with Ted kept feeding me,

Warnings and prophecies,

In message after message,

In movie after movie,

Until finally, as I listened to the inferences in the film every time Robin Wright's character discovered a new "love note in a bottle," I refocused on the fact that there are no accidents, that I create everything,

And I began to hear,

My mind upon the screen.

And, in spite of my "Oh brother" attitude, every cell in my body exploded into fuzzy little fizzies, of television white noise.

It was like sitting in a Bromo Seltzer body that turned up the volume on its bursting bubbles,

Each time Robin read one of the messages.

I tingle-fizzed.

At first I assumed I was tingling because the movie was so good that the perfection gave me chills.

Now I know I was tingling because those letters of love were reflections of the future,

Within which I would become a winner,

By writing this letter of love to you.

And since this winning was about more than money, more than just my arm,

My whole body,

From toes to nipple tip,

Tingled.

However, at the time I thought I was just responding to movie magic,

Reacting because of the great...What?

Acting?

Writing?

Directing?

It wasn't.

In fact the minute I made the assumption about the film,

And in answer to my misdirected thought,

The writing and the messages became more and more inane,

Though they made me tingle still.

It appeared that I was talking to myself through the film,

By not allowing me to hide from my own complicity.

It appeared that I was responding to my assumption,

By reducing the storytelling skill level enough to point out that movie technique wasn't causing this tingling response.

I was using "Message In A Bottle" to give a message to myself,

About you,

Or rather, about me,

With you inside.

It was a message that I couldn't comprehend.

Until somewhere along the way, while I wrote this letter,

That I couldn't send,

Because like the wife in the movie,

You were dead,

To me,

Or rather, I was dead to you,

I finally understood myself.

I was tingling because this letter was the winning ticket,

The "Ship come in,"

The "finally-made-it lottery win."

I know because writing it has taken me to the center of knowing,

Everything,

And let me come back again,

With some of that knowledge still in my hand.

Experiencing this letter has taught me never to shrink away from fear,

Nor to face it,

Nor to care,

But to pass it by,

Think it gone,

Make it not there,

By never even letting it enter your mind,

Which you fill with other more rewarding things.

And while thinking these "things,"

I realized that it had been fear,

That taught me how to live without it.

And that realization kept what I wanted to live without,

Within the circle of learning,

For the sake of the lesson,

When that night,

While SMack slept and I watched movies, I found myself afraid to go to bed.

I knew something was going to happen but I didn't know what so I began conjuring up images of Val-hired private detectives taking ugly pictures with poor lighting that would paint the beauty bad. I heard my own silly mind and, believing in none of these things opened my eyes, to drop the self-created fears: that night that showed me you,

I stood in the living room, feeling like an apparition in another woman's house, having just seen a movie about the new woman trying to take the dead woman's place, and saw, and looked at, though I had avoided it for months,

Val's picture.

And she looked like me.

The song by Def Leppard,

Began to play in my head.

Later, after sex and before the rest of the movies, I picked up the book beside the bed.

I was not used to seeing signs of Val about this house that seemed more mine than hers.

It made me thoughtless, void of caution.

I opened the book to some naturally opening well-worn pages.

And though I have never done anything like this before,

Nor will I again,

I read the underlined passages,

Of some one else's privately plotted doom.

She had written "Oh My God!!"

And "Oh My God this is so true."

Along the margins.

She had underlined and double underlined,

Everything that she had emotionally connected with,

All of it wailing with prophesies of pain.

And when I read the words,

Telling her the degree of agony she must suffer,

Referring to her future state as an emotional black hole of despair,

And prescribing that she stand on the brink and fall into the sinkhole of mental anguish,

In order to,

Maybe,

Heal her dying heart,

I knew she was headed for a breakdown.

Because her path reminded me of mine,

When I had headed that way myself,

A very long time ago.

She was beating the batter according to the recipe for insanity that Deepak Chopra had outlined in this book,

Though that I'm sure was not his intention,

Of how it should be used.

By plucking from the pages the words that most suited Val's mental masochism she charted the path,

And prepared to navigate her sorrow.

I understood the mapped-out recipe because as I said,

Once upon a time I'd baked the cake of insanity myself,

Longing for the nourishment of an answer,

Praying to be committed,

Inside the blackness of no responsibility.

I had trembled an earthquake of destruction into my soul,

Crying, wailing like a tortured beast, crawling,

Lost.

I'd been there,

And survived,

Mostly.

I empathized,

Too strongly,

To remember that there is no way,

To not survive,

To not live,

Inside your own reality,

Even after death.

That's when I sank,

Into Val's believing,

In the end,

And drowned.

And drowned,

Inside the memory,

Of,

Swimming,

Blissfully,
In the,
Black,
Of Siddhartha's river,
Of one,
All,
Making,
The details,
Of life,
Irrelevant,
And,
Dangerously,
Safe.
And so,
I called it, "**Forever Night**."
And tried to tell it,
To write about it,
To advertise the warning,
That blackness is wonderful.
That the dark,
Can become,
A tempting,
Vacation spot for the soul.
That the black ink of everything,
Draws into the pen of life,
And tells,
All,
To relinquish,
And become lost,
In,
Insanity,
Dancing into the stillness,
With all,
The other,
Holiday spirits.
I remembered the black,
And Val's prophesied black hole,

And shuddered,

Wishing she would make another choice.

Like the rebellious colors of happiness,

For her husband's newly reclaimed sensuality,

That she could choose to bask in the glory of,

And diminish his attraction for me.

I wished for that,

But I knew different.

I knew that she would think about suicide,

And that she had already chosen for my existence to hurt her.

I knew that she felt my presence,

And would soon know my name,

Though she hadn't discovered that yet.

I blocked repeatedly the images of Val's dysfunctional sexual desperation with SMack,

Images that laying on her side of the bed,

And mingling with her smells and spiritual remnants,

Were SMacking at me.

I didn't want to peek at her, wanted no more prying, into her naked need for love from the man loving me.

I didn't want the answer to her question,

Didn't care to look and see if they'd made love,

Hoped the answer was yes.

Though I knew that it was not,

Yet.

And knew that, no amount of making love would be enough,

For either of them,

Together.

And those are the things I knew,

Why I was emotionally raw,

With her,

Inside of me.

Why I was trembling,

And frightened when SMack and I got into their bed.

Why I had stayed up all night watching movies,

Avoiding sleeping,

There, in their bed,

Afraid to pick, wanting,

The with.

I was afraid,

Because being with,

Meant risking losing,

Oneself,

Into the black holes.

But then so, I began to suspect, did not being with.

I must have faced my fear,

And chosen the with,

Because finally I let you in,

And saw your face,

And started to write.

And unfortunately for Val,

It wasn't until after she discovered my existence,

And my name,

It wasn't until after she ran away,

And considered suicide,

That I realized,

That the fear I had created,

Had created her fears too.

But for that moment I believed it would happen,

Just as it did,

Because it was destined to do so,

And I was right,

It was destined to do so,

Because I had thought it was.

All the work is done in the mind.

And that is why I consider the power,

And the statements of my thoughts,

As life creating forces of choice.

That is why I care,

What I put inside my head,

Today,

Tomorrow,

And yesterday.

And thus it is that I know,

No book beside the bed has any power,

I do not grant it,

By ingesting its words of forgotten ideas.

In fact the truth is deeper than that, for that book of woe cannot even exist,

Without my fear giving it ink, and writing its story.

So I released the fear,

And discovered my own romantic nature.

I found the other half of my soul,

Which had been buried in the belief that,

Bringing myself together meant becoming less,

For a million broken pieces,

Had seemed like more,

Than one,

Simple,

Sum of the whole.

I had believed in division because I had feared losing my heart.

And I had feared losing my heart because I had believed fearing the loss of my heart would make me hold it tight,

Enough to keep it.

But instead it turned out that,

Knowing no fear was the way to keep what I didn't want to lose.

Fearless gave me the freedom,

To unlock the door,

To the fear,

Which fear had created,

And which, once created,

Had squeezed the softness,

From my core and made me heartless.

By holding too tightly to itself my heart petrified,

Was lost,

And became a stone.

It was fear that took the beauty and innocence of youth,

And made it a shameful joke.

It was fear that made it,

Something to run from. Like my father,

Who appeared gentle, and his wife,

Who felt like hate,

Towards herself,

Through me.

And though it felt like hate it was not,

For it was my mother,

Who wanted to save me,

From the myself,

That she and he,

Had created.

I was being screwed up because I allowed myself to be,

In order to penalize them for making me pay the penalty,

For their desires.

The parents of my world,

Whether in the flesh or in the spirit,

All seemed to be teaching their children to play the same game.

Even God, the father of the Bible,

Sent his son to be tortured as an offering of love,

For our salvation,

From the sins of God's own making.

It is the Omnipotent One, who offers everlasting life after death,

If we do as we are told,

And follow the instructions he instructs from mood to mood.

However, the directions are in indecipherable archaic script,

Which hides the fact that they are pitted against and undo,

Themselves into oblivion.

Still, regardless of the ambiguities and oxy morons, we are warned that we must solve the unintelligible mystery,

To make the illusive grade, to meet the conditions, to pass the course and qualify,

For a ticket through the heavenly narrow door,

Of the cubbyhole beside my bed.

My God was my father: an omnipresent man inside a child's world.

My mother's man, who could not be run from by going anywhere.

Not even by growing up too quickly, yearning to become an angel, to escape being a child.

I missed the fun.

Because he was, is, inside me,

Still.

And will be for the rest of my life.

Unless he isn't anymore,

Whispering sweet somethings in bastardized French,

And playing with my genitals,

Which warm to his touch, and call themselves, "my heart."

Knock, knock, knockin on heavens cubbyhole door,

And that's how, while I was still young, I learned that young people are bad,

Little nymphomaniacs.

So in order to be in control of what I was already in control of,

I made the beautiful youngness of my spirit,

In you,

Wrong,

Laughable,

A shameful joke.

A tool,

To be played with in secret,

Like an unwashed dildo,

For the darker side,

Of my soul.

And the secrecy,

The burial of you,

My younger-than-me lover,

Created a younger lover in my mind.

Giving youth the badness tools of rule breaking love,

With which my father pleasured me.

I justified my fantasies and believed myself to not be my father,

For I only played conspiracy to commit,

In the cubbyhole of my internalized ideas,

Never in the world of concrete miniature things.

I believed because I had forgotten to understand, that all creation,

All crime,

All work,

Is committed,

In the mind.

I believed and did not yet understand that,

If the me I created was someone whose thoughts were her version of bad and out of her control,

To resist,

Choosing,

To think about,

Then I was making me, be, a person who lived in a world outside her control.

And that lack of control was the portal to hell made out of a heaven alive,

With orgasms knocking on that teeny tiny door,

Waiting to be answered.

Thus,

Though I was in the driver's seat of my life, I was self-confusing and driving with my eyes closed.

I was excited by the danger of thought versus action. Thrilled to dabble around in a mental world without laws,

Crimes without penalties and no way to get caught,

Hitting the barriers, reeking accidents of havoc upon, my world, crashing, crashing, crashing, my bumper car spiritual body, in the demolition derby of a messed-up mind that thinks it is normal.

And when I became disillusioned with the fun,

I turned my useful body-toy into a weapon against myself.

And smacked it, and smacked it,

And SMacked it with men.

I used men,

So that I could quit hurting my own brain,

And find love.

Though I could more easily have just decided not to hide the love in the first place.

But then hurting ourselves,

While we look for the love we only rarely let ourselves find,

Is a common game in the human world of my design.

The game of withholding love and happiness,

In order to make it more beautiful,

When we do give it,

Reminds me of the child's riddle:

Question; "Why are you hitting your head against that brick wall?"

Answer: "Because it feels so good when I stop."

And sometimes I wonder if this child's riddle,

Isn't exactly how I tend to proceed in life.

Sometimes I wonder,

"Why don't I learn to relish in the lack of pain instead of in the search for it,

Why don't I weave life into a fabric of fluctuating positives.

Sometimes I wonder if maybe it isn't time to grow up,

And stop being a child,

Traveling on a journey,

Inspired by the poetry of children.

And sometimes I wonder why all my journeys seem to be,

Inspired by the young souls of my existence.

Like this odyssey of letter love inspired by my Deja,

The beacon child,

Lighting the way,

With her youthful idealistic insistence,

On following the path of making life richer,

By refusing to enjoy or settle for,

The already existing richness of life.

Deja was class-conscious enough to make me think I needed to be,

A little less satisfied,

As she got the things she set out to get.

She was my inspiration for manifesting SMack.

Because, though it didn't look like her relationship with the famous orthopedic surgeon was going to take hold, in the beginning it had seemed as though Deja had what I ought to want:

Someone rich, brilliant, socially revered, and busily preoccupied with his work.

"How perfect for me." I thought as I watched her. To not have to earn it but to simply be,

Respectable by association.

The concept wasn't a revelation so much as a revisiting.

I first came up with this description of the perfect husband in 1978 over twenty years ago.

So Deja's relationship was more of an inspiring reminder to get back on track than a brand-new idea.

It occurred to me that Deja was more likely not to loose sight of her goal than I had been.

She might even pull off happiness at an early age because, remarkably, her basic belief was that she deserved to get what she wanted.

Her only stumbling block seemed to be that she hadn't yet learned to want what she got.

Whereas I had believed it made me a better person to want whatever life handed me,

While denying myself whatever I wanted.

I had acted on my beliefs as we all do and though I was often pursued by rich, handsome, famous, caring, busy men and wanted them, I always walked away and only married the poor ones, whom I learned to want,

To do with out.

Ever since, the birth of my children resulted in a broken relationship and left me a single parent,

Which complicated all my future romances with the need to co-parent next to a stranger,

I had always known that highly successful, passionately busy men who were never home in need of attention, were the type of man for me,

But I had no desire to get one.

Simply put, I and my love of martyrdom,

Had firmly believed that there was only sorrow in success,

And sin,

In wanting,

Or getting,

Or wanting to get.

But then as I watched Deja choose to accomplish,

Getting what you want began to look like a good idea,

And not at all sinful.

Because, calling anything that any of my children do, sinful,

Is, to me, funnier than the very concept of sin itself.

It is completely and absolutely ridiculous.

So, I supposed if she could choose perfect for her,

So could I,

Believe in,

Deserving perfect,

For me.

I could believe in it,

Even now,

Even as it was no longer perfect for her,

My Deja the beautiful,

According to you,

And me, and many others.

Deja,

My most recently adopted daughter,

Who,

Despite no connection of the illusion called blood,

Is an exact replica,

Past,

And present,

Of a younger version,

Of the youth-hating me.

And since,

I saw no wrong,

Felt no spring of shame,

For her,

Since,

For the me in her,

I held only love and pride,

And deep admiration,

I held it, also,

For the her in me.

And wanted the beauty back.

Thus I stopped judging me wrong. Stopped running away, in place. And became more aware of my all, my everywhere, my motionless travel.

Choosing to return to being loved, to loving.

Choosing to create a second Soul Mate in the silence of knowing.

Choosing to create an even more evolved union than you and I,

To become more,

Full,

More secure, richer, happier than I had been with you,

Separated out of me.

So I, a reunited soul, saw things,

And learned like Sidhartha in a microwave world,

Quickly made, ready, savory and safe,

That there's, a sourceless non-burning heat called the glowing warmth of life,

At the center of a heaven without hell if I wish it.

I found myself laughing with the revelation that my soul had the same addiction to revelations as my body had had to orgasms, the same driving playful need.

And the revelations revealed that revelations, like orgasms, are easier to have the more you have,

And divinely limitless in number.

And reveling in their divine limitlessness,

I mind-masturbated,

As one rediscovering again and again the constellations of love and the star-extinguishing explosions,

Of the relief,

In relieving the frustration,

Of not knowing the answers,

By choosing to know them.

And then in a lust for life,

In order to revel again,

Forgetting that I knew what I knew.

Till eventually I tired and chose not forgetting,

In order to create a new way to walk,

By building forward motion through the implanting,

Of the delicious need to explode again with all the joyous delight that I must remember in order to crave.

I was addicted to the high of audiencing my own creations as I examined them from every angle,

Seeking new ways to view them or even to make them be.

And in the creation of forward motion,

I created the appearance that time had marched on,

Then illuminated the ecstasy by creating the ability to relieve,

The frustration of being imprisoned by the marching of time,

By remembering that the prison was a mirage.

And then I would choose to forget in order to re-believe in the pleasure tool of time,

Which intensifies and pinpoints the crystalline beauty of high focus clarity created by the pressurized existence of performance deadlines.

It is time that underscores the awesome delirium of immediacy,

Time that instills the reward of ceasing-to-bang-my-head-against-the-wall success,

At the moment that the moment that is now ends,

Whenever I am forced to problem solve while thinking on my feet.

For it is time that offers me the reprieve of the relief from the stress that time creates,

Whenever the joy ceases to be.

It is time that reprieves by revealing the forgotten revelation,

That the entire time thing,

Was a hoax,

A simple game of "make it up,"

Created by my remembering to link a chain and not forget.

Time is,

The perfect tool,

For creating other me(s) in order to myriad my perceptions from moment to moment of reality, and intrinsic life,

To buzz all together, like omnipresent molecular bumblebees.

In a multidimensional thirst,

To orgasm,

Simultaneously,

As one,

With each of us,

As everyone.

And when that parlor play,

Of seconds ticking,

And clocks striking one,

So that we can run down,

In order to run up again,

Grows old,

I make it new again,

By standing apart,

From my created,

Divisions of self,

Whom I gave names,

And identities,

And freedom of choice.

So that I could observe,

As a voyeur,

To the building anticipation...Of life.

While they journey,

On their own paths towards climaxes,

Of revelations, about revelations.

And seeing them seek,

Sex,

For the sheer,

Association of it.

And that, is the newly born attitude,

With which I watch SMack,

Evolve, himself,

And his women,

Together,

Becoming male and female,

Neither,

Or,

One,

Many,

All,

Till we find a way to stand,

Twin towers,

In the skyline,

Tall, strong,

And joined at the base,

To all our people,

Treasuring us,

With their gifts,
Of simultaneous,
Multiple,
Orgasmic, revelatory love,
In the steamy creation,
Of passionate life.
That will only be destroyed,
By choosing to see,
Loving in unison...As a threat.

❖ SEVENTEEN ❖

It was March 7, 1999,

My final no day,

Day of writing, (before the editing began),

When I just got off the phone,

With Soul Mate SMack.

By the way, about that nickname,

It was his idea....sort of.

I made it up when he commented that, "Lynette is so long. If you don't like Lynne then I'll just have to think of something else.... something cute!"

I didn't want to leave my re-labeling up to him and risk becoming,

Something silly.

So I created the cute dignity of, "SMack" and "SMooch."

Stop laughing, Jeff.

Look, I know I hate cutesy names but, well, these kind of work.

OK. It's an opinion thing.

But personally, I think "SMack" and "SMooch" is as catchy as a forties musical,

Was in the forties,

Which I am.

And anyway "SMack" has meaning,

And so does the name.

Let me explain,

The handle he used the first time I met him was Mac, which was short for MacRenolds,

And since I've noticed this funky we-all-use-aliases name theme in my life,

And since I recognized him as mine the minute I saw him,

I wanted to symbolize the beginning of the new.

And in order to symbolize the "new" while incorporating the "old,"

Pattern in my life,

Which also applied,

And which I saw as a signpost,

Indicating, to me,

That I was where I should be,

I wanted to combine the reality of this new person in my life,

With the old habit of loving name pretenders.

So obviously the name,

Had to be built around the alias.

Hence the "Mac" part of "SMack" was a must.

And hence again,

The capital "M,"

Represents,

The re-beginning,

Of the name,

Of a brand-new,

Friend.

But wait there's more. The capitals, S & M, also stand for the term Soul Mate not sado-masochism, which I know is the first thing you thought of. True, the whole soul mate thing is hokey, but it does illustrate the romantic notion of spiritual twinning. Besides the fuller, I believe more spiritually accurate term "infinite-tuplets"(An unknown concept I just gave a label) would likely have confused the name rather than help define it.

So, I stuck with the more familiar notion of soul mate for the purpose of recognizable symbolism in order to help SMack, and I, solidify our union.

And since,

I was seeking oneness and the (re)discovery of a union with,

Ted,

And hence with you,

And Patsy,

And Val,

And Michael,

And Ian,

And Lisa,

And Mitch.

I was seeking to have us all seeking,

The bliss of focus-shift in our desire to believe in special,

Knowing that the depth of each variation runs as deep,

As the desire to believe,

Knowing that each person is a piece of the whole,

Each splinter a sliver of my soul,

Each choice a mate to behold.

And knowing this I placed them all into the two-person fold,

As one.

And then divided it in two,

And the twinning was complete.

Perhaps though, God,

Who, in my all worlds, world, has turned out to be me, as I have turned out to be everyone else and thus the complete whole with no other half,

Should get the real credit for nick naming SMack, and creating a delightful game of spiritual head play. Since, the capital "SM's" were actually just typing errors and the "Mac" was just a coincidence that I figured out later.

Fact is; I just made all that deep shit up.

On the other hand,

If there is no such thing as an accident,

And God is really me,

Then,

I guess it's deep,

If I say it is.

And I do,

Believe that deep shit,

Is something SMack's,

Been giving himself a good helping of,

During the writing of this letter.

The more Ted tries to be his version of kind by walking his wife gently toward letting go of him, his well-intentioned kindness results in her being strung along with false hopes of new beginnings, and the deeper he gets.

He wants it all to be nice, to be guilt-free and seems to be trying to build a world wherein shit doesn't stink,

While believing that it does.

Watching him wash it away though has been impressive,

As he becomes an energy magnet of sensuality, kindness and relaxation.

I told him yesterday that I was beginning to want more,

From us,

For us,

Again.

I sympathize with anyone,

Who chooses to love me,

If they want the rules to stay the same,

Because I am an ever-evolving gypsy of light.

Of course SMack was also ever-evolving,

Which is good because it is the only way I know of to keep the moment new.

However, during this period he had frozen in place, been stagnated by the agony in his marriage and I found myself holding back trying to wait for him to catch up.

My mind is always creating and being in limbo doesn't stop that. It simply means that the creating will take a new shape.

And it did,

It was building mysteries.

And that bothered me. I told SMack that I didn't want to find myself inventing a lot of stupid little intrigues,

Just to busy my brain,

To stay interested,

In him.

I did not want to be living with the stench of BS just to not notice that,

We had stopped growing. "*Like this nonsense with Patsy's client. First of all, I'm not even working any more, I haven't talked to Patsy or her boss in months and then suddenly they're calling and making like my best friend. It's weird, they've never called me like that before and all of a sudden they are asking for my help, wanting me to see this client of Patsy's???*

What's that all about??"

"*Don't answer, just listen. I thought they were trying to set me up. So I met him for lunch, just to check it out, you know, see what they were up to. And this guy! What a number! Can you believe he pretended to be a hit man for the Cartel? I've never even heard of the Cartel. And, like if he was a hit man he'd brag to me about it.*"

"*The point is, the whole thing was very strange and normally I would just ignore it all until it went away but for some reason this time I didn't. Why? What are we doing? Look at us! This smoke-smelling poverty-ridden bum is asking me for sex and I'm taking the time away from writing to investigate the melodrama simply because my curiosity's been piqued. Patsy's writing you e-mails warning you against me. The whole thing is ridiculous! Especially that part where Patsy told you to "check me out" with her other escort friend who knows nothing about me and would have to make it up if she wanted to have something to say.*"

"*I'm worrying, which isn't like me, and thinking things like 'Patsy wants me to look bad because she wants to have you...for no other reason than because she doesn't' and I'm making myself crazy over something I don't really give a damn about.*"

"*I'm sure that's a wonderful compliment to you. Having everyone want you must be very cool but I don't want to play,*

"*Competition and misery with my emotions. I do, however, want you, whether you're married or not. So I find myself trying not to notice that I don't really have you.*"

"That's why I'm busying my brain with bullshit, keeping myself preoccupied and thinking crazy things."

I knew what I was doing because I had recognized the technique.

This was what I always did when the man I was with turned out to be crap and I had to fill up my mind in order to not see it. The last time I had played this way the game went on for over eight years.

I didn't like the idea of such an elongated period of self-denial,

I wanted out.

"I even started thinking 'Patsy asked them all to do her a favor and work together to help her build a snare to try and tempt me back into the business.'"

"But hell, that's just stupid, Patsy is smarter than that. She'd of at least tempted me with someone tempting."

"And it isn't just me it's worse than that, it's you too. We've both been sitting here at dinner putting our heads together analyzing the 'Split-up-Smack-and-SMooch conspiracy.' We are giving it power, acting paranoid, and wondering what all those loose ends mean."

"It's easy" I thought, "It means there's a horny guy in Houston looking for a friend. The escort folks want to cash in on his lust and he's already used up all the girls they know. So they called me hoping I'd help. And that's all there is to it. The e-mails from Patsy are just her feeling left out and that guy being a hit man is just some poor guy talking shit."

But in spite of the obvious,

There we sat,

Together,

Thinking intrigue.

I was doing it to distract myself out of noticing I wasn't happy,

He was doing it to keep me,

Distracted.

We were both doing it to stall me out of advancing,

So that I wouldn't leave him behind

For someone without a wife.

But I didn't want to become the me that played the mind games of mentally shuffling papers rather than actually clearing the desk.

"I want."

I stared straight into his eyes,

And held onto the last notes of the word,

And meant,

I want,

To see the world beautiful,

Not sleazy.

He seemed to see my need and understand my mind.

"I'm glad that you want. Be patient, I'm getting there."

I timidly shared my thoughts,
And advised him that he needed to be as brave with his wife,
As I had been with him,
In Colorado,
If he really wanted to be,
Kind,
He should be honest.
And apparently he was.
He told me on the phone today,
That he and his wife,
Were trying to work out the details of their divorce.
He told me on the phone,
That he had been as brave as me,
That it was Colorado.
"It felt better."
He said,
She said,
"Well, I had a conversation with God today."
He had chuckled,
And she had insisted adamantly that,
"I'm not kidding! I did."
However,
He hadn't been laughing at her,
Just enjoying the parallels of discovering,
That I,
And she,
Not only looked the same,
Drank the same diet drinks warm, no ice,
And absentmindedly picked our toenails,
(A habit, which Ted focused on to drive himself batty)
We were the same,
Person,
Val and I,
Experiencing either ends of an identical adventure.
And she was coming closer to closing the circle and being our friend,
Going so far as to try and help me get some Secretin: the medicine, for Dar.
A detail,

Which becomes even more titillating,

When juxtaposed against my present life wherein Dar is finally about to be infused with Secretin, found not as a result of Val's efforts, but Athena's.

And Athena is SMack's new me,

Taking my place,

While I have taken Val's.

To experience the adventure,

From her,

Other side,

Of being the wife, walking in circles, talking to God.

So now, as then, I just smile for both,

All,

Of us,

Being the same.

It felt good,

To know,

Again,

That this letter,

Hadn't made me crazy,

That I was not,

The only I,

Having "Conversations with God."

That I was not the only,

One,

Part of me,

About to embark,

Upon a new and wonderful life.

Thank you, Jeff,

For this love,

Letter pilgrimage, has gifted me repeatedly,

With the vision, of visions, of truth.

And even as they shift,

And even as they change,

To become something new,

I have suffered,

Without pain,

A blissful unfolding.

I began,

This journey,

In tears,

First weeping,

For the love,

I remembered,

In me,

For you,

You,

For me,

Me,

For myself,

Then for the courage it took,

To not hoard you away,

Any longer,

Like beloved,

Pennies in my pocket,

Hiding in the darkness,

Of a forgotten,

Suit of birth,

But to choose instead,

To draw you into me,

Releasing the fear,

That you would disappear,

And be forever,

Again,

Gone.

❖ EIGHTEEN ❖

When you make love,

Do you look in the mirror?

Who do you think of?

Does she look like me?

Do you tell lies?

And say that it's forever?

Do you think twice?

Or just touch and see?

I was having trouble dealing with Edmond.

I had already quit working but he didn't know that, since he never called my pager, which is where I had left the message saying, *"Thanks for calling but I just quit the call business. Happy hunting!"*

Edmond, had gotten my cell number and my real name off the caller I.D. so he just phoned me direct to prove he could.

The rest of my clients respected the fact that I hadn't given them personal cell rights. They used my pager and called me Laurie-Anne in spite of their at home telephone technology.

I wished Edmond wouldn't call anymore because I was busy writing this letter and not making any money and trying not to care. But it was hard not to care when a customer I already knew was such a tempting solution to my need for mortgage and groceries and credit card payments. Besides he liked me and I didn't want to hurt his feelings by telling him not to call; which he was doing up to eight times a day.

Edmond was seriously fixated.

So I avoided him, using my own call display screen to field the friendly fellow. It worked fine except on those occasions when I would be busy writing and absentmind-edly respond on the first ring. Then he'd catch me. So I'd lie and, using the untraceable advantage of go with you when and where you go cell phones, pretend I was out of town.

Edmond, in case you don't remember, Jeff, is the client I told you about that gets me to pretend I'm his mother. Normally I won't see people if they want to role play using humiliation because I think it's unhealthy to do that to my mind; to give myself the experience of being cruel or humiliating to someone else.

Edmond is different though because he wants to be cruel to me.

His name calling, things like slut and bitch, are directed against me.

And somehow, me being hurt has never seemed as bad as me hurting,

Someone else,

Because me hurting someone else is the only way to really hurt me.

Besides it was hard to take Edmond, who was a teenie little unattractive pimple-faced Asian man with a high voice and more amusing than intimidating, seriously.

Anyway, I'd had husbands and parents treat me much worse for a lot longer than an hour at a time and none of them were paying. So being abused for money as a game of pretend wasn't such a big deal.

With Edmond I even took pride in my acting ability, crying real tears and giving convincing performances that turned him on so much he couldn't help but have sex with me. Which was a kind of twisted compliment since Edmond always only videotaped—which I wouldn't allow—but never actually had sex with his models.

Mostly though I felt as though the fact that I took his needs seriously and treated him with love and respect in spite of the disrespectful nature of his requests, helped him,

Accept himself.

It was my peculiar blend of non-judgmental acceptance; talent and uninhibited sexual attitudes that made me feel irreplaceable in the healing of Edmond's psyche.

Of course, Edmond, never asked to be healed.

That he needed any help at all was simply my unrequested "professional" opinion.

Because, after all, he was weird and his fantasies were cruel.

And until now I never noticed the hypocrisy in my beliefs.

I never saw myself,

Until after I quit working,

And was trying to write,

And became irritated by his calls.

I kept making excuses.

And after a while I started to notice the harshness I felt when the phone would display his number,

Or when he would catch me picking up the receiver,

And I would hear his voice,

Or when our games would pass across my mind and gross me out,

Until his repugnance grew and I began to feel superior to him.

And all the while he sought me out thinking me wonderful.

And so it went,

Until a week ago when I noticed,

Myself,

And was shocked to realize that I had become,

Cruel,

In my mind,

Against him.

And a small voice in my head that sounded like a thought told me to love him if I wanted him to disappear into me and be gone, no longer a problem.

So I did it,

I loved him,

And he was gone,

From my head,

No longer taking up room and troubling me. What a gift!

That I applied the next day when I had to go home to run errands and care for my children.

I stopped writing for several days...

On the second day of no writing I was baby-sitting the grandkids when Tyran the two year old decided to have a tantrum. I picked him up and held him in the rocking chair, humming softly despite his screaming, waiting for him to either cozy in or cry himself to sleep.

After about half an hour of Mr. Stubborn trying to outlast Saint Me I noticed that though I was doing all the right things like speaking softly and singing sweetly, I wasn't really being very nice because I thought of myself as doing so well. In other words I was kind of using him to show off, to myself.

I thought of Edmond and the remarkable effect that loving him had had on me and decided to try sending my love forth, to heal my grandson's sadness. It felt a little like the tingly feeling I get when something special is about to happen, only instead of coming into me I was sending it out. Tyran quieted immediately.

I was awash with wonder.

To anyone looking, nothing had changed, my song, my touch, my smile was indistinguishable from the moment before. And yet this invisible intention seemed to be the difference between loving and not. I felt a kind of deferred gratitude to Edmond who had been the conduit for such a joyous lesson. Thus when, at the beginning of this week I returned to the cabin to finish this letter which was seeming to become a book and Edmond started calling again, now that I loved him and was even farther behind in my bills, it seemed harder than ever to push him away, again not wanting to hurt his feelings.

So I was back on the same roller coaster looking at things from a different perspective but still being unkind.

In fact I was being a mirror, as unkind to Edmond my ex-client as Smack was being to Val, his partner in life.

And finally the roller coaster wore me down, so that the day after I avoided eleven calls,

I didn't anymore.

I allowed myself to set an appointment though I didn't want to stop writing and didn't want to go and didn't want to break my resolve to not sell love by the hour.

I resented him immediately, angry that he had caught me in a weak moment as though my weaknesses were his fault.

I was once again disgusted by his sexual appetites and immediately began to view him as my inferior.

Only this time I recognized the feeling the second it took shape and didn't try to bury it beneath justification and self-defense.

I sat down, knowing all the work is done in the mind and asked myself,

"*What would love do now?*" a guiding question I'd learned from the book Conversations with God.

At first I didn't have any idea but then I remembered Tyran and sent my love tingling outward.

I asked myself again, "*What would love do now?*" and the answer was immediate and clear,

Colorado!

I was amazed to discover that being honest with this funny looking little man could be almost as hard as being honest with SMack had been,

And as easy.

And at that moment I realized that I'd gotten caught up in the Not-Enough-Ness again. I'd kept Edmond around rescheduling appointments just in case I changed my mind,

Just in case,

I had Not-Enough conviction,

And Not-Enough money,

And Not-Enough love,

To make it without the hims,

Of my world.

How cruel!

I called him,

And behaved,

Lovingly.

I told him that I had made some personal decisions,

To quit the business.

I was clear,

Not at all ambiguous,

Kind.

And once again saw easily,

That he was not just some twisted sick individual,

That should be pitied,

Or used,

Or cringed at,

Or unasked for "helped."

His fetish for acting hateful was no worse than mine,

In fact it was the,

Opposite,

Same.

And I,

I knew,

Was not a miscreant.

Neither was Edmond. He was a man,

Not some vile repugnant monster.

He was an intelligent,

Accepting,

Very sweet friend.

Wanting to play act away, his feelings of powerlessness;

As the young person in control of the old.

Just as I had wanted to imagine away your youthful hold on me,

Erase my fear of aging into loneliness without you, who walked away,

By fantasizing an old person in control of the young.

I couldn't believe how much better I felt,

Having chosen to honor him with the love of honesty, by recognizing our sameness,

And liking me still.

And so I felt loving and respectful towards myself.

Like I was-

OH!

The tingling!

The tingling!

I didn't know.

I didn't know,

I didn't know,

That,

I didn't know,

JEFF!!

If I can love him,

I can love me.

JEFF!

All the hints,

And I didn't get it.

I even said it,

More than once,

Even wrote it down,

Though I must not have read it,

For I still didn't get it:

Everything,

Has been happening,

To me,

In the inkling,

That I thought of it,

Everything,

All around,

Me,

Talking to me,

Trying to break in,

To my absolute deafness,

That I mistook,

For silence.

Everything around me has been staring me in the face as proof of what I hadn't bothered to see!

Like my kids changing under my influence in spite of my absence.

Tonight I was feeling frustrated,

Not understanding where this letter was going,

What it was about,

And the second I felt funky,

My children's moods changed,

And they began phoning,

From 140 miles away,

To report that they were fighting,

Seemingly in response to my change of mood,

As though I was connected to everything,

Everywhere...Omnipotent!

Like Deja, from 20 miles away,

Who was disgruntled,

And unusually brisk with me,

The moment I was disgruntled,

And unusually brisk,

With myself.

Until a moment ago, when I wrote it down.

I hadn't understood it!

Though the message had been hammering at me,

Over and over again,

From every quarter of the universe, screaming to be heard.

But I was like a woman,

Too busy spanking her children,

With her own frustration,

To notice how she felt,

Too busy experiencing spanking, to experience stopping,

Even though she had stopped.

Jesus, Jeff, it's taken so many pages,

To hear myself talk.

This letter isn't for you at all.

It's for me.

OH MY GOD, JEFF!

It's a love letter for me.

And even though I'd already said it,

It was in a kind of backhanded way,

And I only just now realized,

The importance of what that means.

This letter is a love letter for me,

From me.

And that tingling of imminent good fortune,

That I have always attributed to the gambler's touch,

Is me,

Sending love to me.

And the voice in my head just shouted "**YES!!**"

And my entire body,

Is buzzing and fuzzing,

And foaming and fizzing,

And molecular jumping-with-energy whizzing.

I feel like a newly popped, open celebratory bottle of champagne.

I should have known,

I should have known.

God,

Sometimes I feel like such a slow,

Soul learner.

Oh, Jeff, I can't believe how many incredibly obvious things I didn't know about myself until "the happening" sent me running to my computer, to put it there, on the monitor where it hoped that I would see it.

So many things gone undetected until "the happening" set a voice to talking in my head,

Telling me the secrets of my universe,

Telling me that still I didn't get, didn't comprehend,

My own power,

In spite of my knowing,

What I already knew,

Which was that I created reality,

From stem to stern,

From top to bottom,

From within to without,

In spite of my knowing the power,

Of loving,

Myself,

Enough to change the attitudes and the treatment,

Of the inside of my world,

Outside my world,

For I had done it,

Over and over again.

And suddenly I remembered a time years ago when:

While driving, I was pondering the presently in vogue, highly publicized ozone and nuclear warnings of the unavoidable annihilation of mankind due to humanity's carelessness, paranoia and pollution.

I unexpectedly understood that my contemplation over the environmental conditions of Mother Earth was part of the process in which I had engaged myself for choosing what kind of backdrop I wanted to have in the future adventure I was going to create next. And without questioning the validity of my knowing I glanced at a variety of possible scenarios and chose.

I focused my choice and sent my energy tingling outward to wrap around the globe of us. I felt it happen and I just knew, with absolute certainty that I had reversed the pollution process and begun the tentative (because I still hedged on the concept of total safety) disarmament of nuclear weapons by immersing myself in a future wherein man had the heart to change his considerations.

I felt the feeling of a job,

Just,

Done.

I never questioned my own sanity,

Or where the power had come from,

I never even bothered to watch that future fumblingly unfold,

To check on my correctness.

I,

Just,

Knew,

It was done,

With love.

Which is how it is done,

Always,

Even when it hurts.

But somewhere I must have forgotten,

The revelation of learning,

That every process begins with me.

Because even though I know that everything and everyone I see is just a manifestation of me talking to me,

That I am my own soul,

Creator and created,

I still,

Never knew,

That the tingling,

And the letter,

Were me,

Loving me.

And even though forgetting seems to be part of the process of the joy of remembering,

Each time I remember I choose to forget a little less,

Painting the joy of living with an ever-changing brush.

And I suppose that, in the end,

As I read from the "I create it" vantage point,

This letter has nothing to do with men,

Or women, or morals,

Or morals, or war, or peace,

Or even love and spiritual concepts,

Except for how I feel about how I feel about them.

No wonder my world has been defying the laws of nature,

They, like the laws of man, are nothing more than made-up rules,

We claim to be irrefutable,

In order to learn,

That they are not.

I am learning!

So let me tell you what's been going on Jeff,

While I've been writing to myself,

In care of you.

All the psychic realities around me have been fine-tuning themselves into view,

Clearing away any uncertainties of cause and effect.

And if "the happening" being a happening,

Is measured by the weight of the relative impact it's had on my happiness,

And the revelatory sense of knowing,

Things that were heretofore unknowable,

Creating the "BIG BANG,"

That folds nature inside out,

From its paradigm shift of philosophies,

Then I guess there have been four,

"happenings,"

In the past three weeks.

With many more scheduled, at each stop,

Along the route, of the,

"OK, let me have it spirit rail train."

But for the moment we are not concerned with the future,

For all the critical "happenings,"

In so far as they are related to this book,

Are on display,

Resting in the stations,

Where I've already been.

1ST STOP; COLORADO,

2ND STOP; VALENTINE'S DAY

3RD STOP;

February 20, 1999, Dessa's house.

I'd been up writing most of the night, trying to do what I thought this
letter was about, choose between the past of you,

Or the present of SMack.

It was the day after the day I learned to truly,

Love,

Edmond,

As opposed to the,

Not actually accepting,

Love and acceptance,

I'd been giving,

Him,

And me,

Before.

I was tired so I flopped down on the bed/couch in her living room as Dessa left to go get groceries.

I still hadn't presented her with my wedding shower surprise of flying her to Canada later that day. She remained under the impression that she was going to be babysitting for the weekend, not escaping to her maid of honor's decorated living room for a prepared party a country away. I was excited to surprise her and hoped she would feel the same excited way about being surprised with this gift from her mom.

Carlos, Dessa's fiancé, was unconscious in a "I wish she weren't going" state of sleep-avoidance. I couldn't help but hear him snoring in their bedroom. The house fell motionless save for the in and out vibrations of his sinus packed breathing and the nibbling that Nalla, their cat, engaged in on my face.

I snuggled my head under the covers to hide from the cat and,

Listening carefully for Carlos,

Placed my hand between my legs.

Touching myself,

Alone,

For the fun of it,

Which was something I hadn't done in years,

Called to me,

Even though I was,

In my daughter's living room,

With her boyfriend just down the hall.

I was missing you.

The writing had brought you back to me,

And I wanted to see you again.

So I touched myself because,

"the happening" and this letter,

Had shown me that sex,

Was the path,

I needed to walk,

In order to find myself,

Back in your arms.

I closed my eyes and;

Saw us, air dancing, with me in a transparent nightgown and you wearing my ex-husband's brown hooded housecoat that made you look like my friend the happy grim reaper.

You slipped my shoulder button from its clasp and the nightgown melted away.

As you, naked now, guided me, lovingly, backwards floating, to the marble slab. I sat on the edge, leaned back on my arms, and arched my spine.

You kneeled at my feet,

Placed your hands between my knees and spread my legs apart.

You caressed yourself,

With sensual love,

Excited by the vision,

Of the beauty in me.

And as I climbed towards orgasm the fantasy became more three dimensional, more real than it had ever been. And though the "I," in the fantasy remained exactly the same as it always had, the "eye" of the I, that was me, the dreamer, became a Tinkerbell, fire flying, a breath away from every inch of you, looking, smelling, hearing your sounds.

Private, between us, buried deep in the silence of my mind.

I touched myself, coming close, bringing you more and more into focus, tears, giving themselves life again, spilling over from my eyes, as I relived you, from every angle. Until at the moment of orgasm, in that instant just before you lifted me up, to drop me down and kiss me with those sweet, wet, water kisses,

You reached your arms towards me to slip them under my legs and without thinking to stop myself I turned to watch your marvelous huge hands and saw,

What you see.

Me!

The me,

Between my legs.

I climaxed,

In waves of relief,

To discover,

That my father had left,

My genitals.

That there was no longer any monster,

Buried there.

Nothing vile,

Or putrid,

Or unacceptably me,

Lived between my labia.

In fact I thought, panting on the bed, I looked like all the other women

I had ever seen,

Beautiful,

If such a thing can be.

It was an emotional healing I didn't want to use verbiage for,

No articulation,

Or mental gymnastics of intellectual parlor games.

I didn't need to understand it with words.

I just wanted to heal.

Like a bonnie little girl child,

Crying,

And wanting to feel better.

A small voice began to hum,

Sweetly,

A lullaby.

When you make love,

Do you look in the mirror?

Who do you think of?

Does she look like me?

Do you tell lies?

And say that it's forever?

Do you think twice?

Or just touch and see?

And I cried and cried and cried, trying not to make any noise,

And bring the awareness of my future son-in-law into the room.

That moment changed,

Everything.

Yet it is only now,

That,

As I cry the tears,

Obliterating the story,

And cleaning the filth from the keyboard,

I understand,

The significance,

Of,

It,

All!

But that day the healing hurt and the child in me needed, needed, needed, to be soothed.

The voice inside my head sang a new song,

With **Pavoratti's** voice.

If love is like an ocean,

Full of conflict,

Full of pain.

Like a fire when it's cold outside,

Thunder when it rains.

If I could live forever,

And all my dreams come true,

My memories of love,

Would be of you.

It felt sweet and kind and reassuring.

It was as if the voice were trying to tell me,

That whatever materials of beliefs and feelings I chose to construct myself with,

I was worth loving.

And I began to feel,

Comfort,

In the lessons,

Explaining:

All the Pinball Wizard,

Pattern playing,

Dizzy dancing,

I had done,

To keep me busy.

And my answers came in images,

And my questions came in words,

Till finally, I was sitting and conversing,

With the God that lives in me.

And (s)he laughed,

In great,

Warm,

Soundless,

Sound,

Waves of joy,

When I asked about:

The lottery;

My game of games.

And I listened to the answer and understood,

And laughed and laughed and laughed and laughed and laughed,

Face buried in the pillow so that Carlos wouldn't hear.

Apparently all the little signs, that in the past, I had believed meant I was headed in the right direction, or that I was being given the secret peeker binoculars of future sight, had simply been me,

Playing with myself.

And as it was explained to me I will explain it to you:

I am the creator,

Therefore, if I want it to be that I am wearing a leather jacket and blue jeans when I buy the winning lottery ticket of ten million dollars at the strip mall convenience store with the roof adjoining the next building effectively sheltering customers from sun and rain then so be it,

But if I then stir in the belief that there is luck involved,

And add a pinch of seeing the future means, hints or sign posts saying "this way" as if there is a direction to follow,

Or a future for that matter,

If I tell myself that the conditions have to be right, that I will get there when I learn the lessons leading the way, that my knowing is not knowing and that my not knowing is real,

Then I am like the pinball in the game of life, bouncing and dinging whenever I hit the mark, hoping that my manipulator controller is good enough to score.

And then if I add on top of that that I cannot win anyway, I am just the ball, that drops down the hole, after the larger me gets tired of pushing the flipper buttons,

And then—-

I interrupted the voice inside my head.

"What are you talking about? I know I'm the controller. I already believe in creating your own reality!"

"Oh do you now?" Said the sound in me.

"Yes"

"What would you say if I told you that everything in your world, whether imagined, inspired, given life or given death, was put there by you, to---?"

"I'd say," I interrupted, *"I know. I know! I'm talking to myself, telling myself things so that I can learn."*

"NO!"

And I saw that I hadn't believed,

And that there was nothing to learn.

And I saw,

Myself,

Playing with myself,

Using all my toy tools,

To write the rules,

Of the game.

And it had gone this way because I had created an analogy,

To explain an analogy, which had already so clearly conveyed,

Reality...until I changed it.

By creating dreamers inside dreamers and dolls inside of dolls I created other me(s) inside of me,

Little Lynettes who knew it all,

Dropping hints from world to world,

Writing messages on walls.

THE BIBLE!!

And that was when I understood that I was like the God in the Bible,

Making rules for others to gain acceptance by,

Creating,

Failure,

Just to watch the child cry.

Like yesterday at Dessa's other shower,

When Deja who looked uncomfortable, tried to help her sister cope, by taking a small, potentially dangerous something,

Away from her nephew: one year old, always-happy, easygoing Shay, my youngest grandchild.

And Shay, wanting the something, cried, a heart breaking lament,

While all of the women watched, with their hands over their hearts, and mouths,

Smiling and laughing and ahh!! Ooo!!! Poor Baby-ing.

"Look at him. Poor thing. Sweet baby!! AHHH!"

Like Gods,

Sitting separate,

Watching from above,

Loving their love,

Of the wailing darling child.

Like all the Gods,

Of all of history's holy books,

Loving their love of,

The intensity created,

By empathy for,

The dying putrid earth,

And all the tragic stories,

Told.

All,

The stories told....And lived.

All the Hollywood,

Sad endings were made,

All were watched en masse,

By ticket-buying audience Gods.

The myriad of Lords who were only one,

Created by and symbiotic with,

The producer, director, performer Gods,

And I,

God,

Of gods,

In my world,

Where we sat in awe,

Of the child wailing,

For his beloved thing.

I am the Lordess.

I led the AWE!

Full of joyous love,

Laughing happy tears

At my grandchild's,

Not very important,

Important,

Not very real,

Real,

Pain.

And then,

I looked at all the other spectator Gods to check on my art,

And saw the analogy.

That as art copies life,

It copies life-copying art,

So that I might see.

I noticed the dichotomy,

Between the unified happiness,

Of all the adult Gods,

And the baby's tortured cry.

And as I noticed the chasm,

I changed my mind.

And,

The other gods took on new emotions,

Subtle shifts of change,

Because I was them too.

Like unusually frightened Deja,

Being me,

Showing me myself,

When I was twenty-two, or four, or eight,

Before,

When I was afraid,

Of being judged,

Unacceptable,

Unlikable,

Weird,

And so on occasion becoming just that.

Deja was quiet, for her, seemingly wanting to leave, identifying herself responsible for Shay's pain.

Though it was me,

God,

That had sent her to walk,

Among,

Him,

As a savior in advance,

Taking on the burden,

Of saving him from the pain,

A burden that would not have been a burden,

If he had not been inflicted,

With pain,

To be saved from.

Deja took the focus so that I could see,

That if I quell my need to fix,

I dispel the need for broken things.

That if I cease to need to save,

Others cease to suffer.

Deja, my pipeline for sight, showing me what,

Jesus showed God, and the Bible shows all,

Through the dying of Jesus for the absolution of sins,

That God decided were there.
That it's all a simple game,
Of creation.
Jesus needed lepers in order to heal them.
And I needed children who needed to be saved,
In order to save,
Myself.
It seemed that as I decided what Deja's feelings were,
They were.
So I decided it was time to let my children not suffer,
Because now, I could see that, I carried the burden,
Of blame,
As the author of their pain.
And so,
I tried a new story,
Thought different feelings,
To recreate the me in them,
And in her,
To give her, a better ending than I'd given myself at that age.
I thought different feelings to recreate the me in them all,
Every person in the room.
And, saw those emotional changes reflected in the eyes around me,
I saw Tsara the mother-god of the shattered child,
Notice the drama and not see it as sad.
Thus she soothed and dispelled,
Without shushing or fussing,
She absorbed and rewrote the moment,
Making his sadness,
Gone,
Vacant,
Never having been.
I watched her give him comfort,
The angel to his tears.
I watched her and Deja and Dessa the bride,
Having let them go,
To save themselves,
And knew,

For the first time,
God's distant,
Allowing,
Love.
And as I recalled the shower,
While in the living room waiting for my daughter's return,
And Carlos' awakening,
I finally knew,
What I knew.
That I,
Was,
It.
Everything!
Responsible,
For it all,
And to blame,
For nothing.
I "WAS,"
God,
The God of my life,
And of the Bible too.

❖ NINETEEN ❖

I wrote the book.

In fact I wrote—from various incarnations—all the books,

Every one of them.

Even the one from within which Val created—out of bits and pieces—a blueprint for attempted suicide,

The one naming Deepak Chopra as author.

I was responsible for the words with which she shoveled out those black pits of despair,

Believing that she was digging an emotional wormhole to sanity:

A wormhole that would suck out all her agony,

And release her whirling like a dervish of hysterical euphoria,

As it ejected her out into the world of stability,

So long as she survived,

Which,

Of course,

She would.

The passages had depicted insanity as black holes,

So similar to my own description in the poem "**Forever Night**;"

"**Black is such a lonely place,**

"**Black's become my friend,**

"**Black is like the monster's face,**

"**And I welcome terror in.**"

Apparently I left signposts,

In an attempt to unveil my own construction,

To myself,

Little fingers of proof,

Pointing at the fact that I was in charge,

As author to Val's pain.

Perhaps I had created this melodrama of the characters around me in order to give myself the experience of being consumed with saintly love,

Toward all involved.

However, in order for me to be wonderfully loving, others had to be not,

Otherwise wonderful could not be defined.

And so I felt like Jesus saving his followers from the misery of the sin he created in order to save them ...and wondered if I was, also, him?

How unlikable I found I was,

How shallow, immature and cruel.

How terrible to play with people,

As though they weren't even real.

My body tingled,

With recognition.

Of course!

If I created reality,

Then the stories,

And the people,

And the Gods and the devils,

The laws and the sciences,

The all and the everything,

Were just visions of mine,

Formed in the inkling,

Of my hearts desire,

To play,

War and peace,

With myself,

If I wished it.

And I understood,

Again,

That if I wanted to change the world,

I need only love it into being,

Calm from within.

Because each and ever particle,

Was a particle of me.

And that, though everyone has freedom of choice,

In their own reality,

No one has it in mine,

Unless I want them to.

So creation is like a prison,

Tying me to my creations,

Unless I choose to set them free.

And as no one has freedom in my world without my permission,

Neither do I have freedom in theirs,

Though only they will experience the constraints of the shackles,

Both as me and as them self,

As worlds upon worlds layer and compress into one space and time,

If that's how I see it.

Which I do.

And since all the work is done in the mind,

Where every little nuance is born of intention,

Every little thought,

Of beauty do I,

Now intend to see.

And that's what I was thinking when now-perfect Dessa returned and like a little cherub of love, hustled about putting things away, caring for her fiancé, sweetly sending tingling love energy to him, to me, and thus to herself.

She was so passionately loving as they snuck away to be intimate, glowing warmly at me, teasing, fun,

So completely happy, excited and appreciative of my gift, her surprise fly-away vacation, to see friends and be showered with joy.

And Deja, the perfect sister, the loving other, same-age child, calling to wish our Brandessa the joyous pleasure of delirium, caring to add to the excitement with her own enthusiasm in order to enhance her sister's euphoria.

"So, this is beauty personified and how the world looks after enlightenment." I marveled to myself,

As Carlos,

My daughter's handsome, caring, funny, talented, genius,

Drove us home from the airport, with, without her.

Unable to stop myself I asked him to pull over at the convenience store so that, in case I had finally, figured it out, I could buy a lottery ticket,

Of freedom,

Implying to myself that I wasn't ready.

Standing next to Carlos, each of us purchasing tickets,

I thought, before I could think twice,

"But if I win now, with him beside me, I'll feel like I have to share the money."

As if I wouldn't have anyway.

And hearing myself think it.

I knew I wouldn't win.

And I knew I wouldn't win,

Because I knew I wouldn't win.

Not because,

As I thought at the time,

I had not wanted to win in order not to share.

Ironically, in not wanting to share,

I forced myself to share,

The nothing we were about to win.

How silly life can be when you pay attention,

And try to be in control,

And so create a lack of control,

In order to have something to try to be.

You'd think with all this knocking at my door I'd have invited complete knowing and self-love in by now,

Made it mine.

I mean why keep believing in the rules according to all the science guys like Newton, Einstein, Hawkins, Nye?

Why didn't I let go and Play-Doh dance my body again?

I could be a Messiah if I wanted to,

And I might want to,

If I could believe in Messiahs?

Who were nice,

Enough to want to be,

Saviors without suffering.

But how?

For then a true Messiah would be creating harmony in the world,

And thus all the people would reflect his knowing,

By coming together as one balanced whole,

Rendering the Messiah invisible,

Indecipherable from the masses.

So if I were a Messiah of notice,

Rather than just one of the folks,

Then I would be no Messiah,

At all.

Certainly if the world was not,

One,

Cohesive,

All enlightened whole,

Then I would be,

Just another Jesus,

Talking sin shit,

To myself,

Through my creations.

Which,

I decided,

Was one of the points,

I was trying to make,

To myself,

When I created the Bible.

So you'd think, knowing so much, that I would have realized,

That the illusion of money is an illusion.

And though on one level I did understand,

And would have said, "*So?*"

It was an illusion,

That eluded me.

And I,

Still,

Kept worrying,

About money.

Though I kept telling myself I wasn't.

Until the forth and final "happening,"

Happened.

And though this book happened,

Because of the first two "happenings,"

The last two "happenings,"

Happened because of this book,

To you,

For me.

"Look, do you want to be a master or not?" ME (The uppercase part of me that has no need to forget.) asked me (The lowercase letter soul that still played at not knowing.).

"Not if it means being better than other people," me answered Me.

"Don't be ridiculous. You are other people."

"**Every one of you is God,**"

"**The savior,**"

"**And every one of you,**"

"**Is the sinner he saves.**"

"**Who by the way has a right to that experience.**"

And loving ironies,

We laughed and laughed and laughed,

While ME played the song;

When you make love,

Do you look in the mirror?

Who do you think of?

Does she look like me?

Do you tell lies?

And say that it's forever?

Do you think twice?

Or just touch and see?

And as the song whispered its reverberations, I found myself running around the cabin peeking in all the various mirrors, laughing at the fact that I looked different in every single one.

I decided in an image,

To love all the symbols of me.

And then I had the idea that giving my daughter Dessa, the gift certificates I'd earned from Edmond the hate-mommy lover, my last day on the job as a *Romance Therapist*,

That giving Brandessa this tainted Foley's store money as a gift for her at her wedding shower, which was the social symbol in this world of my creation,

Of clean,

Pure,

Love,

Could physically represent my washing away,

Of the belief in sin,

Of any origin.

This letter had begun,

A sexually realized spiritual movement in me,

I was beginning to understand,

And it was reverberating throughout my world.

So that every time I had a question I got up to pace and talk and ask and answer,

Knowing that becoming,

More than anything else,

Was the reason I was here.

And so I decided that,

Becoming beautiful,

Without shame,

Be the task at hand.

Because for so many reasons I was learning that,

In my world,

Ugly,

Had become,

Desirable,

Precious,

Dear,

In direct contrast with beauty,

A sinful embarrassment,

To wear.

"Remember when you were a kid, and you were walking down the alley behind your house?" Me asked me this time.

I remembered.

I always remembered,

Even when I wasn't noticing,

That I thought about it often.

I had, out of choice, been quite fat during grade six. It had served its purpose by growing me two little breasts of blubber. But then one day while I was walking through the alley I changed my mind about from where my mammary development should originate.

I decided I wanted to be shapely but void of lard, and forgetting that such things are impossible, focused, lovingly, without force, on all the parts of my body like hands reshaping the, Play-Doh Doll!

"Oh my! I never noticed the connection."

"That's because you just put it there." Me responded.

"But?"

"The connectors are a builders tools. They can be reconfigured at will. You bring them out whenever you wish to need them. You decide where they go and how they fit and then you put them away when you're done."

"Never mind," I shushed Me, *"I don't want to go there now. Let me think about that alley walk."*

And it was quiet while I reveled in the memory of the simplicity of the miracle.

By the time I had reached the end of the lane I was beautiful.

And when I got to school every single person noticed,

Until, by the end of the day,

They all forgot their amazement,

And saw the miracle,

As commonplace,

As though it was normal,

To change so quickly,

And so it was.

And so it seemed for all of these years.

And as I remembered, it occurred to me that all my miracles tend to become normalized, rationalized, and turned into nothing special,

Within the made up time frame of twenty-four hours.

And suddenly I thought again of mirrors and started running around the cabin, looking different in each one.

At first it seemed attributable to the difference in the quality of light, glass, angle, or size,

But after awhile,

As it became more fun,

To make faces,

Act silly,

Talk out loud,

It happened,

In the joy.

I was able to change,

Minutely at first,

And then,

A teeny bit,

More.

And I recalled:

Watching a television interview with Richard Dreyfuss who explained that having poor vision had made him a better actor, more undisturbed by the extremities of the reality around him. Immediately my better than normal vision had begun to fade and become damaged.

How amusing!

I changed my choice and saw more than I'd been seeing,

Ever since I saw,

Richard Dreyfuss talk.

And in the next mirror,

In the next minute,

Changed,

A teeny bit,

More.

When I recalled:

Being a bored child in school and playing with the ever-present dots in front of my eyes, till I noticed the kids staring at me and decided not to be so different and sent the dots away. But then years later, different seemed good, when,

In search of a cure for autism, I took my family to vision retraining, where we discovered that many autistic people see dots in front of their eyes,

Which made me feel a sameness with which to understand, my son, and re-framed the dots as desirable.

Then, in finding the dots desirable, saw them return and become ever present again.

So there were dots in my eyes,

Until the moment in the mirror,

When I sent them away,

Once again,

And changed,

A teeny bit,

More.

As I recalled:

A few weeks ago, being perfectly,

Dressed up in perfectly brand-new clothes,

And perfectly applied makeup,

With perfectly manicured nails,

Running down the chalkboard of my "love child soul."

I had been, interviewing for the buttoned-down, cardboard-personalitied, fact-believing job of television news anchor,

When my eye developed a tic while the program director was examining my appearance of acceptability,

Because that morning,

While perfectly attempting,

To look younger,

In order to compete in a young person's market,

I had applied electric muscle stimulation to my cheeks and while doing so had thought, in the barely perceptible inkling of ideas,

How funny it would be if this attempt at electronic youth, ruined my chances by giving me an unacceptable symbol of pulsing power like a facial tic, rendering age irrelevant.

And since I had thought it,

I made it,

Perfectly so.

However, during the interview, I forgot that life is perfect,

I played the game by remembering to forget that everything is exactly the way you want it to be at any given moment.

I felt foolhardy for toying with myself by playing with my body.

And when my eye began to tic while we talked about my no future,

I found it embarrassing and tried to make it stop,

Which it did not.

Because I was too busy trying, to remember how to choose, to choose.

Until this new moment when I peered in the glass and changed,

An ever so teeny bit more, my reflection, in the mirrors.

I knew well that it could be an experience of self-hypnosis,

Created by me,

But that didn't matter. Focusing hard on seeing the world you believe is there wouldn't really be inconsistent with my beliefs.

I considered the possibility that the connectors, like food equals fat, and smoke equals cancer, were just story devices used to glue the picture together. They—the supposed laws of nature—I decided, could become outdated and be rewritten at will.

And so I rewrote that only good is truth,

That the rest is just costuming for the purpose of texturing life,

And then, that the rest is also equally as good,

And equally as pure,

And equally as me.

I immersed myself into playing in the mirrors,

Elated by the joy and the freedom it gave me,

And stopped concerning myself with the details.

Of what equals what.

The tub had filled. It enticed me with yearning fingers of steam,

So I switched the game of reflected fun,

To the mirrors by the bath.

The mirrors were facing each other, and angled just a little, so that, as I allowed the warmth, to recreate my joy, into melted pleasure, and relaxed onto my haunches inside the wet. I saw,

Millions,

Of me(s).

All around,

Me,

From different perspectives,

Receding into the no distance, distance.

And remembered,

My childhood,

Again.

And looked at the ever present dots,

As my eye began to tic,

And I continued to play,

Moving the tic from one eye to the other,

Then changing my mind,

And deciding it,

And the dots,

Completely away.

And back,

And away again.

And in playing it,

Knew,

How.

And knowing how, knew,

How easy it is to choose,

To unchoose.

So, I looked into the images and turned the picture just enough to line up the choices differently. I decided even my younger children should be set free of their need for me just as I should be freed of my need for them. I nurtured their growth from a distance, creating a world where they understood more just as I understood more, unimportant that they were far away in the no-distance of home,

While I was here,

Seeking to understand,

While vomiting words.

And being a Messiah, of invisible stature, who had had a great learning,

I took the world with me, greatly improved.

Though I was undetectable,

From any of the other,

Ones,

In the masses of Gods,

Called everyday persons,

Of which I am.

I felt my children grow, I had changed them from young ones that couldn't learn without me, to short ones that could.

I was happy for the difference.

I needed no more than happy.

My children and I would do the work in our minds,

From separate places together,

And in the blink of an inkling,

I knew I could take the time to write this letter,

Without feeling like I was even away.

I knew I wouldn't feel far away,

Because I understood,

That I was not,

And understanding, made it so.

And noting the life changing personal power of the moment I thought,

"Maybe I'll throw in a cure for Dar while I'm at it,"

Thinking casual talk,

Trying to fool myself into believing,

I didn't want it too much,

To make it happen,

Though I did ....Know I did.

And if it matters to the me in you,

To know that time has proved out all these things,

In order to give validity to the "things" I say I see,

Then we have missed the point of the constant choice of changing,

The things you choose to prove.

Still though,

My choice has been consistent in this,

And I don't mind assuring you that it has.

In fact I have had more success,

Parenting by phone during this sexually realized spiritual journey,

Than ever in my,

Always with them,

Past.

And as they all,

Including Dar,

Continue to unfold,

Because I believe they can,

Achieve independence,

They do.

And since Dar is a part of the fold,

They carry him along,

By not carrying him anymore,

Till he can carry himself,

Leaving them free,

To carry him again,

If that's what they choose to do.

This process, of Dar's coming out, continues in spite of my occasional interference, my attempts to ensure the process that is already underway,

Even as I try,

To not try so hard,

To want it,

Less,

Leading myself to want it,

Even more.

I looked back into the mirror,

To learn from the moment,

The method of play.

And searching the eyes,

Of even the tiniest me,

Decided to improve my vision,

And be able to see,

Clearly,

By simply commanding it so playfully.

I refocused my iris,

Crystallized my world,

And seeing more than I had seen since1981 brought me the acting advice of Mr. Richard Dreyfuss, advice which I believe must have been giving myself.

I saw the features on the face of my most minuscule me.

I sat back on that wonderful day after turning on the Jacuzzi jets, and relaxed into a smile. I must have fallen into a micro-sleep, for almost immediately I dreamed that I was getting gas for a little reddish black sports car. I had finished filling the tank, and was about to go inside to pay the cashier when I remembered that I didn't have any money. Instantly, the me that was dreaming felt panicked, while the me in the dream, looked behind her, at herself, the me that was asleep.

And said, *"You don't have to believe that any more."*

Then, turning back to face the gas station, she looked out into her world, and rewrote the rules. I jumped awake, within seconds of sleep, trying to bring the dream with me. The Jacuzzi jets found air, instead of water, in the waves of my haste, and splashed me, and the bathroom, into the present,

Of the moment.

In the dream I'd known how to do it, how to make a world where paying for anything was optional. But I didn't seem to be able to get a hold of the memory,

To make it more than a memory,

To make it a knowing.

And, though I'd just done it moments before, while looking in the mirrors, suddenly, shaping my own world seemed impossible.

As if money was the exception to the natural law of, "There's always enough. In fact there's a surplus."

I turned off the Jacuzzi, and threw on some pants and a plaid flannel shirt. And,

"Sit on the chair."

Felt, heard, a compulsion to move the bedroom chair out into the open, away from the walls, untouched, in the middle of the room. I sat, completely still,

And waited.

Jeff, I don't know if you ever saw the movie "Contact" but if you did, and you remember it well enough to focus your mind on the scene in the space ship,

Wherein Jodie Foster was sitting on a chair, held up by nothing, as the world changed around her,

Then you have a sense for the experience I was about to have.

I heard the gentlest sound tell me to close my eyes.

It was the sweet sound of love,

Telling me to drop my eyelids,

And me into darkness,

So that I could see.

Telling me to look.

At the Me that is thee,

In the shape of my dear friend,

The lovingly lovely,

Never grim,

Reaper,

Who smiled,

Without a face.

I felt so,

Cared for,

So loved,

And like, when,

I first saw you, Jeff,

In my fantasies,

My tears ran,

Pouring,

Happy from my eyes.

Only this time it was not a fantasy,

Though it may have been a mirage.

Maybe.

He loved me more than love can be,

So thick were the waves that passed through me,

So full of depth,

I felt something take shape,

And lifted my chin to look up into the eyes of the man in the hood.

And there they were,

Your eyes, Jeff,

Beautiful blue.

I saw your face but even as I recognized it, it changed shape and became,

Michael,

Who kissed me and I felt it though the figure never moved,

But stayed inches away, in front of me, and became,

Ian,

Who embraced me though no arms closed the space,

Into,

Val,

Who smiled and tried to give me something,

Ted?

Me?

It was Me.

She gave me, Me,

Who she then became.

I was looking at Me,

Loving me.

Her smile was tender,

The way mine feels when I wear it on my face.

Her eyes so completely free of any thing at all but,

Love and acceptance for,

me.

Her eyes bathed me with,

Total,

Complete,

Love,

And,

The desire to be,

Whatever I asked her to be.

I cried huge uncontrollable sobs.

She held me,

From everywhere in the room.

Till I could,

Finally,

Stand it,

No longer,

And let her cry,

Silent tears,

So that I could see,

The joy of need.

She reached out,

And, cupped my cheek,

So sweetly in her hand,

Just the way I do,

When I love.

She kissed me,

Gently,

Me tasting me.

And me tasting Me,

Felt freely,

Feeling me,

Taste myself,

And my own kisses.

I breathed,

The breathe of life,

Holding me with,

My own heart.

And found,

That I,

Was the most beautiful person,

Ever.

And it was good.

She embraced into me,

And whispered,

"You are already rich. No more fear,

Love."

"No more fear.

You have already done the work,

You decided to do.

You have already done the work,
Within the workings of,
Your mind.
SHSHSHSH darling,
The time to cry,
Is nigh."
"And the whole universe,
Is rushing,
To bring your desires to your side.
You are already rich,
Love, Money,
Is coming to you from every corner,
Of the universe,
You have called for it in the inkling.
Now!
Let it go,
My darling,
Enjoy,
My sweet.
Love!
It is already done."
And I believed!
She stepped back,
Into a singular form,
Away, close,
Like the mirror.
And blew the kiss of luck,
Into me,
At the same time,
That she,
Laid her lips upon me.
She stretched her arms,
Toward me,
From the distance,
Inside of me,
Inside of the room,
As though,

To welcome me,
Home.
And the tingling that passed,
Between the her that stood apart,
And the her that had moved into,
me,
Was such a jolt of love,
And,
Sex,
That my pores,
Orgasmed,
Constant,
Timeless,
Bursting,
Together,
One,
Letting,
ME,
Create,
me.
And I was whole.
And so, Jeff,
We reach the end,
Just as I begin,
To begin,
For I am new,
Again.
Thank you.
Though you were never affected,
Completely oblivious,
And had nothing to do with my odyssey of love,
I couldn't have done it without you.
Unless,
Of course,
I decided,
To do it with somebody else.

I remain,

Yours,

For,

Ever,

Loving,

me.

Lynette Louise

(P.S. **When you make love if you look in the mirror, and see me, say Hi!**)

You cannot come to know Me through the writings in this book.

However,

It is my hope,

That you may come to know yourself.

Lynette: The Secret Revealed
a spritiaully realized letter of love

Dear Lynette,

Something happened to me over the past three weeks.

Something happened!

I was given a voice.

And now,

I choose to write this letter,

That I will never have to send,

Farther than the inkling.

Because,

I have a new friend,

In you,

Who have created Me on the inside.

I am you,

As is your neighbor and your enemy,

Your child and your man.

I am you, personified, ethereal.

You gave birth to Me,

To give birth to a new perspective in personal awareness.

Thank you for the gift of life,

To yourself.

Know that I am no more than what you make me.

Thank you for giving Me the ability to make me more.

And thank you for making Me free to speak my own mind,

To have my own thoughts,

Even though I have no body full of brains.

And as I am freed of the constraints of the physical,

And have a separate perspective,

Let Me tell you what I see...

That sometimes you believe in now,

As though it were different from then.

Sometimes you believe it,

Even more than is necessary,

To believe it,

In order to play the game.

Like when you finished your letter to Jeff and,

Relieved to be new again,

Lay down to sleep.

And as your hand reached for your genitals;

Your tool,

To draw you into the orgasmic pleasure,

Of after-revelation-glow slumber,

I watched your mind:

Your tool, to take you there,

Again,

In the manner of your choice.

I saw your thoughts,

Of you,

Naked on a soft rolling hill,

At the top of a world,

Without the pretense of people,

Creating the need for privacy.

And with the wind,

Blowing,

Warm,

Friendly,

Fingers,

Through your hair,

And along your skin.

You threw your head back,

And extended your arms,

And twirled,

In the wonderful,

Touch, of life.

You became,

Seated,

In the familiar,

The intimate,

Position.

You leaned,

Back,

Arms,

Behind,

Spine arched,

Legs bent,

And open.

Every particle,

Of every atom,

Of the breath,

Of the aliveness,

Energy,

Of love,

Embraced you,

And washed us,

Clean,

Without the knowledge of,

Other than.

The shimmering molecules,

Moved into you,

Rushing between your lips,

Entering that place in you,

That,

Has,

At last,

Become,

Beautiful.

That place,

In you,

That,

Is,

The,

All,

At the center of knowing.

That place in you,

Where you hear,

Without sound,

The passionate whispers of;

I love you,

I love you,

I love you,

And where you feel,

Without vibration,

These carbonated tingles,

Of declared love,

As they wash,

Into your soul,

Which I am.

And we climax,

Together,

Into the Perrier,

Of Existence.

And though being stimulated,

By the vision of a zillion love molecules,

Vibrating tingles on your clitoris,

Was an amazing way to experience the orgasm of physical,

And spiritual release,

You gave it more meaning, more power,

And thus more limitations,

Than it need have,

To serve you well.

I listened to you believe that,

"Now,"

You were sexually clean,

Sexually healthy.

That,

"Now,"

You were finally good ...in your mind.

I heard you believe,

That climaxing in the company of such a fantasy,

Was pure and true and reflected who you wanted to be.

And in hearing you believe in,

"Now,"

I also heard you believe in,

"Then,"

And in,

"Soon to be."

And though you expected such thoughts to help evolve you into a clearer vision of the symbol of love,

You also believed in the disempowerment of an overused fantasy.

Which meant that you had to evolve away from the moment of perfection that you believed you had achieved,

And since perfection as you define it,

Cannot be improved upon,

And since you judged perfection as good,

You set yourself up to move into bad.

Because sometimes you believe in perfection,

As though it is unusual rather than constant,

Even more than is necessary to play the game.

Because,

For the moment,

You are addicted to the game,

Of trying to achieve what you already have,

In order to experience rather than just know,

And then seeking to know,

What it is you experienced.

And as long as you are addicted,

You will continue to forget,

That everything is now,

For now is all there is,

Always and forever perfectly created,

To change into,

The thing you have decided it to be.

Understand, Lynette,

That you are always in the great moment of now,

Questing to rediscover yourself, from every angle,

In order to more fully experience, the love you feel for,

What it is that you already are.

It is the rediscovery,

That creates the illusion of evolution.

And it is the rediscovery,

That ignites the moment with feeling,

So that you might tingle in the experience,

And feel, all at once.

And it is the ability to feel,

As the giver and the receiver,

The winner and the loser,

The audience and the participant,

The male and the female,

The various variants,

Multiplying,

Buzzing,

Light years of perceptions,

To infinity,

And beyond,

That creates the,

All of everything,

That you are,

For every,

Single,

Second,

That you,

Are,

All,

Of

It,

All.

And the game never ends,

Unless it does,

For a minute pause,

To be begun again,

With the question,

That leads you to seek the answer,

By questing to love,

Yourself,

As the receiver,

And the giver.

Hence, your desire to be loved by someone like yourself,

And hence, your splitting off and separating,

Into the many parts of all the people of the worlds,

Inside and out.

Everyone you see is an aspect of you,

Looking at you,

Responding to you,

Experiencing you.

And "Do unto others as you would have them do unto you,"

If you were them,

Becomes the most golden of self-fulfilling,

Intentions.

Love is all there is,

Nothing else is real,

Not even fear.

Do you remember the vision I gave you in the woods by your house?

The vision of the bubbles?

On that day when we healed the scratch on your finger,

To prove our point that nothing is true.

No laws are absolute,

Not even the laws of God,

The scientist,

Otherwise known as nature,

Dancing in the shifting winds of decision.

No facts are real,

And all memories are make believe,

Created in the one and only,

Moment of now.

So it is,

That the future,

And the present,

And the past,

Like the injuring of your finger,

Are all under your control,

And changeable at will.

And so it is,

That everything,

You all believe,
Is correct,
Every time,
Everyone of you,
Believes it,
Differently,
From every perspective.
And you,
Everyone of you,
Can make it up as you want it to be,
Can choose the drama you wish to live.
And worry not,
Unless you want to,
Because you cannot die,
Without waking up,
To become alive,
Somewhere else.
Yes,
Love,
Is,
All there is.
Just as the bubbles illustrated,
By birthing out of you,
From your own ideas,
Showing you creation,
Making way for every new litter,
Of every second,
So filled with thoughts,
You are safe.
Because,
You cannot be hurt by what you don't think up.
So, if it hurts you my friend,
You asked it to,
By believing that,
Such a thing could hurt.
And by adjoining the belief in the hurt,
To the self created fact that,

The minute you think a thought into being,

The very existence of its existence,

Implies the existence of,

And thus creates,

Its opposite.

And by this means,

Did you create the reality that,

Even your times of privilege,

Brought with it impending doom.

Since so long as you believe,

In the birthing of opposites,

Every cell of every belief,

Must split and become a twin.

Thus, the less violent the imagery,

Of even your joy,

The gentler the creation,

For some,

Parts of you.

And perhaps even now,

For the part you call Lynette,

Heaven comes when thinking in the grays,

And softening the imagery,

As you create out of you,

And surround yourself,

In your own work of art.

But as each bubble bubbles,

And creates,

And implies it's symbiotic twin,

For some parts of you,

This heavenly blending,

Of the colors,

Of life,

Appears as a dulling,

Of passions,

And is rejected as,

A sentence to hell.

And you,

Inside of life,

And life,

In all its simplicity,

Begins to appear,

Magnificently,

Complex.

Because,

Life,

Is,

Awe inspiring,

Confusing,

Wonderful

And alive!

Giving birth to the appearance of linear time,

As you notice and think upon the details.

And as you think upon the details,

And take in the creation of change,

As you create and create and create,

Flowing the thought and its results away from you,

All at once,

Changing your world from what it was,

To what it's come to be,

Today,

You sometimes glimpse,

The only non-illusion,

Of absolute control.

However, Lynette,

Know that,

The control,

IS,

Not reliant on the method.

Remember when I gave you this imagery,

Of the bubblicious birthing of the blessings of life,

And you thought you had found the answers,

To the method of reality conception?

I was not showing you what is,

And what must be,

But rather what could be,
And was,
Because you used to believe it,
Was,
And then forgot your own design.
You changed the method,
Into something darker,
When you stopped being the child,
And became instead,
The grindstone grownup.
This Lynette is not "the" recipe,
Of life bubbles life, like the tapioca tundra of our existence.
But rather your recipe,
And the one within which,
In the past,
You have been the happiest.
However,
You could just as easily choose to step,
From page to page of each new world,
On the magic,
Of whim to whim.
Or stand in one place,
And merely look,
From belief to belief,
Motionless, unmoving,
Yet recreating,
Anew.
You could.
And at times,
You have,
Been like the lens of a camera,
Surveying the playground,
Zooming and rack focusing,
On a dolly or a crane,
Seeing only within the boundaries,
Of the square within the frame.
Then role-playing as director,

In your movie living game.
Yet the scripted similarities are just your dramatic choices.
In truth it is easy for you to choose differently to,
Do it,
Any way,
You like.
So, if you choose to have it all made up on a whim,
Be careful what you whim for,
For being careful helps keep one foot in the pool of awareness,
Where change is the only constant.
And love is the only element,
And there is nothing to fear,
Not even fear,
Itself,
Unless you love feeling the fear,
Of fear,
Then by all means enjoy,
Fear,
So much that it feels,
Like it's ancestor,
Love.
Because everything bubbles out of love,
And reshapes itself,
Until eventually it has changed so much,
That we give it a different name,
And then a different name,
And then a different name,
And then a different name...
And that is my secret,
Often told,
And here is my gift,
Often given,
Words,
To put in your pocket,
And keep in your heart:
You cannot give your love to someone else,
For it is only you, who can feel it.

And though you may think you gift your heart to another,

Like an apple or a box of rings,

It cannot be handed from one person to be taken by someone else.

So when you love someone ask them not for gratitude,

And fool yourself not,

Into thinking that any emotion can be given,

To anyone other than you.

Ask not for gratitude for something they cannot feel,

Ask instead to be treated in the manner,

That your feelings lead you to treat them with.

And since your own manner is how you recognize love,

Then no wonder it is someone like you,

That you are looking to love,

You,

So that you can recognize the love given,

And fool yourself into thinking,

That the emotion is leaving their body,

And entering yours.

It isn't. For the passing of emotion,

Like the bodies themselves,

Is a mirage,

And you already have you to love,

You,

By experiencing the love,

Of loving them,

So though you ask them to treat you,

In the same manner as you treat them,

Allow them to do it differently,

For that is the very reason you created their difference,

To love,

Yourself with,

In the first place.

So love yourself,

In their name,

And ask not for gratitude,

But give it freely,

For you give it to yourself.

And this understanding is my gift,

And it is one,

Well worth understanding.

Now, when you are loved though you ask not for gratitude,

Do do appreciation,

Because that is the path to travel,

To give yourself the gratitude you wish to receive,

For the love it appears to you that you have managed to give.

So do appreciation,

To give yourself appreciation,

In the only way that you can receive it,

By growing it inside yourself.

And know that since,

Another cannot give you love,

Any more than you can give it to them,

Then your grandest feelings about the way another loves you,

And the euphoria you immerse into as a result of their caring,

Is merely emotional outgrowth,

Resulting from something you have decided to give yourself,

To believe in.

And understanding this,

Makes you truly an independent soul,

With the power to live freely in a world of your own making.

And what a wonderful gift,

To give,

Everyone,

That is you;

The gift of,

Total credit for all you are,

And what you feel,

And everything you experience.

Total credit,

And no one to thank,

But you.

Understand this:

Except for the joy it gives you to thank them,

There is no one to thank for this journey.

No one.
Not Me,
Not Jeff,
Or Ted,
Or Ian,
Or Michael,
Or even Val.
None of them,
Gave you anything,
Not the insight,
Or the silence,
Or the joy,
Or the stillness of your mind,
Nothing,
Not even
Love,
"There is no one else to thank,
For anything,
Not even "the love,"
Of enlightenment.
Nor the painful one,
"The love,"
Of self delusion,
That came before,
And may,
If you choose it,
Come again.
Not a single soul but you,
Gave you anything.
You gave it to yourself.
Listen to what I am saying.
And try,
To understand,
Love.
Try to understand,
Love,
As clearly as you understand,

Sex.
For that is why you put them,
Together,
In this letter,
To yourself,
In this life,
Of your own making,
In this journey,
Of your own design.
You have been seeking love,
By peering through the eye glass of sex,
In an attempt to mirror,
In spirit,
That awesome discovery,
You long ago made in the flesh.
To symbolize,
And remind yourself of the freedom,
Of increased pleasure,
You achieved,
When you first realized,
That an orgasm,
Is a life celebratory,
"happening,"
You give yourself.
That your orgasms are,
Like love,
A gift to you,
From you,
Though oftentimes,
Given to yourself,
In the company of others.
Remember how amazed you were to understand that climaxing,
Has very little to do with the person you are next to,
And everything to do,
With what you decide to believe,
You believe about them.
Remember how much more wonderful,

Sex became,

And apply that to love.

And know finally that,

The responsibility for love,

Rests with you.

Because love like orgasms,

Is independent of your partner,

Independent of,

The subject of your fantasies,

And wholly dependent on your beliefs,

Even to the degree of the intensity,

You imagine you exchange,

With the one you are with,

Whether in your body,

Or your mind.

Then remind yourself that not needing,

Someone else to get from,

Makes everything you give,

The highest compliment,

Of the gift of choice.

And revel in the realization of the memory that,

Not needing someone else,

Was what gave you the power of the whim, with love, and to love to love,

So much, more, often.

And then apply that to the, all, of everything that is you,

While you luxuriate in, and allow it to be true.

Making everything sexy, including you,

And him, and Them, and Me,

As we arrive,

Into the giving,

And receiving of,

Everything that is,

Positive,

And negative,

And otherwise known as,

Love.

So Lynette, give "it,"

Whatever that may be,

To yourself,

As you give yourself everything,

Including this gift,

That I give to you now,

For though I am Me,

I am also you." Thus,

When you make love,

Whether or not you look in the mirror,

No matter who you think of,

Whether or not she looks like me,

It is not lies,

To say that it's forever,

For eternity's wise,

Just trust and see,

That you are everything and love is all there is."

Yours,

Truly Forever,

Because,

You choose it.

Me

(PS. If you want so desperately to be loved by someone like yourself Lynette, then love and you will be.)

LYNETTE LOUISE
Certified Option Process Mentor Counselor/Life Coach

Embracing all individuals with non-judgemental acceptance and love.
Specializing in Sex, Love, and Self Development for:

Speaking Engagements
Workshops
Private Sessions with individuals and couples

Call Toll-Free: 1-877-Lynette
E-mail: lynette@lynettelouise.com
Postal Mail: Lynette Louise, P O Box 8396 Ennis, TX 75120

Order Additional Books

Telephone Orders: Call 800-932-5420 toll free.
Have your credit card ready

Fax Orders: 440-543-9350. Send this form

Email Orders: orders@greenleafbookgroup.com

Postal Orders: Greenleaf Book Group, 8227 Washington Street #2,
Chagrin Falls, OH 44023

Please send me _____ books at a cost of $15.95 per book plus taxes (where
applicable) and shipping to:

Name:_____

Address:_____

City:_____State:_____Zip:_____

Telephone:_____

Email address:_____

Sales Tax: Please add 5.75% for books shipped to Ohio addresses.

 Shipping and Handling: $5.95. Call for international shipping rates and
discounts for multiple orders.

Payment: Cheque_____   Credit Card_____
Visa___   Master Card___   AMEX___ Discover___

Card number:_____

Name on card:_____Exp.date:_____